I0808317

SIMON BLAXLAND-DE LANGE has for many years worked as an educator for people with special needs as well as a writer and translator. A keen amateur musician and gardener, he is a co-founder of Pericles Translations and Research, Pericles Training and Work for adults with special needs and the Pericles Theatre Company. Together with Dr Vivien Law, he co-founded the Humanities Research Group in 1997 and the British group of the Humanities Section of the School of Spiritual Science in 1998. He first met Owen Barfield in 1979, and has been a student of his work for the past 30 years.

OWEN BARFIELD
Romanticism Come of Age
A Biography

Simon Blaxland-de Lange

TEMPLE LODGE

Temple Lodge Publishing
Hillside House, The Square
Forest Row, RH18 5ES

www.templelodge.com

First published by Temple Lodge 2006

A catalogue record for this book is available from the British Library

ISBN-10: 1 902636 77 5
ISBN-13: 978 1902636 77 1

Cover photo by Laurel Gasque
Cover design by Andrew Morgan Design
Typeset by DP Photosetting, Aylesbury, Bucks.
Printed and bound by Cromwell Press Limited, Trowbridge, Wilts.

Faithfully mirroring the shining sun,
your soul departed when the moon was full—
true image of your great reflective mind.
No longer need you tarry to reflect;
henceforth your thoughts will shine out of themselves
where word and meaning and the deed are one,
and Christ has raised your spirit to the sun.

Rex Raab

(On learning that Owen Barfield passed away in Forest Row on 14 December 1997, a full moon, a month after his 99th birthday, 9 November 1997.

Engelberg, 14 February 1998)

CONTENTS

FOREWORD
by Andrew Welburn

To some (like myself) who were privileged to know him, and still more I should think to that greater number who knew and extremely admired his work, Owen Barfield remained a considerable enigma. More widely known, perhaps, on the American lecture-circuit than in this country, he was nevertheless always a very 'English' speaker, whose stylish language and subtlety was but little adapted to the brash modern age of the sound-bite and the latest critical theory. Often, those who may have supposed there was nothing but those latest ideas were struck that here was a quiet, well-thought-through perspective which showed another dimension. Audiences were dazzled at his ideas and wondered where he had been till now. I recall more than one academic colleague asking in a puzzled undertone which university he lectured at. But of course he held no academic position, and was proud of his long career in the Law, where logic and life, as he put it, meet. He founded no school of thought (though there have been a few Ph.D. students to take up his leads). His call to think deeply and consistently, and to root out those vestiges of half-truth we normally carry around as a sort of intellectual baggage, meant that he appealed everywhere rather to individuals who recognized his extraordinary width of knowledge, and his life-long search for whole truths behind the conventional semi-shams.

His breadth of knowledge was striking; yet he was anything but a walking encyclopaedia. His manner was personal, affable behind his obvious shyness, and his ideas mingled with a range of experiences he was happy to share but which did not fit any conventional slot. I remember vividly, for instance, his eyes shining as he recalled his youthful part in a song-and-dance act with hats and canes. And his great, significant friendships with such figures as C.S. Lewis were hardly based on finding like-minded reinforcements for his favourite concepts—quite the reverse. 'Opposition is true friendship' is the Blakean quotation which dedicates to his Oxford friend his *Poetic Diction*—a short and brilliant early book of his which now (by librarian's accident or design, who can tell with librarians) occupies an enviable place of honour almost at the fountain-head of all basic works of reference in the reading-room of the Bodleian Library.

I knew him all too little and late, and I was therefore naturally struck when the author of this book, who had had the opportunity to interview him extensively about his life and ideas, made it known that he was putting together a book whose aim—and this was the particularly congenial thought—was to evoke the *soul* of Owen Barfield. In the first place it would be a biography to give us that broader picture of the enigmatic author-speaker: and Blaxland-de Lange tellingly chooses to let Owen tell much of it in his own words and characteristic phrases at the outset, calling him up so vividly that one almost gets again the whiff of his extraordinarily pervasive pipe and hears his old English voice. But still more importantly it would be a *psychography* that would reveal something of the deeper aims and purposes of the man all round. And here too Simon Blaxland-de Lange proves true to the challenge of his theme. Soul is perhaps somewhat lacking in the modern world altogether. The quality of Barfield's creative, imaginative, intellectual, anti-intellectual, artistic, literary, legal, amiable, insistent, argumentative, unpatronizing, never resting soul would be a gift indeed for the future to treasure.

In the case of some of Barfield's important circle of friends, it seems relatively easy to say where their soul really lay. Indeed few people have worn their soul more 'on their sleeve', as it were, than C.S. Lewis! He and J.R.R. Tolkien and others, like the occult novelist Charles Williams, came together with Barfield and the anthroposophist A.C. Harwood at Oxford in the years after the First World War to form the group now almost legendary in local history as 'The Inklings', meeting in the unlikely setting of the pub called the *Eagle and Child* (also known less reverentially as the 'Bird and Baby'). Many large ideas united them: a hatred of the technological, destructive world-order whose fearsome capabilities had so recently been demonstrated, a sense of the impending loss of the England of the 'Shires' and traditional rural life, and equally the need for new sources of spiritual and moral life, whose fount must necessarily lie still in the invisible, the unapprehended—though of its advent one could, as they proclaimed, have an inkling. For Lewis and Tolkien especially, one has the sense that they gave their soul to this little joint venture of ideas and creative writing, which turned out in the end to have a huge impact on the imaginative life of succeeding generations through their enduring fantasy-lands of Narnia and Middle Earth, and that conversely it nourished their own souls and saved, for them, the certainties of their pre-War childhood. But Barfield did not really stand in this line.

The clash is especially clear in cases where Barfield sought to get at the reality of such myths as ancient Atlantis. He came to believe that the key to understanding that reality lay in the 'changing consciousness', as he liked to put it, of humanity over ages of historical time. The universality of the myths pointed to their basis in a kind of world-experience that was different from our own, but appealed deeply to our minds because it formed the very basis from which ours had evolved. Using his insight into the history of language, Barfield argued that abstract ideas were a late development in the way people thought about the world. But that did not mean that early humanity lived in an impoverished, confused, merely sensory landscape. Quite the contrary. It is modern human beings who feel cut off from their environment, who see it passing by them in an unintelligible, alienated way, merely registered on their senses but without deeper significance. Early humanity felt part of the world they knew, and felt every aspect of it—colour, sound, form—to be charged with profound meaning. The history of language showed that human beings were deeply aware of the paradoxes and questions of human existence, but they expressed them in myths, symbols, 'concrete' forms of thought, and ultimately in a consciousness of the world which we can still comprehend, at least in some measure, in its otherness to our own. Barfield looked at words which, in many languages, originally carry connotations of physical moving-power such as the Greek *pneuma,* 'the wind'—but also of the inner moving power in human beings, 'the spirit'. Most theorists of language assume that the development went something like this: people saw that the invisible power of the wind blows about the leaves, or waves, or other objects; they saw human beings moving and acting, and they deduced that there must be a sort of wind, an invisible power, moving them from within. But Barfield saw that such accounts are contradictory and unintelligible. They assume first that ancient humanity saw and thought about the world exactly as we do, i.e. they could isolate physical motions and speculate about possible 'causes' of human motions. Yet the whole point, as the linguists seem to have forgotten, is to explain why ancient people thought concretely—thought differently from ourselves. It is we who can abstract the notion 'invisible motive power' from both the instances. But if ancient humanity had been able to do so, they would not have needed to have that undivided meaning which is *pneuma.* It was precisely because they did not make our modern distinctions that they thought in their concrete, immediate way. Not only the content of their thoughts, but the way they thought was different. It was a different consciousness. And Barfield took from Rudolf Steiner the idea that Atlantis is the representation of a stage of consciousness when human beings still experienced meaning as pervading their whole environment, where sound and form were still a 'cosmic word'. We have gradually evolved out of that oneness the 'inner' meaning and the 'outer meaning' that characterize our own stage of consciousness. But we are dimly aware nonetheless that our own stage depends on, and ultimately only makes sense if we connect it with that original, though unrecaptureable wholeness of meaning. The very words and ideas we use still hint at its existence.

Lewis was never more vehement in his rejection of Barfield than when the latter urged such ideas. He seemed to panic at the thought of bringing the childhood magic-world into question and reality. It was an attack on Narnia. In his explicitly neo-Christian thought-world, Lewis's paradises were supposed to be lost—and we should accept the place we have been assigned, while wistfully sighing. Perhaps also Lewis sensed that if his own fauns and centaurs—the life of nature—were to become real they would be too obviously a return to paganism. What he feared was *not* that his paradise might turn out not to have existed. He knew with imaginative certainty that it had. But what if it were not so certainly lost? Blaxland-de Lange takes us into some of the other themes, too, of the 'Great War' between the two men that resulted. (It is typical of their strange Oxford mentality that this was largely carried on in the Latin of the Scholastic predecessors from six or seven centuries before.) Unlike Lewis, other Inklings were imagining that very step of making the ideal real once more. Charles Williams's fantasy *The Place of the Lion* transposes a Platonic, 'ideal' lion into actuality as a very concrete, startlingly concrete spiritual being. Barfield transposes the goal-posts of the familiar patterns of Christian thought and brings to them a sudden whiff of actuality, engaging with the scientific details of language and modern thinking. Yet for that very reason, it becomes more difficult to sense where he is taking us. He, like Lewis, finds central value in the Christian symbols of the descent of God into his world, revealing his meaning to us finally from within after we have lost that wholeness when it was everywhere outside us and around. But he does not appear at all constrained by the limits of the traditional framework of Christian ideas—or even seems to challenge it deliberately to move on. We find it perplexing that he wants to be both modernist and its opposite, to overturn and question but not to accept the contemporary myth of the meaningless universe that it is generally assumed must result. So where is Barfield coming from—where, in other words, is the soul of his venture? Christian though he is, it does not lie in Lewis's dream of a childlike faith renewed.

There is something of the same paradox in his work on Romanticism. He was most influential here for his study of Samuel Taylor Coleridge, that controversial figure whose thought has been treated both as brilliant and as half-charlatan, as astoundingly original and as pilfered from the safe reservoir of German philosophy that was utterly unknown in his insular homeland. The fact is that it was hard to tell exactly where the truth lay because most of Coleridge's non-literary writings were, until the very end of the twentieth century, available only in his original manuscript form. (Sibylline leaves indeed.) Kathleen Coburn had begun to publish Coleridge's notebooks, then gradually came the *Collected Coleridge* grand edition which includes the jottings he made in other people's books (I mean other authors' but also other owners'!—what he facetiously called, in a typically outrageous mix-up of languages, his *cacoethes annotandi*) and some American scholars in particular were beginning to put together a truer picture of Coleridge's general patterns of thought. The adventurous *Essay on Life* also revealed Coleridge's grasp of the new evolutionary biology (he was a friend of Hunter, whose famous 'Hunterian' museum of specimens fuelled so many nineteenth-century reflections on organic development). With another friend, J.H. Green, Coleridge responded to the new perspectives in a penetrating philosophical and scientific analysis. (On a lighter note: Coleridge had long punned on his own initials, STC, and the Greek-Christian confession 'He is risen!'—*estēse*; now he jokingly put Green into Greek too, and refers among friends to the new 'Chloro-Esteecean' system of ideas.) But few Coleridge scholars were willing, or perhaps sufficiently widely informed as was Owen Barfield, to appreciate the implied coherence and unity of Coleridge's thought in all these varied spheres. They were concerned, on the whole, to estimate whether Coleridge was well-informed or not on certain intellectual issues of the day. But the idea of looking for a clearly thought-out approach to science and philosophical method in his scattered pronouncements was hardly raised. Enough if Coleridge could be said to have been 'on the right lines' in supporting evolution, or if he fitted into patterns of aesthetics or cultural history that had gone on to win the day and so could be hailed as a forerunner of later things.

Many more historians have now become critical of this sort of 'Whiggish' approach to history—so called from the Whig Party which had long advocated steady progress in English politics: previous thinkers or political leaders were therefore all judged by whether they turned out to be on the side which had eventually led to our present point-of-view, and so had been in the vanguard of 'progress'. It hardly stopped to ask what they had stood for in their own time, or on their own terms. But just as Barfield had tried so effectively to recover the original meaning of words in the different consciousness of previous times, so he was determined to understand what Coleridge's ideas had meant in his own mind. It was of little consequence, in his view, whether Coleridge had 'backed a winner' in evolution, but of very great interest whether he had succeeded in showing the essential way the idea of evolution affects our knowledge and indeed our consciousness. As a matter of fact, Coleridge was not in tune with Darwin's notion of evolution as a sort of fortuitous stumbling forward into new forms that turn out to be useful for survival. Darwin did not at all clearly ask the fundamental question—How do *we* need to think differently in order to understand the evolution of forms? But in the *Theory of Life* Coleridge, rather like Goethe in his approach to the growth of plants, had suggested that the relationship at every point between the organism and the whole setting in which it emerges means that we can no longer think in terms of fixed things, counters, so to speak, which stay the same idea as we move them around in different combinations. For Goethe it was the same 'thing' which appeared as leaf or as woody stem, or beautifully coloured petal, at various stages of the plant's development; Coleridge did something similar on the grand scale by trying to understand life itself as the process by which the part assimilates the whole, recreating in itself the original matrix from which it first broke away, and comes to reproduce in its own morphology the totality of its setting in a 'projective identification'. It cannot at any point be detached from its meaning in that whole. And whereas in post-Darwinian thought the notion of anything essential to the nature of man, or other beings, has given way to an assumption of the merely provisional and accidental (human beings are a bundle of responses to growth and the accidents of circumstance, and may become something else in due course), Coleridge's idea of evolution suggest that evolution (and ourselves, as its product) may be revealing something essential about the nature of the universe, or even about God. Interestingly, similar implications about our own value as evidence in this regard are surfacing in recent so-called 'anthropic' science, as well as in advanced modern philosophy.

Barfield has no rival in helping to ease us into the subtle Coleridgean thinking that lies behind these innovative ideas. Yet there is a curious paradox. For that other kind of thinking which Barfield sought to replace, where we evaluate everything coming down from the past as though its sole purpose was to lead up to ourselves, gives us a rather satisfying sense of 'fitting things in', and making Coleridge relevant to our own certainties. Whereas the Barfieldian subtlety of not disparaging the past, and so letting a previous state of consciousness or an independent thinker speak to us on their own terms, leaves us rather with a feeling of floating free and without an easy anchor. Barfield clearly does not want to say—Coleridge was just right. Though he enters so much more fully into Coleridge's mind, Barfield does not submit us to it, any more than he squeezes Coleridge into the shape of our own presuppositions. Some readers have been rather surprised, for example, having realized his evident admiration for the Romantic poet-philosopher's thought and sampled his in-depth exposition of its complexities, to note the title of another of his books: *Romanticism Comes of Age*. Neither in the neo-Christian project of his friend Lewis nor here in the ideas of Coleridge the great Romantic thinker did Owen Barfield lodge his own elusive soul. For him the thoughts of that speculative Romantic age still needed to 'come of age'. Not even in the case of Rudolf Steiner, who influenced Barfield hugely and whose anthroposophy remained a keystone of Barfield's intellectual world, was it ever a matter of mere acquiescence. He was specially fond of the lectures in which Rudolf Steiner urged his audience to be inwardly free and in that sense not to *believe* in the thoughts he was expounding; to believe would be the end of active spiritual engagement, which was the real point of our inner life for that 'philosopher of spiritual activity'.

Yi-Fu Tuan, in his fascinating book on fear, observes that genius often involves doing away with the normal defences we build against uncertainty. Barfield meets that criterion of genius, for he never asks us to rest secure in a system or a set of beliefs. In the opening pages of his *Saving the Appearances,* Barfield likens his method to those ambiguous drawings which can be seen in different ways and depict different things—a duck and a rabbit, to take a case from Wittgenstein. Passing his hand across the familiar outline of modern thought, Barfield reveals that it can show something else. The soul of Barfield's venture therefore lies in this way he has of leading us across boundaries and into liberating new vistas, making us at the same time face up to our modern fears. Simon Blaxland-de Lange's presentation of Barfield at work in the many areas of his biography, and challenging thought, offers a deep and much-needed appreciation of the man's inner life and the significance of his adventurous spiritual journey.

PREFACE

This book is intended to be as far as possible the kind of biographical study that Owen Barfield would have wished to appear after his death. In conversations mainly during the early part of 1996, when he was in his 98th year, he made it clear that, while he welcomed the idea of a volume in celebration of his life, he regarded the task of making his thoughts and cultural insights more widely known as far more important than a large-scale scrutiny of the details of his life. On the other hand, I am well aware that, just as there is considerable scope for more detailed studies of certain aspects of his thought and creativity, not least of his seminal work on language and the evolution of human consciousness, greater awareness of his stature as a thinker may justly invoke a wish to know more about this long and generous life than is presented here. What follows may best be described as a beginning rather than as a definitive statement; and it is my hope that others with greater knowledge of specific areas of Barfield's life and work will thereby feel encouraged to share it. Whether a definitive statement, once written, would take the form of a definitive biography should—if Barfield's wishes are to be respected—presently be open to some doubt. The present volume, however, has both the specific focus and the limitations of having developed almost entirely around what I gleaned from the time I spent with Barfield at the very end of his life—as regards not only its factual content but also its tenor and mood. It is as though Barfield asked me to carry out a particular task, and I cannot emphasize too strongly that a whole wealth of other tasks are prompted by this life—some of which require to be clothed in words, while others are very unlikely to be wholly or even largely confined to the printed page.

Without Barfield's active collaboration—expressed not least by making three trunkfuls of manuscripts preserved in The Walhatch, Forest Row, available to me with what I would describe as a keen enthusiasm—this book could not have been written. I also warmly acknowledge the strong support of four other individuals in particular: Josephine Spence, who opened up a number of vital connections as regards Barfield's personal life, including the link with the late Professor Craig Miller; Dr Vivien Law, who encouraged me both humanly and financially in the entire project and, until her untimely death at the age of 47 in February 2002, read and commented on each chapter as it appeared; Laurence Harwood, who has been a tower of strength in helping to smooth the way towards the book's publication in the form in which it was intended and also made available to me his collection of correspondence between Barfield and his father; and my wife, Paulamaria, without whose loving insistence I probably would not have plucked up the courage to renew my acquaintance with a man whom—apart from a visit to Orchard View in 1979—I had hitherto venerated from afar. Thanks are also due to Dr Andrew Welburn for his generosity in contributing a Foreword; Christopher W. Mitchell and his colleagues at the Wade Center, Wheaton College, for their courtesy and solicitude in the course of two periods of study in the Inkling archives; Fred Denehy for inviting me to the Owen Barfield Centenary Conference at Drew and Columbia Universities in December 1998 and for launching the fund that made writing the book possible; Susan Bealby-Wright, for generously sharing her memories of her father Leo Baker's friendship with Barfield and also their letters; Professor Georg Tennyson, for faithfulness in communication; Professors David Lavery, Verlyn Flieger and Wayne Hammond, for encouragement in difficult times; Clifford Monks, for filling the gaps in my collection of *To Wards*; John Docherty, for keeping me informed about academic events and journals pertinent to the task; Philpots Manor School, for granting me a semi-sabbatical term in the Autumn Term 2000, enabling the book to find its form (the first words, apart from the previously written 'Biographical Sketch', were written during a brief family holiday in Greece about a year earlier); Margaret Miller, for generously fulfilling her late father Professor Craig Miller's wish to send me his correspondence with Owen Barfield; Martin Schmandt and Sevak Gulbekian for reading and commenting on the text; Jane Hipolito, for enthusiastic and supportive conversations and correspondence; and Earl Patrick Castle-Stewart and Jim Willetts for their kind financial gifts.

I also wish to thank all those who have granted permission for the use of copyright or personal material: the Trustees of the Owen Barfield Literary Estate, the C.S. Lewis Company Ltd., the Marion E. Wade Center, Walter Hooper, the *New Scientist*, Professor Lionel Adey, Rudolf Steiner Press, Professor Patrick Grant, the Literary Trustees of Walter de la Mare and the Society of Authors as their representative, John Lukacs, Terence Davies, Margaret Miller and Laurence Harwood. If despite my efforts to contact other individuals whose material I have used I have infringed against any legal codes or personal sensibilities, I extend my apologies.

Simon Blaxland-de Lange

INTRODUCTION

During the last three years of Owen Barfield's life, I made a number of regular visits to the room in The Walhatch, Forest Row, Sussex, where he spent the last twelve or so years of his life. In the course of one of these visits—in June 1995—he referred in animated terms to a book that he had just been sent by its author; and this book, and the doings of its author, continued thereafter to be a theme of enthusiastic discussion in virtually all my subsequent visits.

It should be pointed out that Barfield's mood in his last years could very easily become despondent, especially where the question of his own literary legacy was concerned. This might seem strange in one who had—in the eyes of many of those most qualified to deliver such a judgement, if not of the public at large—been granted the accolade of the highest respect, esteem and even veneration on account of his literary achievements over some 60 years. And yet he was constantly haunted by his awareness—through newspapers, television and general conversation—that the intellectual assumptions and attitudes of mind, together with the patterns of behaviour that they invoke, that he had striven all his long life to counter continued seemingly to exert an ever greater hold upon people's imaginations. At such moments he would sometimes enunciate Barfield's law of book-reading, that 'those who read [something I have written] don't need it, and those who need [the same] don't read it.'

All the greater, therefore, was his joy when Stephen Talbott sent him the printer's proof of his book *The Future Does Not Compute: Transcending the Machines in Our Midst* (O'Reilly and Associates, Inc., May 1995). This is not the place to summarize in any detail the argument of this substantial book (though the title itself does a pretty good succinct job of this). Suffice it to say that Talbott boldly and unapologetically dismisses the claim made by computer-based Information Technology, and the Internet in particular, that it represents that leap forward in human development which so many are hungering for. He argues that what is being manifested in these new technologies are simply the same attitudes already enshrined in our modern world, the main difference being that they are expressed in a far more absolute and uncompromising way than ever before. Such critical analyses of certain aspects of computer technology have been made by others, but it is the distinctive feature of

Talbott's book to have demonstrated that, however revolutionary the technology and the life-style associated with it may be, the underlying *consciousness* that has produced Information Technology is not a whit different from that which 'discovered' perspective at the time of the Renaissance and which has since the Scientific Revolution created an ever more unbridgeable gulf between man and the world that surrounds him. In this sense, 'virtual reality' comes to be seen not so much as a recent technological achievement but as a state of *consciousness* that dawned some 600 years ago, most noticeably in Renaissance Italy.

In order to give substance to his argument, Talbott draws very heavily upon Barfield's work. Indeed, the concluding fourth part of the book and its two appendices are largely devoted to an exposition of the ideas of this thinker who, according to Talbott, has—to a degree unparalleled among modern writers in the English-speaking world—pointed out that what is of the greatest significance in understanding the evolution of human thought is not so much the unfolding through historical time of ideas about the world but the evolution of man's *consciousness* of the world, of his different *experiences* of it (as opposed to different ideas about the same world of experience). Central to Barfield's concept of an evolution of consciousness is his awareness that man participates—whether knowingly or not—in the evocation of phenomena, that the objects of his perception are, in fact, partly of his own creating. Moreover, he argues, only if we become deeply aware that this is the case can we become able to engender for ourselves new worlds of experience and hence free ourselves from the idols—the world which we conceive as having a separate existence outside ourselves—by which we are otherwise imprisoned.

Talbott's book was written for those who, while initially fully enthusiastic about the new technologies under discussion, have come to have certain questions about their effects on personal and social life. The present book is intended for those who, whether or not they have read Stephen Talbott's glowing tribute to Owen Barfield, would like to know more about him. Barfield is, however, notoriously elusive to those who seek access to his ideas but are unable or unwilling to free themselves from the mental habits—or consciousness—belonging to the conventional world-view of modern times. He even had a term that he used to refer to this problem: RUP, or the 'residue of unresolved positivism', the mental condition of those who, while consciously dissenting from the philosophical view (first formulated by Descartes) that there is an unbridgeable gulf between mental experience and the outside world continue to be governed by it in the way they conceive of mental activity as being encompassed within a specific physical body.[1] C.S. Lewis—probably Barfield's most intimate friend—found an apt way of expressing his frustrations when approaching Barfield on the intellectual plane:

> ...the Second Friend is the man who disagrees with you about everything. He is not so much the alter ego as the anti-self. Of course he shares your interests; otherwise he would not become your friend at all. But he has approached them all at a different angle. He has read all the right books but has got the wrong thing out of every one. It is as though he spoke your language but mispronounced it. How can he be so nearly right and yet, invariably, just not right? He is as fascinating (and infuriating) as a woman. When you set out to correct his heresies, you find that he forsooth has decided to correct yours! And then you go at it, hammer and tongs, far into the night, night after night, or walking through fine country that neither gives a glance to, each learning the weight of the other's punches, and often more like mutually respectful enemies than friends.[2]

For this reason, what is attempted here is neither an exposition of Barfield's thought (he is in any case, with his trenchant clarity of expression, his own best expositor), nor a description of his physical existence, which he would have considered either as a futile focus on the uneventful or an unwarranted intrusion into the irrelevant—although, of course, both these elements of physical and mental biography will find expression in what follows. Whenever the subject of conversation turned to the book that might be written about his life, Barfield invariably used the term 'psychography', or 'biography of the soul', the story of the inner life or self; and as a psychography was not only what he wanted but is also, in my view, the most effective way of making him accessible to those whose interest has been aroused by his ideas, my present endeavour is to transform this wish into a reality.

Barfield himself once made the attempt to write his own psychography, or autobiographical reminiscences, but abandoned it in 1948 on the grounds that it became 'too difficult and/or long-winded once psyche had emerged from childhood'. But how is someone other than the subject himself able to write the story of a person's inner life in a meaningful way (as distinct from indulging in fanciful meanderings)? After all, the distinctive quality of a psychography—and what distinguishes it from a more orthodox biography, which largely recounts the past—is that it is the reflection of *present* experience (largely in the form of memories). Now whereas the various physical legacies of Owen Barfield's life—in particular his literary legacy—continue to be available to investigation by the physical senses, his soul, or psyche, quite clearly is not. There is no one, I trust, who would disagree with the proposition that, whatever one's view of the nature of the soul may be, it ceases to be united with the body—or with what the body has fashioned during an earthly life—after death. But what happens to the soul? There are three possible ways of relating to this question. One can either regard it as an absurdity, on the grounds that there is no such thing as a disembodied soul. Alternatively, one might posit some kind of belief as to the destiny of the soul after death but assert the impossibility of gaining any direct knowledge of it. Or it could be that one has the capacity to follow and form a relationship to the unfolding present destiny of a soul that has lived on earth and convey this knowledge to one's fellow human beings. Clearly, the task that Barfield allotted to his biographer would be an impossibility on either of the first two grounds. On the other hand, I have a firm conviction that the third way is a possibility. That was also Owen Barfield's view, avid student that he was of Rudolf Steiner (who had such capacities). The only drawback is that I do not know whether I can achieve it. But, excepting the likelihood that at this stage I may well lose the company of such readers as cannot even grant that such a possibility exists, there is nothing to be lost by giving it a try.

The form of what follows arises out of Rudolf Steiner's indication that, after a brief review—lasting some three or four days—of the life that has been lived, the soul of the person who has died lives in a state of conscious awareness and in a backwards order through the entire content of what has been experienced in sleep, a process that normally lasts for approximately one-third of the life that is now past. The content of one's sleep life, which for most people is largely inaccessible to them during life on earth, is essentially a matter of seeing oneself as though through the mirror of those who were affected by one's words and deeds—one experiences what one has been and meant to others, whether in a positive or a negative sense. On this basis, the present reality of Owen Barfield's soul experience—the earthly present being late October 1999—would correspond very roughly to some five or six years before his death in December 1997, say the year 1991, which happens to have been the year when I came to live near his home in Sussex. This introductory chapter is, therefore, followed by a biographical sketch of Owen Barfield based on a number of interviews that I had with him during this period (largely in the second half of it). This will not only be a rudimentary way of tracing the early part of his present soul journey—in that it recalls and records memories expressed precisely in his last years—but will also serve as a means of giving the reader a general overview of his life.

There then follow the two principal parts of the book, the first (Part Two) taking the thread of Barfield's life back to his first journey to America in 1964 and the second (Part Three) chronicling the years of his dual activity as a lawyer and writer. Each of these parts is organized on a similar basis, with an introductory chapter reflecting Barfield's connection with a well-known, representative figure followed by a chapter on the thinker whose ideas were most seminal for that portion of his life. There then follows a chapter which attempts to give an overall picture of Barfield's own central cognitive preoccupations during these respective phases; and the next three chapters in each part enlarge on this somewhat along the lines of a three-movement work of music, with a threefold statement of—in turn—the fundamental ideas, their inner, reflective deepening and their possible fulfilment or future potential. The final chapter in each of these two parts dwells more on matters of personal and social intimacy, in so far as these are relevant to a psychographical study. The original manuscript also included, as a balancing element to the Biographical Sketch constituting Part One, Barfield's own *Psychography* of 1948, which is of particular value for the light it sheds upon the soul-experiences of his earliest years. However, the Trustees of Barfield's Estate—who have graciously granted permission to quote from his writings—were not able to allow this to be printed here, on the grounds that it is intended to publish this elsewhere. An interested reader might like to look out for its publication and read it in the place appointed for it in the present book. Any further extension of the exploration into Barfield's spiritual background and future destiny is likely to find this piece of writing a valuable springboard. (This paragraph was added in August 2005 in preparation for the book's publication. The book itself had been completed three years previously, in August 2002.)

PART ONE

1. OWEN BARFIELD: A BIOGRAPHICAL SKETCH BASED ON HIS OWN WORDS[3]

Owen Barfield was born on 9 November 1898 in London, at 6 Grosvenor Gardens, Muswell Hill, Middlesex, to Arthur Edward Barfield and his wife Elizabeth as the youngest of their four children. Originally, it seems—although he thinks he may have dreamt his mother recounting this story to him—he was to have been called Humphrey, but his parents changed their minds to Owen while they were on their way to registering his birth. Where the name Owen came from is a mystery, there being no immediate Welsh antecedents.

At the time of his birth, the family lived in the suburb of Muswell Hill. When Owen was six or seven years old, they moved somewhat further away from the centre of London to Whetstone. It was a typically middle-class upbringing in a 'secular' family, where a mood of scepticism reigned with regard to anything of a religious nature. Both parents were from non-conformist backgrounds, most likely Congregationalist. His father, who had had no proper school education and had seven brothers and sisters, was a solicitor. His mother, whose maiden name of Shoults proclaimed a distant German ancestry, likewise came from a large family of six or seven. Apart from being an ardent feminist, she was also an excellent pianist and had a great love of music. Owen himself was the youngest of four children; he had a brother four years older than himself, and two sisters who were some nine or ten years older.

Barfield's memories of his early years centre mainly on his mother's two principal preoccupations of music and feminism. After painting a picture of the family circle, which included a nanny-like figure called Daisy, and two maids, a cook and a housemaid (fairly standard practice in those days), he describes an event which made a considerable impression on him at the time shortly before he began attending school. His mother was in the habit of taking her tea in the dining-room, and Daisy would as a kind of special treat take him down from the nursery—he was by now its principal occupant—to be with his mother, either during or after tea. On this occasion, however—and it must have marked a time when his father had become a bit better off—he was in the drawing-room, and some men arrived with a grand piano. 'I was sitting on the floor, probably with a toy of some sort. At last the men finished putting it up and they went off. My mother sat down and played a Schubert impromptu or a Chopin nocturne. I remember that awfully well.' His mother's feminism arose out of her feeling that women were downtrodden. Nevertheless, she was not content with simply holding a view on the subject but was active in proclaiming it. Although she did not quite dare to join the WSPU (the Women's Social and Political Union), she took part in open-air meetings in Hyde Park. Sometimes she would take the chair, while never actually speaking herself. 'You put up a little stool or something, there was nobody there at all, you started addressing the British Public. Then a few stragglers would come, and there would perhaps be some barracking... She was terrified of drunken men. But she stuck that for a time. She dropped it because my father—who wasn't out of sympathy with her cause—thought it might interfere with his reputation as a solicitor if she got known.'

Barfield was educated at Highgate School, where he started in 1906. 'It meant going by train, with a season ticket. My brother was already at the school, and he was Barfield one and I was Barfield two. Then after a year or so he left... The preparatory school was in a separate building on the other side of the road. The headmaster was a man called Kelly, an Irishman. We wore red blazers, red caps. The lowest form was taken by a woman, a Miss Long. I was about seven or eight when I first went there, I think—certainly not more ... I remember my father taking me before I actively joined the school to see the headmaster of the Junior School, Kelly. I remember him giving me a book to read—I did read quite a lot... I remember him saying, "He can certainly read!"... We began our multiplication tables in the lowest form in the old-fashioned way; we all shouted out in chorus: twice one are two, twice two are four, twice four ... and so on. Another thing we also used to shout out—not shout, exactly—she taught us the capitals of Europe, also the counties of England. I can remember hearing their voices: Norway Christiania on the Christiania fjord, Germany Berlin on the Spree... We started Latin straightaway, Latin and French included, although we were still doing that basic stuff as well.'

One particular memory stands out from this time. The grounds of the Junior School were separated from the road by a long stretch of wall. 'I remember—why I did it God only knows—that I chalked on the wall in large letters, "Mr Kelly is a fool". I didn't really think he was a fool... I was terrified of what I had done, I cried I think; and either my mother or my father, brother or uncle advised me to go and wash it off very early in the morning. Which I did, I got there before the school opened, and before anybody came wiped it off... It was a sign that I had learned to show mischief, I suppose ... I didn't dislike him, I didn't have much to do with Mr. Kelly. I don't know... People call each other fools, you know what small boys are ... For some reason, I do remember that very clearly.'

By the time he had reached the age of 12 or 13, Barfield was in the top form of the Junior School, and was top of it for one term. It was then time for him to cross the road to the old Public School founded in 1565 by Roger Cholmondeley, and—as was the custom for those who came from the Junior School—he by-passed the first three forms into the Fourth and Remove. 'And there you started ... well, not started, you had learnt Latin of course, but you took it seriously, you learnt Latin verse, and you had to write some Latin verse. I remember the master teaching us the rhythm of the hexameter and pentameter and making us all say: "Dum-dum-dum-diddle-dum, dum-diddle-dum-diddle-dum." Well, I went further up the school. Then I began to have trouble with stammering.' This became an increasingly serious affliction as he passed from the Shell (the form after Fourth and Remove) into the Fifth Form, when it became necessary to decide whether to specialize on the classical side (Greek and Latin) or the modern side (German language, commercial geography 'and things'), and on into the Sixth Form. 'For a time it was really terrible. Not only did I stutter but couldn't say anything. And it sometimes irritated the master, the classical master—there were two of them, there was the form master Doughton, an English gentleman, and a classical master called Simmonds, rather strict but also very capable—and he sometimes got very irritated with my stammering. Anyhow, I felt it more and more because it also came out when I was talking to school friends, and it was when I was still at school—I was probably in the Sixth Form by then—yes, it was from 1914, when the First World War was declared; and it got so bad that in despair one night when going to bed, when asking myself if on the whole I would prefer not to wake up again, I came to the conclusion that I would ... I believe that I mentally—I'm not sure whether I wrote it down—composed the first poem I wrote, it was addressed to sleep: 'Sleep has a brother...' Sweet sister sleep—the idea that you didn't want to wake up again. I don't think I experimented with poetry again for a long time after that! That doesn't mean that I was like that the whole time, all day and every day. You had your games and larks, but it was a great shadow in my life from that point of view ... I think the sudden increase in 1914 may very well have been suppressed fear, I don't know.'

Barfield thinks that his stammering could very well have been associated with the onset of war. At any rate, it did seem to have a purely psychological origin, and did not respond to therapies based on focusing upon the physical organs of speech. Reciting poetry, singing and acting never presented any problem. Thus, for example, he recalls a regular family custom: 'At Christmas time we always did charades . . . It became a custom on Christmas Day that we entertained the uncles, aunts and cousins on my mother's side and on Boxing Day we entertained the cousins, uncles and aunts on my father's side. My two sisters and my brother and I put on charades or did a play—they published little plays for actors to do—and then I could manage all right. I played the principal part in one, an invalid in a nursing-home; I put on a special voice, a sort of quavering voice, and with that I got away with the stammering, I remember that very well.'

His stammering didn't affect his academic work, but was more of a social affliction. He recalls vying with Cecil Harwood—whom he first encountered as a fellow pupil in the Fourth and Remove who had, unlike Barfield, not attended the Junior School and had passed through the bottom three forms of the Upper School[4]—at the top of the Classical Sixth, by which time there were only some 12–15 pupils left in the class. (At the time the modern side was increasing, while the classical side was decreasing relatively in numbers.) The classics master—the fondly remembered Doughton, who was in Holy Orders without having a living—would dedicate an hour or more to conversing freely about English literature, and Barfield was very grateful for this. The pupils on the classical side didn't study English literature as such, however, just classical literature, Latin and Greek; and it was clearly very important for Barfield that he had this foundation in classics, both language and literature. He recalls one success with a certain tinge of amusement: 'In my last Summer Term at the end of the academic year—I suppose it would have been 1915, probably—I got a Governors' Gold Medal for Latin verse. Now that was a thing—the prize and the Gold Medal that went with it—donated not by the Government or by the finances of the school but by the Governors. I don't know how many years back it went. Anyhow, with the Governors' Gold Medal for Latin verse you had a passage set for you over the holidays, 100 lines of English poetry, which you had to put into Latin verse. They got fewer and fewer candidates for that. I was actually the last one who did it. I got the Gold Medal! And I was assured that my work attained a high enough standard—but I wasn't competing with anyone else at all. I don't suppose it was ever given again—pretty unlikely, I should think.'

The World War exerted an influence in other ways on Barfield's last years at school. 'I was still in the Upper School, fairly high up in it, getting on towards leaving. I had to join the Officers' Training Corps . . . We went out on exercises, some kind of route march around Highgate . . . It was a strain, because we lived some distance from Highgate. I had to go by train and return by train at night; and after a full day at school on either one or two days a week I had to go on a route march or whatever they called it, in khaki uniform, khaki puttees I think they called them. Anyway, by the time you'd had a day in school and all this military exercise afterwards and the train journey home you were pretty well worn out. A bit of a strain all that time. And then of course older boys were joining up, and I remember one boy in the Sixth Form—I think that by that time I was also in the Sixth Form—joined up, and we heard after a few weeks I think it was that he was dead, not at the front but in some kind of accident when he was teaching or learning. This cast a great shadow over everything . . . I was also critical, partly because my family were not madly jingoistic; they rather viewed it from a detached point of view, they thought the patriotism was a bit phoney. I remember the Officers' Training Corps had to go to a church parade, and I was very embarrassed because we never went to church[5] and I didn't quite know when to stand up and when to sit down. I also remember very vividly our own Sixth Form master, Doughton . . . he took the service and preached the sermon. Oh yes, we were doing Aeschylos' *Agamemnon*, and he quoted the English translation of the chorus, 'Cry aloud for the world, and let the good prevail'—and he applied this to the situation of the Allies against Germany. He also said, addressing the boys in the congregation: 'If I know anything of the spirit of a public schoolboy, and I think I do, they're all longing to be in the thick of it'; and I remember criticizing this mentally very strongly . . . Of course in the early days of the war it was all very jolly, and everybody joined up and gave their ages as older than they were, went marching off to Germany to the horrors of the front, the slaughter . . . I remember one of the politicians or somebody who . . . specified three years as the duration of the war, and I remember—I think it was in a newspaper—it being said that everyone was horrified at the idea that the war might last as long as three years. Of course, the youngsters that were joining up would say they'd be back in six months, they'd roll up the Germans . . . It was a dark time, and it got darker and darker somehow . . .'

In the normal course of events Barfield would have gone on to university after leaving school, but the war prevented this. Finally, his own summons came, even though, characteristically, his war service lacked any real military element. 'Well then, about 1917, early 1917 in the spring, I was called up. They had introduced conscription by then. I should have joined by then anyhow, my brother had done; and I remember that because my brother was in what is now called the Signals Service, which was then a section of the Royal Engineers, I also got into the Royal Engineers. I was quite anxious not to be in the Infantry . . . because I think the average expectancy of life of a young infantry officer by the time we'd got to 1916 or 1917 was about three weeks after he had got out there. Anyway, I joined up and was posted to start with—I don't quite know why—to a unit in Worcester, a unit of the Royal Engineers, the Signals Service.

I'd hardly been away from home before, I never stayed long away from home, and I was mixed up with men of all ages and was pretty homesick. I was also rather proud of being independent, earning my own money and so forth. In Worcester, where we were for some time, for a few months, I had got quite a number of books from the Lending Library, a good deal of lighter literature, Charles Lamb's *Essays* and so forth . . . In the early part of the time one spent quite a while learning Morse Code . . . For quite a time I was just a private. You weren't called a private in the Royal Engineers; you were called a pioneer to start with, and then you were promoted to sapper—you got a slightly higher weekly wage—I think you got 14 shillings a week as a sapper, quite a lot in those days. I must have been there[6] the best part of a year, I should think. Then I was made a lance corporal . . . and one of the things we did was to take men who had come back temporarily from the front through a short course in wireless telegraphy. I came into quite close contact with a number of colonials in that way. You got a group of South Africans, a group of Australians, New Zealanders coming over at different times . . . Some of the men had really had tough experience on active service; they hadn't been actually wounded but they'd been right through the strain of combat. They were much older than me. I was rather a baby-face in those days, and I had to give classes to men back from the front. I lectured them, I suppose, on wireless telegraphy; then I marched them from one room to another, and so forth . . . They rather joked that I was like a baby, really! They regarded me as a bit of a joke, but they were decent, really. Not obstreperous at all.

By then I had applied for a cadetship, which is on the way to becoming an officer. This was to take me into the wireless section of the Royal Engineers. My brother was already an officer in that, and he helped my application along. But they must have lost the papers, because I remained in England . . . for something like 18 months. Ordinarily I should have been posted abroad long before that, or I should have started training as a cadet. But as I say they lost my papers, and that was why I remained so long as what corresponded to a private soldier in the ranks and then became a lance corporal. At last the application came through, and I went through a course as a cadet in the Royal Engineers, and that meant going to riding-school, learning to ride a horse and various things, and that must have taken me about three or four months I suppose. I was then commissioned and became a second lieutenant and was hanging about in the officers' mess waiting to be sent abroad when the Armistice was signed! But I was sent abroad just the same. You see, the machinery went on grinding. I was quite used to this by then ... I think I may have mentioned before that on active service if you wanted to send a message from one part of the line to another you could do this in various ways. Sometimes you could use an actual line of sticks, sometimes you could use telegraph, sometimes you could use a runner to send a message. The one thing you never used was wireless telegraphy, because it was in its infancy then, it was almost experimental, there was no reliance on it at all. But once the Armistice was signed and there was no active service, it was never used. So there I was just kicking my heels in Belgium, for ... the Armistice was signed in November and I was demobilized in June—just doing nothing! There were some advantages. I had a horse to use for my own pleasure; and I used the time for brushing up my French, because you can learn French at a school—at least you could then—quite attentively and thoroughly and it would be of no use to you at all for practical purposes. So I got hold of Hugo's French grammar and really worked hard at it while I was there, I didn't have much else to do.'

During this period in Belgium, however, a further 'distraction' was dreamt up for Barfield. 'After the Armistice the army couldn't be demobilized all at once, there were soldiers hanging about with nothing to do, spending their whole time playing football; but somebody started a scheme that there should be education for them, and I was chosen among others as one of the officers who would look after the education of our unit. For that purpose you had quite a number of books sent out from England, what you might call the classics, Charles Dickens, Sir Walter Scott ... but they also provided a course of three weeks at Oxford to teach you how to teach English ... And I was sent over to Oxford—actually, I was already a scholar at an Oxford college; I was longing to go there as an undergraduate (Harwood was already there at Christ Church as an undergraduate; he was demobilized much earlier than I was). And here was I planted at Keble College in uniform ... Well, I got particularly interested in poetry, I think before the war broke out; my sister was quite interested. I was quite interested in the Georgian poets . . . And I think by the time I was sent abroad I had started occasionally to write some poetry, only very occasionally and very sporadic. It was very odd. During the three weeks' course that I was sent to while still in the Army, there was a daily hour or more with a man called Rene Lambourne, who was a real enthusiast for English literature. And I must say that he woke something in me or encouraged something in me that hadn't quite been got hold of while still at school or in the Army. It was perhaps the result of that that, while the scholarship I got for Oxford was in classics, Greek and Latin and ancient history, and I ought to have read what they called Greats (which is also philosophy and classics), I asked permission to change to English language and English literature, which was kindly granted. I've never been quite sure since whether I was wise to do that. I had a lot of contact with C.S. Lewis, who was a real classical scholar . . . I used to envy him; he had read about three or four times as much Greek and Latin as I had. On the other hand, I don't know—but that's what happened. I did struggle through to get a first class degree . . . One very trying feature of the English course as it then was, one of the things that the School of English Language and Literature demanded of you was the study of phonetics. And there was an enthusiast for phonetics called Wilde—I found it an awful bore, somehow. Talking about the larynx and—I don't know.'

Barfield was at Oxford (Wadham College) between 1919 and 1923. He has little to say about his actual studies, though quite a bit about his literary and other activities. 'I think I'd begun to write some poetry myself then, or certainly wanted to. I think I wanted to write myself, I hadn't written anything serious by the time I'd left the army. My first publication of an article in an English journal was I think in my first year at Oxford.[7] I should have first gone to college in I suppose November 1918, but I was still in the army then doing nothing, and that went on until June . . . That meant that my first entry to Oxford was in September (1919) . . . The two first things I published, one of them was in the *Cornhill Magazine*—I don't know whether it's still going—called "The Reader's Eye", and that tried to tell about the effect that is presented by a really exciting piece of poetry when you read it, almost suggesting that you got more aesthetic experience from reading than from hearing it spoken—heterodox. There is something that you get in reading a poem with the particular combination of words that leap out of the page. And the other one appeared round about the same time, in *The New Statesman*, called "Form in Poetry".[8] . . . It was a man called Clive Bell, I think, an art critic who wrote a book where he raised the question, "How do you distinguish art from something that isn't art at all?". He said that art must have "significant form". And you mustn't say significant of what, the whole point is that it should just be significant . . . Now there was interest in that kind of thing . . . Of course, the point was, he was saying by "significant form" that everything of value depended on the form and not the matter. Someone then suggested that perhaps the same applied to poetry. In that case, what exactly is a poem? All sorts of stupid ideas were advanced—should one write a poem in a special shape on some sort of paper? And I pointed out that form in poetry lies not in the sense-perceptible world but in consciousness, the human consciousness between the poet and his reader.' As Barfield points out in the afterword to *A Barfield Sampler*, writing the article in question 'was in fact the occasion of my beginning to contemplate human consciousness as a field, a category, a thing to be thought about and studied in its own right. From there the step was a relatively short one to the evolution of consciousness, which has always been my major theme.'

After mentioning some of the leading lights on his literary horizon, amongst whom were in particular Walter de la Mare and Yeats, Keats and Shelley, he suddenly turns to chronicling another activity of his Oxford years: 'Either in my first or second term I noticed an advertisement for the English Folk Dance Society . . . And I thought I'd try what they were like. I remember very well that in my own family at Christmas time—we had a lot of relations—we always finished up dancing Sir Roger de Coverley, which is a folk dance. It always stuck in my mind that when I saw this I thought that the more there is of that kind of thing the better and that I'll try it. So I went to the first class there—as a spectator of course—and then I joined. I got very keen on it, especially Morris dancing, which is only men. It is traditionally only danced by men, but of course women were in the class as well. And that led quite soon—I don't know if it was my first summer vacation—that I had this invitation. There were three sisters in Cornwall—the other side of the Fal from Falmouth—who were very keen on taking music to the villages all around. They thought, quite rightly, I think, that the Cornish people had a special appreciation of music, and they wanted to add some dancing—not folk dancing so much, not classical, but court dancing, out of which many of the movements of the concerto, symphony and so forth were written. So they took these round—they first of all took the music only, one played the violin and one played the piano, a third played the cello, and they added some dancing which they did themselves or with women friends.

They had an unhappy experience at one of the concerts, I think in Truro, with some rowdy sailors, and they said at a meeting afterwards that they must have some men. How would they get them? So they notified the English Folk Dance Society of their requirements, and they passed it on to me: the offer was to whoever wanted to stay in their coastguard cottage, on the coast of Cornwall, and be taken round to various places to dance to their music. They would pay your expenses. So I offered *myself*, and had a lovely time. Purcell, Handel, Bach ... minuets, gavottes, correntos ... sarabandes. They had quite an ordinary cottage; they'd built a large studio at the back, just a wooden building, merely a room. So I rehearsed the dances with them there, and took them round with their programme of music to five or six villages. That became a kind of habit; we went out the next year as well.'

After a brief pause, Barfield goes on to speak about an experience which arose out of these visits to Cornwall: 'I fell in love, or thought I had fallen in love, with a girl ... a cousin of the two sisters who ran the place ... not requited ... I don't really know how much I was in love with this woman, girl, or just in love with the idea of love ... I was in despair, and the despair was not simply because of this, for I had no confidence in the meaning of life, that life had any meaning; and I was very much oppressed. That was mixed up in it ... Looking back at the past, I realize I wasn't really in love with her but either in love with love or with what I hoped to find in the world of nature in general and so forth. Anyway, she turned me down, and at the time I got very, very miserable, utterly depressed—I must have been rather trying for friends of the family, I should think. But what was really at the root of the misery, I realized afterwards, was this being caged in the materialism of the age. I was interested in poetry, and was of a very romantic disposition, I suppose. Anyway, I did go through a very painful and depressing time for months, I don't know for how many months but quite a long time. Rather suddenly one evening, one fine evening, at the end of a holiday in Switzerland, the clouds sort of lifted—I know this sounds very dramatic, but it is rather essential—all the misery that I had felt, all this lifted with it, because I felt I would be able to find all the beauty I had fallen for in this woman in the whole world of nature. I wrote a sonnet sequence—this was before the relief I have just mentioned, I was in despair—nine sonnets, which were published in the *London Mercury*, then the leading literary journal in English[9] ... I got to know in a fairly superficial way the editor of the *London Mercury*, J.C. Squire, very well known in literary circles, and also the literary editor of *The New Statesman*. I got a little bit into the outer fringes of literary circles . . . After this lifting of the heavy cloud of the depression, the misery almost, I added another couple of sonnets to the sequence, which were never published. I tried to give expression to this lifting of the depression from the bereavement . . . I remember the last line of one of them:

O Eve, my soul, my eyes with which I see![10]

Now I'm not saying that they're particularly good sonnets. But why I thought I couldn't just leave this out was because it was what led into the whole shape and development of my literary and philosophical work, because at the time I had the love-affair and the sequel to it I was deeply involved with poetry, both reading and writing it, especially the English Romantics, Keats and Shelley, Shakespeare's Sonnets and so forth . . . My book *Poetic Diction* was, in a way, looking back to that time, a kind of development from this—what I call—Sophia experience. I pointed out that the realm of material nature which can be experienced in poetry was formerly—it can only be expressed nowadays in the form of metaphor—not a metaphor but an actual experience. That was the basis of my philosophical work.'

The third strand associated with Barfield's visits to Cornwall was his marriage to the lady who taught the dances. Maud (christened Matilda) Douie (1885–1980) was several years older than Owen. Like his mother, she had a great love of music. 'She had a delightful faculty for singing Scots songs, ballads and things. She could talk exactly like an Edinburgh Scotswoman . . . We married in 1923 . . .'[11]

Again and again in his reminiscences, Barfield returns to the three or four summers that he spent in Cornwall while a student at Oxford. In a later conversation he brings these experiences into connection with a more general review of his life:[12] 'It occurred to me, as a general observation, that I've been very fortunate in my physical body: I've never had a surgical operation—and am terrified of having one—and have only been under anaesthetic twice, each time in a dentist's chair, not in a hospital, and apart from all the usual childhood illnesses I haven't really had anything. I've been very lucky, really. But I think it's also true that my physical development around puberty time was rather swift. I was rather late, and I think to start with I was rather underdeveloped, rather a skinny, undersized little boy, you know; and then when development did come it came with rather a rush. I was in a public school where games were compulsory. I didn't care for them very much. My father got me an exemption from games, so I was free in the afternoons. The headmaster at

Highgate School was against that, but he had to agree because my father asked for it. He had me up for interview, and he had this phrase: "I should have thought a fellow of your physique could do with something like that." I assumed he meant that I was a skinny little thing and I needed football to buck me up; so I went home and told my parents what he said, and they instantly said: "Oh no, you've got a very good physique!" Apparently I had by that time. I'd suddenly developed—I won't say handsome but—quite sizeable. And not because this had happened or had been said but I found I got very keen on gymnastics—the real gymnastics, with apparatus and horizontal bars, parallel bars, vaulting horse, etc. The school didn't pay a lot of attention to it and I don't think their standard was very high. So in a year or two I became practically the senior gymnast in the school—not that I was very advanced either but their standard was so low! The public schools used to send two representatives to Aldershot every year to compete with other public schools, and the year when I would have been the right sort of age the war broke out. Had it been as usual I think I should have represented the school. It was quite a thing—I was quite an experienced gymnast. It was this late development. I don't think I was conceited at all, but I was rather well developed, had rather a good figure and held myself well and so forth.

Then of course there came about 15 months' military service and everything was in abeyance. After that, in 1919, I went to Oxford. I hadn't been there long before I spotted an advertisement for the English Folk Dance Society. This rather attracted me, as I was keen on things to do with the body generally. I joined them, I got especially keen on Morris Dancing . . . Country dancing is fun, but Morris Dancing is a bit more. The characteristic of it is that you remain in the same spot, your body is always vertical, except for your arms, and the music plays through you horizontally. I remember having a vivid experience at the end of one of the movements. You stand there, arms going up and down in one rhythm and your feet tapping in another—and I had a very strong experience of the music flowing through me, so to speak. I was motionless, but the music was flowing through me. It was very strong. I got very keen on Morris Dancing, and did quite a lot. I also attained a prominent position in a group of people who represented the Folk Dance Society at Oxford. We used to give performances in the grounds of big houses and so forth occasionally, that sort of thing. I did quite a lot of it. Well, that led to something quite different, a different part in my early life, anyhow.

There were two sisters who lived near Falmouth called Radford. They were very keen on Cornish people, they thought that the ordinary

Cornish people had something musical in them. They were both very musical, and they organized a kind of party in the summertime, a concert party; they took concert performances round various villages and some towns as well, such as Truro. So there were those two, and they had also ... during those concert tours or concert performances the lady who afterwards became my wife, Maud Douie. She was Scottish by birth ... she had a lot to do with historic dances, she had worked with them, had worked with Gordon Craig at one time. She joined them for these concert arrangements. Well now, they had an unhappy time on one occasion—I don't remember where it was, Truro or somewhere—but they were very keen on having dancing as well as music, you see. Of course, they only had themselves and two other women. They had to have women dressed as men, and that led to some rather ribald comments. They ended up after that performance saying: Ah well, we must have men! They didn't know how to get the men, so they wrote to the English Folk Dance Society in Oxford. Then I was asked if I would like to go down there and join them for the next performance, also staying beforehand—they would pay expenses. Well, I jumped at that, I'd always wanted to go to Cornwall—for one thing, I'd never been there.

They had a sort of cottage right on the sea, on the Fal, opposite Falmouth, the other side of the Fal from Falmouth; there was a big studio attached to it. We'd spend about a week or a fortnight rehearsing and getting used to the music beforehand; then we'd tour around—generally it was by boat I think in those days, there weren't so many cars—to these various villages and one or two towns. I jumped at it, rather, and had a lovely fortnight there. There was a tremendous lot of music. They were both very musical. And I got to know the kind of dances that they incorporated in their programme, the country dances or contradanses, not done now—you hardly ever see their names except as the title of movements, or suites. Things like galliard, pavane, bourrée, that sort of thing. We learnt and actually practised them. One of them played the piano, the other played the violin, and they had a friend who did the cello. Altogether, it was a kind of new world for me—not that we'd had no music at home... But all this was—I don't know—delightful. I repeated that experience for three or four years, I think. We also got to know them very well. Maud Douie, who did the costumes and taught the dances, was an old friend of theirs, they had met her before. She specialized in the history of dancing and studied a book all about the history of these old dances... Anyway, I was in touch with her, she lived in town—in touch with her there... There was a great deal of music and dancing.'

Maisie and Evelyn Radford had a third sister, Marian, who lived at Bath. All three had been to university (Evelyn had a First in classics), besides being very musical. 'Then of course there was Maud Douie... After three or four years we married. She was a good deal older than me; and she was also engaged as the dancing instructor to a thing called the Oxford Ballet... A very curious idea it was. I don't know whose idea it was. Anyway, they produced I think mainly Bach's music; and Maud Douie was engaged to produce the dances. So she would come down to Oxford a good deal. So as I say we married; and we were both keen on doing something like what the Radfords had been doing. We had plans for getting a caravan, going round—all that sort of thing. There were one or two people in Oxford who would have been interested to join us... My wife and I produced a little show, we called it a Children's Theatre. We did intend to run it as a profession and charge for entrance. I think we did have it for one performance. The idea was to go round the children's parties, the children of the wealthy part of the population, and do these nursery rhymes and so forth. We did "The frog he would a-wooing go"—I was the frog and she was the mouse. We hoped to develop that. Nothing became of it much. The trouble was with the music. We were determined not to have mechanical music, but if you had real performers it got frightfully expensive... So I was very much involved with the whole business of dancing and producing something along the same lines as the Radfords in Cornwall. My wife and I wanted to do this... The Radfords went on and did quite a lot. We used to go down for the summer holidays and used to see them fairly often.'

It is clear from Barfield's recollections that these activities—in Oxford and (in the summer) in Cornwall—played a large part in his life during the 1920s. 'The picture I'm trying to convey is that during the whole of this period—say, most of the second half of the 1920s, not necessarily all of it—I was really more involved with this than with writing anything. I must have been writing, because *History in English Words* was published in 1926; and I must have started on the novel ['English People'] by the end of the 1920s. Yet the kind of picture I have of the sort of thing my mind was full of—it wasn't literature, it was all these possibilities of dancing and so forth... In those years—the late 1920s and the first part of the 1930s—my mind was more involved with that kind of thing than it was with writing.'

Writing during this period consisted largely of composing articles. 'After my marriage, of course, I was finishing *Poetic Diction*, well, almost writing it, I don't think I'd got anywhere with it as a book until after we'd married... Then I got this temporary job on the weekly periodical called

Truth. It was a curious periodical, with its roots deep in the past. It had started off in Victorian days but was still going in the 1920s and on into the 1930s. Quite unique really, a serious kind of political comment but also rather cheeky. A kind of ironical attitude to the world in general. I had a queer job on that, about one and a half days a week. Before the weekend I used to get one section which was Church Appointments—it was a kind of society or high-class paper as well as being cheeky, and they always had these Church Appointments. It was sent to me by the man who wrote it. I had to sub-edit it over the weekend and take it up on the Monday to the office of *Truth* in London; and by Tuesday mid-day my week was over! I got about £4 a week for that, I think—quite a lot in those days. I got to doing a bit more than that as well. I did an occasional article I think, but there were also news paragraphs in every week's issue with a little heading and then some incident and then very often a caustic comment on it by the editor. And as time went on the editor used me more; he asked me to find things to write about, to write these kinds of columns. I remember one in particular—I had rather a job because I didn't read the papers a lot and didn't easily find the sort of things that would be interesting to readers. I remember once finding something very suitable. There was a magistrate in London somewhere who used to try to prevent parents who were objecting to vaccination of their children. They had a statutory right, but he wanted to try to prevent them using that statutory right. *Truth* got on to him and he didn't know what to do with it. I remember I did a couple of paragraphs on the lines of what they wanted . . . I also made contributions to the *New Statesman* and the *London Mercury* . . . I was associated with *Truth* only for one or two years. They didn't kick me out; they wanted me to join the staff as a permanent member. Well, I didn't want to do that, because if I did I'd have to gradually trim my personality to the paper. I was rather sorry because I liked the people, and got on very well with them. They wanted me, but I said no. Good thing I did, because it wouldn't have suited me really . . . Yes, I certainly had a shot at making a living of a literary career. I couldn't be independent. I knew I would have to fall in with one of the current schools of literature—either the old Georgian one or T.S. Eliot. I didn't have any real feeling for either of them. (The Georgian poets wrote lyrics about the English countryside and that sort of thing, domestic life—all very strict, established forms.) . . . After we'd married—I wasn't earning anything, my wife had a little money—I wrote a few articles for literary journals and so forth. Had I not had my other central interest and possible activity in the theatrical world and dancing I suppose I might have become much more integrated into the literary circles of the time ... I was a bit detached from the current fashions of the time, was completely outside them ... Middleton Murry and his gang... And of course the Bloomsbury Group were no use to me at all.'

A third crucial strand in Barfield's life during the 1920s was anthroposophy. The place of encounter was, again, Cornwall. His old school-friend, Cecil Harwood, had joined him as man and dancer during his second summer with the Radfords (1921); and in 1922 (and also the following year) Harwood was accompanied by Daphne Olivier, who—in addition to being a singer and fiddle player—was a schoolteacher who was to become his wife. As Barfield reports in his obituary of Harwood (Supplement to Members' News Sheet, Anthroposophical Society in Great Britain, February 1976), Daphne at some point either prior to or during this period attended an education conference in Stuttgart at which Rudolf Steiner lectured, and she had become deeply interested in Rudolf Steiner's ideas on education. Through her, Harwood and Barfield began—'rather sceptically', as Barfield records—attending some weekly lecture-readings[13] which George Adams (then George Kaufmann) was conducting at 46 Gloucester Place (near Regents Park). Things moved fairly rapidly, as by 1923 (probably in that year, or maybe 1924) Barfield had joined the Anthroposophical Society. His reason for doing so was characteristic: 'When I first joined the Society I still wasn't really a committed anthroposophist. Quite a number of the books that are now published weren't published then, only in typescript form, and also the leading thoughts that Steiner was giving every week, which were translated into English dutifully and published—I shan't say they were top-class but they were good enough; and I read a tremendous lot of them in English translation. I realized how much I owed to the Society, and I really joined because I thought it wasn't fair not to... My membership card has actually got Rudolf Steiner's signature on it, so that must have been before he died [in 1925]... Well, I must have joined in 1923, probably', a few weeks or months before Harwood also joined. In his obituary of Harwood, Barfield records the next development: 'Very soon after this came the 1924 Torquay Conference,[14] which changed everything. Daphne, with whom Cecil had remained in touch, was of course going; and both he and [Walter] Field decided to attend as well, I myself, to my lasting regret, not being free to do so. I recall very vividly a telephone conversation after his return, in which he briefly informed me that Rudolf Steiner was a simply astounding man, and that he himself had decided to become a teacher in a school that was still to be founded. He did not say so, but it was clear, even through the microphone, that he had become a dedicated man.' Immediately after this conference at Torquay, Rudolf Steiner gave two lectures in London on his way back to Dornach, and Barfield attended the first of these (24 August 1924). 'I've got quite a clear recollection of that of course, very clear. I didn't know German at that time, but George Adams, a very good translator, used to go around with Dr Steiner. I don't know how he did it. He didn't actually use shorthand, he used some kind of semi-shorthand of his own. Steiner would speak for twenty minutes, George would get up and summarize, or more than summarize, he would more or less repeat what he had said . . . I think Steiner was very aware of what he owed to George Adams in that way, or of what the Movement owed anyway. I remember that lecture very well, because he started talking about Laurence Oliphant. I'd never heard of Laurence Oliphant before . . . His previous incarnation was Ovid (with one intermediate female incarnation) . . . Steiner was of course pretty ill at the time. I remember him getting on to the platform, not actually tottering but looking pretty weak and white. And then he lectured himself into vigour and health; by the end of the lecture he was not quite striding up and down the platform but walking up and down, gesturing and so forth. When he first came onto the platform one really felt quite anxious whether he would be able to keep it up. George Adams asked me if I would like an interview with him. I stupidly said no. Actually at that time I'm not sure I was a member then, it was certainly an elementary stage of my anthroposophical connection. I think I thought it wasn't fair to take his time if I didn't have anything to say to him. But I've realized since that he could see things in you, give advice; and I'm rather sorry I missed that chance.'

Poetic Diction, published by Faber and Gwyer in 1928, represented the synthesis of, on the one hand, Barfield's own observations of his experience of the enjoyment of language (especially lyric poetry)—both as a result of his own appreciation of, and wonder at, the natural world and his literary studies—and, on the other and, his study of anthroposophy. As he makes clear in a lecture delivered at Rudolf Steiner House in 1976 or 1977,[15] these two elements ran on parallel paths for some time before they finally came together in this book, which sets out his philosophy of language and lays the foundation for all his subsequent writings. This is not the place to describe this book in detail. However, it is worth recording what Barfield refers to in the lecture just mentioned as to the source of what came to fulfilment in *Poetic Diction*. When he was eleven or twelve years old, attention was being drawn in a Latin lesson to the way that the accusative case is used to express duration of time; and the particular sentence chosen to illustrate this point was 'Cato, octoginta annos natus, excessit e vita' (Cato died aged eighty). 'Nevertheless', recalls Barfield, 'the boy sitting next to him [the subject of his lecture, i.e. himself] suddenly observed: "Cato at the age of eighty *walked out of life*—that's rather nice!" or words to that effect'. Barfield continues: 'You see, what this friend (whose name incidentally was Cecil Harwood) was drawing attention to, because it tickled his fancy, was a *metaphor*. You can say "Cato died". You can also say "Cato walked out of life". Well, of course the Subject himself was familiar with other metaphors, with figurative language, figures of speech; but it had never occurred to him before that it was possible to *enjoy* them, to relish them, for their own sake . . .'

Poetic Diction itself was the fruit of a B.Litt. thesis: 'I had vaguely asked to study for a B.Litt. I got my ordinary degree like everybody else [in the Summer of 1921]. Then I chose to go for a B.Litt. (among all the other possible degrees). If you go for a B.Litt. you have to write a thesis or dissertation; you choose it yourself and submit it to the examiners, and you generally have a supervisor. They accepted my proposition that I would do a thesis on poetic diction. But the question was the supervisor. In the end they decided it wasn't at all what they were used to. The kind of thing they were used to was the very scholarly sort of question, whether Coleridge had an unusual number of toenails, for example. In the end they said that I'd better do without a supervisor. I got the degree all right,[16] and it turned into the book *Poetic Diction*.'

During their first year at Oxford, Barfield and Harwood were in different colleges (Barfield at Wadham, Harwood at Christ Church). In their second year, however, they shared a house together with two other men, in Pembroke Street. When they returned to Oxford in the autumn of 1921 for their postgraduate studies they shared rooms for one term in Grove Street and then for the remainder of the academic year they took a furnished cottage in the village of Beckley (the first time either of them had lived in the country). Among the many visitors who bicycled from Oxford during this time was C.S. Lewis. Lewis was almost exactly the same age as Barfield, being born 29 November 1898, and was still an undergraduate at University College, whence he took a Double First in Greats in the summer of 1922. This was the beginning of a friendship that lasted for some 40 years until Lewis died in 1963, and was probably the most important in Barfield's life. The two men shared a love and appreciation of literature and poetry and in many other ways had much in common. But they maintained sharply differing views as to the ultimate source of what they appreciated and its accessibility to the human imagination. Barfield—following Steiner—affirmed in this respect the existence and knowability of a world which for Lewis was ultimately (except at the very end of his life) a closed book. This dispute took the form of a series of letters and academic treatises—known affectionately as 'The Great War'—which the two friends shared with one another principally between 1925 and 1927. Its rumblings, though, continued until around the time of Lewis's conversion to Christianity (1929), after which he (Lewis) regarded the subject as closed and the difference of opinion unbridgeable. After affirming that Lewis was so central a figure in his life, Barfield goes on to characterize the fundamental difference in their world-views: 'The difference between Lewis and myself in our thinking went right to the heart of the matter. He wouldn't abandon the materialist paradigm—although at the end of his life I think he did. He had no conception of the epistemological significance of the imagination, although he valued it . . . But right at the end of his life he really did get the notion of imagination as a vehicle of knowledge as well as feeling through his idea of the Sacrament—one or two sermons he preached in the university church did rather suggest the idea that imagination is a part of reality and not just an entertaining comment on reality . . . He says, when he deals with our friendship in *Surprised by Joy*, that I influenced him more than he influenced me—and I think he's right as far as change of outlook is concerned; but his influence on me was very strong in compelling me to think responsibly and logically. I'm not sure that at one time, in the early stages of our conflict, he didn't pull me up and stop me developing a theory of two kinds of truth.' It remains only to add at this stage that it was entirely characteristic of their relationship that not only did Barfield dedicate *Poetic Diction* 'to C.S. Lewis: Opposition is true friendship' but Lewis similarly dedicated his first *magnum opus*, *The Allegory of Love* (1936), 'to Owen Barfield: Wisest and best of my unofficial teachers'.

At the time of the 'Great War' with Lewis, Barfield and his wife were living at Long Crendon, 15 miles from Oxford. From here they tried to build up the travelling entertainment business mentioned earlier. In addition to trying to create something of a living out of the children's theatre, Barfield was also seeking to establish himself as a writer. It was in this respect unfortunate that the first edition of *Poetic Diction* appeared at a time when romanticism was thoroughly out of fashion and was to remain so for a couple of decades (the second edition was received more favourably when it appeared in 1952). 'There was a kind of taboo not simply on specific religious belief or faith but on any suggestion in anything you wrote that there might be some meaning in the world—there was a kind of taboo on it, it was almost indecent . . . The idea was that any alleged perception of meaning in the world was due to wishful thinking. And I more or less accepted that before I began to think seriously. C.S. Lewis certainly did, we both did. While I was working all this out, participation and so forth, I had the uneasy feeling that it might all be wishful thinking . . . But I decided just to go on with it, see where the thoughts led me, and it seemed to work out all right . . .' In the summer of 1929 Owen and Maud spent some time on holiday in Germany, staying in the 'nice little university town' of Bonn for two or three months, and it was during this time that Owen recalls beginning the writing of his long unpublished novel 'English People', an intellectual tapestry of English life in the late 1920s, a kind of spiritual odyssey in which the struggles referred to above are explored in various ways by the characters in the novel. The writing of this novel appears to have been done by degrees over a period of years rather than months, and it was the rejection of the manuscript—hardly surprising, perhaps, in view of its unfashionable philosophical range and depth—by several publishers which led Barfield to the conclusion that he would have to earn his living in some other way.[17] It was also in this period that the Barfields adopted two children, Alexander and Lucy (their third child, Jeffrey, was fostered by them during the Second World War).

It is not really possible to follow the course of Owen Barfield's biography after this point with any understanding without some reference to his domestic circumstances. For while he was possibly too independent a thinker to find a niche in some established academic or literary circle, his wife's views about anthroposophy—which greatly stimulated and enhanced this independent spirit—were such as to rule out exclusive involvement on his part with those who shared his enthusiasm for and devotion to the ideas of Rudolf Steiner. Thus, for example, it would not have been possible for him to join Cecil Harwood as a teacher at what was to become Michael Hall (though he taught for a brief period of a few weeks at The New School in Streatham). Even attendance at conferences on one or another aspect of anthroposophy can never have been an easy matter (as was the case with the Torquay Conference mentioned earlier). 'The outstanding features that characterized my marriage were twofold, I think. The first was the big difference in age—my wife was some 16 years older than I was. And the other thing was that I discovered anthroposophy and joined the Society almost in the same year I was married; and she reacted very strongly against anthroposophy. I suppose I was getting more and more involved, members of the Society were coming to see me, and . . . she didn't think they always had as much sense as she had! She continued to be strongly averse to anthroposophy . . . but I felt I couldn't give it up or cease to interest myself in it . . . It was a kind of sword through the marriage knot, right through, almost right through; though we had enough in common to get on pretty well together. It was hard, hard for her too. And then right at the end of her life I was astonished to learn that she had applied to join the Society [she died in 1980]. Kind of making amends. Well, I tried at that time—her mind at that time was not very receptive, her mental capacities were going, she was getting old—I did try to read some anthroposophy to her and that didn't work at all. Nevertheless, she had taken this step to join, and that did make up for something. It was rather touching . . . She was influenced a bit by my contact with America. On more than one occasion she stayed in America with me and came to my lectures, even made notes on them. How much she understood I don't know. I think she was impressed and, if you like, comforted by the sort of reputation I had there, the kind of men that one met in the academic world there. She saw that I wasn't just a fanatic or a fool. I don't suppose she ever thought I was, but she might have thought rather in that direction when it came to anthroposophy. And of course, when you first come up against anthroposophy, you aren't very capable of expounding it convincingly to anyone outside . . . In the early stages I came across a note that she'd written. She'd come across the account of the two Jesus boys, and she either thought it was wrong or ridiculous or hated it; and she made up a little rhyme about it:

> Little doll Steiner
> Sat in a corner
> Eating his anthropop pie;
> Two Jesus and Marys
> As some astral canaries . . .

I can't remember how it went on after that! . . . Her standpoint was the church—not that she was extremely devout or a very active church member. The circle in Scotland where she was brought up—the kind of people in the church she would have met with, brothers-in-law and so forth—were educated and thoughtful. She was interested in a movement in England which was interested in introducing art, in particular dramatic art, into the life of the church. A man called Geoffrey Dearmer [one of the editors of and moving spirits behind *The Oxford Book of Carols*] was rather the leading spirit in that. And that of course made the clash over anthroposophy worse in a way, because she thought she was already doing what Steiner was doing. Not that *she* was, but the people she was interested in. That comes in somewhere as well.'

The novel 'English People', with its rich gallery of people and their thoughts, might be considered as a magnificent attempt by Barfield to hold all the different aspects of his life together. Thus, for example, there is an anthroposophist, Humphrey (modelled, according to Barfield, on his friend Walter Field), but also a devout Anglican priest, John, who is in addition an enthusiast for Douglas's Social Credit philosophy. And yet it would be hard to imagine that Maud would have appreciated either its trenchant critical insights into British politics or its apocalyptic ending ('The Rose on the Ash-Heap'). Ultimately it is a thoroughly uncompromising book, which is perhaps why it has still not been published.

Exactly when Barfield decided to join his father's legal firm of Barfield and Barfield is not completely clear. According to Walter Hooper (*Oxford Dictionary of National Biography*), this happened in 1929. Barfield's recollection (not necessarily reliable where dates are concerned) suggests a date later than that given in the introduction to the *Barfield Sampler*, namely, 1930: 'The next change in outward circumstances [after marriage] I suppose was when I went into the law. That wasn't until the middle of the thirties. Of course, the early years were taken up with getting familiar with the law—taking the final exam is quite an essential thing for solicitors—and then practising with my father in his firm . . . Those early years when I used to go into the office every day, I remember reading the paper on the train on the way to the office, all this outrageous behaviour of Hitler. The papers were trying to hush it up—*The Times*, for example. Only *The Daily News* (which no longer exists) really gave away what he was actually doing. I gave up *The Times*—like a good many others, I was so disgusted with the way they were engaged in this hushing up business, and I wrote to them to tell them why. Things were hotting up then, Hitler was making all these promises, positively his last demand, and so forth. Chamberlain and most of the English newspapers and media were trying to appease Hitler. Appeasement was the great word then. It's depressing all this somehow . . . But whether I had been admitted [to my father's firm] I don't know. Either I was already practising or I was learning the law as an articled clerk—I don't know. That would have been some time in the late thirties that I took the law seriously . . . It was a small firm with three partners—mainly conveyancing and probate, a certain amount of litigation as well. I think I once took a case in the County Court as an advocate! But generally it was office work, conveyancing . . .'

The firm was in Old Broad Street, later moving to the Strand. (The Barfields were at this time living in the Golders Green/Hampstead area.) Barfield's father died shortly before the war, whereupon a man called Reynolds, who was younger than Barfield, became the senior partner. He got on well with Reynolds, although there does not seem to have been a deep connection, despite Reynolds having literary interests and a particular appreciation of Shakespeare's Sonnets. During the bombing of London (1940–2) the firm moved out to the suburbs. For a short period Owen and Maud (and family) had a country abode in Buckinghamshire in the form of a bus or coach in a field; thereafter they lived in Chalfont St Giles. Barfield has virtually nothing further to say of more than anecdotal interest about the work that brought him in his income during this period until his retirement in 1959. However, his account of how he managed to bring some semblance of calm to a situation where a doctor at a school on whose council he served had exchanged one wife for another offers a little glimpse of his methods: 'There was a very fiery meeting, with people disagreeing violently with one another. I was in the chair, and I said everyone should stand up and make his or her statement, how he or she saw it. If they did, it would smooth things over a bit. I can remember—I think we decided to break off when things had got to a kind of maximum rupture state at the meeting, to break off for half an hour and cool things down—I remember strolling up and down the garden wondering what to do next. I had this idea of making them all get up and make a statement, and I think it worked fairly well . . .' The only other window he offers an interested enquirer is his humorous little book *This Ever Diverse Pair*, written to stave off depression and breakdown.[18] The 'ever diverse pair' of the title represents a couple of partners in a legal firm, one of whom, Burgeon, is as reasonable and humane as his alter-ego, Burden, is sour and unsympathetic. (In this connection, it is worth mentioning that Barfield did not bring in as much business as Reynolds, who had a middle-class clientele; and he agreed to—or more likely suggested—the proposal that Reynolds take more than an equal share in the profits.)

Finally, Barfield clears away a possible misunderstanding associated with his work as a lawyer: 'I was at Wadham College. It's quite a small college, but it is rather famous for having sent out a large number of distinguished lawyers, people like F.E. Smith. When people concern themselves with my biography, they are apt to assume that, because I went to Wadham College and later on in life practised in law, I was always training for the law. This is not so. So I thought I'd tell you how it came about that I went to Wadham . . . One had the scholarship system. Every year a group of colleges come together and issue this scholarship exam to classical scholars in public schools up and down the country. You go in for that, and then the Oxford colleges join, so to speak, in examining the papers and make a list of those who have won a scholarship. Up to now there had been no choice of a college. But when you apply to enter a school, you have to put your order of preference. You may get a scholarship award for any of the colleges in the group (or you may not, of course); and I was advised by my classics master that one stood a better chance of getting a scholarship if one didn't put at the top of one's list the large and famous colleges but one of the small colleges. That was the only reason I went to Wadham. I'm very glad I did, because it's a very nice college, I liked it. But it had nothing to do with the fact that I went into the law afterwards.'

His friendship with Lewis meant that, even after taking up legal practice in London, Barfield's connection with Oxford remained unbroken until after his retirement as a solicitor. Generally, his visits to his former university would have been in his capacity as a member of the 'Inklings' circle, a group of like-minded (but also thoroughly individual) people who met in Lewis's rooms—and afterwards at the Eagle and Child ('Bird and Baby')—between 1922 and 1945. Tolkien and Charles Williams were also influential members of this circle, which had many adherents too numerous to mention here, all of whom, however, had some kind of an interest in mythology and occultism from a Christian point of view. The friendship between Barfield and Lewis—the latter being the mainspring of the circle throughout its existence—provided the original nucleus and thrust for these meetings. Barfield offers some brief recollections: 'During this time [the late thirties and early forties] I used to go up to Oxford about once a term I think to spend a weekend with Lewis. Very often on the Friday night there would be a meeting of the Inklings . . . When I was well into the law—I'd got my finals and so forth—one thing I did, a sort of island of literature in the midst of a raging sea of law, was to give a paper to a meeting of the Inklings in Oxford organized by Lewis. It was called 'Poetic Diction and Legal Fiction'. That must have been in the early 1940s I suppose. Afterwards it was printed in *The Rediscovery of Meaning*, but it was first of all printed by Lewis in his *Essays Presented to Charles Williams* in 1947. It struck me that if you were looking for some signs of a link between my immersion in the law and literary production it was in a way a kind of landmark . . .'

A quality which the other Inklings did not, by and large, share with Barfield was his passionate concern not merely with visionary ideas but with their implementation. Barfield comments: 'I don't think any of them had any real interest in society as a whole. Lewis never read a [news]paper or anything of that sort, and I don't think Tolkien did. Charles Williams—I'm not sure; he was more wide awake to the world around him than the other two. I didn't know him all that well, of course...' One striking characteristic of Barfield's long novel 'English People' is that it ranges through all three main realms of the social organism. There are groups of people on a quest for truth and understanding (rather as the Inklings were), but also—in addition to those endeavouring by fair means or foul to uphold the political status quo—individuals who embody the aspiration to tackle the challenge of transforming the underlying social and economic fabric. At the time when he was working on the novel, Barfield was very interested in the ideas of C.H. Douglas.[19] It is also striking how many articles and other writings he published between 1929 and the outbreak of the Second World War on what may broadly be termed the economic question. Moreover, it is not fortuitous that he was a co-translator of Rudolf Steiner's lecture-cycle known as *World Economy* (published in English 1936–7). Nevertheless, it was the ideas of C.H. Douglas and his Social Credit movement which were in vogue at the time in question. 'I met Douglas more than once,' Barfield recalls. 'His assumption was that all the poverty and shortages were due to the ineffective and fallacious financial structure, and if you got that right... His picture was that the potential supply of goods was now unlimited, the only problem was that there wasn't enough money to buy the goods. His idea was to supply the consumers with a kind of bonus all round, I think. It rather faded away when a good time after 1935 one could no longer be so sure about there being enough for everybody ... the environmental business, the question as to whether the earth can support its population. But in 1935 the general feeling was that there was enough for everybody, it was just a question of the distribution of it being held up by the financial system. There is something wrong with the financial system, obviously. These huge debts ... I don't remember whether he also had Steiner's idea that capital shouldn't bear interest for ever but only for a limited period. I don't think he did. I would think it's very important. Because when you've got these huge debts, the original debt keeps on piling up because they can't find the interest. How it relates to the trade union movement I don't know...[20] Someone was trying to engineer a meeting between Douglas and Rudolf Steiner if Rudolf Steiner came to see him! So that fell through...' One further point should be mentioned in this connection. As a result of his interest in the work of C.H. Douglas and his articles on the theme of Social Credit in the early 1930s, Barfield embarked on a university degree in economics at London University. He passed all the economics and mathematics but failed in geography. By this time this phase had passed, partly because it had become apparent that the notion that there was no problem on the production side in meeting humanity's needs but only a problem of distribution, in that the poor couldn't afford to buy the goods, was a fallacy. So he did not retake geography, as he might well have done otherwise.

The other main area of activity in Barfield's life in the 1930s and throughout his career as a solicitor in London was the Anthroposophical Society. For many years he was active on the Executive Council and was secretary of the Anthroposophical Association, which was the 'business arm' of the Society. Quite apart from anything else, his legal skills were helpful in securing a considerable reduction in the rates that had to be paid for Rudolf Steiner Hall. However, it is to the split in the worldwide Anthroposophical Society in 1935 that his memories constantly return, together with the great difficulties which this entailed. 'When these difficulties started, I was a member of the Council of the English Society. At an early stage in the difficulties they held this meeting in Dornach for members of the governing bodies of the different national societies, and Harwood and I went to this very fiery meeting, which went on until about 3 am . . . [Albert] Steffen was taking the chair of course, and I sat in the front row and watched it all the time. I didn't feel there was anything of profound substance there somehow. Mind you, I didn't know German then. I felt at the time that Dr [Ita] Wegman seemed to be the profoundest anthroposophist among those people, a very deep one . . . Steffen in the chair was quite unable to handle it, it wasn't his job to be a chairman at all. I suppose in a way that was the touch-point of the whole struggle, they were beginning to distrust each other. There was a very strong antagonism present in the meeting between the chairman, Steffen, and Frau Doktor [Marie Steiner] on the one side and Dr Wegman—she was a kind of villain of the piece, they kept on saying things about her which were kind of elusive. I once boldly got up and said that as I couldn't speak German would I be allowed to speak English. They kindly said yes. I said that we'd come all this way and we really don't know what you're talking about. Is there anything Dr Wegman is accused of? Has she committed murder? That rather flung the stone in the middle of the discussion, really. I can't remember how it went after that, but it was after that that the total break between Dr Wegman and Dr Vreede and the others came about . . . It was all rather elusive. There was a terrible man called Roman Bos who accused her [Dr Wegman] ... I remember him saying, "Es handelt sich um einer *Raub* des Esoterischen"—the anti-Wegmanites accused her of some kind of wrongful action, piracy ... after that things just got worse and worse. I can't remember in detail. I don't think that particular meeting led to anything.' Eventually, Ita Wegman, Elisabeth Vreede and several others were excluded from the Anthroposophical Society, an event which constituted the split of 1935 and which (at least in outward terms) had essentially to do—on the one hand—with the administration of Rudolf Steiner's legacy of books, lectures and other esoteric material and—on the other—with the future destiny of the Society founded (or re-founded, to be more precise) by him at the Christmas Conference of 1923. Barfield was one of those who—like Ita Wegman—adhered to the view that Rudolf Steiner's deed at Christmas 1923 had not lost its validity through his untimely death in March 1925, and that this re-founded Anthroposophical Society continued to have a deep esoteric significance—not only for anthroposophists but for the whole of mankind as a source of social and cultural renewal. On the other side were ranged those who, like Marie Steiner, could attribute validity only to the legacy of Rudolf Steiner's own teachings. In the English context, the former group continued to be known as the Anthroposophical Society in Great Britain (founded by Rudolf Steiner in person in 1923), while the latter were the English Branch of the General Anthroposophical Society. 'The Frau Doktor party regarded themselves as the true successors of Rudolf Steiner's legacy, and she of course had the copyright under Steiner's will. There was all that trouble as well. You had to get permission to publish anything from her, really. It was a terrible time. A lot of personal hostility, a terrible time ... The Museum Street people were the English Branch of the General Anthroposophical Society. They had their separate headquarters, a different periodical. They hardly recognized us ... They were the smaller group ... We endeavoured just to carry on with Anthroposophy in our own way and not to listen to the interferences that tried to come from Dornach. At one stage they wanted to dismiss quite a number of our members, including George Adams and probably D.N. Dunlop [at that time the Chairman of the Anthroposophical Society in Great Britain]. We simply ignored their demands and went on developing our own Anthroposophical Society in Great Britain, which the Dornach people—or those in England who represented them—didn't really recognize at all. There was the trouble with the books, of course. Steiner's copyright was still alive in those years, and if you wanted to publish a [translation of a] lecture you had to do it with the consent of the Dornach publishing section, which was more or less run by Frau Doktor...' Barfield himself made many contributions to anthroposophical journals during the period of his legal practice, some of the most important of which were published in book form in *Romanticism Comes of Age* (1944). Then towards the end of this period, in 1957, Faber and Faber published his treatise on the evolution of consciousness, *Saving the Appearances*, a book which brought to clear expression what had merely been implied in *Poetic Diction*.

In the meantime, however, an event had occurred which on the surface represented a severe disappointment to Barfield. At the end of 1954 C.S. Lewis left his teaching post at Magdalen College Oxford, and he wanted Barfield to take his place (Lewis had been offered a chair at Cambridge, the specially created professorship of Medieval and Renaissance English). Exactly when the negotiations for Barfield to take his place were being conducted is not completely clear. Barfield recalls that this was in the late 1950s, but it may have nearer to 1954. 'It was all practically fixed up . . . There was the dinner. I'd been to see the Master of Magdalen, anyway I went to see some don or other and was accepted, was assumed to be a gentleman!—and Lewis had fixed up a kind of farewell dinner for himself and an introductory dinner for me all together. And then of course I had to decide whether I was to call it off or go on when the idea of my going to Oxford had fallen through . . . You see, different subjects or schools are run by the dons themselves on a democratic basis; and anything like an appointment is decided by the dons themselves. But when it comes to choosing someone they appoint a committee of two or three to put forward candidates to select. I don't know who the two or three were that the committee consisted of, but they put me forward; and once the committee had put me forward it was assumed by Lewis and others that I was elected. Actually, it has to come before the whole of the dons, not only the school, to be ratified—and they turned it down! A great disappointment at the time, a tremendous disappointment . . . Of course, those on the committee who had put me forward would have naturally voted for me. I don't know how big the majority was—probably fairly slender. But no one quite knew why. Some suggested that it was because Lewis wasn't very popular with his colleagues; I think they rather envied him then, the name he had outside our circles . . . so I think it was quite reasonable. The ground they gave was that it was because I was too old; they would have to have another appointment pretty soon. I must have been about 60 then. But it was a pretty big disappointment, because I'd looked forward very much to actually living in Oxford, to the kind of society you get there—my wife was also looking forward to it very much. But then a year after that I got this letter from America suggesting that I should go over there, which I accepted, and that was the beginning of any literary reputation in the outside world that I established there (and still is) . . . America is my home really, in that sense. I couldn't have accepted the invitation to America if I'd had the Oxford job. So in a way it was karma working together for good, but it was a great blow at the time . . .'

This leads naturally into a consideration of what is perhaps the most outwardly successful but also unexpected aspect of Barfield's life, namely, his period as a celebrated guest of a whole series of academic establishments in the United States and also Canada. The unexpected nature of this fame has probably much to do with the fact that Barfield, both in his manner of expression and his outward demeanour, would seem to be so characteristically English and bereft of that quintessentially American verve and charisma. Indeed, it would be fascinating to try to understand why it is that, even now, he is celebrated far more widely as a deeply original thinker in America than he is in his own country, where he is of interest almost solely to devotees of anthroposophy. Suffice it to say at this point that Barfield has always been deeply grateful for the esteem which he has been accorded by the American academic world (or at least a portion of it). It is also significant that, of Barfield's four literary executors, three reside in America and the fourth is an American living in England.

'I first went to America,' he recalls, 'in 1964. So all that part between what I've already spoken to you about and this time when I went to America is all rather colourless in my mind. Quite a lot was happening, I was writing a lot of articles, I suppose—but then it was rather like starting a new life in America. Although I had no reputation in England, a certain part of the academic world in America, the English departments, quite a lot of people . . . were already interested in my books. It was a strange experience, rather like the "ugly duckling"! . . . "I've read your books, of course"—that sort of thing, you know. And of course it was useful from a financial point of view; they paid you awfully well. I had no responsibilities other than teaching. That went on until 1974–5 . . . The last time was at SUNY [State University of New York] . . . It went on for over ten years, I was going fairly regularly to America.'

By the time he actually began going to America, Barfield had thoroughly relaunched himself as a writer. Not only had *Saving the Appearances* appeared but *Worlds Apart* (1963) and *Unancestral Voice* (1965) were either published or imminent. Nevertheless, the original intention to visit America would appear to have predated all of these—at least, this is how he remembers the situation. 'There was a man called Stanley Hopper who ran the English Department of a graduate school at Drew University in New Jersey; and one or more of the students in the graduate seminar read one of my books. It can't have been *Saving the Appearances*, because it wasn't out then. Anyway, he read it[21] and got interested and invited me to come and teach at Drew. That's how it all started. There was a surprisingly large salary attached to it—which I rather jumped at! He hung fire for some time, curious—he didn't answer letters. I wrote again to say that if I didn't hear I should assume it was all off and make my arrangements accordingly. Then there was a telephone call, or a cable, I can't remember which. I got to Drew—very nice little university, Drew. As is the case with more than a few American universities, it was a Methodist foundation. Well then, while I was there I got this invitation from Brandeis University near Boston, and I think the main reason was that one of their staff couldn't do the first term of the year and so in a hurry they got me! They called me a Professor of American Literature. I warned them I hardly knew anything about American literature, but that didn't matter much! I forget where I went from there—Hamilton College I suppose, in upstate New York . . . Well, Canada, of course—I went to British Columbia . . .' There was a brief period when Barfield became something approaching a cult figure, but—unlike with Tolkien, for example—this did not last very long, and Barfield recalls that a degree credit-course on 'Barfield studies' only lasted for one term. However, he is being a little modest in his recollections as to the length of the 'American period' in his life. Thus, for example, *History, Guilt and Habit* (published 1979) consists of lectures given in Vancouver in 1978; and his last visit to America as a guest lecturer, when he visited four universities in the space of a few weeks, was not until the spring of 1981. Not that the connection with America came to an end then, of course, for Barfield's work continued to appear in a number of American university journals during the 1980s, and also in more specialist journals like *Towards* (founded in 1977 'to explore and make better known the work of Owen Barfield, Samuel Taylor Coleridge, Wolfgang von Goethe, Rudolf Steiner and related authors'), which published among many other articles by Barfield his novella 'Night Operation' (1975), a futuristic tale displaying awesome insight into the present state of culture in the West. Nor was this the last time that he visited the New World. Characteristically, Barfield declares that 'my greatest achievement lay not in writing books but in my skill in bringing Americans together', a remark which indicates pretty clearly the level on which he has been working for most of his life. To conclude this section on America, mention may be made of two recent accolades. In 1994 he was given an award from the Conference on Christianity and Literature, which 'classified my book on Coleridge [*What Coleridge Thought*, 1971] as the most important Christian writing of that year', and in 1995 he appeared as the central 'hero' of Stephen Talbott's treatise on the drawbacks and dangers of the Internet, *The Future Does Not Compute*.

After his withdrawal from this 'post-retirement' life of travelling and lecturing, Barfield had the unexpected opportunity which his extreme longevity offered him to survey both his own life and work and the world around him. His physical base had latterly been his room in 'The Walhatch' in Forest Row, Sussex, whither he moved from South Darenth, Kent, after his wife died at a ripe old age. Again and again he referred to the importance of seeing through the reductionist assumptions underlying materialistic thinking, thus in a certain sense carrying to its logical conclusion the scepticism imbibed from his agnostic background. This, not some kind of suspension of disbelief, underlay his commitment to anthroposophy. 'I think it was more a strong feeling that I had, a revolt against the whole materialistic paradigm, which underlay my exposition of anthroposophy. I could never accept that. And the tone or manner of my anthroposophical writings was a strategy to undermine the materialistic paradigm . . .' There are, as he states with his usual transparent clarity in, for example, his article 'The Coming Trauma of Materialism' (1974), small but growing circles of people nowadays who would agree with what he says about the materialistic paradigm. There are, however, far fewer who have been able to follow him in his commitment to anthroposophy, as he attests in an important lecture given in 1984 entitled 'Anthroposophy and the Future'[22], where he refers to Rudolf Steiner as the Aristotle of modern times, as the one figure in the whole 'counterculture' or 'post-materialistic' culture whose thinking holds the key to a viable future for mankind. 'I came to the conclusion some time ago,' he says referring to this lecture, 'that it won't be enough for the world to get rid of materialism or for large numbers to pursue the teachings of the alternative people. There's no real hope for civilization unless, whether under that name or not, anthroposophy is the accepted *Weltanschauung* of the majority. I compared that with what happened in the Middle Ages with Aquinas, who centred everything on Aristotle . . . Unless everything centres on anthroposophy—not in a doctrinal way but by accepting that its teaching is somehow essential to the whole process of evolution—it will fail. That doesn't mean that everybody, or the majority, will have to join the [Anthroposophical] Society or accept all the teachings, but [it will fail] unless the central core is accepted or, if not accepted, is used as a working hypothesis to shape civilization. That could happen, but it doesn't...'[23] As Barfield indicates with quiet but trenchant clarity in his Afterword to the fifth (latest) edition of *Poetic Diction*, even many of his friends and intellectual admirers have not been able to banish RUP (the residue of unresolved positivism), with the result that 'although they would distinguish between spirit and matter, when they think about or imagine spirit they make it out to be a very thin form of matter'. He refers in this sense to Jung: 'Well, Jung was pretty profound. He was more free from RUP in his private life than he was in his writing, I think. He kept mum so to speak about what he really did believe about the difference between spirit and matter in his published work because people wouldn't read it... Didn't I [in the Afterword to *Poetic Diction*] draw attention to the fact that he spoke of primordial archetypes, and then immediately afterwards said that they are "psychic residua of numberless experiences at the same time"? I asked how primordial is a residuum!' It is one thing to believe in the idea of spirit, quite another to conceive of a spiritual world so real that it can come down to earth and transform it and hence enable a union of these two polarities to come about. But of course the struggle to affirm the latter against all the odds has been familiar to Barfield since the time of his 'Great War' with C.S. Lewis. Apart from his beloved Coleridge, one thinker whose work was dedicated to this same end was Novalis. At the time of one of our conversations, Barfield was rereading Novalis' novel *Heinrich von Ofterdingen*, and this prompted a discussion about this writer and his place in world history. Barfield's novel 'English People' is also deeply imbued with the spirit of Novalis.

An extension of this same theme which remains of crucial importance to Barfield is its application to the challenge of social transformation, an idea which becomes enormously more relevant if one really believes—as he does—that since the Incarnation it has begun to be possible for not only human beings and human society but also the earth itself to be gradually spiritualized. 'I do feel very strongly that we shan't get out of the materialistic assumption which is spread over the whole civilized world now except by the realization of the difference between threefold thinking[24] and ordinary ratiocination. It's probably because of my own experience, for when I first became acquainted with anthroposophy one of the books I read first of all was the one about the threefold state... It made quite an impression on me. I felt it was a new idea which might be interesting; and then seven or eight more years later, when I had really studied anthroposophy and had understood threefold thinking, I reread the book and it was a different book altogether, much deeper than I thought... Perhaps it's all rather wild speculation, but I suppose one should keep one's mind open to possibilities. But the more people I talk to—and there aren't very many of them nowadays—they seem to feel that something's got to happen fairly soon, something rather fundamental and spectacular, catastrophic possibly, in the near future; and the more that comes through on the news the more convincing this seems to me to be. This development of bombing in Japan [there had just been a bomb explosion in the Tokyo Underground] and what they call militias in America, together with the development of new explosives that are very easy to make, easy to transplant and use—there's no defence against them really, however efficient the police force is. If someone can make lethal explosives in a test tube and is not especially concerned to protect his own life, you can't do anything about it... Is that going to be a kind of axe laid to the root of western civilization? I don't know ... I'm rather glad I'm not a young man, that's all ... I'm worried about our children, what kind of life they've got to go through... When one raised that kind of issue in the past the answer sometimes was that children would be born with the forces to deal with it. But how *can* they? I don't know...'[25]

During another conversation the impulse to establish a community-based biodynamic farm on associative rather than market principles in the Forest Row area was discussed: 'It occurs to me that thinking or working along those lines might be a step in the direction of solving *the* great difficulty in further development generally and of anthroposophy—the whole threefold conception, the social aspect, the threefold commonwealth. You can't really make anything of that unless you also have a threefold imagination, an understanding of threefoldness, including polarity.[26] Coming up against a practical problem might possibly help to make something along those lines work... It might come about that it is through that channel that the threefold organizing of society comes about, instead of the threefold idea being introduced as a political theory, so to speak. It could come into being almost unnoticed...'

The conversation continued to range over the field of politics and economics, and included some reflections arising out of the then current revival of J.B. Priestly's play *An Inspector Calls*, which seemed to have a considerable bearing upon the theme. Barfield expressed his view that no change for the better in the political realm was likely 'unless there can be some real changes in the predominant economic theory—it's all market now. Maybe people will grow out of that and find that it doesn't work. There might then be a bit of room for growing more on threefold lines, but as things are now the market is a kind of god, an answer to all problems. And of course it's pure selfishness.' And as for the National Lottery: 'I can't understand that lottery, I really can't. It appeals to all the worst instincts in human nature; and also economically, from the sound of it. The way it has developed enthusiasm for it is quite horrifying.' An account—or impression—of this last decade or so of Barfield's life would not be complete without mentioning the only piece of imaginative literature belonging to this period, the novella 'Eager Spring' (hitherto unpublished). The theme of this story adds further confirmation of his conviction stated above, that a new social order can only arise out of a determination of those few for whom it is important to address the land issue and, hence, attempt some kind of response to the environmental crisis currently facing mankind. Nevertheless, 'Eager Spring' contains much more than this; for it also sets Barfield's view as to the centrality of anthroposophy for the future of civilization against the background of an apocalyptic struggle between good and evil.

One theme which came up not infrequently in the course of conversations was that of Information Technology and the so-called revolution in communication. The main tragedy of so much of this new technology, according to Barfield, is that it is bound up with 'the ordinary reductionist view that there is just one reality, that of the senses, and that everything else is mental'. The result is that the people who are involved with it begin to feel that they have contact with a world which is more real than the ordinary world of the senses but which of course is not the spiritual world. On one occasion, Barfield had cut out an article from the *Sunday Telegraph* that reported on research indicating that it might be possible to overcome the hold-up in the research that has been going on in this field by having three master chips instead of one; and the writer of the article asked whether the Trinity might possibly have a relationship to computer technology. 'This seemed to suggest,' he commented, 'that there is a realm of knowledge you can't get with one chip but you can with three. Is that the first sign of a realization of threefold thinking, a kind of caricature of the essentialness of threefoldness in thinking, forcing its way through even this very materialistic communications outlook?' The immense gulf between Barfieldian thinking and that of the proponents of Information Technology has been portrayed in, for example, the book by Stephen Talbott referred to earlier, *The Future Does Not Compute* (published at almost exactly the same time as the conversation just quoted from, 17 May 1995), but this is not the place to elaborate further on this theme. What seems so striking is the contrast between the solitary, virtual-reality world of non-communication[27] represented by these new technologies and the warmly welcoming, and deeply stimulating, world of Room No. 3 at 'The Walhatch'. It would be interesting to enumerate those who have been welcomed to partake in the art of conversation—which was the essential hallmark of the Inklings circle—both in Forest Row and in South Darenth, and so share in the creation of that tapestry of twentieth-century life which is the life of Owen Barfield.

It seems appropriate to conclude with a few thoughts about the way that this life might best be enabled in a certain sense to live on into the future. Barfield himself attempted to chronicle his own life at one stage by means of a 'psychography', a biography of the inner life or the soul. In some ways it is a remarkable document, but he abandoned it (in 1948) because it 'became too difficult and/or long-winded once psyche had emerged from childhood' (according to a note written on the manuscript). After breaking off the narrative, Barfield then continued to struggle with defining the spiritual and mental experiences that he had sought to record, concluding the attempt in mid-sentence with the words 'cetera desunt (abandoned)'. What he was left with was an absolute conviction as to the meaningfulness and validity of spiritual experiences (which were for him no less real than those of the sense-world), together with what must have amounted to a despair at his seeming inability to communicate them. Biographically, this struggle belongs to the years culminating in the writing of *Saving the Appearances* (see the chapter entitled 'Language as a Key to the Past'), the book which represents his answer to this dilemma. Psychographically, what we have in this document is merely a fragment, pointing not forwards in his earthly life but backwards, reaching tentatively towards the spiritual source of the life that Owen Barfield was to live.

He would sometimes say that his life—his outward life—has been too humdrum to be of any interest to anyone, and he would add that the bits that were not humdrum he would not want to be shared by all and sundry. In one conversation—which took place after I had been making unsuccessful efforts to fund the project of writing his biography—he expressed some thoughts that should, I think, be recorded here. 'More important than the biography is to get the existing material more widely known ... more important than the biography.' (The context of this remark was that he had been asked by his American publishers—he does not have a publisher in Britain—whether he wanted to buy up stock of some titles which were to be discontinued once they, the publishers, had been taken over. This prompted him to enunciate, with his usual humour, Barfield's law of book-reading: 'Those who need don't read it and those who read don't need it'.) On hearing about an initiative proposed by Stephen Talbott called 'Bridges', the aim of which is to further dialogue between anthroposophy and its surrounding cultural milieu, he commented: 'If this "Bridges" should really go ahead and take hold, I think you'd be much better employed using your energies there than in worrying about my literary remains and producing a complicated biography. I don't think it's going to help anthroposophy to do that.' He continued in a similar vein later on in the conversation (on 10 April 1996), when I had been speaking about my active enthusiasm for the Tablehurst and Plaw Hatch Community Farm: 'I should be sorry if you got bogged down in a lot of niggling research work over my biography when you might be doing something along the lines of what you're talking about now. It's much more important from the point of view of the dissemination of the fundamental anthroposophical world-view... If somebody claimed that *Saving the Appearances* had been written by someone else, I don't think it would reduce its chances of making an impact. It's the impact I'm interested in, not the association with the name of Owen Barfield.'

This biographical sketch was drafted in the early part of 1997 and finished at Whitsuntide that year. On 14 December 1997, at around 1.30 pm, Owen Barfield died. He had for some months been feeling that he had been on earth for long enough, and had been experiencing a recurrence of an old digestive problem which—coupled with pneumonia—brought his long life to an end.

PART TWO

Elucidation and Recognition: The Lecturer (1964–97)

2. *OWEN BARFIELD AND AMERICA*

Barfield's first journey to America as a Visiting Professor (as far as I know, his first visit altogether to the New World) was in 1964, the fruit of that gradually maturing connection through Stanley Hopper forged initially by his essay 'Poetic Diction and Legal Fiction' (1947).[28] The last time that he gave a lecture to an American audience was in 1984, when on 3 August he spoke to the Rudolf Steiner Institute at Chambersburg, Pennsylvania, on 'Anthroposophy and the Future'. Just over half of the way through this period of 21 years Barfield had his first personal contact with the man who might with some justice be described as the most highly esteemed, honoured and therefore in a certain sense representative American novelist of his time. The relationship between these two men as expressed in the available correspondence and elsewhere is so deeply symptomatic of Barfield's relationship with America—and of much else besides—that Barfield's American period, which to all intents and purposes encompasses the last third of his life from 1964 onwards,[29] can be illumined most fully if the dynamics inherent in this highly significant personal correspondence are considered by way of an introduction.[30]

Saul Bellow, the American novelist in question, made the initial contact by writing this brief letter dated 3 June 1975:

> Dear Mr Barfield:
>
> I've read several of your books, *Saving the Appearances*, the collection of essays on Romanticism, a long dialogue, the name of which I can't remember just now and, quite recently, *Unancestral Voice*, a fascinating book. I am not philosopher enough to argue questions of rationality or irrationality, but there are things that seem to me self-evident, so markedly self-evident and felt that the problem of proving or disproving their reality becomes academic. Like you I am tired of all the talk about what matters, the avoidance of what *really* matters.
>
> Sincerely yours,
> Saul Bellow

The hoped-for meeting evidently took place, as the following appreciative letter confirms:

Dear Mr. Barfield,

That you should come down to London to answer the ignorant question of a stranger greatly impressed me. I daresay I found the occasion far more interesting than you could. You were most patient with a beginner trying to learn his A-B-C's. I continue to study your *Unancestral Voice*. It's hard going—some forty years of thought and reading condensed—but I have a strong hunch that you are giving a true account of things. In these matters illumination counts for as much as the sort of 'handproofs' we have been brought up to demand, and lately I have become aware, not of illumination itself, but of a kind of illuminated fringe—a peripheral glimpse of a different state of things. This makes little sense to you perhaps.

Thank you for coming in to talk to me.

Sincerely,

Saul Bellow

Bellow's intensity of interest in Barfield's work, as exemplified especially in *Saving the Appearances*, *Unancestral Voice* and *Romanticism Comes of Age*, is confirmed by the letter he wrote shortly afterwards in response to one from Barfield:

Dear Mr. Barfield,

Your letter was very welcome. I'm glad you saw some merit in *Herzog* . . . I continue to pore over *Unancestral Voice* and it is most important that you should be willing to discuss it with me. I can readily see why you would take little interest in contemporary fiction. Those who read it and write it are easily satisfied with what your Meggid calls lifeless memory thoughts. For some time now I have been asking what kind of knowledge a writer has and in what way he deserves to be taken seriously. He has imagination where others have science, etc. But it wasn't until I read your book on Romanticism that I began to understand something about the defeat of imaginative knowledge in modern times. I don't want to labor a point which you yourself have brought to my attention; I only want to communicate something in my own experience that will explain the importance of your books to me. My experience was that the interest of much of life as represented in the books I read (and perhaps some that I wrote) had been exhausted. But how could existence itself become uninteresting? I concluded that the ideas and modes by which it was represented were exhausted, that individuality had been overwhelmed by power or 'sociality', by technology and politics. Images or representations *this* side of the mirror have indeed tired us out. All that science did was to make the phenomena technically (mathematically) inaccessible leaving us with nothing but ignorance and despair. Yes, psychoanalysis directed us to go into the Unconscious. From the dark forest of its Ucs.—a sort of preserve of things unknown—painters and poets like good dogs were to bring back truffles . . .

Tomorrow my Spanish holiday ends. My wife and I are returning via London and will be there for about ten days. I hope you will be kind enough to give me a few hours more of your time.

It was very good of you to send me the Steiner book. Will you have lunch with me (as my guest this time) in London? You speak of yourself as the servant of your readers; but this reader, though eager to talk with you, hesitates to impose himself.

Sincerely yrs,
Saul Bellow

At the time of the first meeting between the two men in London in June 1975, Saul Bellow's highly successful novel *Humboldt's Gift*[31] was, as Barfield put it in a letter to Bellow of 5 January 1976, 'in the pipeline and near its mouth'. In the intervening six months Barfield had received, read and annotated a copy of an article from *Newsweek* magazine dated 1 September 1975 entitled 'America's Master Novelist'. This article, by Walter Clemons and Jack Kroll, in addition to being an informative eulogy to Bellow, and an appreciation of his latest novel, contains more than a passing reference to Barfield, who clearly valued the comments ('with its very generous allusion to O.B.', he wrote in his January 1976 letter). It is worth quoting the passage marked in Barfield's copy for the light that it sheds on some of the underlying themes in the relationship under consideration:

> The life of the spirit is very much on his [Bellow's] mind these days. Some early readers of 'Humboldt's Gift' have been startled by Charlie Citrine's espousement of anthroposophy, the creed of the early twentieth-century occultist thinker Rudolf Steiner, who believed in the transmigration of souls and opposed the dominant scientific view of the universe. How seriously are we meant to take these passages in the novel? Answer: very seriously indeed. Bellow discovered Steiner through a book called 'Saving the Appearances' by Owen Barfield, a remarkable British writer who now lives in retirement in Kent after a long career as a lawyer. One of the main purposes of Bellow's trip to England this summer was to talk with Barfield.

For Bellow, Barfield's work represents a vigorous claim for the importance of poetic imagination. 'Read "Saving the Appearances",' he says, 'and then Rudolf Steiner's little book on theosophy—your hair will stand on end! I was impressed by the idea that there were forms of understanding, discredited now, which had long been the agreed basis of human knowledge. We think we can know the world scientifically, but actually our ignorance is terrifying.'

When he discusses these matters, Bellow's face lights up with youthful enthusiasm. Like Charlie Citrine, who receives a message left behind by his deceased friend Humboldt: 'Remember: we are not natural beings but supernatural beings,' Bellow in this most open-hearted of his novels embraces, at least as an imaginative possibility, the notion that '*this* could not be it . . . We had all been here before and would presently be here again.'

Bellow's next letter gives greater emphasis to the inner struggles underlying his initial euphoria, as expressed both in his early letters and in the *Newsweek* article.

Dear Mr. Barfield:

It's not a case of out of sight, out of mind. I think often of you and compose quite a few mental letters. But I have no progress to report; much confusion, rather. I mustn't be altogether negative; there are trace-elements of clarity. I continue to read Steiner and to perform certain exercises. I am particularly faithful to the I Am, It Thinks meditation in the Guidance book you so kindly gave me. From this I get a certain daily stability. I don't know what causes so much confusion in me. Perhaps I have too many things going on at once. I had promised myself a holiday after finishing the last book. I think I told you last summer that I was going to Jerusalem with my wife. She gave some lectures at the Hebrew University in Probability Theory. My intention was to wander about the Old City and sit contemplatively in gardens and churches. But it is impossible in Jerusalem to detach oneself from the frightful political problems of Israel. I found myself 'doing something'. I read a great many books, talked with scores of people, and before the first month was out I was writing a small book about the endless crisis and immersed in politics. It excites me, it distresses me to be so immersed. I can't mention Lucifer and Ahriman, I don't know enough for that. Neither can I put them out of my mind.

I didn't mention *Humboldt's Gift* to you because I thought you weren't greatly interested in novels. I thought it might even displease you. Besides I tend to think of a book just completed as something that has prepared me to do better next time. You asked me, very properly, how I thought a writer of novels might be affected by esoteric studies. I answered that I was ready for the consequences. That was a nice thing to say, but it wasn't terribly intelligent. It must have struck you as very adolescent. You asked me how old I was. 'Sixty,' I said. Then you smiled and said, 'Sixteen?' It was the one joke you allowed yourself at my expense, and it was entirely justified. It's a very American thing to believe that it's never too late to make a new start in life. Always decades to burn . . .

I'm a bit ashamed to present such a picture of confusion. You probably knew it wasn't going to be easy to change from one sort of life to another. This is not a very satisfactory letter but I feel that I owe you some account of myself—I feel it because I respect you and because you tried so generously to help me.

Best regards,

Saul Bellow

On the back of this letter from Bellow are written the following words in Barfield's handwriting: 'For me the clinching argument was that the impulses of higher love were corrupted into sexual degeneracy.' (*Humboldt's Gift* p. 294.) This quotation from Bellow's novel comes from a passage where Citrine is reflecting intensively on the content of a 'pamphlet' which his anthroposophical advisor Dr Scheldt had given him to read. It is not difficult to recognize in Citrine's reflections a lecture given by Rudolf Steiner in Zurich on 9 October 1918 entitled 'The Work of the Angels in Man's Astral Body', where Steiner was speaking about the dire consequences that will result if human beings in the twentieth century are unable to take conscious heed of what higher beings are seeking to impart to them. Barfield would doubtless have also recognized these very striking thoughts, not least because he assisted in making the published English translation of this lecture. These thoughts clearly made a deep impression on Bellow, since they appear again in his novel *More Die of Heartbreak* (1987), though this time they are assigned to a Russian exile in Paris called Yermelov (see, for example, pp. 72–3, Penguin ed.). But why did Barfield write these words on the back of Bellow's letter? He goes some way towards explaining this in the letter that he wrote in reply, the implication of which is that—to him (Barfield)—Bellow is making excellent use of anthroposophy as a tool for analysing the modern world but is failing to understand its true significance. For his part, Bellow was clearly also struggling with something that he was unable to fathom, something which could not be assimilated by his panoramic, novelistic eye.

A further letter from Barfield followed shortly after, and contains some typically Barfieldian frank remarks about a novel which was being universally acclaimed,[32] not least in anthroposophical circles:

> Dear Bellow,
>
> (I feel uneasy with 'Mr.' but have never got comfortably acclimatized to the contemporary practice of jumping straight from there to first names.)
>
> I was glad to get your letter. Would it be an exaggeration to add 'and a little relieved'? I'm not sure. You evidently read into that 'sixty' and 'sixteen' exchange a whole lot of meaning that simply wasn't there. All that actually happened was that I did for an instant actually *hear* 'sixteen' and thought the error ludicrous enough to be worth sharing. All the same you *are* a pleasantly young sixty. I agree with the *Newsweek* man. My most vivid recollection of your visit is of your jaunty little hat floating along the railings of the footbridge at Farningham Road station.
>
> I did get hold of Humboldt's Gift and may as well confess that I couldn't get up enough interest in enough of what was going on to be held by it. If it's any comfort to you—and the possibility that you don't particularly need comforting ought not to be altogether ruled out—I had very much the same experience with the Lord of the Rings. Later I met a man who for some reason had typed out all the references to Steiner and Anthroposophy and he lent me his extracts. I read them through and then sat back and asked myself what exactly you had got from Anthroposophy; and I found I couldn't answer. Your literary mind is so active—or perhaps agile is the word I really want—that it was like trying to catch a flea!
>
> Because it evoked certain rather deep-seated and arcane vibrations, I was especially struck by a sentence on p. 293: 'For me the deciding argument was that the impulses of higher love were corrupted by sexual degeneracy.'[33] One should not forget that the correlative to 'corruptio optimi pessima' is 'redemptio pessima [sic] optima'. Only of course it has to *be* redemptio, and that is something I fancy even Blake never managed to get quite clear about.
>
> The I am: It thinks meditation has meant much to me too before now. By the way I don't think I ever asked you if you are familiar with

the 'Foundation' meditation (given at the founding, or refounding, of the World Society in 1923). You have probably come across it somewhere, but in case not, as I typed it out for someone years ago and kept a carbon I don't want, I am enclosing it. It is central to everything. If you haven't already got it, perhaps it will make amends for a maybe rather trivial letter. I daresay you noticed, during our two conversations, that, whatever I may have somehow managed to write in some book or other, I am not personally much at home in a 'wise old Dr Barfield' role.

Let me know some time, if you feel like it, whether you are engaged on another book and how you are getting on with it.

Kindest regards,

Owen Barfield

A few months later, the following letter arrived from Bellow:

Dear Mr. Barfield,

By now you will perhaps have written me off as someone who straggled in and then faded out in pursuit of other enthusiasms. The fact is that I continue as well as I can with Steiner and that I am still trying to train myself. I haven't been able to do this steadily. Last autumn I decided—I took it as a duty—to write a short book about Israel ... I worked myself into such a state of fatigue that I was unable to pull myself together physically, much less write thoughtful letters. The morning meditations, which I continued faithfully, helped somewhat, although there were days in which I could only ramble through them in a promissory way. Later, I would do them properly.

I didn't mind your dismissing *Humboldt.* I expected that. It is a comical and very American examination of the cares and trials of 'civilized' people in a civilized country. These cares are by now plainly ludicrous and one can be truly serious about them. The ultimate absurdity is that it is the spiritual matters which alone deserve our seriousness that are held to be absurd. Perhaps it was wrong of me to put this longing for spiritual fruit in a comic setting. I knew that you could never approve and would think it idiotic and perhaps even perverse. But I followed my hunch as a writer, trusting that this eccentric construction would somehow stand steady.

I shall send you the little Jerusalem book when it is published in October.

With best wishes,

Saul Bellow

In reply to a further letter from Barfield, Bellow describes his continuing difficulties with Steiner:

Feb 5, 1977[34]
Dear Barfield,

On the contrary, I should have written to you long ago. Nor did I expect you to acknowledge the Jerusalem book, which I sent in lieu of a letter, thinking that it would explain why I was so poor a correspondent. I find it most difficult to pull myself together. It is all too bewildering. Steiner makes matters sometimes easier, sometimes much harder. This is not because of the new perspective he gives me; in some ways I am drawn to him because he confirms that a perspective, the rudiments of which I always had, contained the truth. But to reassemble the whole world after a different design isn't easy for a man of sixty. I keep my doubts and questions behind a turnstile and admit them one at a time, but the queue is long and sometimes life is disorderly. Besides I can't put into what I write the faint outlines I am only beginning to see. That would muddle everything, and it would be dishonest, too, in a novice. Writing as a comic novelist, I am capable of anything, mixing desperation and humor just as I like (in my own mind, defining Herbert's 'wearie' in The Pulley, as weary with one's own absurdities). But I was serious in the Jerusalem book . . .

I am looking forward to your collection of essays. Thank you for telling me about Guenon. I shall inquire at the library about his books.

I passed through London just before Christmas but didn't want to announce myself. I thought it might be inconvenient for you to see me just then. But I will be in England again in April. I'm going back to Jerusalem via Edinburgh and London. I'm due in London on the 17th or 18th. I very much want to see you, I need hardly say. Eager, is the word.

With many thanks for your letter, and every good wish,

If the April meeting took place, it probably contributed significantly to the very evident warmth of friendship expressed over the following couple of years. Barfield must have appreciated the humour in the next extant letter:

Dear Mr Barfield,

If you hadn't let me know that you were coming, I wouldn't have thought it in the least churlish. I am old enough to begin to understand how difficult travel is for people of advanced years. Unfortunately, I shan't be in the Midwest. My wife and I are teaching at Brandeis, in Waltham, Massachusetts, this autumn. But I would be most willing, even eager, to fly down to New York if you can spare the time from your schedule at Drew University.

Wesleyan University Press did not send me your book, but I obtained a copy through channels and have read most of it, admiringly. 'Read' is not the word for it; I am obliged to study your essays, and I have with a certain amount of difficulty come to understand some of them reasonably well. Writing novels does not prepare one for all this hard work in epistemology. In London I embarrassed myself by asking you several stupid questions. That, unfortunately, is how I learn. I humiliate myself, I grieve, and the point remains permanently with me. I think you will understand how hard this work must be for a man who has led the life that I have led. I count on you to forgive me (as well as you can). The other day I received a letter from a lady who had heard the talk I gave in Edinburgh and who reproached me in the name of what she called all the 'anthropops' in the front row. They had come to hear a great and stirring message. Instead, I spoke merely of what it had been like to become a novelist in the city of Chicago. What? Waste everyone's time with streets and slums and races and crimes and sex problems (I hadn't mentioned sex, by the way). I must learn to do better, and she appealed to me to take more instruction and draw more inspiration from Owen Barfield. She is, in her way, bang right. But what am I to do? I can't pass myself off for a sage, and it wasn't as a sage that the Arts Council invited me to Edinburgh.

I thought you might be mildly amused by this.

In any case, I would welcome the opportunity to see you in New York, between planes.

With best regards,
Saul Bellow

A year later he sent a further expression of his dedication and respect:[35]

Dear Owen:

I think I had better stop waiting for a tranquil moment. There is no tranquil moment.

What I wished to tell you at some length I will tell you briefly. We read *Saving the Appearances* and *Worlds Apart* in a seminar last April and May. It's too soon to say how well I succeeded as your interpreter. The participants were Wayne Booth of the English Department, Professor

Wick, a philosopher who specializes in Kant, a young mathematician named Zabel, one of my wife's colleagues who had seen a copy of *Saving the Appearances* on my table and was keen to discuss it with me. There were also two graduate students, one of them interested in anthroposophy. Booth and the Kantian found the book 'interesting but tough', as Huck Finn said of *Pilgrim's Progress*. Booth was extremely sympathetic, keenly interested, Wick was laconic and pulled at his pipe and told us that we didn't really know Kant; we would be hopelessly muddled until we had put in a year or two at the Critiques of this or that. But even he found you an attractive writer. I thought I would get this brief interim report to you while my recollection of the seminar was still fresh.

For the rest, the usual difficulties—no, worse than usual. I am being deprived by the courts of all my possessions . . .

I asked you in London whether you might be willing to look at the manuscript of a novel, or a portion thereof. Are you still of the same mind, or would you rather be spared? As a friend, I would advise you to take the easier option. As one of those 'writing fellows' (the term used by the indignant old lady in *The Aspern Papers*), I hope you may find it in your charitable heart to let me send you a hundred pages or so.

Very best wishes,
Saul

However, Barfield was nothing if not consistent in his opinions, and incisive about the way he expressed them. In a letter written on 15 August 1979, Bellow made him aware that he was genuinely perplexed and, even, shaken, by Barfield's continuing dislike of his novels:

Dear Owen—

It's been a long time—and one thing and then another. It was kind of you to send the C.S. Lewis book, but I've not been able to read it as attentively as I'd like. Shortly after it came we were called to Bucharest. Alexandra's mother was dying. The circumstances—well, I shall spare you the full description, but my wife was allowed to see her mother no more than three times in ten days. Then death, and another mysterious struggle with the bureaucracy about property. Alexandra came back sick with grief. Some three months of illness—and then more difficulties. I know it's not kind of me to speak to you of difficulties, you have so many of your own which, with English restraint, you don't speak of. But I am only trying to tell you why there have been no letters. I continue to read your books and to think about you, and go on reading Steiner and working at Anthroposophy. I wouldn't like you to think that I am fickle and that I've dropped away. No, it's not at all like that. I am however bound to tell you that I am troubled by your judgment of the books I have written. I don't ask you to like what you obviously can't help disliking, but I can't easily accept your dismissal of so much investment of soul. It may have come out badly, but none of it was ever false, and although I can tolerate rejection I am uneasy with what I sometimes suspect to be prejudice. And my 'heaping of coals', as you expressed it in a letter last year, quite turned me off. I didn't know what to say to that. You don't like novels?—very well. But novels have for forty years been my trade; and if I do acquire some wisdom it will inevitably, so I suppose, take some 'novelistic' expression. Why not? A juggler 'illuminated' would go on juggling, wouldn't he? I find some support in Steiner: '. . . if a man has no ordinary sense of realities, no interest in ordinary realities, no interest in the details of another's likes, if he is so "superior" that he sails through life without troubling about its details, he shows he is not a genuine seer.' (*Anthroposophy: An Introduction*)

Having gotten that off my chest, I want to tell you that my affection for you is very great, and I am sure you know how much I respect you.

For my part, I feel safe with you—i.e., I know you will forgive my idiocies.

Ever yours,

Saul

Barfield responded immediately, and with great warmth:

My dear Saul,

I had been very pleased to get your letter. I had been wondering a little at having heard nothing especially as the last time you wrote you had suggested sending me some pages of your current work and I had (I thought warmly) welcomed the suggestion. But I put it down to your being submerged in personal preoccupations, a supposition which appears to have been roughly correct, though the preoccupations appear to be of a rather difficult sort—much sadder and more violent that anything I have been imagining. Does my single brief encounter with Alexandra qualify me in offering her my sympathy in all she has gone through . . . ? That you have it shall go without saying.

As I say, I was very pleased to get your letter, but I doubt if you have been much more troubled by anything I have said about your novels than I was by what you say about its effect on you. You speak of my judging them. I thought I had made it clear that I did not feel confident enough to do anything of the sort, and a little later I thought I had finally checked the subjective nature of my response by reporting the very different one of my fellow anthroposophist: seriously, I imagined you regarding it as something of a joke that in spite of all we have philosophically and spiritually in common my personal limitations (you know I was born in the reign of Queen Victoria) prevented me from seeing in *Humboldt's Gift* what nearly everyone else sees plainly enough. Evidently I was much mistaken but I still do not understand how you can have got the impression that I found anything 'false' either in *H.G.* or anything else I read. Not the shadow of a dream of anything of the sort.

Maybe you have not fully realized what a Nobel prizewinner feels like from outside. I wrote as breezily as I did because I supposed that any lack of appreciation from this quarter could do about as much damage as a peashooter will do to an armoured car. If what I read had been sent to me in MS or otherwise by a relatively unknown author to whom I owed something and who might conceivably get some help out of me, I should (a) have taken a lot more trouble in reading and reflecting on it and (b) have worded whatever I had to say with much greater care. Actually you had not asked me for an opinion, and I only recorded—not an opinion, but a frank statement of my reaction because I felt it would be somehow disingenuous to make no reference at all to the novels, the more so as they were much in the news at the time.

When all that is said I remain feeling unpleasantly guilty in the light of your letter. I told you quite truly that I could not help envying your success. Possibly that feeling was a more serious factor in my unconscious than the passing ripple of it that appeared in my conscious mind—and misled me into a sort of cantankerous exaggeration of the remoteness and imperviousness of an armoured car. Whatever the cause I am seriously distressed by the thought of having wounded you, however slightly, though I cannot help being glad to learn that you care for me enough to make that possible.

With all this I nearly forgot to thank you warmly for the generous paragraph on my forthcoming little book, of which the Wesleyan University Press have sent me a copy.

I suppose there is no chance of your attending a conference in East Lansing from October 11 through 13? I don't know the exact title, but it is something like The Individual Poet and Language. My own lecture, as the title 'Poetic Licence' suggests, will be mainly literary, or perhaps exclusively so. I am dashing to Michigan and back for a single week, and even so in fear and trembling as to whether I ought to be away for so long; and I am likely to be spending the last night (Oct. 16) at Hope College, Holland. I can't promise that you would gain much wisdom, but it would be nice to have a chance of meeting and talking . . .

Affectionately,

Owen

Bellow's response confirmed that Barfield's letter had made the impression that he had intended:

Dear Owen:

With my 'meaning to write' I am like a drunkard who says he will reform: going on the wagon, as drinkers here say, and the wagon is very different from the winged chariot. Your letter moved me by its warmth, kindness and candour. I have too much respect for what you have done, have made of yourself, to answer lightly and easily. Four or five years of reading Steiner have altered me considerably. Some kind of metamorphosis is going on, I think, and I am at a loss for words when I sit down to write to you. You will think it absurd that I should make a judge of you. It is absurd, and you must find it disagreeable as well, but the position carries no duties, you owe me nothing. I see you—it came through in your letter—as a man who has learned what to do with the consciousness-soul, has managed to regenerate severed connections and found passages that lead from thought to feeling. I won't embarrass you by going on about this; you may think it bad form. I've observed in your books how you shun all such claims yourself, and that just as the Meggid calls himself the least of Michael's servants you prefer to diminish yourself. The best of us have been destroyed in the wars of this century. Among the survivors there's only the likes of ourselves to go on with. 'I am myself indifferent honest, but . . .' Yes, it is like that. I am even more 'indifferent honest', myself, so it amused me to be described as a tank surrounded by pea-shooters.

I wanted to see you in Michigan, but it was impossible to go just then. I wouldn't have had much time with you in any case. I have to satisfy myself by re-reading your books. I don't think I shall be coming to England very soon. In Edinburgh two years ago an Anthroposophical lady, admonishing me, said, 'Mr Barfield will have to take you in hand in kamaloca.' But perhaps I will have made some progress by that time and you won't have to be quite so severe with me.

Yours most affectionately,

Saul

After this letter from Bellow of November 1979, there is no further evidence of any correspondence between the two men until 1982. In this year Bellow's next major novel, *The Dean's December*, was published; and Barfield was invited by Clifford Monks, editor of *Towards* magazine, to review it. Judging by the copious handwritten notes, Barfield went to a great deal of trouble over this review, which was duly published in the Spring 1983 issue of *Towards*. However, it must have been completed well before then, since on 21 August 1982 Bellow wrote a considered response to it in a personal letter to Barfield, who had written to Bellow about *The Dean's December* on 23 July. This is the last record of any correspondence between Bellow and Barfield (other than some dates appended to Bellow's letter in Barfield's handwriting: 15.9.82 and 13.4.86).[36] It could therefore be surmised with some justice that there was—at least eventually—a mutual agreement that there was no point in trying to take their intellectual and spiritual relationship any further. The review under consideration would therefore appear to represent a kind of end-point.

As this is a book about Barfield rather than Bellow, there is no need to reproduce Barfield's review in full. Barfield makes three general criticisms of the book. First, the theme is too heavily weighted towards social and political matters. Bellow, says Barfield, prefers to regard the modern disintegration of the individual human spirit as an incentive to study the disintegration of society to being inspired by a perception of the latter to study the former (which would by implication be Barfield's way). Secondly, the book has a certain formlessness, both in its literary structure and in its use of language; and he considers there are too many undeveloped metaphors in the book for the reader's imagination to be truly nourished by the experience of reading it. Thirdly—and related to his second point—he complains that the book is dominated by a narrowly focused self-consciousness:

> Extremity of self-consciousness, together with unwillingness to essay the leap beyond it, is the general problem of the age in which we live. Its inherent antagonism to any sort of form or structure is the particular problem of literature and the arts; and there are those who believe that the correct solution is to abandon structure altogether. The author of *The Dean's December* drops an occasional hint that he is well aware of

> the problem . . . He has confirmed as much, too, in interviews given since the Nobel Prize, and he had already disclosed in the novel that came before it, *Humboldt's Gift*, that he is no stranger to the writings of Rudolf Steiner. In *The Dean's December* he has chosen to remain, with most of his contemporaries, perched on the apex of excruciating self-consciousness at which the Western mind has arrived, ignoring any prospect of taking flight above it. Whether or not it was a wise choice is a question I should not like to be called on to judge . . .

The review ends with a kind of backhand compliment to Bellow for having done an excellent job of what he *did* choose to do.

Bellow's response was not so much an answer to the points—the critical points—made by Barfield as the expression of someone who has been deeply hurt. He accuses Barfield of not having understood what the novel is essentially about or, indeed, what modern life altogether is about:

> Dear Owen,
>
> Clifford Monks sent me your review of the Dean with the suggestion that I write a reply—take issue with you, perhaps? It would be inappropriate to do such a thing. I wouldn't dream of trying to overturn your opinion. Perhaps your understanding of the book is better than my own. After all, one can never answer fully for what one has written. Besides the Dean is not a 'fiction' in the conventional or formal sense. It is, as some people have told me, people whose judgment I value, a very strange piece of work.
>
> I was touched by your close reading of the book and by your interest in (affection for?) its oddball author. It's natural, however, that I should read my reader, criticize my critic, even the friendly and affectionate critic, or try to make out the shape of his thoughts. Besides, I am an apprentice Steiner-reader whereas you are a respected veteran, so I am bound to take an immense interest in your views. Here is a man who has been studying anthroposophy for fifty years. What effects has this had? What is his vision of the modern world? etcetera. And I felt as I read your review that you found me very strange indeed. I was aware from our first meeting that I was far more alien to you than you were to me. American, Jew, novelist, modernist—well of course I am all of those things. And I wouldn't have the shadow of a claim on anybody's attention if I weren't the last, for a novelist who is not contemporary can be nothing at all. Rimbaud's *Il faut être moderne* is self-evidently true, for me. Perhaps for you, too, but you would qualify modern in so many ways that it would no longer be the same thing. In any case, the

fact that you find me so alien proves that it is not the same. And why do I say that you are less alien to me than I to you? Well, because you have qualities familiar to me: English, of an earlier generation, educated in classics, saturated in English literature. Your history is clearer to me than mine can ever be to you. I have led an 'undescribed life' as it were. Few Europeans really know anything about America. Brogan knew a bit, and so does Barzini, but there is something *very* different (not in every respect a *good* difference) on this side of the Atlantic. And I hope you won't take offense at this, but in my opinion you failed to find the American key, the musical signature without which books like mine can't be read. You won't find anything like it in any of the old manuals. There is nothing arbitrary in this newness. It originates in one's experience of the total human situation. But there is no point in lecturing on the self-consciousness of Americans and how it is to be represented, or why the reflections in the Dean are 'crowded' into small corners of sentences. Without the signature the Dean is impossible to play. Reading becomes a labour, and then of course one needs frequent rest, and the book has to be put down. And what is this mysterious signature? It is Corde's intense passion. If the reader misses that he has missed everything.

And this is where I think your reading goes wrong, for you see 'extremity of self-consciousness' rather than passion, Henry James in shorthand. Not at all. Nothing like it. The Dean is a hard, militant and angry book and Corde, far from being a brooding introvert, attacks Chicago (American society) with a boldness that puts him in considerable danger, but he is far more concerned to purge his understanding of false thought than to protect himself. Indeed, what is there to protect when the imagination has succumbed to trivialization and distortion?

Autobiography? Only in the vaguest sense. If I had been writing about myself I would have recorded that the Dean was reading Leading Thoughts and The Michael Mystery, and that he saw himself between Lucifer in the East and Ahriman in the West. It's not so much 'unwillingness to essay the leap beyond' extremity of self-consciousness as it is dependable [on] certain knowledge of what the leap will carry you into that is the problem.

I'm quite sure that I haven't changed your mind about anything. I wasn't really trying. I esteem you just as you are.

Yours with best wishes,

Saul

> About the 'leap beyond': certain knowledge isn't it either, but it would have to be a leap into a world of which one has had some experience. I have had foreshadowing very moving adumbrations, but the whole vision of reality must change in every particular and the idols dismissed. Then one can take flight. It can't be done by fiat, however much one may long for it.

From Barfield's perspective, there could be no reconciliation with such a standpoint. American culture, as chronicled in Bellow's novels, was to Barfield merely an extreme and one-sided development of a particular stage in human consciousness which he traced back to the Renaissance and associated especially with those Western European peoples which have been in the forefront of establishing the world-view of scientific materialism and the particular life-style that is characteristic of 'today's world'. Far from representing a new step in the evolution of human consciousness, it has served merely to give the particular geographic stamp of the American continent—with its tremendous growth-forces and natural energies—to this characteristic observer-consciousness of the European West, with the result that everything has become bigger and 'better' but also considerably more fixed and, even, conservative. In this sense it would to him have been an illusion to think of the twentieth (or twenty-first) century as the American century; and at the back of his mind he would have had Rudolf Steiner's prediction that there will indeed be a time in the far future (beginning around the sixth millennium) when America will hold the reins of cultural development, but that the next cultural epoch following on the present Western European period will be one when not America but the Slavic peoples of Eastern Europe are to bring their particular cultural gifts to mankind. The significance to him of anthroposophy in this connection was to prepare for this more spiritual Slavic cultural epoch by bringing about a widening of the mental horizons of the Western European scientific quest. He therefore saw it as heralding, and seeking to inspire, a genuine new step in human cultural development, in the evolution of consciousness.

It is also unlikely that Barfield was surprised by Bellow's letter. He well knew how easy it was for people, and especially highly intellectually aware individuals like Saul Bellow, to feel an enthusiasm for both his and Rudolf Steiner's ideas and insights, while nevertheless in their general consciousness—in the way that they apprehend the world—remaining firmly within familiar territory (the 'RUP' syndrome: see Introduction). That Bellow, who as a novelist held in great esteem clearly sees himself as an interpreter of his time, should consider—as it would seem he does—that the way to deal with the existential condition of spiritual loneliness is to 'go [out into the world] and see in detail exactly what is happening'[37] is somehow symptomatic, for it shows that he genuinely regards this outer reality as fundamental, maybe not in his deepest thoughts but for the purposes of every-day life. Barfield, however—at any rate by the time he met Bellow in his late seventies—was deeply imbued with the living reality of the primal moving quality of the individual human spirit as manifested in man's thinking activity. This was to him the source—and in terms of the natural earthly world the sole source—of new spiritual impulses flowing into the world. This is why he began his review with the lengthy quotation from the novel itself (p. 161, Penguin edition) which led him to his first critical comment.

On the basis of the example of Saul Bellow, it is I think a fair supposition that, for all the initial euphoria and somewhat more lasting enthusiasm that greeted Barfield in the New World, his hour has no more really dawned there than in his native land. His thinking, especially when compared to that of someone like C.S. Lewis, who dominated Barfield almost into oblivion in a major conference at Wheaton College, near Chicago, celebrating their joint centenary year of 1998, was so far-reachingly radical that it can only be gradually assimilated by one who has not already had prior preparation for it. Bellow himself, with his endlessly engaging honesty, was shrewd enough to recognize this. It is also a measure of his faithfulness to Barfield that he wrote a very illuminating foreword to a new translation of a set of lectures by Rudolf Steiner entitled *The Boundaries of Natural Science*, published in 1983.

3. BARFIELD AND COLERIDGE

Although Coleridge, who was something of a lifelong passion for Barfield, formed the subject of some of the latter's early writings,[38] it was only in the period of his American journeyings that the initial forays into the mind of this most seminal thinker of the English Romantic movement, as reflected in the essays mentioned below, were developed into a full-scale expedition. The fruit of his findings was set forth in what was Barfield's most substantial book from this period, *What Coleridge Thought*, which was published in 1971 in America and in Britain the following year. Moreover, it was his Coleridge studies which in a certain sense underpinned all his very considerable work as a Visiting Professor in America and Canada, forming the foundation of much of his seminar work and, by implication, also of his many lectures.[39] It was as though his arrival in America in 1964 marked the point where he was no longer forming his own conception of man and the world but seeking ways in which his particular message might be communicated to a wider audience than the select few who could appreciate, say, *Poetic Diction* and *Saving the Appearances*. *Worlds Apart* and *Unancestral Voice* represent in this respect a kind of transition from one phase to another, being both a further refinement of the 'message' and a quest for a form in which it might become more widely appreciated. As the particular audience whom he sought to address in this wider way was essentially the academic world in general (as opposed to a very small number of figures in it and in the world of publishing), it made sense that he should—whether consciously or not—build on the very evident affinity that he felt for Coleridge's ideas in order to establish a real rapport with that world, not least because in this same period the *Collected Coleridge* was being edited and published under Professor Kathleen Coburn's guidance in Toronto, thus giving further weight to a figure who was in any case one of great academic respectability.

Barfield's relationship with Coleridge over the period in question may best be traced through a series of some 76 letters which he wrote between December 1964 and January 1992 to Professor Craig Miller, Associate Professor of English—and leading Coleridge specialist—at the University of British Columbia, Vancouver, Canada. The correspondence continued until 20 November 1995, the date of Miller's last letter to Barfield, who had by this time come to find letter-writing extremely difficult.

The initial contact was on Barfield's side, through a letter written on 22 December 1964 from Drew University, Madison, New Jersey, where he was residing for his first stint as a Visiting Professor from the autumn of 1964 until May 1965. The purpose of Barfield's letter was to thank and compliment Miller for his article on 'Coleridge's Concept of Nature' in the Spring 1964 number of the *Journal of the History of Ideas*. The warmth of Barfield's approach in this brief letter has to be understood in the context of his earlier explorations into the more recondite aspects of Coleridge's writings, a Coleridge who—as he asserted in his 1932 lecture at the Goetheanum (see Note 36)—was at that time '(in my country at any rate) almost entirely unread and to a very large extent unpublished'. Indeed, he had studied the *Treatise on Logic* from which he had drawn 'a great part of the material for this lecture'—from the unpublished manuscript in the British Museum (as the British Library was then called). It was therefore a somewhat bold, pioneering step that, in lecturing at Drew University on 'Language, Imagination and Knowledge', he should have elected to base his whole course 'round STC's Epistemology, his doctrine of Imagination and his Concept of Nature'.

Miller was deeply touched by Barfield's letter, and the foundation was laid for what was possibly the most fruitful instance of academic collaboration in Barfield's life, even though much of the colleagueship had to be dependent on the vagaries of the postal service between Kent or Sussex and Vancouver.

Barfield's next letter, dated 28 February 1966, was also written during an autumn–spring Visiting Professorship, this time to Brandeis University, Waltham, Massachusetts, where, in addition to giving a few lectures,[40] he gave a seminar on 'Coleridge and Imagination'. In this letter he refers to Miller's proposed book (mentioned in his article) on *The Unity of Coleridge's Thought*; and this leads him to write about his own plans in this regard.

> I have for a long time been meditating a book myself, in which STC's 'dynamic philosophy' would be properly expounded in a more contemporary idiom and should probably start work on it this summer when I get back to England . . . I think [my book] would be primarily psychological, literary and scientific (though of course it would also have to be philosophical) exposition, with Coleridge scholarship incidental—the latter less exhaustive than yours, though I should hope neither superficial nor inaccurate.

Earlier in the same letter he gives a frank appraisal of his own and Miller's position among students of Coleridge:

> I fancy you and I are one of a very, very small number of people now living who have really got inside, so to speak, of Coleridge's thought ... or do you know any others? I wonder if you feel, as I do, that he was speaking no more than the truth when he said (*Table Talk*, 28th June 1834): 'You may not understand my system ... but ... if you once master it, or any part of it, you cannot hesitate to acknowledge it as the truth. You cannot be sceptical about it ...
>
> I think I know pretty well why so few have stumbled on the unity of his thought. First, it is because abstract ideas about polarity are a different matter from an imaginative grasp of polarity; and secondly because of an inveterate contemporary disease which I have got into the habit of referring to as 'R.U.P'. 'R.U.P.' stands for 'Residue of unresolved positivism', by virtue of which, to put it very briefly, people who have explicitly rejected (and even publicly refuted) the premisses of positivism nevertheless continue to accept its conclusions. I don't think Kathleen Coburn, whom I not only like personally but admire tremendously, is free of it ...

The second main function of Barfield's letter of 15 March was to convey the suggestion that he, together with his wife Maud and daughter Lucy, visit the Millers in June as part of their holiday tour before returning to England. This visit did indeed take place as planned between 14 and 16 June.

Personal acquaintance clearly brought a bond of true friendship into the correspondence thereafter, and it never flagged. This is evident in the next substantial letter from Barfield's then home, Westfield, Hartley (near Dartford, Kent), dated 31 October 1966. Two sections of this letter should be quoted for the light they shed on the way that Barfield was preparing for the writing of his book on Coleridge. After referring to a piece of 'pukkah research' in which he was engaged on some annotations made by Coleridge in his copies of two works by Giordano Bruno, he makes a bold statement about Coleridge's relationship with his alleged sources which has a certain affinity with the way that, in his turn, he first encountered the work of Rudolf Steiner:

> Actually sources are not much in my line, but I want, especially when writing of the 'two forces of the one power',[41] to be doing so with background knowledge of any sources or alleged sources. In *fact*, Col's 'sources' were, I am perfectly convinced, more often than not confirmations and new and/or convenient ways, recognized as soon as spotted, of formulating what he already knew because he had thought

> it out for himself. But of course the idea that anybody ever thought anything out for himself is not likely to be broached in our great centres of learning. As for the possibility of *two* people doing it and arriving independently at the same conclusion—if a guy'll believe that, I guess he'll believe anything![42]

He also passed on to Miller the following definition—offered to his students at Drew while lecturing on Coleridge—as 'a principle basic to his [Coleridge's] epistemology, his philosophy, his psychology and his aesthetic': 'Polarity experienced is the root and ground of imagination no less ultimately than identity experienced is the root and ground of abstract thought: the root in either case of their psychology, and the ground, in either case, of their validity.'

By the time he wrote his letter of 13 May 1967 he had completed 'three difficult chapters' of his book. He also confirmed that he would be back in the United States in September that year, first at Drew and then moving on to Hamilton College, Clinton, New York in the spring, where *before* he began his course he was made Doctor of Humane Letters. At Hamilton he was to take a further seminar on Coleridge, in addition to giving four public lectures.

The letters from both men over the next three years contain numerous debates about various Coleridgean terms, with Barfield generally acting as a lucid interpreter of Miller's arduous scholarly attempts to make sense of what Coleridge meant by them. His capacity to do this lay in his ability to put his own definition ('polarity experienced . . .') into practice as opposed to cherishing it as a nice abstract idea. For example, in his letter of 17 September 1969 he refers to a recent stint of research in the British Museum which included consideration of the famous 'order of the mental powers' inscribed by Coleridge in the margin of a philosophical treatise by Tennemann:[43]

> I have also managed to get a little—not nearly enough—time in the MS Room at the British Museum, most of which I spent on the Böhme and the Tennemann marginalia respectively (from the latter of which K[athleen] C[oburn] quotes extensively in the Notes to her edition of the Philosophical Lectures). In the last 2 chapters I have written, one on Understanding and one on Reason, but of course also both on both, I have found myself making very full use of the scheme of the 'order of the mental powers' on one of the Tennemann volume flyleaves, which I had already obtained from Florence Brinkley, who quotes it near the end of her book:

Reason
Imagination
Understanding

Understanding
Fancy
Sense.

And in the same letter he uses this scheme to make a very perceptive comment—beside which the recipient wrote 'good!' in pencil—about some Coleridgean terms that had been puzzling Miller:

> Reason being 'much nearer to sense than to understanding' (as the extremes of polar opposites are nearest of all to ... identical with ... one another), I suppose natural instinct and spiritual instinct may be said to coincide whenever Reason is fully conscious of herself within a finite being, the result of which would be total alignment of the finite will with the infinite Will. How does that strike you?

We also learn from this letter that:

> I had a good semester at the University of Missouri (Columbia) in the Spring [January–May 1969], with a very small seminar (5 students plus 2 faculty members and one faculty wife), all keen and open-minded: and I stuck entirely to STC and we made some headway. Since reaching home on June 11 I have been working again on my book, which I shall probably call 'What Coleridge Thought', and have just sent off Chapter IX to the typist. I almost begin to think I may finish it—if trouble continues to hold off. I am not going abroad next year.

His letter of 19 January 1970 contains a passage about Kathleen Coburn which is valuable for its concise expression of the views of each about the other:

> From the personal angle, she [Kathleen Coburn] inscribed an offprint she gave me of her article 'Coleridge and Restraint' in the *University of Toronto Quarterly*, April 1969: 'Owen Barfield, whom Coleridge would have loved', and I am dedicating my book to her ... I find in her a gentle, affectionate, unassuming, dedicated and astoundingly able human being. Or, putting it another way, she is a dear.

After several more letters where—among other things—terms such as Primary and Secondary Imagination are discussed and the latest scholarly books on Coleridge are commented upon, Barfield announces in his letter of 31 October 1970—the first from his new home at Orchard View, South Darenth, near Dartford—that his Coleridge book was finished on 27 October. It was published in America in the autumn of 1971 by Wesleyan University Press, by which time (letter of 10 October 1971) it had become clear that Oxford University Press had agreed to publish a British edition, which they did the following year. On 28 December 1971 Miller wrote warmly and approvingly to Barfield about *What Coleridge Thought*, a judgement to which he would add, in a letter of 29 April 1973, that '. . . your book on Coleridge, *What Coleridge Thought*, is the best book on Coleridge in existence'.

By the time of Barfield's letter of 16 January 1972, no one had 'breathed a word about it [the book]'. He was well aware of having written a book that would not necessarily be liked in literary-critical circles, a point of which Miller was thoroughly aware:

'You have opened an attack on Coleridge critics which is most perceptive and dangerous. I suspect that some critics will attack the book because it is such a different approach to Coleridge and to normal ways of thinking. They may not have the patience to listen to what you have to say. The loss is their's [*sic*], and time is on your side . . .' Regarding this Barfield commented:

> I expect you are right in what you say about critics attacking the book. Or they may adopt the alternative, and more effective policy of ignoring it altogether . . . The dangers are: 1. that literary men won't read it because there is too much about science in it and scientists etc. won't because it is mainly about Coleridge. 2. That philosophical critics of Coleridge, who have long been enjoying themselves detecting sources and assessing debts, will feel that it fouls their nest by coolly implying that all that doesn't matter very much.

While to Miller's mild complaint that he would have liked more about the relationship of Coleridge's ideas to modern (especially scientific) thought, Barfield made the following point, thus anticipating (and rendering irrelevant) one severely critical reviewer's judgement (Professor Owen's, see below):

> I was particularly anxious to make the book a true exegesis of Coleridge and in no sense a stalking-horse for Barfield. According to my view of the nature of thought, and therefore of true scholarship, however hard I aimed at pure Coleridge I could not prevent it being

> Coleridge through Barfield. What I was determined it should *not* turn out to be was Barfield through Coleridge. That made me specially cautious and even reticent in developing the relation between Coleridge and modern thought, as I feel I clearly see it . . .

The reviews *did* come, of course, some 36 of them if one includes both full-length articles and brief notices. Barfield was especially grateful for a 'truly magnificent 5 page review of *WCT* in the summer [1972] number of the *Arizona Quarterly* by a man called John Ulreich', whom he had first met at Hamilton College when he was teaching there in 1968. He must also have been grateful to Professor Ulreich for his efforts to answer the trenchant criticisms which duly appeared in the May 1973 issue of the (Oxford) *Review of English Studies*, in a review by Professor W.J.B. Owen, which, for all its crass bone-headedness, must have quite substantially influenced the way that the book was received in British academic circles. Barfield was stung not so much by the accusation that 'the topics discussed are [Barfield's] own, not Coleridge's, or only incidentally Coleridge's' (which he knew was not the case, see above) but that—in Professor Owen's eyes—he was failing to point out that very 'wholeness' of Coleridge's thought (in the sense of its relationship to living, organic reality as opposed to abstractness) which it was the main thrust of his book to describe. So strongly did he feel the injustice of Professor Owen's comments that on 7 September 1973 he wrote a letter for publication to Professor J.B. Bamborough, Editor of *The Review of English Studies*, which he concluded as follows:

> Without boring your readers with a plethora of pointed quotations, please enable me to inform them that the issue which your reviewer believes *What Coleridge Thought* does not discuss, together with the conclusions thereon which are expressly and emphatically drawn and frequently referred to, forms the main topic of about two-thirds of the book.

Bamborough did not publish the letter, not least because Professor Owen stuck firmly to his guns even after receiving both Barfield's and Ulreich's comments. There was therefore little left for Barfield to do other than to say exactly what he thought to both editor and reviewer, the former letter being nevertheless as much a model of good form as the latter was—in the politest possible way—devastating. His letter of 8 November 1973 to Professor Owen concluded the correspondence:

> In reply to your letter of November 3 I am afraid I fail to see how anyone can fail to see that the two questions: (a) Is the language

ordinarily used of biological organism literal or metaphorical, when it is being used of mental activity in poetry or elsewhere?[44] and (b) Are the physical and mental worlds one single homogeneous organism or are they not? are in fact one and the same question. Or that *What Coleridge Thought*, whenever it is discussing Coleridge's answer to the second question . . . is also discussing the first.

If therefore, when you claim to be entitled to disagree with me, you mean disagree with my book, of course I gladly concur. But if you mean disagree with my letter to the RES, then candour precludes the comfort of acquiescence. I am no great admirer of C.P. Snow, but I feel he coined a rather pregnant phrase when he spoke of 'the technique of the intricate defensive'.[45]

In addition to Ulreich's perspicacious review, two others deserve particular mention. Professor R.K. (Roger) Meiners, of Michigan State University, focused especially upon the skill and intensity with which Barfield through his book enables Coleridge to speak directly to our time. And Professor M.H. Abrams, of Cornell University, presented a masterly summary of Barfield's own account of Coleridge's thought: 'The result is by far the clearest, best organized, and most comprehensive account yet written of the intellectual premises and procedures that inform all the work of Coleridge's maturity—work that includes *Biographia Literaria, The Statesman's Manual*, the *Theory of Life*, the revised *Friend* of 1818, the *Philosophical Lectures*, *Aids to Reflection* and *On the Constitution of Church and State.*'

One could say that, in the end, Barfield must have been satisfied with the book's reception. Even his particular complaint about the book's high price—and hence inaccessibility—was assuaged by its appearance in paperback in 1983 (alas out of print for several years). There were enough scholars willing to acknowledge, firstly, the significance of what he was trying to do[46] and, secondly, his view of the significance of Coleridge. Meiners, for example, concluded his review by framing another passage from Barfield's Introduction with some words of his own:

'Where does Barfield locate the significance of Coleridge (and, by inference, of his own book)?

' "It will become apparent to anyone who has the patience to reach the end of this book that I find the relevance of Coleridge's thought to our time where he himself located its relevance to his own. It resides, above all else, in his radical critique of one or two major presuppositions, upon which the immediate thinking, and as a result the whole cultural and social structure of this 'epoch of the understanding and the senses' (*including supposedly radical revolts against it*—Meiner's italics) is so firmly—or is it now infirmly?—established. As long as this is ignored, I doubt if he has much to say to us, whether as philosopher or as sociologist.''

'You can't get much more *radical* than that, for it digs down into the roots of thought itself.'

Barfield himself contributed what might be thought of as a kind of introduction to, or a brief and incisive statement of, the essence of *What Coleridge Thought* in an essay called 'Either:Or', which appeared in *Imagination and the Spirit: Essays in Literature and the Christian Faith Presented to Clyde S. Kilby*, ed. Charles A. Huttar (1971).[47] In this essay, which is focused on the famous truncated Chapter XIII of the *Biographia Literaria*, he contrasts the dualistic either:or which 'began with Greek philosophy and culminated in the seventeenth century in the great Cartesian *either/or* between matter and mind—*res extensa* and *res cogitans*—on which the whole of modern science is implicitly based' with Coleridge's view of polarity, emphasizing that in the latter's thoroughgoingness it reaches beyond any system of thought that is still thinking in terms of opposites—even one that would replace the materialistic model of modern times with a more spiritual perception (he is referring to Romantic Theologians such as C.S. Lewis and his fellow 'Inklings'). Such 'pioneers', he says, 'have not yet caught up with Coleridge'. The book itself—a detailed summary of which would belong more to a study of Coleridge than to one of Barfield—supplies the substance upon which such a statement can be based.

Barfield's subsequent letters to Craig Miller, between April 1976 and August 1978, were largely concerned with preparing for his prestigious visit as a Cecil and Ida Green Foundation lecturer to the University of British Columbia in October 1978,[48] an event which came about through Miller's dedicated determination. They contain numerous references to his work on Coleridge's *Philosophical Lectures*, or *Lectures on the History of Philosophy*. He informed Miller in a letter dated 9 December 1978 that he had agreed to edit these lectures for the *Collected Coleridge*. They had originally been made available through the research and editorial skills of the General Editor, Kathleen Coburn, and had then been entrusted to Thomas McFarland, author of *Coleridge and the Pantheist Tradition* (1969), who had apparently (in Barfield's words) 'decided that the *Opus Maximum* [which McFarland had already taken on] is enough for one labourer in the vineyard'. At first he made reasonable progress, but after a couple of years his letters begin to reflect his struggle with this task. By 12 October 1981 he had 'done' nine out of the twelve lectures, but he was already seeking guidance in the kind of matters with which a professional editor would have been well familiar but which interested him relatively less and tried his patience in the extreme. The problem was that Kathleen Coburn, who could alone be his mentor for the particular volume he had taken on, was always either on the wrong side of the Atlantic or laid up in hospital because of a fall or serious illness. By December 1983 he is informing Miller: 'As to the Coleridge job, it drags on rather and I get very tired of it'; while in January 1984 he wrote to Thomas Kranidas: 'The Coleridge job drags on and *entre nous* I am sick to death of it and devoutly wish I had never taken it on.' By August 1985 the '*Lectures on the History of Philosophy* are in the doldrums', quite a strong remark to make to Craig Miller. Professor Coburn finally died on 23 September 1991 without having been able to give Barfield the guidance he needed, and his last recorded comments on the subject consist of some despairing remarks in a letter of 18 July 1993 to Thomas Kranidas.[49]

One of the most precious features of Barfield's correspondence with Craig Miller is his ability to produce every now and then a flash of insight into Coleridge's restlessly creative mind, a quality that was elicited to no small degree by Miller's painstaking, though somewhat ponderous, scholarship. Usually these insights are a distillation of that crucial fifth chapter of *What Coleridge Thought* entitled 'Outness', itself a re-expression in Coleridgean language of the crux of the epistemological argument of *Saving the Appearances*. Thus, for example, in his letter of 6 March 1982 he recorded the following note he had recently made 'apropos of STC generally':

'The future of science, perhaps of civilization, depends on how many minds become able to think the preposition "in" without furtively imagining spatial encapsulation.'

Similarly, it is highly significant that, when commenting in a letter of 8 May 1988 that he was not 'altogether disheartened by the response to *What Coleridge Thought*', he made the observation that '... abandoning the received assumption concerning the subject-object relationship is a tough nut for most people to crack, and may even be a frightening one'.

As a final excerpt from this correspondence, Barfield's letter of 23 November 1989 included a 'shorthand summary of the world as I conceive Coleridge saw it, and as I see it'. This was prompted by his reflections on an essay by Miller on Coleridge:

Time

Space

Metaphysical: Will	Phenomenal World	Multeity of individual wills derived from (but not cancelling the distinctity of) Will
Theological: Father	Son	Holy Spirit
Ecclesiastical: God	History (descending to, and ascending from the incarnation, death and resurrection of Christ)	Communion of Saints

However, Barfield's affinity with Samuel Taylor Coleridge was not confined to the realm of ideas. This can be discerned in the passionate sense of personal commitment pervading *What Coleridge Thought*, especially in some passages in the Notes. It is this quality that enables his book to bring Coleridge so eloquently into the twentieth—or twenty-first—century (and I cannot find anything in the book to suggest, as does Professor Owen, that this striking empathy is in any sense a misrepresentation of the book's subject). What is being shared with Barfield's readers is a vibrancy of *experience*, of ideas that are a matter of life and death. It is a quality which—albeit from a more biographical rather than philosophical point of view—also radiates from Richard Holmes's deeply intimate two-volume biography of Coleridge, *Early Visions* (1989) and *Darker Reflections* (1998); and the thoughts that follow have been stimulated largely by reflecting upon Barfield's biography in the light of Holmes's picture of Coleridge.[50]

In the first place, Barfield was a true Romantic, with all that that implies. Essentially, this epithet refers to a quality which leads a person in our modern times to stand against the prevailing trend of scientific reductionism or materialism, against a non-spiritual view of the world and of man's place in it. By implication the term may often be associated with conservatism, a wish to go back to the past and to subvert 'progress' (hence the designation 'Wrong but Wromantic' attached to the Cavaliers in *1066 And All That*, in contrast to the Roundheads, who were 'Right and Repulsive'), and with an anti-rationalistic standpoint. However, this raises the question whether what purports to represent progress in our time—most obviously, the tremendous pace of technological development and outward change currently in evidence—is really progress of any kind in human terms or merely an elaborate way of *avoiding* a step forward in inner development. The characteristic Romantic position of finding oneself at odds with one's time does not, therefore, necessarily imply a retrogressive or, for that matter, anti-intellectual attitude. Both Coleridge and Barfield, indeed, were outstanding examples of this. Coleridge, for all his extreme inner turbulence and outward disorder, was one of the most intensely rational men of his time; and while some may complain of Barfield's devotion to Rudolf Steiner, his writings are imbued with a depth of lucidity unparalleled among his contemporaries. Similarly, both men were intrepid social reformers, although Barfield never became as involved with political journalism as was Coleridge. It would also be possible to point to a number of other similarities, such as their refusal to accept any sort of compartmentalization of knowledge and their ability to range freely between the humanities and the sciences, their interest in German philosophy, their love of walking expeditions, their marital struggles, their innate generosity of spirit and capacity for friendship. What I would particularly emphasize here, however, is that Barfield discerned in Coleridge someone who in the early nineteenth century was fighting the same spiritual and intellectual battle that he was to wage throughout his own life, a kindred spirit who

> approached the problem of knowledge from the pole of Pure Reason or Spirit. He had *grasped in pure thought* the fact that Reason was the very substance of his mind, of his soul, of his self-consciousness. He knew that Reason was his mind and his mind was Reason. He experienced Reason as the very being of his own Ego—and since *Being is one* everywhere and at all times; since Being is the being of all things, of nature no less than of man, Coleridge in his knowing did really approach nature from the point of view not of a creature but of a creator of nature . . .[51]

Moreover, his was a mind which, when its attention was directed towards a study of this same nature, concluded that

> for cognition (however the case may be for immediately technological purposes) physical process cannot be isolated from mental process, nor natural science from human and ethical psychology

and which, in his *Theory of Life*, developed

> a full-fledged theory of evolution alternative to, and largely incompatible with the received [in modern parlance, the Darwinian] theory.[52]

Coleridge had, in a word, through his relentless quest for truth and his refusal to idolize any particular view of it, perceived the reality of the evolution of consciousness, a theme which, as Professor Shirley Sugerman has rightly observed,[53] was utterly central to Barfield's entire mental and spiritual endeavour. It was therefore not for nothing that, when introducing Barfield to his audience at the University of British Columbia in 1978, Craig Miller remarked: 'Of all the men I know, he comes closest to being a modern-day Coleridge. What praise can be higher than that?'

4. *THE VANCOUVER LECTURES: EVOLUTION OF CONSCIOUSNESS*

If Barfield's Coleridge studies represented the background to his thinking over the period of his life under consideration, the theme of the evolution of consciousness—with its particular modern focus on the rediscovery of meaning—lay at the heart of what he sought to build upon this foundation. Even where he was not explicitly focusing upon this theme, he would usually be turning his attention to the effects of a lack of awareness of the evolution of consciousness—either to currently prevalent assumptions or theories about human existence and their effects upon people's lives or to challenging these ideas in one way or another. It is therefore by no means without significance that, roughly at the chronological heart of the correspondence with Craig Miller, there is a considerable body of material relating to the preparation for a conference which had this theme as its central focus. Its position in the correspondence is like a picture of the relationship in Barfield's intellectual life between the vessel of his Coleridgean scholarship and the distilled spiritual substance of his evolution of consciousness studies which he poured into it, studies which were themselves the mature fruit of his many years of research into the history of language (as evidenced in, most notably, *Poetic Diction* and *Saving the Appearances*). The lectures which form the subject of the present chapter contain a highly concentrated expression of the evolution of consciousness theme, thus providing a key to his entire thinking during the closing decades of his life. In the chapters that follow, the thoughts cogently summarized in these lectures will be elaborated upon further.

Roughly half-way through the year-long correspondence with Craig Miller over the titles for his important Vancouver lectures in 1978, he suggested some topics in a letter of 16 November 1977:

> Topic 1: Science and Humanity (or 'the Humanities')—with special reference to current assumptions concerning evolution.
> Topic 2: The Rediscovery of Meaning and the Evolution of Consciousness.
> Topic 3: Reactions against the Scientific Establishment and the presuppositions on which it is based; both past and present (Roszak *et al.*)

and what they signify—along the lines of 'The Coming Trauma of Materialism'.

Miller and Sol Kort (Director of the Humanities and Sciences Programs at the University of British Columbia) then set to work translating these formulations into attractive lecture titles, drawing inspiration from certain phrases in *Poetic Diction* and *Saving the Appearances*. The net result of this quest for titles was that Barfield's second topic emerged unaltered as his central theme (and its original position as a second topic in Barfield's mind should best be understood as pointing towards this centrality). In the letter of 12 April 1978, which he wrote by way of finalizing his titles, Barfield formulated his central theme thus: 'The History of Ideas: Evolution of Consciousness'. It is interesting to note that the ambiguity noted above between the relative significance of a number in a sequence and a position in a group extended in this case to the manner in which this lecture was delivered. Although Barfield conceived it as the first of the series of three lectures that he was to give, it turned out to be the central one in order of delivery—for the reason that the public lecture (which this was) had for purely pragmatic reasons to be sandwiched between the two expressly intended for the University.[54]

Barfield's first topic metamorphosed into the title 'Modern Idolatry: the Sin of Literalness' (encapsulated, somewhat cryptically, as 'Guilt' in the title of the published version of the lectures); and his third topic became 'The Force of Habit'.

With this background in mind, the lectures themselves may now be examined as keys to Barfield's overridingly central theme during the period under consideration and to the subsidiary themes arising out of it.

The title of the first of the Vancouver lectures as published under the title *History, Guilt and Habit*, 'History of Ideas: Evolution of Consciousness',[55] neatly summarizes its theme; for in this lecture Barfield is juxtaposing two radically different ways of regarding human history and evolution. He concludes that, while both segments of his title refer to valid and worthwhile pursuits, the second opens up far wider and deeper vistas than the first. However, this 'evolution of consciousness' which it is his principal object to explain remains an inaccessible mystery to all who are unable or unwilling to question the assumption that human beings have—at any rate throughout recorded history—merely been giving different (and increasingly accurate) answers to the same questions, having different (and steadily better) ideas about the same perceptions. Barfield's aim in this lecture is to help his listeners to question this assumption. His first step is to point towards the distinction between the essentially passive function of perceiving and the activity of thinking. It is essential, he says, that these be distinguished, even if they cannot normally be divided in what is generally experienced as an act of perception. The former is something that happens to us, the latter is something that we do. He draws attention to this feature of our normal way of (as we call it) perceiving the world around us by exemplifying what happens if we fail to keep both of these two elements in view and in balance with one another. In this respect he cites, on the one hand, the 'blooming, buzzing confusion' which William James suggested would fill the mind of someone who had all the organs of perception but had never done any thinking and, on the other, the physicists and philosophers who assert, more dramatically, that, once one has succeeded in distinguishing what one perceives from what one thinks, one must necessarily rigidly divide the one from the other and, in the process, consign the former to the realm of the inherently unknowable. While evolutionists and historians may be reassured that, in studying the familiar, macroscopic world, they are indeed studying the actual world and not the chimera that some physicists and philosophers might lead them to suppose, they must never forget that 'what we perceive is structurally inseparable from what we think', or that we participate in the evocation of phenomena. Barfield then goes on to point out a consequence that follows for the historian from the realization that what man perceives is in fact the product not merely of his senses but of his own thinking. For it becomes clear that his subject is not merely the examination of changes in ideas about or consciousness of the world but of changes in the world itself. Looked at in this way, history is only superficially a record of changed ideas (history-of-ideas changes) and is fundamentally a chronicle of changes in perception (evolution-of-consciousness changes).

Having established this, Barfield proceeds to examine the actual nature of these changes of consciousness. He is able to do this at the end of the lecture by drawing upon a distinction that he made at its beginning between the terms 'evolution' and 'history', when he concluded that what one may think of as the dawn of history represents the incursion of a consciously directed human process into the stream of an unconscious natural one. However, only now that he has elucidated for his listeners the mysteries of the act of perception does it become possible for him to assert that, simply because there was no thinking as we know it going on in the pre-historical period, it does not follow that there was no perceiving, or no consciousness of *any* kind. From the vantage-point of our present consciousness, the only thing of which we may be absolutely certain is that the world which we intellectually conceive may have existed, a world which is unfailingly conjured up in museums and geological picture-books quite definitely never existed. How, then, are we to gain some kind of an inkling of the nature of this consciousness? Through studying language, says Barfield. If we engage in such a historical study of language, we find a variable relation between perceiving and thinking, which comes to expression in the relation between, respectively, the poetic and prosaic elements of language, poetry having a more perceptual element and prose a more intellectual character. It transpires that early language has a greater perceptual element, while later language is more intellectual. If we were to go back to a time beyond language, it would be reasonable to surmise that what we would have would be a wholly perceptual consciousness. Barfield then goes on to show how the historian of consciousness—as opposed to ideas—may set about his task within the temporal context open also to the historian of ideas; but then, he says, he can move on to other and wider issues, exploring the essential difference between the period before the birth of philosophy and the period after it. He concludes this magisterial lecture by affirming that there is no doubt that evolution-of-consciousness changes continue to be at work beneath the surface also in the historical period of modern times.

The theme of Barfield's second lecture ('Modern Idolatry: the Sin of Literalness') is the modern soul-experience of alienation which arises out of the inability which most people in modern times share to grasp the central idea of the evolution of consciousness which he has presented in the first lecture. For if, he says, we fail to take seriously the evidence which a study of the history of language presents us with (and he helpfully recapitulates the main outlines of his findings in this respect)—evidence which plainly tells us that our remote ancestors had a very different consciousness from our own—we will remain imprisoned in the particular reality principle of modern times, which Barfield here labels for convenience 'the age of Darwinian man'. This reality principle, or 'common sense', 'assumes that it is the outer world that is real and permanent, while the inner experience we call consciousness, or subjectivity, or our own, or our self, is a fleeting unreality to which it somehow gives birth from time to time'. This is in stark contrast to the reality principle of our remote ancestors, for whom there was no such thing as a merely 'outer' world; for them, 'the outer and material [was] always, and of its own accord, the expression or representation of an inward and immaterial'. What were once sacred images have become things; and yet in modern times these empty things continue to be worshipped and 'have become, in fact, idols', the worship of which constitutes the 'sin of literalness' in the title of the lecture.

The main substance of the lecture as it unfolds from this point is an analysis of the inner experience of thus living the lie of revering empty idols. For what this behaviour amounts to is a determination at all costs to run away from the reality of the true, existential self in favour of that false self which feels in harmony or united with the idols (which in our time are increasingly represented by the world of the electronic media). The most insidious effect of this evasiveness is guilt—a guilt which begets paralysis of will where the viewing of images of suffering exceeds or is irrelevant to one's capacity to do anything about it, and which arouses contempt and outright anger towards those of one's fellow human beings for whom one truly is responsible in one's personal, existential life but of whom one is failing to be adequately aware.

The third lecture of this tri-unity of lectures, entitled 'The Force of Habit', is concerned with finding a way out of the mental prison of habit described in the second lecture. The problem is that we have to wrestle not only with our own philosophical conceptions but with the assumptions that are ingrained in the very fabric of ordinary life, most especially in the words that we use every day. The only way to break such a habit is to develop a new one—'the habit of thinking *actively*; of choosing to think, instead of letting our thoughts just happen'. Barfield proceeds to expand on this by citing one of Rudolf Steiner's basic exercises in achieving greater inner discipline, control of thoughts, an exercise that soon leads to a head-on encounter with what Coleridge called 'the mind's self-experience in the act of thinking'. These exercises can facilitate the development of the imagination—'imagination is really thinking with a bit of will in it'—in the sense of Coleridge's view of it, in contrast to the passive quality of fancy.

With such a tool of enlivened thinking, it becomes possible to venture in a more illuminating way into the world of scientific knowledge; for such a faculty of imaginative perception is better fitted by far to investigate the life in nature than is 'an imprisoned thinking that is in truth only applicable to the inanimate part of it'. And only when scientific enquiry incorporates such a faculty can there be any hope that the 'common sense' of modern times will significantly widen its perspectives to encompassing a genuine sense of responsibility for the natural world as a whole (for, as Barfield says, 'you do not change the inside of a living organism without at the same time changing the outside'). He concludes this third lecture by emphasizing how crucial it is that the world should be changed from the inside, from the side of the Humanities—a task which includes scrutinizing so-called 'laws of nature' as the mental cerebrations which they can easily become if regarded as facts of nature—rather than changed through the application of technologies whose true motivation is not so much the advancement of knowledge as it is personal power and the manipulation of others.

* * *

In a letter of 11 August 1978 to Craig Miller, Barfield indicated that these three lectures had given him 'a good deal of trouble' to prepare. This is scarcely surprising, in view of the immense weight of content with which he invested them.

His efforts were rewarded by the appreciation that the well-attended lectures received. In a letter to Barfield of 27 November Miller wrote that 'you gave us the courage to speak more openly about the ideas which mean most to you, and to attempt to make your vision a part of our students' lives'. His daughter Margaret had commented that everything about Barfield's visit was 'inspirational'. Miller also passed on an observation made by a lady in the Anthropology Museum, that Barfield had made her 'braver'.

Taken together, the three lectures are rather like a musical symphony, with a first movement containing the main statement of the ideas, beginning with a grandiose theme leading to a complex development section and ending in a recapitulation and coda; a second movement which, while taking up the same ideas, has more the reflective, deeply felt poignancy of a lyrical adagio; and a third and last movement which metamorphoses the same thematic substance into a more light-hearted statement of what can be done about it all, banishing present shadows and sorrows with the reasoned affirmation that a new world can indeed be forged out of the old.

5. POSITIVISM AND ITS RESIDUES

This and the next two chapters will be concerned with elaborating on, and developing the themes of, the three 'movements' characterized at the end of the previous chapter. With the present chapter we plunge directly into the heart of the intellectual battle that dominated the closing decades of Owen Barfield's life—a period when he was graced with the opportunity to direct the light generated by the research of his active working life upon the world around him. For while in *Saving the Appearances* he had been able to develop the insights into language and its origins described in *Poetic Diction* into a graphic and coherent picture of the evolution of human consciousness over the ages, the majority of the people of his time—and the same could be said of the present situation—were unable even to conceive of such a mechanism of evolution because, whether consciously or not, they were already convinced of the truth of the very different picture that is generally associated with the name of Charles Darwin (1809–82).

During the later 1950s and 1960s Barfield went regularly about twice a year to Devon to speak with the zoologist and writer E.L. ('Peter') Grant Watson (1885–1970) about biology and in particular about its unifying[56] idea, evolution. Grant Watson was a field naturalist and explorer who had since his student days at Cambridge developed the conviction that 'the Darwinian theory of evolution through chance variations and natural selection is too simple to meet the complicated and evasive patterns that Nature presents' (from the Introduction to his book *The Mystery of Physical Life*, 1964 and 1992), and went on to propound—on the basis of his discoveries—a theory of the descent of spirit or, as he put it, 'gradual incarnation of the Logos', arguing that, in contradistinction to the Darwinian view, the germ of all future possibilities was there in the beginning awaiting the right environment to be made manifest. He goes on to tell his readers that his thinking had, like that of other students, been firmly grounded in the accepted dogmas of the time until he encountered the then Professor of Zoology, Adam Sedgwick, who indicated in a private conversation that he did not believe in any of the theories of evolution. 'Archetypal forms of plants and animals were, he said, precipitated. *Precipitated*, he seemed to relish the word; and he added that it was bad form in scientific circles to mention the word *creation*. From these precipitated forms the existing genera and species had come into being through processes of devolution. He stressed that for biologists *facts* were of supreme importance: no theory had yet been put forward that could not be contradicted by groups of facts that refused to fit in. For himself, he looked at the facts, and he advised me, as a young man, to do the same.' Looking back over his long life, Grant Watson proceeds to characterize the effects of a general failure in the scientific community and elsewhere to heed Adam Sedgwick's advice: 'The philosophy that lies behind Darwin's theory has been taught as a dogma in schools and colleges for the last eighty years. It has had a far-reaching effect, since most students believe what they are taught, and some apply their belief to their general outlook, if not to their immediate conduct. The idea prevails that it is proved that men are descended from monkeys. During this time, a great de-bunking process had been in operation. The implications which life within the thought of a world in which no creative principle is either emergent or in process of self-revelation, is [sic] such that men are not stimulated to look for meaning in their own lives, or in the life of the universe . . .'

However, the source of the particular dissenting judgement against the Darwinian view of evolution which Grant Watson came across in his Cambridge student days and proceeded to amplify in his books and in his conversations with Barfield can be traced back to another Cambridge scholar, who curiously had the same name as the Professor of Zoology (died 1913). This other Adam Sedgwick (1785–1873), the great-uncle of Grant Watson's professor, was one of the great pioneers of field geology and was Woodwardian Professor of Geology at Cambridge from 1818 until his death. It was he who had originally awakened Darwin's enthusiasm for field geology by taking him on a field trip to North Wales in 1831. He strongly objected to theories that were not supported by reasonable empirical evidence; and it was this preference for intellectual clarity and open-minded argument that led this deeply sincere and intuitive man, whose integrity, solid humanity and deep spirituality were as massive as the huge block of roughly shaped granite which stands at the focal point of his native village of Dent in the Yorkshire Dales as a testimony of the love and respect of his fellow dalesmen, to be regarded as Darwin's most serious and well-respected antagonist.[57] Sedgwick also opposed Charles Lyell's notion of uniformitarianism (of which more later). But his opposition to both uniformitarianism and natural selection was not based on a fundamentalist belief in the Scriptures. Rather was it inspired by a clear instinct that such theories would ultimately evoke a sense of meaninglessness and threaten to undermine all civilized values. As Colin Speakman points out, he opposed Darwin's *Origin of Species* '... because, more acutely than those around him, he foresaw the emergence of an inhumane materialism—"he feared that the specious plausibility of its all-embracing naturalistic 'development' would undermine that sense of personal responsibility that he believed was basic to the nature of man in society"—a fear with which, after two World Wars and a Hiroshima we can have more sympathy'.[58]

It was, therefore, a strongly flowing underground spring which Barfield encountered in the work and, most especially, in the person of Elliot Lovegood Grant Watson, a spring bearing tidings which, as Barfield indicates in his Preface to the 1964 edition of *The Mystery of Physical Life* (he wrote different prefaces for both this book's two editions), 'the *Zeitgeist* has seen to it that they remained largely unheard'. It now remains to see to what extent he was able in his own lifetime to lead it out into the open.

Darwinism is probably the most significant and influential single aspect in the English-speaking world of the philosophical system known as positivism, associated especially with the French philosopher Auguste Comte (1798–1857). Thus in the title essay of *The Rediscovery of Meaning*, which first appeared in article form in the *New York Saturday Evening Post* in 1961, Barfield focuses on positivism in general rather than on its massive influence upon evolutionary theory. Here he defines positivism as 'the philosophical name for the belief more widely known as "materialism" ', which is itself the result of systematically interpreting the facts of nature purely in terms of physical cause and effect. As a doctrine, positivism would claim that this way of interpreting the facts of nature is the only possible one. Barfield points out, very reasonably, that 'a proposition that only one method of scientific investigation is possible cannot itself (except for devout believers) be based on scientific investigation by that method. The proposition is, therefore, in fact a dogmatic belief; although it has been so thoroughly absorbed into the thought stream of Western humanity that it has come to be regarded not as a dogma, but as a scientifically established fact.' Barfield goes on to demonstrate how in the twentieth century this nineteenth-century scientific materialism or reductionism has been extended into the realm of language itself, with the result that 'logical positivism' and 'linguistic analysis' can assert that the very language that we use to refer not only to sense-perceptible phenomena but to any other experience or insight that we seek to communicate by means of it is altogether meaningless. He then sums up our modern dilemma in a few brief words: 'At last the choice is plain. Either we must concede that 99 per cent of all we say and think (or imagine we think) is meaningless verbiage, or we must—however great the wrench—abandon positivism.' The remainder of the essay is largely devoted to exploring what this latter course of action implies, a theme which will reappear in the third 'movement' of this Barfieldian symphony which is the subject of these chapters.

The theme of positivism in its Darwinist form reappears in the last of the lectures given by Barfield in 1965 at Brandeis University, although these lectures[59] for the most part represent a succinct distillation of the output of his central phase. He points out that the reason why people almost invariably make assumptions about human history and the development of language that are completely at variance with the actual evidence afforded by these disciplines is that their thinking is dominated by certain modern tabus—no less potent than the tabus of traditional societies—whose source lies outside philology, aesthetics or history. These new tabus derive from modern biological theories, in particular theories of evolution which emerged during the nineteenth century. There is a great need to distinguish between the observed facts and the theories erected on them or, more specifically, between the incontrovertible observation that the vegetable, animal and human kingdoms appeared physically on earth in that order and the wholly unwarranted assumption that non-consciousness preceded consciousness and then developed into human consciousness. Such an assumption, says Barfield, is based on two presuppositions which he defines as follows: 'The first of the two presuppositions is that "inwardness", subjectivity of any sort, is not merely *associated with*, but is always the *product of* a stimulated organism. The second, arising out of it, is the presupposition that in the history of the universe the presence of what is called "matter" preceded the presence of what is called "mind".' The line of thought presented in this lecture then culminates with the recommendation to the listener (reader) that he consult the writings of E.L. Grant Watson, in particular *The Mystery of Physical Life*.

A further example of the development of Barfield's thinking about positivism and its ramifications comes from the last of the essays chosen by him for inclusion in *The Rediscovery of Meaning*. 'The Coming Trauma of Materialism' (December 1974) was conceived as a review article on Theodore Roszak's book *Where the Wasteland Ends* (1972), although Barfield admitted subsequently that it was 'a convenient peg' on which to hang some of his own most cherished thoughts. The main thrust of the essay is an examination of the cracks appearing in the apparently solid surface of scientific materialism and a reflection upon the challenges which this growing uncertainty presents; but it also contains a further extension of Barfield's analysis of positivism. Building on Roszak's arguments and using some of his terminology, Barfield dates our contemporary 'mindscape' back to the Scientific Revolution and designates it as 'Cartesianism', on the basis that Descartes was the thinker who, fairly near its beginning, 'most competently formulated the felt alienation of matter from mind, and thus of nature from humanity, of which [our modern Reality Principle] consists', in the same way that Aristotle gave his name to the 'mindscape' which preceded our own. He then takes up Roszak's challenge to the Western mind that it abandon Cartesianism.

The main obstacle in the path of such an abandonment of Cartesianism is not so much that people are convinced positivists in our time but that materialism has by now become 'the mental habit of taking for granted, *for all practical purposes and most theoretical ones*, that the human psyche is intrinsically "alienated" from nature in the manner indicated, a habit so inveterate as to have entered into the meanings of a great many common words and thus to have become accepted as common sense itself. Materialism in this sense is not, for instance, incompatible with deep religious conviction.' Barfield then goes on briefly to trace a line of development which he elaborates upon further in a lecture to be considered later in this chapter. For Darwinism could not have developed out of its Cartesian antecedents without the doctrine which did more than anything else to alienate man 'from his own origin and *history* as man'. This was the theory of uniformitarianism, formulated by Charles Lyell in his *Principles of Geology* (1830–3) as the maxim 'that no causes whatever have, from the earliest time to which we can look back to the present, ever acted, but those now acting, and that they never acted with different degrees of energy from which they now act'.[60] All causes have, therefore, according to this unprovable hypothesis, always been as purely physical as they are now. As the article on 'Evolution' in the 13th edition of the *Encyclopaedia Britannica* asserts, uniformitarianism depends on Cartesianism and Darwinism depends on uniformitarianism. And as for Darwinism itself, it is entwined in virtually everything that is written about anything nowadays, with its tenets of the struggle for existence, sexual selection and the animality of man. Barfield offers a long list of subjects and departments of knowledge outside biology where these tenets lie at the foundation of what is propounded.

With this we arrive at what was probably Barfield's most significant single statement on positivism—or the materialistic paradigm—as such, even though he was constantly referring to it throughout the period under consideration in one way or another. Because of this, and because the lecture in question (for it was a lecture) has not been published in book form, it will be worth examining it in some detail. Before doing so, however, it would be good to say something about the context of the lecture. Fortunately, an excellent account of the event during which the lecture was given has been preserved in the journal which published it, *Towards* magazine, founded in 1977 out of the inspiration of the course given by Barfield at a Summer School in Detroit in 1976[61] (the last issue appeared in December 1989) to celebrate the work of Owen Barfield as a modern expression and interpretation of the spiritual impulses of Goethe, Coleridge and Rudolf Steiner. (Its editor and publisher, Clifford Monks, for many years a teacher at Highland Hall Waldorf School, Los Angeles, has earned the undying gratitude of the scholarly community that cherishes Barfield's work.) The event was the Fullerton Conference held at California State University, Fullerton, 26–28 February 1980, and the lecture was—at least in its original form—entitled simply 'Evolution'.[62]

The Fullerton Conference was the joint initiative of Jane Hipolito, then a member of the English Department at CSU, Fullerton, and Bruce Weber, of the Chemistry Faculty at the same college, who in 1973 had conceived the idea of inviting Barfield to attend and be a main contributor to a scholarly conference on evolution, the essential object of which would be to bring the different perspectives of the Humanities and the Sciences into a single focus on this theme. Maria Linder, then Professor of Biochemistry at Fullerton, was also an active participant. The substance of the conference, which was fully reported in the Summer 1980 issue of *Towards*, consisted of Barfield's public lecture on 'Evolution' on the first evening (26th), a working lunch with individuals preparing papers in Barfield's honour, an interview with Barfield by Clifford Monks and a 'Worlds Apart' colloquy on the theme of evolution. And in addition Barfield gave a public talk to members of the Southern California C.S. Lewis Society and the Mythopoeic Society on 'The Inklings', which dwelt in particular on Lewis himself. Apart from the two public events, attendance was limited to a small number of invited individuals, mostly from the academic world.

Barfield begins his lecture—to which we will now turn—with a definition of his famous 'RUP' (Residue of Unresolved Positivism) referred to above (see Introduction and Biographical Sketch), which 'denotes the persistence of inherited positivism in the subconscious, after even the imagination has rejected it, or claims to have rejected it'. He goes on to assert that his lecture will be primarily concerned with unmasking some of the difficulties and absurdities to which the unconscious assumption that positivism is true has given rise—he here defines positivism as 'the dogma that nothing really exists except what is actually or notionally perceptible by the senses'. He then launches his argument by citing a prime example of this 'unresolved positivism' in the otherwise inexplicable refusal of most biologists to countenance the activity in organic processes of any forces other than mechanical (or mathematical) ones. 'But why [he asks]? Why has the paradigm of a fundamentally mechanistic materialism clamped itself so inescapably on the life sciences, and not only on them but on nearly every department of contemporary thought?' The carefully considered answer that he would give to this question 'can be given in one single word, evolution'.

According to its etymological meaning, the word evolution signifies 'a gradual and uninterrupted process of change from one form into another . . . through a whole series of intermediate forms, the one imperceptibly merging into the other', the typical instance being a seed or embryo evolving into a plant or animal. In today's vocabulary, however, the word 'always means Darwinism or Neo-Darwinism', which is a 'hypothetical account of the history of the natural world, not in terms of uninterrupted transformation of form into form, but of abrupt substitutions of a new form for an old, rather in the manner of Aladdin's lamps'. However unsatisfying such a concept of change may be, one is enjoined to accept it on the grounds that the only notion of causality conceivable to the modern positivist mind is the mechanical push-and-pull variety. Future generations will consider the way that the very simple theory of Darwinism seized hold of the popular imagination initially of the English-speaking and then of the whole Western world as 'a startling historical phenomenon'.

Barfield proceeds to trace the three steps in the development of Western thought which enabled this remarkably unsatisfactory theory to become the 'common sense' view of humanity's origin. These have already been enumerated in the summary of 'The Coming Trauma of Materialism', but it is worth repeating them in the slightly different form in which Barfield presents them in the present lecture. 'First, the formulation by Descartes of the principle of an absolute dichotomy between matter and mind and of the mechanical constitution of the former. Secondly, and arising naturally out of that, the adoption by the geologist

Lyell, as an axiom of scientific investigation, of the hypothesis that what we today ascertain as the laws of nature have always existed, have never changed and will never change ... And thirdly, the Darwinian theory of natural selection as not only a cause, but the *whole* cause of biological development through the ages. Again, the third arose naturally out of the second, since Darwin's drama of natural selection requires as a stage for its performance the solid, extra-mental, extra-spiritual earth, stretching millions of years back into the past.'

In the next section of his lecture Barfield returns to a consideration of the etymological aspect of, in particular, the word 'evolution', on the grounds that a study of the history of language—or, using the word in its older sense, of the evolution of consciousness—is the best way to understand these relatively more recent developments in human thinking at greater depth. He illustrates what he means in a very telling way by recounting the story of the encounter between Max Müller, the well-known philologist, and Darwin.[63] 'Müller did not question the primary Darwinian thesis that the human form has evolved or emerged from animal forms. What he did refuse to accept was the tacit corollary that human consciousness has biologically emerged from animal consciousness. As a student of ancient languages, and of the development of meaning in speech, he told Darwin that, whatever else his theory of evolution explained, it could not possibly be taken as explaining the origin of speech. And speech is of course the endowment that most obviously distinguishes the human species from the rest of the living world.' Moreover, Müller did not merely tell Darwin this through the medium of a series of lectures to the Royal Institution in 1873 (entitled 'Mr. Darwin's Philosophy of Language') but called on him in person. Darwin listened attentively, raised no serious objections and stated, in the kindest possible way: 'You are a dangerous man.' Barfield's concluding comment about this story is to point out that it illustrates the extent to which the light of reason was not Charles Darwin's guiding star. He was someone who had, in his own words, made up his mind 'that man is descended from some lower animal' and was therefore 'almost forced to believe, a priori, that articulate language has been developed from inarticulate cries' whatever arguments he might hear to the contrary (quotations from a letter of Darwin's to Müller). More generally, the story also exemplifies the opening up of the—now much wider—gulf between two different conceptions of the nature of reality which, in Barfield's words, could be called 'investigation from without' and 'investigation from within'. 'Müller's penetration into the history of language, and thus into its intrinsic nature, had shown him that if you want to investigate the nature and above all the origin of human consciousness, you can only do it from within that consciousness. You will get nowhere by first of all forming biological and physiological theories which take no account of consciousness, and then basing on those theories your ideas about consciousness.' And then Barfield extends this thought into a specific judgement about the validity of Darwinism: 'What I now have to affirm is that an unprejudiced contemplation of [the history of language] compels the abandonment not only of Darwinism as a satisfactory account of the origin of human consciousness, but also of those other two steps in the development of Western thought, of which it was the culmination, and which I mentioned earlier, namely the Cartesian dichotomy between mind and matter and the uniformitarian hypothesis of eternally unvarying laws of nature. Because, sooner or later, a certain truth is brought home to you, to which nearly all your contemporaries are blind—I mean the fact that mind or consciousness is not the *function* of an organ, though it makes use of organs, the brain among others; that it is not a mysterious something spatially encapsulated within a human or animal skin; that it is the inner side of the world as a whole, just as an individual mind is the inside of one human being.'

Much of the remainder of the lecture is devoted to thoughts concerning the basis for a second scientific revolution, which would be brought about through biologists, and scientists in general, deciding to supplement their research into the outer world from without with exploration of the inner world from within. This would, among other things, unveil the mysteries surrounding organic forces, which 'are as much mental, or noetic, or spiritual ... as they are physical'. These thoughts belong more to the third 'movement' of this Barfieldian symphony. However, it is worth reflecting briefly at this stage about the phrase 'a second scientific revolution'. Many would say today that we are in the midst of precisely such an event, and they would refer us to the Information Technology which is currently 'revolutionizing' our lives. But it takes very little thought to realize that this is a completely different scientific revolution to the one that Barfield is talking about. He envisaged a mode of scientific research (and related ideas circulating in the popular mind) with a greater measure of imagination, of mental or spiritual activity, than is evident in, say, the Darwinian theory of evolution. What is most striking about the fruits of computer-driven research is that there is not more but considerably less thinking activity of the kind referred to by Barfield involved in its generation and stimulated by its results; human ingenuity is being harnessed to the desire to create a world where such thinking is not merely not necessary but not even possible. Were Barfield alive today he would quite possibly describe the technological revolution of our own time as 'the wrong second scientific revolution', and he would add that he warned us of the very dangers to which we seem to be happily succumbing (and this includes some who ought to know better): 'We should do well to reflect that the presence among us of a powerful impulse no longer to deny the spirit but to impound it, or rather no longer to doubt it but to deny it, to materialize as it were the immaterial itself, or in other words to turn from theoretical to practical reductionism, may be pregnant with the gravest possible consequences for humanity as a whole.'[64]

It is, at any rate, very striking that Darwinism, which ought to have suffered its *coup de grâce* from the various assaults directed towards it up to, including and shortly after Barfield's 1980 lecture,[65] continues to be defended by the media today with the same vehemence that greeted the criticisms of a generation ago. In Britain one can only marvel that the dogmatic Neo-Darwinist effusions of a Professor Richard Dawkins were by and large favourably compared in the 'quality' Press with remarks made by Prince Charles in the BBC Reith Lectures (May 2000) which were critical of Darwinism.[66] Yet one of the leading popularizers of modern evolution theory, the Harvard Professor of Genetics Richard Lewontin (mentioned by Barfield in his 'Evolution' lecture), wrote the following in 1997: 'We take the side of science *in spite of* the patent absurdity of some of its constructs, *in spite of* its failure to fulfil many of its extravagant promises of health and life, *in spite of* the tolerance of the scientific community for unsubstantiated "Just-So" stories, because we have a prior commitment, a commitment to materialism. It is not that the methods and institutions of science somehow compel us to accept a material explanation of the phenomenal world, but, on the contrary, that we are forced by our a priori adherence to material causes to create an apparatus of investigation and a set of concepts that produce material explanations, no matter how counter-intuitive, no matter how mystifying to the uninitiated. Moreover, that materialism is absolute, for we cannot allow a Divine Foot in the door.' All in all, there is a sense nowadays that it is no longer even possible to win the argument (as Barfield and others surely did in their particular spheres) by rational debate. In the 'post-modernist' intellectual world of the new millennium the jousting field is empty, the combatants have withdrawn into isolated citadels of intellectual titillation where—in the absence of any sense of, or respect for, absolute truth—anything goes and everything is permissible.[67] The problem is that reality, however painful and problematic, does not simply go away. This legacy which an unredeemed, untransformed positivism has brought to the inner life of human beings in our time forms the subject of the next chapter.

6. THE EFFECTS OF IDOLATRY

In the second lecture of *History, Guilt and Habit*, Barfield diagnosed the soul malaise of modern times as a general failure to acknowledge the validity of the broader picture of an evolution of consciousness as presented by him in the first of these lectures. Now that these prevailing ideas and assumptions have been enlarged upon in the last chapter, it is possible to share more intimately in his analysis of their consequences. Before focusing on the writings where he dwelt particularly on these consequences both for the inner life of human beings and for their outward, material existence, it will be worth while briefly to recapitulate his argument.

Our age is one of individual self-consciousness, where individual human beings become aware of themselves as independent, self-directing entities for whom individual freedom (in the sense of liberty, which is an external kind of freedom) is a kind of touchstone of their existence. This individualized consciousness brings with it a sense of isolation from the world or alienation. Barfield does not see anything wrong with this; on the contrary, he regards it as an essential stage in the evolution of human consciousness over the ages, while also wholly appreciating the equal validity of the very different states of human consciousness that prevailed in former times. For him, problems arise where this state of isolated self-consciousness is experienced as something permanent which should be perpetuated, or even as a kind of end-point in human evolution. And he is at pains to point out that this sense of permanence, of being an individual entity surrounded by other entities from which one is wholly separate is only possible if these surrounding entities—the world, that which is not I—are mentally conceived as 'idols'. 'Common sense today,' he observes, 'assumes that it is the outer world that is real and permanent, while the inner experience we call consciousness, or subjectivity, or our own, or our self, is a fleeting unreality to which it somehow gives birth from time to time.' Further reflection enables one to realize that the driving force behind modern life is a determination on the part of 'liberated' human individuals to maintain these idols of external reality in existence at all costs. In other words, it is not our individualized consciousness but our wish to escape from the experience of it (and still more from the challenge of developing it) that has on the one hand turned us into outward materialists and given our modern life-style its distinctive stamp of unparalleled destructiveness and, on the other, been responsible for the considerable increase in mental illness and psychological instability.

In most of his writings and lectures of the period under consideration, Barfield was usually focusing on either establishing a clear diagnosis of pathologies of modern life or offering a remedy for them. Only rarely did he feel moved to reflect more deeply on the phenomena which he saw before him in the form of a fictional narrative; and when he did so he invariably had great difficulty in persuading publishers to share his ponderings with a wider audience. Thus of the two pieces of extended writing falling into this category written subsequent to his first visit to America in 1964, 'Night Operation' (1975) and 'Eager Spring' (1985), only the former has been published, after several rejections by publishers.[68] This is probably because they are essentially didactic poems with a message to impart, rather than perfectly constructed stories with a racing plot. Barfield, as always, has something to say, and being Barfield this something is both original and in places thoroughly challenging and uncomfortable; and he has chosen the genre of fiction because this offers him the best opportunity to present not merely his ideas but his own *experience*.

'Night Operation' is, on one level at least, an extraordinary piece of writing for a man in his late seventies, especially one so civilized and genteel as Barfield. As there is no apparent explanation in his personal life for the extreme unpleasantness of some of its content, one needs to form an impression of the circumstantial context whence it came. Three aspects in particular come to mind. In the first place, he had recently written the already cited 'The Coming Trauma of Materialism' (December 1974), an essay which culminates in a passage where he describes some of the likely results of significant cracks appearing in the modern mind-set of materialism:

> Let us nevertheless suppose that the resistances [to a breakdown of the materialist paradigm] are eventually overcome and try to imagine a second stage of transition [following the kind of challenges represented by a book like *The Velikovsky Affair* (1966)]. This must surely be a climate of extreme depression amounting in many quarters to despair. Certainly if I myself, forsaking generalities, endeavour to focus on particular goings on at the point of time where it shall at last have become incontestable that the age of post-materialism has dawned, I am simply forced to envisage an epidemic of something like nervous

breakdowns, with probably some suicides, within such solid fortresses of conformity as M.I.T. or the London School of Economics and among their alumni.

There will be problems for the many as well as for the elites. And here I seem to see not so much depression or despair as a period of total confusion. For example, what exactly will happen to popular sexology, as the cracks start [to] widen between habits of behaviour and habits of mind; if it becomes as much a matter of common sense as the converse is now that an individual human being is a unit of dignity transcending birth and death and not a lump of galvanized meat? Darwinism, directly and through Freudianism, has been responsible for the artificial abstraction of 'sex' from gender or humanized sex. One's imagination boggles at the convulsions that must accompany any struggle of anal and oral eroticism to turn into something like romance or the marriage of true minds or even something altogether new; at the incertitudes, the qualms, the misgivings, the deflated egos, the sagging self-assurance of a permissive society, as its whole vast monkey ethic of solemnly inculcated sensuality, masturbation, perversion, abortion, hitherto fed to it from school, university, parliament, press and sometimes pulpit, begins to subside beneath its feet.

And then, as if to predict his own miniature offering in 'Night Operation', he adds the following thought: 'One way or another there is an opportunity here for a good book in the genre of science fiction by a really imaginative writer, who should fill out in terms of concrete events and experiences the issues I have merely glanced at, and no doubt introduce others.'

A few lines further on he refers to another article, which he had written for the same journal (the *Denver Quarterly*) in the winter of 1972. This earlier article, entitled 'The Politics of Abortion', opens up the second of the three strands of experience which together created the context out of which 'Night Operation' was written. Although, in the article referred to, Barfield is less concerned with expressing his views about abortion than with trying to orchestrate some kind of continuing dialogue between pro-abortionists and pro-lifers, he was wholly supportive of the aims of the Society for the Protection of Unborn Children (SPUC). According to Elspeth Chowdharay-Best,[69] Barfield was a friend of Lord Patrick Barrington, the founding Chairman of SPUC and the chooser of its name (it had been founded in 1967, the year when the Abortion Act was passed in Britain); and he attended several committee meetings of this society, which had its origins largely in the Anglican Church. What is of particular relevance here is that in 1974 and early 1975 he was engaged in preparing first a memorandum and then some oral evidence on behalf of SPUC for the Royal Commission on Civil Liberty and Compensation for Personal Injury. Again, the details of Barfield's legal arguments are not of prime importance in the present context, in that he was trying to establish parameters for possible insurance claims made by individuals with handicaps against parents and others alleged to be responsible. What is transparently clear is his stance that the rights of a human individual begin at conception as opposed to later; and he adds a wry comment on the question—raised in Paragraph 16 of the Royal Commission Circular—as to 'whether there should be a cause of action for "wrongful life" (i.e. for being allowed or even caused to be born defective instead of being aborted)': 'In the age of W.S. Gilbert the idea of an action at law for having been born would have been good for a laugh. Its absurdity would have escaped neither a music-hall audience nor an academically trained mind. I suspect the same would have been the case as recently as twenty or thirty years ago. Yet today it is the sort of idea a Royal Commission is prepared to spend time solemnly discussing! So rapid has the drift become in intellectual as well as moral sensibility' (quotation from Barfield's Memorandum of April 1974). While his evidence for the respective hearing on 21 February 1975 dwells on the need in our time to extend the property rights accorded to women from the time of the first Married Women's Property Act of 1870, which led to a woman having a legal existence distinct from her husband's (thus transcending the common law dictum that 'husband and wife are one person, and that person is the husband'), to the unborn child. 'May it not be the case that many of the technical difficulties by which the Law Commission was confronted in developing a law of liability to unborn children will only disappear when legislating intelligence ceases to confound spatial inseparability with actual identity; and therefore no longer feels bound (as the Law Commission avowedly did) by an unexamined general rule that "mother and child are one individual—and that individual is the mother"? In fact there are two individuals, not one and . . . in equity the relationship between those two is one of trusteeship or guardianship, not one of unqualified ownership.'

The third element of experience prompting the writing of 'Night Operation' was most likely the outward socio-political tensions in Britain at that time. Towards the end of 1973, OPEC (the Organization of Petroleum Exporting Countries) had agreed on a dramatic increase in the price of oil, an event which underlined the extreme fragility of the

Western world's complex and highly interdependent life-style. In July 1974, Barfield drafted a contribution to a proposed symposium on 'Rudolf Steiner's Threefold Commonwealth'. The symposium did not take place, but Barfield's preparatory essay on 'Industry and the Law' has preserved what he was thinking in this respect at the time and, more important, the way that he was thinking it. Although the basic ideas in this essay are not new,[70] Barfield's introductory words strike an almost apocalyptic mood:

> The complex industrial society of the Western world is at the moment waking up to a deadly serious problem. It is the fact that, because of that very complexity, small groups of individuals here and there are in a position to enforce their will on a whole community. Terrorists holding nations to ransom with kidnapped hostages are only the extreme example. The power does not depend on outright lawlessness. Workers in a single industry for example need only threaten to withhold their labour indefinitely and, so intimate is the interdependence between one industrial structure and a great many others, that ruin may stare us in the face.

Curiously, this chapter is being written amidst a not dissimilar crisis in Britain, with a national blockade preventing the distribution of all but emergency supplies of petrol. 'Britain grinds to a halt,' reads today's *Guardian* headline, as an interruption to the bulk of the 3000 daily tanker deliveries—supplying 100,000 litres of petrol to motorists every day—that keep the country on the move begins to take effect. What is being emphasized here is not the political aspect of the situation in either 1974 or 2000 but the sense of crisis and, of course, opportunity and challenge which such a time of instability and questioning engenders. 'Night Operation' is, as Prof. Jeanne Hunter indicates in her prefatory note to the story in *A Barfield Sampler*, 'a contemporary allegory on the fall and potential rise of humanity represented in the character of Jon, a voice crying in the wilderness of modern humanity'. In other words, Jon is to all intents and purposes Barfield trying desperately to show his contemporaries the way out of the abyss into which they have largely unknowingly fallen.

Thus it is symptomatic that the story begins not with an elaborate description of some sort of futuristic environment (which in fact we never get from the author) but with an account of Jon's birth which could well be contemporary: 'It was simply that the gynaecologist's prognosis had indicated no special reason for aborting him and his mother's distaste for the messy business of child-bearing had not been quite strong enough of itself to make her opt for it. Somehow or other he had slipped in.' The reader is then led by way of the process whereby Jon learns to develop a verbal and practical relationship with his environment to the awareness that the world that he inhabits is a sewer, and that our familiar natural world, with its lamps of sun, moon and stars, is one which in the course of his education he is only allowed by his teacher to glimpse for a few minutes through a thickly glazed window reachable via a lift and a narrow stone staircase. As for the reference to the supposed location in time of the twenty-second century, this is mentioned merely in passing in the course of a section describing the replacement in educational practice of the three Rs by the three Es (ejaculation, defecation and eructation, or, as most members of this society put it, 'fucking, shitting and puking'). One of the two main elements in the first of the two parts of the story is essentially an amplification of this statement in the form of a picture of a society where all trace of culture may be said to have died, at any rate in the sense of what is outwardly apparent. Barfield lays it on thick, and makes full use of the opportunity to caricature certain very evident tendencies in modern life and thought. In the society that is described in the story, the encouragement of learning or erudition of any kind is regarded as undesirable, since 'it is agreed on all hands that the primary purpose of education is to avert elitism by scotching discrimination'. This is seen as one of the great advantages of the three Es, on the grounds that—in the words of the Principal of Jon's school—'we cannot all think, but we can all excrete'. The other main reason why the three Es came to overcome a powerful movement to return to the three Rs was that the former represented the actual direction in which contemporary habits of social behaviour, and also art and literature, were heading. This line of analysis is subsequently extended into a lengthy quasi-sociological description of how people, out of their increasing boredom with the various sophisticated delights centering on the penis (E1), were claiming that the future progress of humanity lay in exploring the sexually inclusive realm of anality (E2); while a small avant-gardist section of the public, the 'Nauseants', were extending their research to the pain/pleasure dilemma posed by E3.

Meanwhile, Jon himself was following a distinctive path of his own which was eventually to lead him out of this graphically loathsome subterranean environment. Prompted by a 'minor peculiarity' in the speech habits of one of his teachers, an elderly woman who insistently avoids voguish linguistic vulgarisms and clichés, he develops the habit of pondering words and their meanings, and as a result enthusiastically takes up the opportunity to learn about the origin of the civilization in which he lives through 'applying for History (Ancient and Traditional)'. Barfield then gives us an account of Jon's researches behind the locked doors of the Inner History Museum into the history of humanity, a quest that he was able to pursue solely by dint of his endeavour to understand large numbers of words which had become obsolete or had contracted in their meaning. The convincing ring which pervades this passage is a tacit reminder that this was also Barfield's own path, as we shall see in detail later on. It is this research—the key to the world of light—which leads Jon to the conclusion that he must find his way to Aboveground if he is to remain sane and withstand the great repugnance that he feels towards his surroundings. It also enables him to persuade his two close friends, Jak and Peet (who, respectively, bring a feeling and will element to complement Jon's emphasis on thinking), to come with him.

As we learn at the beginning of the second part of the story, which is concerned with the friends' visit to Aboveground, it is the policy of those at the Top Level of this sewer society to prevent anyone leaving it if at all possible. Nevertheless, every citizen has a veiled inalienable right to do so, even though the official way involves making good all transgressions against State policy preserved in the computer bank in the Personal Records Office, a condition that effectively discourages most applicants. However, Jon and his friends manage to find a way out that circumnavigates the Personal Records Office; and one has the impression that this manner of egress was always open to anyone with the determination to go that way (characteristically, this was Peet's contribution). On reaching the mouth of the cave, they are terrified of the great open space around them; and only Jak's image of his 'winsome lady' gives them the courage to go on. There follows a relatively brief description of Aboveground and of the friends' initial experience of it, which, like much of the story, can be read on two levels: first, as a more literal, futuristic image of our familiar earthly world as it might become by the twenty-second century in the wake of the economic collapse and the dread of airborne invasion referred to in the story; and secondly, somewhat more imaginatively, as an impressionistic evocation of a wholly *contemporary* world of spiritual experience, which is only accessible from the metaphorical foulness of the degraded culture of modern times by way of the mysterious guardians of the threshold of Aboveground whom Peet somehow manages to circumvent or satisfy on his friends' behalf.

And then 'the monstrous happening began'. After spending a few hours in their unfamiliar surroundings, Jon, Jak and Peet share in what they agree is the most crucial experience of their visit to Aboveground. At first they are aware of a number of parachute-like objects descending to the earth from the sky, growing smaller and smaller as they approach the ground. Upon landing, the little spheres borne by the parachutes disappear into the ground, and the parachutes rise up and fade into the starry background whence they had come. Each of the friends has a different experience of this event, although all three accounts are descriptions of the souls of human beings incarnating on the earth. Jon sees the little spheres as golden balls, and equates what he saw with pictures that he had seen in old books in the library of 'a wide-winged bird flying downward and, pendant from its bill, a long loop with a new-born baby in it. *Stork* I believe they called it . . .' And he goes on to express his vision in the image of a 'little ghostly Cup', which, as he indicates on the verge of descending once more into Underground, 'would need refilling from time to time' and 'was a vessel that could be brimmed with no other substance than its own magic Provenance awfully beheld'. In Peet's view, Jon was perceiving the past of humanity, the humanity to which the Gods gave birth through the Word, and the birth of individual human beings. As for himself, he says that the balls he saw were not golden but black, and they crumbled into dust and vanished rather than sunk into the ground. Peet claims to be seeing the future: 'And what have the Gods started doing *now*? Blackballing; excreting humanity; spewing out their own creation; "emptying the contents of the womb", as the businesslike abortionist puts it, when he is converting a baby into excrement!' Jak perceives what happens every night; for the silver balls that he sees are the ' "bodies" of men and women now living . . . The silver cannot stay silver. Either it will turn black, or it will change into gold. I don't know. Perhaps, when the little spheres disappeared into the earth, they were finding their way back to the skeletons to rouse them from sleep. And perhaps they were bringing down, compacted within them, something of the Beginning itself, or something at least of its tremendous energy.'

The three friends agree that what they have seen represents something of sufficient value to bring back with them to Underground (they had agreed that on encountering such a thing they would return to their subterranean home, at least for a while). Jon does not want to return at all. Peet—who had insisted on this condition—is determined that they should. The balance is, again, tipped by Jak and his memory of his beloved who has remained behind in the sewers. They return to Underground united by the firm conviction that they will blaze a path for others to join them in Aboveground and work unceasingly towards the vanquishing of the stultifying darkness and stench by which they have always been surrounded. Barfield ends the story as honestly and as openly as he can: 'What happened after that, how far they maintained their joint resolution, what influence they were able to exert, and what effect, if any, it had on the destiny of that closed society of sickness and the smell of sickness, from which they had momentarily emerged, is a tale that cannot be told for the sufficient reason that it is not yet known.'

By the time that Barfield wrote the work of fiction that is the other main subject of this chapter, 'Eager Spring',[71] the focus of his attention was in the process of switching from giving lectures and writing articles to reviewing or writing prefaces and afterwords to other people's books, a large number of which were either by Rudolf Steiner or by students of his work. Thus to the years 1984–5 there belong his review essay on Rudolf Steiner's lecture-cycle *The Boundaries of Natural Science*,[72] his introduction to Steiner's lecture-cycle *The Origins of Natural Science* (the introduction was written in October 1984 and the volume published in 1985), his introduction to Steiner's lecture-cycle *The Karma of Materialism* (mailed in April 1985 and published later that year) and the introduction that he wrote in May 1985 for a volume of essays by his late friend John Davy.[73] However, these years also witnessed two events which represent a kind of culmination of Barfield's lecturing activity. The first was his lecture 'Anthroposophy and the Future', delivered at the Summer Session of the Rudolf Steiner Institute, Chambersburg, Pennsylvania on 3 August 1984 and published in *Towards* (Vol. III, No. 1, Fall 1987). Then there was, as far as I know, his last lecture, his contribution to the Summer Conference of the Bio-Dynamic Agricultural Association at Hawkwood College, Stroud (5–7 July 1985). Some of the thoughts expressed in these contributions will be enlarged upon in the next chapter. But before proceeding to 'Eager Spring' itself, it is worth dwelling for a moment on the remarkable phenomenon of Barfield's presence at the BDAA Conference, 'On the Road to Bio-Dynamics', in July 1985.

It might have been thought that there was something incongruous about the presence of this 86-year-old philosopher of language as one of the leading speakers at an annual conference of farmers and gardeners. However, the 50 members of the BDAA who gathered at Hawkwood College over this festively sunny weekend (I was one of those present) were able to appreciate and, judging by the report written of the conference, understand the intensity of Barfield's awareness both of the overriding importance of the work of this small but active group and of the obstacles to its growth. He spoke of the increasing threat to the whole earth from pollution, deforestation, chemical sprays, factory farming and so on, and emphasized that its salvation will depend on what he described as 'a breakthrough into the *general* consciousness of what is already present in yours. I see the fact that you are putting your awareness into practice as an indispensable contribution towards the coming about of such a breakthrough. But I also see that it will hardly suffice of itself to bring that about. You will need help from elsewhere.' The context of this last remark is his conviction that, while there seem to be many others who are equally aware of the threats that he has referred to (environmentalists, conservationists, ecologists, Friends of the Earth), nearly all of them 'are limited by the same mental shackles as the enemy they are fighting. So I have thought or at all events *hoped* that you might welcome it if I spoke to you not about BD farming but about those mental shackles, and about any signs there may be of their loosening a little.'

He then goes on to speak about the mental shackles of the positivist assumptions already discussed in the previous chapter and their partial loosening through the work of scientists such as Rupert Sheldrake, who in his book *A New Science of Life* had developed the concept of a morphogenetic field or field of formative forces. However, he asks his audience not to get so carried away by the ideas of 'Sheldrake & Co.' as to imagine that we are on the verge of the breakthrough to which he has referred. For 'there is something that stands in the way ... that maintains a wide gap between *theories about* formative forces and actual *perception*, actual *experience* of them (as by Rudolf Steiner). A habit of thought can become so deeply ingrained that it goes down into the unconscious and prevents people from seeing the obvious consequences of their conscious thought. The habit I refer to is the assumption that nothing is real that cannot be actually *or notionally* perceived by the senses.' After referring briefly to the origin of this assumption in the divorce, formulated by Descartes, between matter and spirit (the latter of which in this view is to be found only in human consciousness), he discerns its tenacious presence in the would-be inaugurators of a new approach to the life sciences: 'When biologists are more and more forced to admit that there must be invisible forces behind natural phenomena, *they cannot possibly conceive of them as being in any sense of the same nature as the forces at work within human consciousness*. Invisible, yes. Imperceptible, yes—but still physical forces. They are conceived to be of the same nature, if not actually the same, as electro-magnetic forces.' The existence of a 'life-force' is acknowledged, but not 'mind in nature'. And yet, he continues, 'etheric forces *are* operative in human consciousness as in physical nature. There's the rub. *Re-thinking biology will not prevail without re-thinking the whole phenomenal world*... Science has been busy reducing biology to physics. There *could* be a very different marriage between the two! But only if both of them acknowledge, not merely invisible forces in nature, but *mind in nature*.'

This deeply personal appraisal of the actualities—as opposed to the ideal possibilities—of the present situation facing mankind concludes with a frank estimation of the difficulties and challenges that lie ahead: 'But I fear [there is] a long way to go. Why? The gap between fancying an imperceptible life-force of some sort, on the one hand, and, on the other, accepting and *working with* the presence of mind in nature is a formidable threshold. If I really accept it, I am forced to accept a new concept of what I mean by myself. It means I am no longer wholly in my body, and the consequences of that are momentous indeed. For the scientist it means: no scientific progress without self-discipline and self-development. [It is] no fallacy to equate that threshold with the threshold of which Rudolf Steiner writes in *Knowledge of the Higher Worlds* and elsewhere. We learn from him, too, that just now the evolution of consciousness is pushing humanity as a whole towards that threshold. Some of the straws in the wind I have mentioned are no doubt instances of that fact. What is desperately needed is *recognition* of that fact. It seems that, without recognition, man may be pushed nearer and nearer to the threshold, and even pushed over it *in the wrong way*.' It was out of this carefully considered, but uncompromising interpretation of contemporary conditions that 'Eager Spring', the last work of any substance that Barfield wrote and in many respects his final testimony, was born.[74]

As Barfield makes clear in the Foreword that he wrote for its intended publication, 'Eager Spring' was the joint initiative of himself, as author, and his illustrator, Josephine Spence; and it was a visit to Gilham Spring in the Wealden village of Forest Row, Sussex (where Josephine Spence had lived for some time and which was to be Barfield's home after November 1986) which gave him the idea for the story. He also sought to acknowledge in his Foreword that the systematic tree-plantation schemes of Harry Coppard were no invention of his own but were derived from a factual account of events that took place in Provence in the early years of the century.[75] The first chapter sets the scene for this parable of the modern environmental movement. Two young university students, Leo(nard) Brook, who is studying archaeology, and Vi(rginia) Fisher, who has just graduated in English Literature and has a particular interest in the medieval period, are walking in the Sussex Downs and come across a spring which has been dry for some time. Leonard explains that this is because all the trees which used to cover the area have been cut down over the past centuries to satisfy the local iron industry and the immense requirements of shipbuilding. They then encounter the secluded cottage of Harry Coppard, which mysteriously is set amidst a richly wooded area of deciduous trees. When they return to his cottage, the shy, retiring Coppard reveals that this forest is his own creation, and that on securing the necessary means he decided to dedicate the remainder of his life to restoring life to nature in the very place where the first wholesale deeds of destruction had begun. 'For centuries past,' he told Vi and Leo, 'humanity had been despoiling the Earth for its own purposes. But the Earth was a living creature, and living creatures can die. It was time for man to start giving back to the Earth as well as taking from it . . .'

In the second chapter, which recounts the events of the marriage of these two young people and explores their very different interests, we learn that, while Leo is a somewhat conventional archaeologist, Vi is developing an ever greater interest in and respect for ancient myth and allegory and has a more imaginative approach to life in general. The next few chapters tell on the one hand of her growing openness to a spiritual interpretation of human existence along Barfieldian lines (a line of enquiry encouraged by her university colleague John Herapath, who in his turn is well versed in Rudolf Steiner's anthroposophy), and on the other of her burning conviction that there is something profoundly wrong about man's present destructive and parasitic relationship to the earth, views which on both counts establish an ever greater rift between herself and Leo. 'As I understand it,' she tells Herapath, 'the spirit first created mankind, and the Earth, and then *entered* them. But then it retired from the natural world in order to constitute man a free autonomous being. It then became his task to give back to the Earth the spiritual life with which it had been endowed.' At this point she is able to form a very clear and unbreakable connection between these far-reaching thoughts and her experience a few years previously in and around Harry Coppard's cottage; and she becomes determined to do something to counter the rape of the earth symbolized by the dried-up nature of Eager Spring.

The next phase of this central element in the story arises out of a subsequent visit to Harry Coppard by Vi, who has by now joined a group called the 'Earth-lovers'. Thanks to his efforts, Eager Spring is now flowing again; and he has 'retired' from his patient planting of acorns on the Downs around his cottage. But he now tells of a new threat in the form of a particularly effective but also particularly dangerous biocide used by the larger farms for animal treatment. Despite the adroit lobbying of the pesticide manufacturers, the 'Green' people had succeeded in persuading a reluctant Government to temporarily outlaw it pending an inquiry into its negative side effects on cattle; and it had been decided to 'dump' surplus quantities of existing stocks in remote places with appropriate safeguards to prevent leakage. The location of the dumps was secret. Harry, however, had come across one on the neighbouring heathland. Not long after he has made Vi aware of this, she discovers that the newly flowing water of Eager Spring has been contaminated by the poison. Moreover, Harry strongly suspects that something even more sinister is going on, and Vi sets out to investigate. A chemist friend of her husband's is able to establish that the poison contaminating Eager Spring is indeed the same by now notorious biocide. The next step—which leads her into environmental activism—is to investigate Harry Coppard's suspicions that the biocide is not merely being dumped in England but is being in part surreptitiously transported to unsuspecting Third World countries. As a result of an ingenious and highly dramatic exploit, which she contrives together with some friends, she succeeds in obtaining the necessary proof to confirm Harry's suspicions. But some of the deadly substance gets onto her clothes while she is raiding the lorry conveying crates containing the biocide to Southampton, and she becomes seriously ill.

As Vi hovers between life and death, the manufacturers of the biocide are taken to court and found guilty; and they are required to pay a fine (which is no great problem for them). She reflects that, although her campaign has led successfully to the suppression of this particular product, what did this success actually amount to? 'One tiny ingredient in the venomous mix of uncomprehended matter and empty or deluded mind that was threatening mankind and the Earth itself had been neutralized, one cluster-bomb out of the mass that carpeted the target had been defused. That was how she saw it. Vague shadow-pictures of huge social structures, whether totalitarian states or multi-national corporations, not so much haunted as crushed her animal spirits. More and more impregnably, because more and more globally organized. And round what principle? Not the "life" that maintains natural organisms in being with the help of death, its polar twin, not even an imagined abstract "life-force". Round an empty idea called "growth" that now ruled all speculation and all planning, an Eleventh Commandment that had wormed its way into the Stone Tables and, one by one, was steadily obliterating the other Ten: "Thou shalt increase and multiply the total of material goods and services". It was useless. She herself and those like her were attacking a giant with a pea-shooter, an armoured giant, secure therefore even against far more powerful missiles than theirs. They were dreaming that it is possible to wound the invulnerable . . .'

She eventually finds peace in the idea of herself as a tiny cell in one vast organism, and that she 'had been one long before she was born and would still be one after her death'; and with Harry Coppard's and Herapath's help she is freed from the terrible burden of being responsible for putting everything right. As for her physical condition, the only indication is that there is a deficiency of iron atoms in the haemoglobin of her blood. Iron is a theme that has run through this whole story, as the substance that inspired the industrial revolution and the spoliation of the Wealden hills in Elizabethan times and earlier,[76] as the substance which—in its meteoric form—Vi has learnt from Herapath to associate with the vanquishing of this same darkness; and it forms a central element in the *conte* which Vi now proceeds to write, as her way of laying to rest the turbulence that haunts her. This *conte*, which forms about one third of the length of 'Eager Spring', concludes the novella.

In her *conte*, Vi transforms the terrible weight of the assault represented in her case by the biocide manufacturers into the human figure of Godfrey, the zealous but obsessively greedy ironmaster who, at the culmination of the *conte*, throws himself upon Maria—the central figure in her imaginative retelling of her own story—in a determination to kill her. Godfrey is resolved to take away from Maria the home and land bequeathed to her and her older sisters by their late father, a kindly and enlightened figure whose vagueness in legalistic affairs has made them highly vulnerable to Godfrey's rapacious demands in the name of technological progress, demands which are spurred on by his own monetary greed. Whether or not Maria actually dies in this incident we are not expressly told, although it would appear highly likely. What is clear is that another force, stronger than that which it opposes, is able to overcome the otherwise invincible Godfrey; and the *conte* culminates in the transparently Michaelmas image of a dragon slain by a dagger made of meteoric iron. The dagger that kills Godfrey is wielded not by Maria herself but by Paolo, a young Italian troubadour who, out of his love for Maria, has over the course of the *conte* developed his original naive innocence into steadfast devotion. However, he does not himself have the requisite insight or knowledge to forge the weapon with which he is able to kill Godfrey. The source of these qualities is the wisdom which the family physician, Dr Gropewell, has garnered from his many books, from his travels to East and West, from his acquaintance with early Christian traditions derived from St Patrick and St Columba and their predecessors as far back as the birth of Christ and beyond it; and it is Dr Gropewell who has the connection with 'a quaint old man called Welland, a retired ironmaster' (the name is a thin disguise for the mythical Wayland Smith), who lives near a large fallen meteorite and had been amusing himself for years by smelting this metal from the sky.

It is not difficult to discern in these leading characters in the *conte* a relationship with those in the main story. The existential drama out of which Vi has written the *conte* has already been related to Maria's murder (or attempted murder) by Godfrey, after whose death the workmen at the forge see 'a cloud of smoke that positively became a dragon before it drifted westward against the prevailing wind, losing its shape as it went'. Through creating this image in her mind, Vi is enabled to resist the oppressive, seemingly all-encompassing assault on her environmentally awake conscience by the prevailing forces of technocracy and materialism. But it is also possible to see how the relationships that Maria has with her father, with Paolo and with Dr Gropewell in the *conte* are not merely a fanciful pseudo-historical recreation in Vi's (or Barfield's) mind but are the actual precursors of those that she has with Harry Coppard, Leonard and Herapath. Moreover, there is a certain progression in terms of individual qualities from the characters in the *conte* to the corresponding figures in the main story. This is especially striking in the case of Harry Coppard, who seems to be making up for a lack of astuteness and foresight displayed by the three girls' father in the *conte*. But it is also illuminating to view the character of Leonard as having its roots in the innocent naivety of Paolo. Like the young Italian troubadour, Leonard's strength is his loving heart; but whereas there is little indication that Paolo has any intellectual grasp of what going on around him, Leonard's devoted love for Virginia virtually forces him by the end of the story to start to think for the first time in his life, and we are told that 'he had just started on a journey that was to take him a very long way'. And Herapath, while sharing Dr Gropewell's deep interest in esoteric knowledge, has developed a strongly individual moral quality in the way that he puts this knowledge into practice and shares it with others. Finally, one may sense that Vi's life is at the end of the story about to continue from where Maria left off after her very similar courageous journey into the darkness. Barfield's technique of relating characters to one another resembles Rudolf Steiner's depiction of different incarnations of the same group of individualities in his Mystery Plays (written 1910–13 and performed on the

Goetheanum stage in Dornach, Switzerland); and he was in all probability consciously engaging in a reincarnation drama of his own in the way that he chose to end 'Eager Spring'.

Just as 'Eager Spring'—and, in particular Vi's state of mind at the end of the story—reflects with a large degree of accuracy the way that Barfield was feeling about the world in which he still unexpectedly found himself at the end of his creative life, so are there strong grounds for concluding that Vi's recourse to exploring the karmic connections that reach beyond the narrow confines of a single earthly life was also Barfield's way of dealing with what he found. He considered that there was no other way of going *through* the darkness to the light that lay beyond. This is why the unique importance of the anthroposophical path of knowledge as a truly *creative* response to the modern positivistic world (as opposed to acquiescence with it on the one hand or reaction against it on the other) came to occupy an increasingly central part in his thinking over that last third of his life which is the subject of these chapters. In the chapter that follows, an attempt will be made to present the essence of the remedy that he proposed for the sorrows and sickness that he felt were besetting the modern world.

7. *THE FORCE OF IMAGINATIVE THINKING*

In his 1961 essay written for the New York *Saturday Evening Post*, 'The Rediscovery of Meaning', Barfield indicated the choice that confronts human beings in our time: 'Either we must concede that 99 per cent of all we say and think (or imagine we think) is meaningless verbiage, or we must—however great the wrench—abandon positivism'.[77] The previous chapter has concerned itself with the results of our not having abandoned positivism. The present one will be devoted to what Barfield had to say in the last decades of his life about taking the other path of trying to free oneself from its shackles, and represents an expansion of what he expressed in the third of the Vancouver lectures, *History, Guilt and Habit.* Although the introductory groundwork of this chapter has already been covered in the chapter on the Vancouver Conference, it will be as well to recapitulate it by summarizing the relevant concluding portion of 'The Rediscovery of Meaning'.

Barfield leaves us in no doubt that he regards a study of language as the best starting point for anyone wanting to make the 'great wrench' of abandoning positivism. It is not difficult to show that all or virtually all words originally referred both to outward natural phenomena and to inner psychological states, even though in a great majority of cases this duality of meaning has now been lost and the meaning contracted into a reference to either the outer or inner worlds of human experience.[78] In this sense, 'the further back you go in time, the more metaphorical you find language becoming'. Once we have grasped this we realize that symbolism, far from being the exclusive attribute of religion and art, 'is an intrinsic element in language itself'. For words are the bridges connecting our outer and inner worlds; they are the emblems or signs embodying our memory of our outward sense impressions and the *symbols* of our internalized thoughts or concepts. Moreover, 'it was out of man's rich awareness of this meaningful relation between himself and nature that language originally came to birth'.

Barfield then poses the question that follows from an impartial study of the history of words and language. 'How is it, then, that early man possessed this rich awareness while we have lost it? In answering this question we already begin to feel the great wrench; for we find that the abandonment of positivism involves a drastic revision of our whole conception of prehistory.' And he goes on to demonstrate that the same body of linguistic evidence indicates that early man, far from observing nature in the detached way characteristic of modern man, 'participated physically and mentally in her inner and outer process... It is this fact which underlies the world-wide tradition of a fall from paradise; and it is this which still reverberates on in the nature-linked collective consciousness that we find expressed in myths, in older forms of language, and in the totemic thinking and ritual participation of primitive tribes. It is from some such origins as these and not from an alert, blank stare of incomprehension that we have evolved the individual, sharpened, spatially determined consciousness of today.'[79]

However, it is one thing for poets and philosophers (and at this point Barfield refers expressly to Coleridge and other representatives of the Romantic Movement, both past and present) to have the idea of the possibility that modern (scientific) man does not necessarily have to continue becoming 'more and more a mere onlooker, measuring with greater and greater precision and manipulating more and more cleverly an Earth to which he grows spiritually more and more a stranger'. For the problem that tends to arise in this situation is that such individuals are (with the notable exception of people like Coleridge and Barfield) liable to think their enlightened thoughts and continue to leave the detailed investigation of the book of nature to positivist science. Hence the third stage of the process outlined by Barfield of 'abandoning positivism' is to make a plea that the quality of imagination celebrated by the Romantics as an instrument of knowledge is employed also by scientists at each point in their research and in the act of observation itself. But, he asks, 'is such a development even conceivable?'

Barfield answers this question by concluding his essay with a reference to Goethe. In addition to being 'possibly Europe's greatest poet', Goethe pioneered a method of scientific investigation which, by means of 'a perceptive faculty trained by systematic practice', was able to penetrate to 'the creative thoughts which underlie phenomenal manifestation'. For in contrast to ordinary science, which derives its unifying ideas or laws through making generalizations from particular phenomena, Goethean science regards such a unifying idea as 'an objective reality, accessible to direct observation. In addition to measuring quantities, the scientist must train himself to perceive qualities. This he can do—as Goethe did when he saw the various parts of the plant as "metamorphoses" of the leaf—only by so sinking himself in contemplation of the outward form that his imagination penetrates to the activity which is producing it.'

The first two of these steps—the study of the history of language and the picture of an evolution of human consciousness which arises out of it—had been detailed in the major works whose publication more or less framed Barfield's career as a solicitor (see Part Three), and Barfield would not infrequently be asked in the course of his visits to America to reiterate or elaborate upon certain aspects of this research. However, what concerns us in the present chapter, which will be the last in this sequence of chapters whose object has been to present a picture of the working of Barfield's creative mind over the concluding portion of his life, is more the spiritual-scientific path of knowledge which he saw as a genuine alternative to positivism in all its many guises (including the variety that was veiled by its notional rejection, as in 'RUP'), and in particular in so far as it pertains to the redemption of science itself.

As has already been mentioned in the previous chapter, it was in the early 1980s that Barfield was particularly preoccupied with the possibilities inherent in a spiritualizing of science. However, this theme is already visible in a paper which he read to some homoeopathic doctors in Queen Square, London, on 15 November 1980 called 'Science and Quality', which had originally been presented at a medical conference a few years before (he included it in *The Rediscovery of Meaning*, 1977).[80] This essay is important mainly because of its broad historical overview of the foundations (whether consciously philosophical or not) of scientific method, ranging from the pre-Copernican or Aristotelian view to that of modern times, and for its attempt to define in these terms the contribution—both actual and potential—of spiritual science. Barfield's opening sentences summarize the essence of what he goes on to say: 'Modern science is inseparable from the voluntary decision out of which it arose three or four centuries ago; namely the decision to exclude what were called "occult qualities" from its purview. Modern scientific *method* remains based on that rule, and technology owes all its strength to a rigid observance of it.' The key point made by Barfield as he seeks an extension of modern scientific method to include the notion of quality as well as that of quantity is that 'the qualities formerly treated as inherent in nature have, as far as any scientific theory is concerned, disappeared from it, and [that] they have reappeared on the hither side of the line between subject and object, *within* the experiencing human psyche' (i.e. as the so-called 'subjective' experiences of our subconscious). This, in turn, represents the path through which man can also rediscover an inwardness in nature (for 'mind is in fact the inwardness of nature as well as of ourselves'). The German *Naturphilosophen* and of course Coleridge are mentioned as earlier pioneers of such a method of bridging the Cartesian gulf between the individual human mind and nature, while Goethe is cited as one who pursued such a method in his botanical and other studies.

Barfield emphasizes the importance of the individual element in this picture of the modern human mind, indicating that even only as comparatively recently as Plato's time 'minds were ... somewhat *less* individualized, and thus less capable of self-originating activity than they are today'. He then goes on to make an explicit link in this methodological sense with Rudolf Steiner's anthroposophy, observing that 'it is just this principle of an *evolution* of individualized mind or spirit (as the "occult" or unconscious basis of personal human consciousness) which is the first thing that distinguishes the methodology and the cosmology—or, as I prefer to say, the findings—of Steiner's spiritual science from the work of the *Naturphilosophen*, of whom I have spoken, and of which it can from one point of view be seen as a development ... One way of characterizing Anthroposophy would be to call it "a systematic treatment of the evolution of consciousness".'

Interestingly, what Barfield says turns out to be constant if we endeavour in this way to rediscover 'occult qualities' in our scientific methodology is the anthropocentric nature of its standpoint (in common with the anthropocentricity of the pre-Copernican view of the solar system). Man has been restored to the centre of his own universe, albeit in a very different way from before. Indeed, he affirms, we can adopt the term 'evolution of anthropocentricity' as a more graphic way of referring to the evolution of consciousness—a historical sequence of the different *experiences* of their relationship with the world around them that human beings have had over the ages.

From what has thus been summarized so far, it might be supposed that Barfield is presenting Steiner's spiritual-scientific impulse largely in terms of a kind of antithesis to modern science, with its rejection of qualities—whether occult or not—and anthropocentricity. However, a large part of the rest of this lecture is concerned with showing how, in beginning 'from where [the *Naturphilosophen*] left off', Steiner was also wholly at one and in tune with the scientific revolution. Barfield's key insight here is that 'the really vital contribution of science to humanity [is] not (up to the present) its knowledge-content' but that of enabling us to acknowledge that 'if qualities are "occult", or apparently unknowable, that is precisely because they are one with ourselves, or better say our Self'. Elsewhere in the lecture he summarizes this thought as follows: 'Rudolf Steiner was, as far as I know, the first to point out that the scientific revolution betokened the culminating point in that long drama of individuation which is the evolution of consciousness, and further to maintain that this will be seen in future to have been its most important feature—far more important than any of the technological discoveries that have resulted from it, though he did not underrate the importance of these.' Anthroposophy encompasses both the life-principle (Coleridge's *natura naturans*) and the death-principle (*natura naturata*). This is why, at the end of a lengthy passage demonstrating the onesidedness of dwelling exclusively on mechanism and physicality, on the one hand, or on organicism and the etheric world, on the other, Barfield is able to bring these strands together in what may be considered as his general definition—at least within the limited confines of the content of this lecture—of the tasks of the spiritual scientist: 'For spiritual science, mechanism does indeed reflect the death-principle in the universe, but the death-principle is itself indispensable to life, and particularly to human life. It is to the death-principle that we owe the existence of a *conscious* mind, in addition to that *unconscious* mind which is hardly distinguishable from life itself, and is one in us with the life and instinctive intelligence present in nature. It is at this point that a research worker in spiritual science has to take into consideration, and to investigate with exactness, not only an "etheric" world and "etheric" body ... but also a form-giving "astral" world and "astral" body.'

Before we proceed to consider the lectures and writings of the early 1980s where Barfield developed this general methodological outline into a foundation for a science freed from the shackles of reductionist materialism, it will be helpful to focus briefly upon the nature of the great obstacle which he saw as impeding the path from the one into the other, from the familiar 'mind-set' of modern times to the wider mental world of a spiritualized science. This is that same barrier which Jon, Jak and Peet had to penetrate in order to reach Aboveground (see previous chapter), or, as it is generally known in esoteric terms, the threshold into the spiritual world. Barfield spoke in a remarkably succinct way about this threshold in a lecture offered, it would appear, as a contribution to a consultation at Drew University on 22 April 1966. The lecture was entitled 'Imagination and Inspiration'.[81] After setting the scene for his deliberations by describing the conversation between Arjuna and his charioteer, the god Krishna, at the heart of the battle scene in the *Bhagavadgita*, Barfield refers to the dilemma of a neuro-physiologist who, as a professor from the Department of Electrical Engineering at MIT, had given a lecture at Brandeis University during his (Barfield's) stay there as a Visiting Professor in 1965. The professor's problem was that in his particular discipline, which from the very outset is confronted with this duality of vision, he found there was no satisfactory way of making a transition from (in Barfield's words) 'a context in which you are talking about "matter" to a context in which you are talking about "mind"'. Barfield goes on to speak of this dilemma as just one particular example of the 'impassable barrier' between mind and matter which pervades the whole of Western thought; and he relates this to Arjuna's 'threshold experience' where he is able to perceive Krishna for a moment in his universal, divine nature. In this way he forms a connection between the modern Cartesian dichotomy, 'according to which all that is not a human self is matter', and the ancient Eastern distinction between self and not-self: 'You get, in other words, a new awareness, and a greatly enhanced one, of that threshold before which, when he was invited to cross it, Arjuna experienced such overwhelming terror that every hair of his head stood on end. And I believe *our* terror at the thought of being called on to cross it is no less than his. Indeed, I would say it is greater. Only in our case it is disguised from us—or rather its intensity has led us to conceal its true nature from ourselves. Something of this terror I detect, for instance, in the emotional overtones which accompanied the rejection of the so-called "occult qualities" from the field of scientific enquiry and which still often accompany any reference to them. It is a commonplace that violent hatred generally has fear somewhere beneath it.'

Having thus defined and evoked within his listeners some notion of what he means by the threshold, Barfield goes on to enumerate some of the reasons why it has been largely ignored by, or for whatever reason has become invisible to, the Western mind (with a figure like Coleridge being a remarkable exception to the general rule, as he is at pains to point out).[82] What is more pertinent to the matter of the present chapter, however, is the capacity with which he invests the two concepts that figure in his title to illuminate the world of experience beyond the threshold. For in his hands, imagination is transformed from a quality 'founded on the assumed intransigence of [the] threshold between mind and matter' (and hence wholly consistent with post-seventeenth-century scientific method), one which leads us to think of an image or symbol as 'impassably divided from *that of which* it is an image', to one which—in common with Coleridge's view of it—enables us to transcend the threshold between conscious and unconscious mental activity (and likewise between mind and matter and between self and not-self); while inspiration is no longer so much the state of being possessed by a being from yonder side of the threshold (as it was indeed in the ancient East and more recently than this) as a capacity which—like Coleridge's 'philosophic imagination', which he conceived as an interiorized transformation of the more outwardly directed 'poetic imagination'—enables us to communicate 'with individual entities, individual beings beyond the threshold'.

It is against such a background of a clearly defined position as regards scientific methodology (as described in 'Science and Quality'), on the one hand, and the fruit of many years of philosophical and literary questionings (as is evidenced in 'Imagination and Inspiration'), on the other, that Barfield's carefully considered and conclusive statements in the early 1980s about the central importance of a spiritualized science for our time need to be understood. Although these statements are scattered fairly liberally over the reviews of and introductions to a number of books over this period,[83] he expressed himself most fully and forcefully in two lectures given at this time. One of these was 'Anthroposophy and the Future', which will be considered shortly. Two years before, however, he gave a substantial contribution to a Lindisfarne Association Conference in 1982, which will repay close attention.[84] As he says in his concluding words, his endeavour was to set forth his own perspective—'reached at the end of a rather long life'—'as clearly and unequivocally as possible'.

After a short introduction recapitulating the central theses of *Poetic Diction* and *Saving the Appearances*, Barfield emphasizes a theme that he was to take up increasingly strongly in this period, namely, the radical difference of the picture of human and earthly evolution presented in these two books not merely from the dominant Darwinian or positivist hypothesis (see Chapter 5, 'Positivism and its Residues') but from the view of orientalism, 'which sees the predicament of each individual human soul as one of exile rather than travel' and the goal of human existence as one of 'return rather than advance', the aim of the wise man being that of 'shedding rather than enhancing his individual identity'. His reason for stressing the importance of this was that 'at the time I am speaking an increasing number of dissatisfied Western souls were beginning to turn away from their own cultural inheritance and to welcome with open arms the kind of transcendentalism which I have called orientalism . . .'

Having thus briefly delineated his own standpoint, Barfield boldly introduces Rudolf Steiner, on the grounds that 'the subsequent development of my own ideas on the evolution of consciousness is so intricately connected with what I learned from his work that it will not be possible to keep them separate'. He then expresses his surprise that Steiner's name is not more frequently mentioned in books dealing with the kind of subject-matter with which the conference was concerned. But he is no longer content to leave this matter in a mood of hopeful anticipation that one day it will be different. Instead, he develops the theme of orientalism which he has just broached, indicating that 'intellectual rebels against the kind of reductionism that has descended on the Western mind, whether they move towards some sort of revived Neo-Platonism or towards a more definitely oriental conclusion, such as we see in Fritjof Capra's *The Tao of Physics*,[85] all seem to end up in a position which I would include under the general heading of mysticism'. He contrasts this 'mysticism' with the 'occultism' which he discerns at the heart of Steiner's work, and on this basis is able not only to explain why Steiner is so often overlooked in such circles but also to define the fundamental difference between the majority of these 'intellectual rebels' and Rudolf Steiner. Thus on the basis of this occult knowledge, Steiner put forward a detailed account both of earthly evolution from its very beginning and of the historical development of humanity (something which is very far removed from a mystic rapture or nirvana, 'to which the experience we call *knowledge* is irrelevant'). Especially with regard to investigating the pre-historical period, this occult knowledge entails 'a cognitive process not based on inference from the phenomenal world, nor merely on imaginative extrapolation from it, but on direct perception of the noumenal or pre-phenomenal world'.

Barfield now goes on to say something about 'the steps by which this "higher knowledge", or brain-free thinking, brain-free cognition, is arrived at', a training which involves not only the intellectual faculties and imagination but the whole personality. He indicates that he will make no further reference to the training in higher knowledge itself or to the philosophical grounds for thinking that such a cognitive training is possible. Instead he concerns himself merely with the steps themselves, which Steiner termed Imagination, Inspiration and Intuition—and specifically with the first two and the relationship between them.

Coleridge and Goethe are again referred to with great respect. Barfield, however, is here seeking to focus on the step which Steiner took beyond Goethe. For Goethe would not allow his attention to be drawn away from direct observation of the phenomena (and heavily criticized other scientists for becoming lost in a fog of abstract theory). His imagination 'stopped short at imagination'; he could not even conceive that this means of his knowledge was itself capable of further development. Whereas 'in Steiner's epistemology ... imaginative cognition is only the preliminary step leading to a further and different kind of cognitive faculty, or rather experience, which he names Inspiration . . . In imaginative cognition the image-creating faculty of the knower allies itself with, merges with, and thus penetrates, the phenomenon-creating inner life of nature, as a means to understanding it. But, inasmuch as it is based on phenomena and remembered phenomena, it is still subjective. Although terming it imaginative the knower is surrounded, as with a kind of membrane, by images dependent on his own mental activity. In order to reach the further stage of Inspiration, the knower must learn to apply the mental *activity* he has developed by enhancing his imagination in a different direction. He must use it to *obliterate* those very images. It is only then that he will come into direct contact with, will *know*, the spiritual in its own right so to speak, by direct experience; an experience for which, as I have suggested, the least inappropriate term seems to be "perception", though it is a perception more akin to hearing than to seeing.'

The result is that, whereas not even figures like Coleridge and Goethe are able to say anything about the imaginative world lying behind the finished product we perceive as the phenomenal world except *as it becomes phenomenal*, what Steiner presents us with is 'not simply a new way of knowing but also a new *field* of knowledge altogether'. Barfield gives as an example the detailed information that Steiner gives about the four ethers, as distinct from merely stating that there is such a thing as a realm of formative forces. 'The point is that in Steiner the four elements [which can be discerned through these four ethers] are being cognized by the European mind *after* it has lived through the scientific revolution and in consequence is now able to maintain that sharp Cartesian distinction between mind and matter, between the supersensible and the sensible, in which that particular step in the evolution of consciousness has trained it so rigorously.'

At this point Barfield recalls a definition which he quoted earlier by Henri Corbin[86] of a 'phenomenon', a concept which for the purposes of the definition he equates with an image, a symbol, and even a word: 'The phenomenon is that which shows itself, that which is apparent and which in its appearance shows forth something which can reveal itself therein only by remaining concealed behind the appearance.' Barfield's comment—now that he has led his listeners through a description of some of the steps in the spiritual-scientific path of knowledge—is worth quoting in full: 'Why does it say that the immaterial pre-phenomenon can only reveal itself by remaining *concealed* behind the phenomenon? It does so because it is determined to maintain that very Cartesian distinction between mind and matter, and to maintain it, not as a distinction but as a divorce. It says in effect that we can never speak, or never speak discursively, about the supersensible; we can only suggest it. This, I think, is where Steiner differs from all others whom I have encountered who are aware of, and speak wisely about the necessity of overcoming our contemporary reductionism. He does speak, discursively and in detail, about the supersensible.'

As he surveys the great evolution of consciousness drama recounted in this lecture and elsewhere (notably in *Saving the Appearances*), Barfield views Steiner's legacy as no mere further step but a 'giant stride' forward, 'a re-ascent from the nadir of non-participation, of total alienation from *natura naturans*, towards a renewed participation' comprising a 'full *self*-consciousness which the older original participation, and even the relics of it that disappeared only with the scientific revolution, had kept unattainable'. And yet his contribution has 'been largely ignored'. Barfield attributes this in large part to this giant step having been taken by one individual who seemed to be so far in advance of his time. And yet there are other examples in history of great initiates having forged a path for others to follow; and he goes on to cite one particular and very striking example:

> The more you study the individual history of the Graeco-Roman age, the more you are forced to recognize the startling extent to which the mind of one man brought together, and brought order into, its fruits and enabled them to become the seed of the age that was to follow. The age of Alexandrian and Roman philosophy was the age of Syncretism [Eclecticism]—of bits from one philosophy fitted in with bits from another like a sort of jigsaw puzzle. It was not without its merits, but it had no future and it must, I believe, have disappeared like water into sand if there had been no Aristotle: he was the conduit through which the old age passed on into the new, and he became the trunk of the whole wide-spreading tree. He is there throughout, not only in Scholastic philosophy where it is most overtly apparent, but in the very way we think, whether scientifically or otherwise. The scientific revolution, which rejected him as an authority, could no more have occurred without him as an abiding influence than the Copernican astronomy could have come into being without the preceding Ptolemaic one.
>
> The syncretism of the Alexandrine age was at least limited to the academic community, or to a philosophical elite. It is otherwise today. When I look round at the immensely varied output of the 'human

potentials'[87] movement, or the Aquarian Revolution, or whatever you like to call the ferment, I seem to see a sort of super-syncretism, with everyone nibbling bits of religion and philosophy and science from everywhere. Symptoms—perhaps healthy symptoms—of the death of one age, and of the need for the birth of another. But I do not see any sign of their growing together to form the nucleus around which such a new age could first come to life and then increase in form and stature.

The fact is that, if my general picture of an evolution of consciousness is sound, if a descent into individuation followed by a re-ascent towards participation in the universal is the case, then it is not startling, it is even inevitable, that individual consciousnesses, individual minds, should appear from time to time with a wider and wider fullness of real content. I am not a prophet, but for what it may be worth the dim vision I have when I peer into the future strongly suggests that the redemption of civilization will depend in a very great degree on whether its intellectual structure comes to centre around the contribution of Rudolf Steiner to much the same extent as that of the Aristotelian age centred round Aristotle. To the same extent, not of course in the same way. Not in the prior acceptance of authority, with endless quotation, dissection and analysis of texts and so forth. If you should ask me: in *what* way then? I can suggest one answer beyond the vague one, that it will be more like a nucleus than a blueprint.

The thoughts expressed at the end of this lecture about the central importance of Rudolf Steiner for our time matured over the (approximately) two years that separated it from the lecture 'Anthroposophy and the Future' given at Chambersburg, Pennsylvania in August 1984. Barfield begins by recalling a conversation that he had had in the early 1920s with George Adams (then George Kaufmann),[88] in which he compared Steiner with Aristotle, likening both to track-laying vehicles. He used this rather striking image to distinguish both philosophers from other philosophers, who are more akin to ordinary wheeled vehicles which do not create the foundations of their own propulsion. He then recounts the picture—outlined at the end of the Lindisfarne lecture—of the centuries that succeeded the crowning age of Greek philosophy (the time of Plato and Aristotle) and of Aristotle's centrality in enabling an intellectual bridge to be built to the ensuing age.

As he is addressing an audience familiar with Rudolf Steiner's work, he is able to describe the unfolding of this entire period, which Steiner referred to as the fourth post-Atlantean age (the classical and medieval period when Graeco-Roman philosophies and intellectual attitudes were dominant, i.e. between the eighth century BC and the early fifteenth century AD), in terms of a gradual descent of the Cosmic Intelligence into the personal intelligence, a process whereby the human mind begins to experience that sense of total separation from its surroundings which characterizes our present 'scientific' age, referred to by Steiner as the fifth post-Atlantean age. Although this process will be examined more closely in Part Three, it is worth quoting a few sentences from Barfield's description of it, if only because this is how he himself understood it:

> The 4th post-Atlantean age was the age of the Intellectual Soul, a phase of the human psyche which Rudolf Steiner has described from many points of view, spiritual, psychological and historical. One way of characterizing the Intellectual Soul, by contrast with the Consciousness Soul, which is the phase on which our own age concentrates, would be to say that there the individual human intelligence is not yet detached, isolated, separate from the Cosmic Intelligence out of which it originates in the way that characterizes the Consciousness Soul. And, since it is also the Cosmic Intelligence out of which the phenomenal world originates, the Consciousness Soul loses all sense of affinity with the outer-material world. René Descartes gave full expression to the philosophical basis of the Consciousness Soul, when he divided the world into 'extended substance' on the one hand and 'thinking substance' on the other. The human mind feels itself detached from, and set over against, the material world, because it no longer has any inkling of their common origin.

Roughly half-way through his lecture, he abruptly turns from thus surveying the classical and medieval period to the present day and takes up, and further deepens, what he had presented by way of insights into modern culture two years previously. After describing the results of some research that he had recently conducted into the 'human potentials' movement and indicating Steiner's revered place in this movement as one of many contributors to a growing array of mostly spirit-based alternatives to mainstream materialistic culture (or anti-culture), he again refers to 'the truly unbridgeable gap between any of these thinkers and Rudolf Steiner'. He adds that this gap 'is in danger of being overlooked because one would really like to be able to overlook it. One resists acknowledging it. One would much rather things were otherwise. But they are not. One resists partly because one does not want to be a fanatic—or to be called one. It is a bad thing to be a fanatic; but it is a worse one to refuse to look facts in the face for fear of being called a fanatic.' To illustrate what he means, he compares Rupert Sheldrake's 'deeply interesting' book *A New Science of Life* (1981), where the author posits the existence of a realm of immaterial forces which he terms the 'Morphogenetic Field', with Steiner's wealth of detail about what he calls the etheric world; and he compares 'the contribution of a certain Owen Barfield', whose life-work has been to establish that 'there really must be such a thing as an evolution of consciousness', with the scale on which Steiner used this concept in his work. 'It is the airstrip from which the flight, the whole squadron, takes off...'

One particularly interesting aspect of Barfield's restatement of the notion of Steiner's central importance in this lecture is that the analogy which he draws with the classical age had come to him 'only in the last year or so', which suggests that it really dawned on him only as he was preparing the Lindisfarne lecture (the condition of the draft of which indicates that an intellectual ferment was taking place). After the passage of the intervening time between the two lectures, he clearly felt confirmed in his view that the plethora of symptoms (such as Sheldrake's book) indicating a resurgence of interest in spiritual things—which he regarded as denoting that an evolution of consciousness was indeed taking place—serve merely as value 'for the individual souls who feed on them'. The problem is that, as was the case in the Alexandrine age and would have remained so without the coalescing figure of Aristotle, there is no unifying element: 'But for the future of human *society*, for the future of civilization itself, these praiseworthy efforts will have little or no effect because there is variety everywhere and cohesion nowhere. We are about a quarter of the way through the 5th age; and it was at around a quarter or a third of the 4th age that that spotty outbreak of Eclecticism appeared. I confess to drawing considerable support from this analogy for a conviction I had been forced to without its help: namely that the future of Western science and Western thought does really depend on whether or not it is impelled to crystallize round Steiner—to the like extent[89] that it once crystallized round Aristotle.' Had Barfield still been alive today, it is highly unlikely that, in view of the growing sense of disfunctionality in the social and environmental organisms of the world and, in particular, of the partial replacement of analytical materialism by a post-modernism where all trace of a common culture or language of *any* kind has ceased to exist, he would have spoken any less strongly.[90]

The last published piece of writing where Barfield referred to the crucial importance of anthroposophy as a remedy for the modern condition was his review of Fritjof Capra's book *Uncommon Wisdom*. The review was published in the last issue of *Towards* magazine to appear, Vol.

III, No. 2, Winter 1989, together with the author's response to the review of his book. In Barfield's words, Capra's book is essentially a 'demand for a "paradigm-shift" (in T.S. Kuhn's terminology) in the scientific outlook and an estimate of the extent to which such a shift is already taking place both in the realm of science—more particularly physics—and to some extent in the general consciousness, the latter being evidenced by such an ecological phenomenon as the Green Movement'. In other words, it is an excellent example of the kind of symptoms of renewal referred to in the previous paragraph. On the other hand, it also bears all the hallmarks of the shortcomings of which Barfield has been speaking. Barfield is generous where he considers praise to be due, especially in connection with the bridging of the Cartesian split; but he is deeply ill at ease with the very evident 'post-modernist' stance of the book and, by implication, of its author. One particular, and extremely limited, intellectual form (that of reductionist materialism) has been replaced by a mental formlessness, where there are no fundamental entities, laws or equations, where—to quote Capra—'things exist by virtue of their mutually consistent relationships'. Barfield sums up his disquiet on this account as follows:

> What then are we to think of this valiant attempt to blaze a trail into that [new] vision and that [new] science? I would not unduly stress the first and obvious objection, which many would regard as fatal, namely the logical absurdity of some of its fundamental principles. Relationship is *between*. If things exist by virtue of their relationships, there must be able to be a relationship between nothings—which is inconceivable. True, but the inadequacy of logical thought to contain it is part of the new vision. There are other forms of cognitive language besides logic, and some of these forms—notably metaphor—actually make use of logical contradiction. My doubts are deeper rooted than that. Language that purports to transcend logic will *ipso facto* sometimes lack logical substance; but if it is to *mean* anything it must, instead, have what I will call imaginal (which is not the same as pictorial) substance. And that is what I find lacking in the vocabulary of the new vision, as Capra seeks to present it. To put it crudely, as I close the book, I find myself loaded up with a kind of hurly burly of abstract entities and nonentities, to which I can attach neither logical nor imaginal significance. As so often with anti-reductionist books, the diagnosis is shrewd and penetrating: the suggested remedy, *by comparison*, is infantile.

Barfield then goes on to express his amazement—tempered by his awareness that Capra is 'in distinguished company' and 'merely keeping step with the vast bulk of his contemporaries'—that Rudolf Steiner's name is 'not even mentioned, not even for the purpose of repudiation'. Barfield's comment on what he regards as a strange anomaly is eloquently and succinctly descriptive of his view of Steiner's profound relevance to the questions implicitly raised by Capra:

> Here is an unquestionably well-informed genius, dead now for more than sixty years, who at the outset of his career disposed in two or three books of the Cartesian split, and went on to develop and expound a method, both mental and practical, of freeing 20th century science from the fetters of mechanomorphism and building up a supplementary science capable of handling the immaterial as well as the material world; who has illuminated, as no other has done, the relation between oriental and occidental thought; who has met the demand made by one of Capra's advisers and endorsed by him that 'we should be able to combine information that comes from inner states with knowledge gained through objective science and technology into a totally new vision of reality', inasmuch as he himself prosecuted researches into the immaterial realm and reported their result in a language wherein the *terms* (since modern language is semantically determined by subliminal Cartesianism) are intended metaphorically, though their syntax and the conclusions it enables are not.

Barfield suggests that Capra, having wrestled fairly successfully with Cartesianism, remains thoroughly in the clutches of other subliminal propositions, notably uniformitarianism and Darwinism;[91] for nowhere in his book is there any sense of an evolutionary development in time of the laws of nature themselves, or of anything to challenge the assumption that nothing has ever occurred in the past which could not be observed in the present. A buried, unchallenged assumption of this nature is a barrier to acknowledging the possible validity of a cosmology which views the present material world as but a stage from one spiritual condition to another.

In his response to Barfield's review, Capra, while emphasizing his familiarity with Rudolf Steiner, indicated that he regarded him as 'a visionary and mystic much more than a thinker'. This was probably why he did not find in Steiner 'a key contribution to the emerging new paradigm' that he was studying; for, as Barfield has been stressing again and again in the many quotations from his writings in this chapter, the entire significance of Steiner is that he was not a mystic but an occultist (i.e. he was nothing if not a thinker). Capra could hardly have provided a clearer confirmation of the validity of the critical points in Barfield's review or, indeed, of the relevance and appropriateness of his remedy for the intellectual and spiritual turmoil of our time.

8. *'SIR, I THANK GOD FOR YOU . . .'*[92]

The intention of the last few chapters, which have arisen out of Barfield's correspondence with Craig Miller and its central theme of his deep interest in the thoughts of Samuel Taylor Coleridge, has been to engender a certain insight into Barfield's mind—his ideas, intellectual preoccupations and spiritual aspirations—during the last phase of his life. But this study of his 'American' years would be incomplete without an attempt to present a more overall impression of the range of his friendships and, most especially, his correspondence. The present chapter—the last in the sequence dealing with these years—will therefore have a somewhat more biographical character than the foregoing ones, even though biographical details as such, being of secondary importance in a psychographical study, will emerge only incidentally and not as a chronological narrative. A detailed chronology of, say, Barfield's visits to America would be the worthy object of a separate study, which the present writer is not necessarily the best person to undertake.

Inevitably, such an impression has to be highly selective. Barfield was a man gifted not only with an acute intelligence but also with great generosity of spirit, and somehow managed to combine a considerable capacity for solitary intellectual work with a well-nigh insatiable gregariousness. Visitors to his home were always welcome (provided they made an appointment), and he made many new friends during his visits to American universities. He also received a number of letters from persons previously unknown to himself who had read and admired one or another of his books; and these letters would not merely be acknowledged but would receive a full and carefully considered response which usually elicited a further lengthy letter, thus initiating an ongoing correspondence. Each one of these friends and correspondents could tell a detailed story of his own—and there are probably several of whom I have not even heard. The source of much of what follows is Barfield's own repository of manuscripts and letters. If one makes the fairly reasonable assumption that he kept what he regarded as most significant and most in accordance with his own thoughts and preoccupations, such a means of selection may be seen as the most appropriate for the purposes of this psychography.

Perhaps the best way to gain some kind of orientation amidst the multifarious strands of friendship woven over the course of the last third of

Barfield's life is to begin at their temporal focal point in the mid-1970s. Two very important earthly relationships came to an end in the year 1975, which was when both Cecil Harwood (b. 1898) and Philip Mairet (b. 1886) died. Barfield's friendships with these two men represent, in very different ways, links with the earlier part of his life, and they will therefore be considered at the end of this chapter. On the other hand, 1975 was also the year when he met Saul Bellow, and, perhaps more significantly from a biographical point of view, approximately coincided with his first encounter with Professor Thomas Kranidas (autumn 1974), a meeting that led to what was probably the most intimate personal correspondence of Barfield's last years. This was also the time when many of the acquaintances that he had formed during his early visits to Drew and Brandeis Universities were in their fullest flow. Not for nothing was this point in Barfield's life marked by the appearance of that elegantly produced volume published to mark his seventy-fifth birthday, *Evolution of Consciousness: Studies in Polarity* (1976). This 'Festschrift', edited by Shirley Sugerman of Drew University, one of Barfield's four Literary Executors,[93] was both a celebration of his literary achievement and a symptom of the human warmth that was to accompany him until the end of his life from across the Atlantic. Although with certain exceptions[94] the contributions do not add significantly to one's understanding of Barfield (any more than the book as a whole illumines the theme of its main title, a comment which he himself made to me in conversation), each author warmly acknowledges his debt to Barfield's inspiration in whatever academic field he may be specializing. It is this same range and breadth of interest and approach that is so striking as one surveys even the fraction of correspondence that Barfield preserved. We shall first dwell upon this pivotal point of 1975 and survey those epistolatory dialogues in which he was then engaged.

Perhaps the most well known of Barfield's then correspondents (other than Saul Bellow, whose letters have featured in an earlier chapter) was the American poet Howard Nemerov (1920–91). Nemerov, who was Poet Laureate from 1988 to 1990, was deeply influenced by Barfield, having first encountered his ideas in 1963 when he read *Poetic Diction* (he met him in person at Drew University in 1964). His letter of appreciation initiated a correspondence which lasted for over 20 years, although Barfield kept only a sequence of letters from Nemerov (and a copy of one of his own) dating from 1968 to 1981. The letter to Nemerov of which Barfield retained a copy contains several suggestions of books or lectures by Rudolf Steiner which he thought might deepen his friend's interest in anthroposophy. Nemerov for his part admitted that his 'usual melancholy affinity for any distraction' had contributed significantly to his lack of success in this direction, although what he describes as 'distractions' were mainly commissions for poems, or lectures about poetry, or bouts of poetic inspiration, which—because of their fleeting quality—he would always seize with alacrity. By any standards, however, he was an avid reader of Barfield's own books, especially *Saving the Appearances*, which he reread every year ('it holds up splendidly', he wrote on 18 May 1976); and he incorporated a detailed study of Barfield's book *Worlds Apart* in his students' course on Twentieth Century Criticism and Poetics at Washington University, St Louis, Missouri (whither he moved in 1969 from Brandeis University, Massachusetts). As Donna Potts points out in her book *Howard Nemerov and Objective Idealism: The Influence of Owen Barfield*,[95] the two men frequently took pleasure in pointing out examples of Nemerov's implementation as a poet of Barfield's philosophical principles, and in December 1967 Barfield referred to Nemerov as his 'ambassador at the court of contemporary poetry, with which my relations are somewhat strained'. They shared a rejection of the positivist notion of a detachment between the perceiver and the object of his perception, and were equally convinced of the crucial role that language has in mediating between the two, thus confirming in Nemerov's mind recent scientific experiments that 'implicate the observer in the phenomena'. Although it is perhaps taking the scholarly approach too far to label Barfield's philosophical standpoint a 'theory of objective idealism', it is nevertheless the case that the title of Donna Potts's book derives from a verbal description which Barfield once gave to Shirley Sugerman and upon which she encouraged him to enlarge in her published 'Conversation with Owen Barfield' in the 1976 Festschrift: 'Objective idealism contends that that distinction [between subject and object, between man and nature] is itself an unreal one, and that reality, individual being, however you think of it, consists in the polarity between the subjectivity of the individual mind and the objective world which it perceives. They are not two things, but they are one and the same thing and what you call the objective world is merely one pole of what is a unitary process and what we call subjective experience is the other pole, but they are not really divided from each other.' This insight was the philosophical core of what Nemerov appreciated, even revered, in Barfield's work.

Barfield's correspondence with the celebrated research physicist David Bohm (b. 1917), who came to England as a research fellow at the University of Bristol in 1957 before taking up the post of Professor of

Theoretical Physics at Birkbeck College, University of London in 1961, was conducted over a somewhat shorter period (1971–6), although they maintained some sort of contact at least until 1982, when Barfield acquired a copy of the transcript of conversations between Bohm and the English biologist Rupert Sheldrake.[96] Bohm was a quantum physicist who could not accept the orthodox view of this subject as championed notably by the Danish physicist Niels Bohr in the 1920s. He wrote his book *Quantum Theory* (1951) in an effort to understand quantum theory from Bohr's point of view; but he was deeply dissatisfied with a view which ultimately claimed that we cannot know more about the nature of reality than is predicated by Werner Heisenberg's uncertainty principle, that in other words we cannot really know anything about anything. From this point Bohm came to focus increasingly upon the endeavour to understand the philosophical implications of his work as a research physicist, a quest which was initiated by his book *Causality and Chance in Modern Physics* (1957). Not long after the publication of this book he became interested in the Indian philosopher Krishnamurti. In an interview published in the *New Scientist*,[97] he describes in a very illuminating way what this encounter meant to him: 'I first became interested in him in 1959. I came across a book of his in the public library in Bristol, *First and Last Freedom*, which interested me because he referred to the observer and the observed, which is of course the thing in quantum theory. He said there is no distinction between the observer and the observed, which quantum theory is always saying, which really I felt was one of the essential new features of quantum theory. He was referring of course to the psyche, but I felt a great similarity. I met him in 1961 . . .' Thus Krishnamurti's ideas encouraged Bohm to think in terms of 'wholeness' both in nature and in society. He was deeply aware of the atomistic fragmentation evident in every realm of modern life, and made it his life's task in some sense to develop the quantum physicists' wish to transcend the mechanistic Newtonian picture of the universe in the distinctive (to him) direction of focusing on processes rather than separate objects. To this end, he developed the linguistic concept of the 'rheomode' (*rheo* is a Greek verb meaning 'flow'), which is essentially an endeavour to introduce a more verb-based mode of language and, hence, a mobile, living kind of thinking. Like Barfield, therefore, Bohm was something of a polymath, although they began from, as it were, opposite ends of the spectrum of knowledge. Enough has perhaps been said to indicate why Bohm would have appreciated being sent Barfield's *Speaker's Meaning* in 1971, and why Barfield was more than a little interested in Bohm's heroic endeavour to think through to their ultimate end the philosophical and social implications of his research as a physicist.

And yet there is no suggestion either from the correspondence that Barfield retained or from the considerable quantity of Bohm's lecture typescripts and articles which he possessed and had carefully read and annotated that the relationship between the two men developed beyond a mutual interest and respect on the intellectual plane. There is no evidence, for example, that Barfield tried to acquaint Bohm more fully with the ideas of Rudolf Steiner; and the only letter of his own of which he retained a copy (dated 23 October 1971) consists of his comments on Bohm's papers entitled 'An Inquiry into the Function of Language', based on a colloquy held at The Institute of Contemporary Arts, London, on 28 March 1971.[98] If one then peruses the conversations previously mentioned (see Note 93) between Bohm, Rupert Sheldrake and Renée Weber (Professor of Philosophy at Rutgers University, New Jersey and a specialist in Hindu and Buddhist philosophy), especially if one has a certain knowledge of Rudolf Steiner's many descriptions of what he referred to as the etheric world, one understands that here is the source of that deep frustration and perplexity expressed by Barfield in the two substantial 1980s lectures summarized in the previous chapter. For when compared with the authoritative weight of what Steiner says based on his spiritual-scientific research (whether or not one chooses to attach any validity to it), the recorded conversations between Bohm and Sheldrake seem shallow and theoretical, like the tinkling of a cymbal rather than the booming of a gong.

Apart from Cecil Harwood, the only other individual who both contributed to the 'Festschrift' of 1976 and whose letters Barfield also preserved was Norman O. Brown, who by this time had become Professor of Humanities, University of California at Santa Cruz. His piece 'On Interpretation' is the most distinctively individual contribution to the book—a wholly personal poetic utterance, handwritten (beautifully legible) complete with deletions. The slender amount of correspondence preserved by Barfield (dating from 1966 to 1970) is remarkable for a letter written to Professor Brown by Barfield on 21 May 1966, which contains the most sharply critical words I have come across in anything that he wrote. Although the letter was addressed to Norman Brown, the criticism was directed not towards him but towards the composer John Cage (though it concerned not his music, which Barfield had never heard, but a book by him which Brown, in his enthusiasm, had sent to Barfield). For sheer sustained eloquence in devastation, the letter would be hard to beat.

What is of most relevance for present purposes, however, is not Barfield's view of John Cage's unfortunate (though doubtless highly successful) book, whose title is not mentioned in the correspondence,[99] but the open, candid way that he was able to communicate with the—in his words—'acute and combative author of *Life against Death*'. Brown, who at the time taught at the University of Rochester, New York, clearly admired John Cage as an author and naively thought that Barfield would like the book as much as he did. His reply to Barfield's letter (dated 11 August 1966) has a fiery Nietzschean, or Blakean, apocalyptic quality to it ('speaking philosophically, Nietzsche is a holy man to me', he writes). After sharing three deeply searching, existential questions, he concludes his lengthy letter by confirming: 'And nothing, not even anything you may say, can alter my veneration and debt to you.' By 1970 he is busily rereading Steiner's *Cosmic Memory* and hoping that Barfield can guide him further in his studies.

To illustrate the remarkable contrasts in the individuals with whom Barfield was corresponding over this period (with 1975 still being regarded as the temporal focus), we will now turn to a correspondence ranging from 1968 to 1981 between Barfield and the Hegel scholar and translator Arnold Miller, who lived in Gloucestershire. The contact was made by way of a letter from Miller to Barfield dated 30 May 1968, which he introduces by saying that while not himself an anthroposophist he is 'not unfamiliar with Rudolf Steiner's teachings'. He adds that 'all your books are on my shelves'. After thus describing the common ground he reckons to share with Barfield, he proceeds to his complaint that Hegel seems to be 'almost totally ignored' in the chapter on Coleridge in *Romanticism Comes of Age*. Barfield replied gratefully, courteously and constructively, while pointing out that the chapter in question had been written over 30 years previously, at a time when he had not had the opportunity to appreciate Hegel's stature as a teacher of spiritual things so fully as he did now. This did not altogether satisfy Miller, who continued to argue that Hegel's centrality had not been sufficiently appreciated by Barfield. However, in his next letter he makes the revealing statement that he was 'widely unread in philosophy apart from Hegel', on the grounds that 'Hegel was the first philosopher I came across and he provided all I needed'. As the correspondence proceeded (there were some 13 letters from Miller in all, including copies of one to Cecil Harwood and one to the *Anthroposophical Quarterly*, both dating from 1973), it must have rapidly become clear to Barfield that this self-imposed limitation meant that he would have to do all the bridge-building to Miller's philosophical citadel and that ultimately the bridge could not be built anyway. This would have been clearly apparent to him from, for example, Steiner's characterization of the limitations of Hegelian thinking in his preface to the 1923 edition of his book *Die Rätsel der Philosophie*,[100] where he describes the philosophical positions of Hegel and Haeckel as contradictory extremes, with Hegel viewing everything through its relation to the world of thought and Haeckel seeing only what is accessible to external sense perception. Steiner, and likewise Barfield, wished to embrace both these extremes and show how they can mutually fructify one another. The correspondence between Miller and Barfield continued to be thoroughly cordial after the former's retrenchment of his position in his 1973 letters about Hegel and Steiner, although no attempt was made to revisit the disputed philosophical terrain.

Another lively correspondence straddling the year 1975 was that with the historian and writer John Lukacs. The letters retained by Barfield are dated between July 1968 and March 1983, there being some 21 letters from Lukacs, together with copies of two of Barfield's own (there were, according to Lukacs, at least 20 letters from Barfield in all). Professor Lukacs regarded Barfield very highly ('you are among the half dozen people whose writings influenced my thinking most profoundly, and they include Pascal and Toqueville'). According to Lukacs's own testimony to the present author, he originally met Barfield around 1962. Thereafter Barfield was on two occasions a guest at his home in the 1960s; and Lukacs recalls two further meetings in England in the early 1970s, at Barfield's home and when they dined together at the Athenaeum Club. But in his letters—which brim with his most intimate thoughts—he shares much more of himself than his ideas alone, and Barfield learnt in some detail about his joy at the birth of his daughter Annemarie Gabrielle on 25 October 1968 and the tragic death of his wife from lung cancer some two years later. Again and again he returns to his conviction regarding the primacy of mind over matter: 'For years I have tried to impart to my students my view, according to which the modern materialist and Marxian view is not merely 100% but 200% wrong, since what people think and believe *is* the basic reality, and the material and bureaucratic institutions of society are but the consequences (what Marx called the superstructure) thereof. So it is not only that Marx was wrong but the very obverse of what he said is true.' In this same letter of 16 April 1975—the first addressed to 'Dear Owen' rather than 'Dear Mr. Barfield'—he goes on to express his deep concern that what is needed is far more than 'a mere change of accepted ideas', and indicates his disappointment at being unable to discern any significant characterological difference between most professed anti-reductionists and those whom they oppose. 'What matters,' he concludes, 'is how [people] think . . . the relationship of their minds to themselves.' Lukacs's comments about the 'counterculture' in his letters of this year (1975) harmonize both with Barfield's criticism of Theodore Roszak's work[101] and with the spirit—if not necessarily the letter—of his further criticisms in his 1982 Lindisfarne Association lecture; for this craggily individualistic thinker had no intention of jettisoning clarity of thinking together with the pre-suppositions of reductionist materialism and the bureaucratization of intellectual life which he so roundly rejected. It should also be recorded here that, in another context, Lukacs referred to Barfield as 'perhaps the greatest living English thinker of our time'.[102]

In a letter dated Good Friday 1979, Lukacs poses a question to Barfield which I cannot forbear from including in the context of the present study: 'Have you ever considered writing your own intellectual autobiography? I literally CANNOT think of a more important book; yet "intellectual autobiography" is only an all-thumbs expression [of] what I mean. What I mean is something like the history of your memory, and not the reverse . . . I would say "the evolution of your imagination", since to me memory and imagination are inseparable but no, this won't do, because I prefer history to "evolution", the latter having little or no suggestion for free will or choice . . .'

To conclude this section on correspondence in process around the year 1975, brief mention may be made of three more individuals with whom Barfield was consistently exchanging letters around this time. The first of these is Patrick Grant, of the English Department at the University of Victoria, British Columbia. He wrote to Barfield on 8 November 1972 at the suggestion of his colleague Lionel Adey, whose monograph on Barfield's 'Great War' with C.S. Lewis will be considered in the appropriate place. Grant had a particular interest in religious symbolism in literature, and gratefully acknowledged Barfield's inspiration in the books that he published during their correspondence, which would appear to have culminated in 1981 in an article which Grant wrote on Barfield for the 1982 edition (Volume III) of the journal *VII*.[103] Barfield kept a copy of one of his letters to Grant, dated 7 June 1977, where he wrote about the symbol of the Cross:

> As I see it, it is impossible to separate the idea of the true nature of human being from the symbol of the Cross. This was so long before

Christianity, that is the Crucifixion embodied the symbol as history. Plato in the *Timaeus* speaks of the soul of the world being stretched upon the body of the world in the form of a cross. Again, as the essential sign of space, it symbolizes the whole of phenomenal existence.

I think it has long been felt, in the East as well as in the West, that within the plane of spatial manifestation (on which *imagery* depends for its existence) vertical direction symbolizes the Man & God relation and horizontal direction the Man & Man relation, and clearly the two meet in the intersection of the arms of the cross. Both relations are, to my feeling, best understood as polarities, and the 2 polarities intersect at their point of maximum 'tension', that is, midway between their extremities. Psychologically and theologically one would say—all too glibly: Maximum love of one another is reached at the same point or in the same movement as maximum love of God.

Coleridge's endeavour was to express mystical truth in intelligible thoughts as far as that can be done. And my own endeavour, as far as I can claim to have hold of mystical truth, has been the same, I think.

The letter concludes with the strong advice to Grant that he read René Guenon's book *The Symbolism of the Cross*, which Barfield had recently read with 'something like amazement at its combination of depth with width of knowledge'.

The last letter written by Patrick Grant to Barfield—or at any rate the last one preserved by the recipient—contains, in addition to references to his books *Images and Ideas in Literature of the English Renaissance* (1979), *Six Modern Authors and Patterns of Belief* (also 1979), which includes a chapter on Barfield, and *Literature of Mysticism in Western Tradition* (then in process of publication), a few words arising out of his studies of John Donne's *Anniversaries*, which communicate something of the quality of what he shared with Barfield in his letters. Speaking of this collection of poems, 'which I think are mainly about the heart ("the world has lost its heart," etc.)', Grant writes as follows: 'They are troubled and disturbing poems because the heart of which he speaks is, as it were, disenfranchised, no longer the potent symbol of man's spiritual and physical unity with the sun (which used to shoot its beam into the foetal heart at four months) and the heavens, but of his peculiar isolation, tormented alike by sensualism (to which all the hard evidence points), and by the deficiencies of sensualism to satisfy his incurably metaphysical hunger.'

The other two correspondents whose letters complete the tapestry of human bonds being actively woven around the year 1975 are Walter Hooper and Charles Davy, letters from each of whom have been preserved by Barfield between the years 1970 and 1983. Hooper's letters are for the most part about literary and practical questions arising out of the two men's shared task as literary executors of C.S. Lewis and have a quality of engaging *bonhomie* redolent of Barfield's friendship with Lewis. Barfield kept a copy of just one of his own letters to Hooper, that of 17 May 1979, the theme of which is Lewis's book about his bereavement, *A Grief Observed*. What is most interesting for present purposes about this letter is Barfield's clear statement to the effect that, since his own Christianity 'seems to be based almost entirely on experience (plus of course judgements about the experience) and hardly at all on believing something it is difficult to believe', he cannot imagine a shattering emotional or physical blow affecting what he believes in the way that would appear to have been the case with Lewis over his wife's death. Because of this, Barfield writes to Hooper that the theme of loss of belief and its recovery, which he says is one of the two main threads running through Lewis's book, 'does not convey much to me personally'.

Charles Davy (1897–1985), who was a lifelong journalist working initially on the *Yorkshire Post* (after the Second World War as a leader writer) and then on the *Observer*, becoming a close friend and associate of the editor David Astor, encountered anthroposophy at a Summer Course in the early 1930s and remained closely associated with the movement for the rest of his life. The preserved letters from Charles Davy—whose son John (1927–1984) was also a close friend of Barfield's—are mostly concerned in one way or another with the *Golden Blade*, an anthroposophical annual publication co-founded by him in 1949 to which Barfield contributed fairly regularly (by 1975 he had had ten articles published in this journal). Davy continued to be an editor of this journal until 1978 and maintained his involvement in it until his death. He took a great interest in everything that Barfield wrote and was keen to use his influence to popularize his work by way of reviews. Barfield for his part also liked to share his literary enthusiasms with this warm-hearted and open-minded editor. The correspondence may best be characterized by the first letter in the sequence from Davy (dated 3 May 1970). Topics in this letter include the usual publishing updates (Davy has managed to get a letter from Barfield to the editor published in the *Observer*, and he responds to Barfield's positive news about his Coleridge book's forthcoming publication); news of Davy's move to Forest Row and of his golfing skills relative to his grandsons Thomas and Sebastian; a comment—in response to Barfield's previous letter—about Marshall McLuhan being a 'narrowly dogmatic' Roman Catholic; a few lines about fashionable words, with Davy indicating that Barfield's example 'psycho[so]matic' may be getting 'a shade out of date' and suggesting 'structured' and its variants 'structuralist', 'structuralism' as alternative candidates; and some words about summer holidays on Formentera, possible courses by Barfield at nearby Emerson College and good wishes to Barfield for his and his wife's impending move (from Westfield, Dartford to Orchard View, South Darenth). Finally, and most interestingly, Davy questions whether Barfield's point about the logical inter-relationship between the ideas of the evolution of consciousness and reincarnation in his 1970 *Golden Blade* article, 'The Disappearing Trick', may not have 'a loose link' in the argument; and he accompanies his letter with a question from the article and some comments of his own. It strikes me that Davy has not fully grasped the point that Barfield is making in the quoted passage (the passage in question is reproduced in the chapter about Rudolf Steiner, see p. 197), and although his comments are interesting in their own right they serve to confuse rather than clarify Barfield's argument. Suffice it to say that Davy's analysis is in terms of the soul-manifestation over the course of successive earthly lives of the supersensible journey to which Barfield is referring in his potent argument in favour of the logical necessity for reincarnation.

* * *

Following this cross-section through Barfield's multifarious correspondence around the mid-1970s, we shall first trace some of the friendships and acquaintances of his later years before building a bridge via his correspondence through to the period prior to his first journey to America.

Underlying virtually the entire period between 1975 and Barfield's death in 1997 is a deeply intimate correspondence with Professor Thomas Kranidas, of the Department of English at the State University of New York, Stony Brook. The mood of these letters, dating from 28 July 1974 (Orchard View) to 10 September 1995 (The Walhatch),[104] is epitomised by a remark of Barfield's in a letter dated 22 March 1986: 'You would be surprised how often my mind surveys with a kind of amazement the rapidity and the completeness with which Maud and I "linked" with our unknown Stony Brook landlord in 1974'.[105] The friendship prospered to such a degree that by 18 July 1993 Barfield is writing the following words to Kranidas: '*Why* is it that I always feel more "at ease" with you than almost anyone else, including members of my own family?'

Barfield shared both professionally academic and personally intimate details with Kranidas, whom he would sometimes affectionately address as 'Themistokles' (Kranidas was of Greek origin), and deep seriousness is throughout interwoven with rich humour. Reference has already been made in previous chapters to Barfield's travails with Coleridge's *Philosophical Lectures* (an ongoing theme between December 1978, when he took on the task of editing them, and Kathleen Coburn's death in September 1991), and to Saul Bellow's gift of an armchair and his (Bellow's) marital troubles. The main professional issue binding the correspondence together is that of an anthology of Barfield's unpublished literary output (poems and prose), which idea Kranidas launched in the correspondence in 1979 and which, after a number of publishing impediments, finally resulted in Barfield's giving his 'unqualified consent' in June 1992 to the publication of what appeared the following year in the form of *A Barfield Sampler* (State University of New York Press, 1993). Another frequently recurring strain in Barfield's letters is that of the absence of communication from John Ulreich, who—in addition to his heroic work on Barfield's behalf, not least in connection with his play *Orpheus*—had offered to write his biography. Although in a letter of 14 November 1983 Barfield stated that he was contemplating adding Ulreich's name to the list of his Literary Executors,[106] Ulreich 'sounded distant' when Barfield finally managed to get through to him in October 1984 and never resumed communication of any kind with Barfield, who for his part, while not wishing to bind Ulreich to his word, never entirely gave up hope of hearing some news from him.

Regarding *Orpheus* itself,[107] Barfield makes the following revealing comment in a letter of 16 January 1984:

> I am sorry *Orpheus* looks like turning out what Lewis once called one of his books—a *flop d'estime*. The *Golden Blade* will certainly review it, and the journals respectively of the English and American Anthroposophical Societies have one in hand. I suppose Chris [Bamford, publisher] will have sent a copy to *Seven* [*VII*]. (My *Towards* has arrived since I wrote this yesterday, and I am disappointed to see there isn't even an announcement, let alone a review!) All chicken feed of course in the publicity stakes. If I have any painful feelings, they are those of *guilt*, when I think of all the trouble you and John, not to mention Chris Bamford, have taken with the blighter. Chagrin hardly noticeable. Whether based on experience or on self-conceit, and you can take your choice, I have become accustomed to meet absence of *réclame*

with the reflection: 'Oh well, it will find its readers in ten or twenty or thirty years or so.'[108]

Two other quotations from these letters will serve to give some additional flavour of the more 'professional' aspect of what Barfield imparts to Kranidas. The first of these concerns his review of Julian Jaynes's book, *The Origin of Consciousness in the Breakdown of the Bicameral Mind*:

> I have done my review of Julian Jaynes's book, and am fairly pleased with it. Also rather obsessed by it. When you are writing against the main stream of current presuppositions every word, and the placing of it, seems to count: e.g. either too much or too little irony is likely to weaken the impact. It is just about as tormenting, and in the same way, as writing a poem. And if you do solve a problem satisfactorily, you go on so long feeling so infernally pleased with yourself! At least I do. And all this fuss for the *Teachers College Record*, which does not even pay its contributors! I have no idea when they are likely to be printing it . . . [from the letter of 1 January 1978].

This gives some insight as to the seriousness with which Barfield approached the writing of book reviews, especially when—as was the case here—the author of the book in question was expressing a view tantalizingly—or infuriatingly—close to his own. And the following comment from the letter of 9 January 1989 about Samuel Beckett's famous play likewise deserves to be recorded here, for the light that it sheds on the context of Barfield's early formative literary experiences:

> As to *Waiting for Godot*, I did see it when it was first published. No. Not hatred . . . I was totally untouched by it, and the tedium of watching it was such, I am ashamed to say, that, when the 2nd Act turned out to be as drab as the first, I actually nodded off during part of it. My brother, who was with me, felt the same. You must remember that the period when I was first awakening to literary awareness had been the one when the intelligentsia was just deciding there was nothing to be done except to capitalize on mental disintegration; and, as you know, reaction *against* that decision had been the determining factor in my own endeavours. So I was very unfertile soil for Beckett to cultivate . . .

On the more personal side, Barfield makes frequent reference to members of his family and his other close friends. In a letter written shortly after his wife's death on 13 February 1980, for example, he writes: 'I don't feel wholly cut off from M[aud]. In some ways less so than during her loss of mental grip during the last years.' Although this is not actually stated in the letters (and certain portions of them from around this time have been excised possibly for this reason), it is very evident from their mood that he must himself have experienced considerable relief when Maud (born 1885) finally passed through the portals of death. There is one particular (undated, because amputated) letter from around June 1986 where he most likely gave frank expression to what he had been feeling, and this is in any case the impression that one gains from reading a sequence of letters formerly coloured by gloom and latterly overtly exuberant.

There are a number of references to his adopted daughter Lucy (born 1935), beginning with her move to hospital in 1977 (her multiple sclerosis had begun to take hold in the early 1970s) and her wedding in June 1978; some appreciative comments about his foster son Jeffrey (born 1940) who was 'a tower of strength' in driving him about and 'always remained faithful in his way'; and some rather less appreciative remarks about his adopted son Alexander (born 1928), who was 'not helpful' over his move to The Walhatch (November 1986) and always seemed somewhat distant.

Two other close friends who figure from time to time are Josephine Spence, the daughter of the zoologist E.L. Grant Watson and the artist with whom he collaborated over 'Eager Spring' (see Chapter 6, 'The Effects of Idolatry') and the Bookmakers Guild (1986) version of *The Silver Trumpet*; and Marguerite Lundgren (1916–83), the widow of his close friend Cecil Harwood, whom she married after Daphne Harwood's death in 1950, and energetic leader of the London School of Eurythmy of which Barfield was an active supporter.

Barfield also shared his cultural loves with Kranidas, there being many references to musical performances that he had attended or heard on the wireless—indeed, his letters to Kranidas are somehow permeated with a musical quality. There are also some delightful flashes of humour, as for example a definition of a unit of measurement called a 'milli-helen', which is apparently 'the amount of female beauty required to launch one ship'.

To conclude this section on the Kranidas correspondence, it seems appropriate to cite some of the last thoughts which he expressed to his friend in written form. After a somewhat melancholic letter dated 28 September 1994, where he says that he feels more like a *has been* than an *is*, he wrote the following words about the kind of posterity that he hoped for: 'By the way, I am not in the least concerned about literary fame. That is definitely *not* the spier that this clear spirit doth raise. What I want for my books etc., or some of them, is that they may be *used*, where appropriate, to help jog things along in the right evolutionary direction . . .' (from the letter of 19 November 1994). Finally, he sent the following greeting to Kranidas on 10 September 1995 after the latter's visit to The Walhatch on 8 July that year:

> Dear Tom, I have no news. I suppose because the sheer weakness incident to extreme old age prevents one from *doing* anything; one also has the feeling that nothing *happens* . . . How I should love to see you and hear you again!
>
> With my blessings, Owen.

Other letters from this post-1975 period retained by Barfield include ten from Luke Madole, a young law student/practitioner from Texas who wrote to Barfield in May 1978 to seek guidance because of his newly awakened feelings of emotional emptiness and his awareness that words seemed to have lost the meaning that they formerly had for him. He was also struck by the possible relationship between these experiences and the loss of childhood imagination; and he begged Barfield—whom he had begun to read through C.S. Lewis's recommendation—to help him find a way of rekindling the vividness of his mental pictures. Barfield obliged with a sympathetic and warmly encouraging letter, which included some suggestions for remedying the problem based on exercises given Rudolf Steiner. By his own admission, Madole was no literary expert or academic high-flyer (Barfield must have had a chuckle when he encountered *This Ever Diverse Pear*!), and he viewed Barfield's (and also Steiner's) ideas about certain religious concepts such as reincarnation and evil emphatically from the standpoint of an evangelical brand of Christianity. And yet this young man not only read everything that Barfield wrote but had also visited him in England a couple of times together with his wife by the time the preserved correspondence came to an end in September 1982.

If Luke Madole comes across as a searching Christian soul, Steve Neumeister, from whom nine letters exist from 1976 until 1979, describes himself quite straightforwardly as a Christian fundamentalist and a great admirer of Francis Schaeffer. In his introductory letter of 9 June 1976, the highly academic Neumeister, who unlike his fellow Texan Madole betrays a tendency towards declamation rather than putting questions, is mainly wishing to acknowledge his debt to Barfield as his spiritual father alongside Schaeffer and C.S. Lewis. Although as the correspondence proceeds this English faculty member turned theological seminarist comes to emphasize the utter incompatibility of Steiner's (and Barfield's) interpretation of the Gospels with the New Testament, the letters from

Neumeister grow in warmth and affection, and culminate in the strongly stated wish for an opportunity to make Barfield's personal acquaintance. (I am not aware whether he did so.)

Before turning to the pre-1975 period and building the bridge to the time before Barfield set foot in America in 1964, mention should briefly be made of the 1986 letters to and from the Prince of Wales already cited (see 'Positivism and its Residues'); a letter from the Czech President Vaclav Havel dated June 1991 thanking Barfield for sending him a copy of the German translation of *Saving the Appearances* ('Evolution—Der Weg des Bewusstseins'); a couple of news and question-filled letters from 1992, including numerous clippings and conference programmes, sent by Joe Kelly, an American anthroposophist from New Jersey; and a series of formal letters dated 1986–1993 from James E. Person about an introduction that Barfield had agreed to contribute to volume 5 of the publication *Literature Criticism from 1400 to 1800.*

* * *

We now resume the backward journey from the pivotal year of 1975, when two of Barfield's intimate friends died, Philip Mairet and Cecil Harwood. Barfield's correspondence with Philip Mairet takes us back to the works that he wrote prior to his first American journey in the autumn of 1964, *Unancestral Voice* (published 1965), *World's Apart* (1963) and *Saving the Appearances* (1957), although the two men originally met in the 1920s at the wedding of Barfield's Oxford friend Leo Baker (of whom more anon). Mairet was a quiet, scholarly figure whose active life had involved him in literary journalism and criticism: from 1919 he was A.R. Orage's deputy as editor of the *New Age*, also of the *New English Weekly*, and after Orage's death in 1934 continued as editor until the latter ceased publication in 1949. Through Orage he became interested in the ideas of C.H. Douglas, whose Social Credit Theory figured strongly in Barfield's thinking during the 1930s. He was also associated with T.S. Eliot when the latter was editor of the *Criterion*, and he reviewed books for Eliot's firm Faber and Faber. A further journalistic connection of Mairet's was with J.H. Oldham's *Christian News Letter* (founded 1939), and with Dr. Alec Vidler, who edited *Frontier*, another Christian journal, jointly with Mairet until 1953. Mairet, who went to great lengths to escape conscription—for conscientious reasons—during the First World War and had an association with the anti-mechanization group centred on Eric Gill, was in addition engaged in the craft of glass-making and the art of drawing (he had meticulous handwriting until the very end of his life), and acted on the stage of the Old Vic between 1921 and 1924. Finally, he had a strong interest in Rudolf Steiner's anthroposophy, and it is on record that he was one of the first members to join the Anthroposophical Society in Great Britain after its founding in 1923.

Barfield's collection of his correspondence with Philip Mairet consists of 15 letters from himself and 20 from Mairet, together with commentaries/reviews by the latter on two of Barfield's books, *Saving the Appearances* and *Unancestral Voice*. The first extant letter is one from Barfield dated 14 May 1956 acknowledging an invitation from Mairet to renew their acquaintance, which, at Barfield's suggestion, they may have done on 23 May. Almost exactly a year later *Saving the Appearances* was published and was acclaimed by Mairet as a work which points the way towards an understanding of the modern scientific mind in terms of—rather than as a means of denying—the Christian mystery of the Incarnation: 'The practical bearing of this treatise is summarily indicated in its observation that Christianity will renew its power in the mind of man when any introduction to Science will have to begin with an account of the Incarnation of the Word (in the sense of the Divine Logos).'[109] In September 1957 Mairet is asking Barfield if he would be willing to address a group of people at St Anne's House, Soho—'a house of Christian discourse'—on a weekly basis during the autumn on the subject of his book, a proposal to which Barfield agreed to do from 30 October onwards. The next letter from Mairet of direct relevance to Barfield is dated 10 September 1962, by which time Mairet had nearly finished reading *Saving the Appearances* for the fourth time 'with renewed pleasure and admiration'. By 20 March 1964 Mairet is expressing his 'unqualified enjoyment and appreciation of your dialogue *Worlds Apart*', where 'the position that you defend in *Saving the Appearances* is now presented with great enrichment in dialectical interplay with characteristic contemporary assumptions about cosmogony and, I think, with a considerable gain in lucidity and expository power'. Barfield responded on 28 March 1964 with references to the three books with which the present section is mainly concerned, lamenting the lack of general scientific interest in *Saving the Appearances* while gratefully noting the 'long and warmly appreciative notice' on *Worlds Apart* in *Nature* on 8 February. He also mentions that he has just sent off the manuscript of another book to Fabers which 'is much more explicitly anthroposophical in content than anything else I have done'.

By 23 May 1965 Philip Mairet is writing to Barfield with news of his initial response to the third of these books: 'A fortnight ago I received a copy of your *Unancestral Voice* from an editor who asked me for a *short* notice of it, or, if I preferred, he kindly suggested I might just lose the book; from which I suppose he had peeped into it and didn't like, or think much of it. So he may not like my notice either, which will doubtless be short, but to the effect that I shall take special care not to lose a book worthy of several re-readings.' In his review, which accompanied the letter in the preserved correspondence, Mairet comments that the book, for all its apparent diversity of themes on a superficial level, 'has a remarkable unity; it is a well-sustained defence of a very consistent theme—that of the "evolution of consciousness"—a conception which is upheld as the necessary correlative and corrective to current dogmatics in physical and biological evolution'. After informing his readers (of the Christian journal *Frontier* referred to above) that 'Mr. Barfield ... has produced two previous expositions of the same general theme, *Saving the Appearances* and *Worlds Apart*', of which he says that not only he himself but also others 'have been impelled to re-read [them] perhaps with a similar suspicion that they point towards something that may one day prove to have had prophetic value', he recommends that 'they had better read the present work three or four times as I shall, and find illumination in the labour of deciding exactly what, if anything, is wrong with this remarkable approach to the contemporary tension between Christianity and contemporary humanist thinking'.

After a few further epistolatory exchanges about certain details in *Worlds Apart* and *Unancestral Voice* (which will be mentioned in the appropriate place) over the next eight years, the year 1973 witnessed a last considerable intensification in the correspondence between Mairet and Barfield. Mairet's 'addiction' to rereading Barfield's books had not abated, and in a letter of 3 January he is able to state that this method of assimilating Barfield's thoughts has yielded the insight that '*Unancestral Voice*, which I had hitherto regarded as the least rewarding to read of your recent productions, now strikes me as the *most* illuminating of the lot'. In his letter of 24 January Mairet informs his correspondent that the aforesaid addiction had persisted through the past calendar year, which he had spent mainly in hospital or nursing homes recovering from a cerebral stroke: 'One effect of all this has been to deepen my interest in what you call the evolution of consciousness and my enthusiasm for your writings thereupon.' After again referring to a particular aspect of biblical scholarship referred to in *Unancestral Voice* which held a peculiar fascination for him, Mairet goes on to relate an experience which, he says, 'will give a *better* clue to the reasons for my interest in your recent writings'. He then describes how when he had been working as a labourer on the land during the First World War he had, in addition to studying anthroposophic and theosophic authors (notably Rudolf Steiner's *Philosophy of Spiritual Activity*[110] and his studies on German mystics), carried out some exercises in training the imagination, one of which he recounts in detail. He now relates the experience which taught him the great value of training the imagination in this way and which, in turn, led him to understand what Barfield was ultimately driving at:

> Near the end of the war, when I was in solitary confinement in prison, I practised these exercises with considerable assiduity. It was a little triumph to me, which I now still remember, when, for the first time, I did the exercise of following a moving spot of light round the complete circle and back to the starting-point, without a break or stoppage or diversion of attention. I do think that this discipline did much to make the period of imprisonment harmless (if not slightly beneficial) to me psychologically. I may add that, some few years later, I returned definitively to the faith of my parents, and became a communicant of the Church of England. The good priest who admitted me to instruction for confirmation, listened with a good deal of interest to what I told him about this prison experience I had had, of a psychological discipline . . . I guess that perhaps you, my dear Barfield, may see something more rational in my prison behaviour than my priest did—this in view of what you have written about the possible value of training the imagination . . .

By the time Mairet writes, on 8 February, Barfield has sent him a copy of his book on Coleridge, *What Coleridge Thought*. Barfield must have replied immediately to this letter, with its reflections about the shortcomings of Teilhard de Chardin's 'cosmo-conception' on the one hand and Freudianism on the other, since on 11 February he wrote a further letter gratefully echoing Barfield's citing of the Psalmist's words about those 'who, going through the vale of misery use it for a well, and the pools are filled with water' in relation to the travails brought about by his recent stroke. Barfield again replied on 15 February, confessing that 'like you, I remember "falling in love" with those words from the 84th, and I remember choosing that psalm for my father's funeral, in 1938'. (This is the first letter where either of the two correspondents addresses the other by his Christian name, thus setting the trend for the remainder of the exchanges.) By 17 February Mairet is taking up his elegant pen again (the rapidity of the dialogue brings considerable credit to the efficiency of the postal system!), still preoccupied with his critique of Père Teilhard de Chardin and richly appreciating *What Coleridge Thought* ('Sir, I thank God for you . . .'). Because of other pressures, Barfield was unable to respond with such alacrity. By 24 April, however, he has reread Chardin's chapter on 'The Within of Things' in *The Phenomenon of Man* and finds that he still feels the same about it: 'It seems to me to be infected with what I once called . . . R.U.P. (a residue of unresolved positivism). It is one thing to speak, as Coleridge does, of a "within-ness" of Nature as a whole, quite another to attribute separated "within-nesses" to materially separate units—"particles of consciousness", as Chardin calls them . . . Whatever he propounds intellectually, it seems to me Chardin is *imagining* matter as an ultimate. Hence, too, he accepts as a matter of course the Lyell-Darwin-based fantasy of the extreme age of the physical—and indeed the *solid*—earth.' This letter, which arrived on Mairet's 87th birthday, received an immediate, and grateful, response.

A lull then followed in the correspondence until 16 October, by which time Mairet had carefully read the whole of Barfield's book on Coleridge; and he now encloses a copy of a letter that he had written to his friend Tom Heron, which contains the fullest picture of his impression of *What Coleridge Thought*. The letter to Tom Heron is long, but a portion of it demands to be included here:

> One of your letters, Tom, said something about Barfield having put more of himself than of Coleridge into his study of the latter. If this means that something of himself is substituted for S.T.C. so that we lose a value, I can only say I didn't feel it. And the book, *What Coleridge Thought*, prompted me to read the *Biographia Literaria*; which then made one feel very grateful for what Coleridge gives me and to Owen Barfield for a work of interpretation and demonstration without which I might not have had this most valuable intellectual instruction.
>
> To name one outstanding thing I feel I have learnt from Coleridge. Other writers have failed to make clear to me *why* it is that we *can have* the insights into nature which inform our 'natural science'—how it is that we are able to have the right hypotheses and the right ways to verify them. In other words, *Why it is* that our modern science *works* when you apply it, whatever else we may think about it. For this isn't easy to see, when you really enquire into it. S.T.C. does answer it absolutely convincingly, and the more so if you follow O.B.'s exposition of it. But of course it is really the metaphysical genius of

> Coleridge himself that is so comprehensively illuminating . . . I have . . . *never* come to grasp the outline of a philosophy with a deeper feeling of its wisdom, truth and authority—no, not even in contemplating Hegel's (I suppose, however, that I must exclude from this the *greatest* classics, Plato, Aristotle et al.) . . .

Barfield replied shortly afterwards, on 23 October. His reaction to Tom Heron's view of *What Coleridge Thought* is worth recording here: 'One or two reviews have suggested that there is more of Barfield than of STC in my book, though I should have thought the plethora of supporting quotations rules that out. As they were already Coleridgeans, I rather assumed that what they really meant was, that what I revealed was so unlike their own, or the "received", interpretation that it just *must* be B. and not C.—whatever evidence might be adduced to the contrary!'

When Mairet wrote again on 5 February 1974, his theme has reverted from Coleridge to *Unancestral Voice*: 'If I am the only person to have twigged it—that *Unancestral Voice* is the weightiest and most arcane of your works—this is not surprising. I may well be the only reader to have devoted *adequate* study to your entire *opus*!' He adds that Fabers (the publishers) should ' "lay down" the remainder for posterity, like so much Napoleon brandy! For besides being the most esoteric, it happens also to be the most *topical*—and most *typical* of the anxieties of intelligent people in its day'. In what would seem to be his last letters to Barfield, dated 14 February and 11 March, Mairet continues to reflect upon certain aspects of Christian mystical tradition prompted by this same book of Barfield's, and writes approvingly and gratefully about his lecture *The Light of the World* which he had given at Rudolf Steiner House in 1953.[111]

This correspondence with Philip Mairet has not only forged a link with those works by Barfield which we will be considering in the next part of this book but has also enabled us to revisit those Coleridge studies which were described in Chapter 2 as being fundamental to everything that he thought and wrote in his 'American' period.

The last correspondent to figure in this kaleidoscopic chapter on Barfield's human associations over the latter part of his life can form a living link not only with Barfield's early years but also with the friend[112] who was—and is—the most familiar member of the scholarly group with whom he was associated in the England of his adult working life, in the same sense as Saul Bellow may be regarded as a symptomatic figure of the America which he visited so often during his retirement. In using the word 'correspondent', I am conscious that Barfield does not seem to have retained any letters between himself and Cecil Harwood (though fortunately Harwood did—see Chapter 15). As Harwood himself attests in his contribution to the 1976 'Festschrift', *Evolution of Consciousness*, the two of them had met as pupils of Highgate School, North London, 'where we sat next to each other for many years'. In his lecture 'Owen Barfield and the Origin of Language' (given on 21 June 1977), Barfield recalls a scene in a schoolroom just before the master was due to come in to take a lesson in Latin syntax, the aim of which was to illustrate points in syntax by quotations from a Latin author. The particular sentence that was the focus of the pupils' attention at the time was: *Cato, octoginta annos natus, excessit e vita* (Cato died aged 80). Although the point of the excercise in question was to focus on the use of the accusative case to denote duration of time (as exemplified in this case by the word 'annos'), the boy sitting next to Barfield suddenly observed: 'Cato at the age of 80 *walked out of life*—that's rather nice!' Barfield comments: 'You see, what this friend—by the way the Subject [i.e. Barfield] was 11 or 12 years old and so was his friend—what this friend (whose name incidentally was Cecil Harwood) was drawing attention to, because it tickled his fancy, was a *metaphor*. You can say "Cato died". You can also say "Cato walked out of life". Well, of course the Subject himself was familiar with other metaphors, with figurative language, figures of speech; but it had never occurred to him before that it was possible to *enjoy* them, to relish them, for their own sake. That is the proper moment to identify, if you want to place the origin of the Subject's interest in, and feeling for, the nature of language.'

In his short memorandum in the 'Festschrift', Harwood recalls that he and Barfield met again after the war at Oxford, although they were in different colleges, and belonged to the same circle of friends. 'Here began his long and fruitful association with C.S. Lewis, on whom he had a profound influence, and who later characterized him as the "wisest of my unofficial advisers".' Harwood adds that 'we crowned our association in Oxford by an idyllic year in a thatched cottage in the (then) purely rural village of Beckley, to which our friends used to bicycle out for long walks and long discussions. In the Winter we lived with the rigours of an open Tudor fireplace, but the Spring—surely, we felt, the most glorious ever known—brought all the beauties of a still uncontaminated English countryside ...' He then recalls those vitally important summers—recounted in such detail by Barfield in the Biographical Sketch—when, as members of the English Folk Dance Company organized by the Radford sisters, first Barfield (1920) and then he himself (1921, 1922 and 1923) took an active part in touring villages in Cornwall and Devon. Moreover, it was through a member of this Cornish concert party in the latter two years—Daphne Olivier, who became Harwood's wife—that 'we were introduced to the works of Rudolf Steiner and came to recognize him as the—still unrecognized—genius of the modern age'.

Harwood devoted his life to Rudolf Steiner education and to Michael Hall School in particular (founded by him and others as The New School in 1925).[113] He was also the Chairman of the Anthroposophical Society in Great Britain from 1937 until 1974, the year before he died. Although Barfield's outward life followed a very different path after the many shared experiences of their early years, the importance of Harwood as one who helped to initiate virtually all Barfield's most seminal early experiences, friendships and spiritual enthusiasms can hardly be overestimated; and as Harwood's son Laurence observes in his contribution to the 1998 monograph referred to above, the two men's commitment to anthroposophy 'cemented this bond of friendship through thick and thin' despite their outward separation until Harwood's death in December 1975.[114]

PART THREE
The Forging of a Key: The Man of Letters (1919–64)

9. OWEN BARFIELD AND C.S. LEWIS

When in the course of one of my many conversations with Barfield at the end of his life I asked him which of all his friendships was the one that he treasured most, he thought for a while and then stated unequivocally that it was his bond with C.S. Lewis on which he looked with the greatest affection.[115] As this friendship, which began during Barfield's first term as an undergraduate at Wadham College, Oxford in 1919 and continued until Lewis's death on 22 November 1963, encompassed virtually the entire period under consideration in this part of the book, it seems appropriate to introduce this section on the period of Barfield's adult maturity before his first visit to America with a chapter on his relationship to the most celebrated of those twentieth-century Christian mythmakers known collectively as 'the Inklings'.[116]

The first point to note about the relationship between the two men is that the feelings of deep affection were mutual. As Walter Hooper points out in his biographical note on Barfield in Lewis's *Diary 1922–1927*,[117] '. . . although Barfield and Lewis disagreed about many things, especially Anthroposophy, there is probably no one Lewis admired so much'. This sense of admiration of his friend is one of the most striking themes permeating this early Diary, where not only his other academic contemporaries but also eminent writers such as Charles Dickens and W.B. Yeats are subjected to Lewis's mordant, critical wit. An entry dated 9 July 1922 includes the following characteristic remarks:

> D[118] and I sat up late. She said it was strange that I liked Baker[119] more than the Bee Cottage people:[120] we concluded it must be because Baker liked me more than they did, also he is my equal, while Barfield towers above us all . . .

Barfield himself, in his foreword to Lewis's *Diary*, expresses surprise that Lewis made no reference to what he referred to in *Surprised by Joy* as 'the great war' over their intellectual disagreements (which was underway towards the end of the diary years). He points out that the nearest Lewis comes to mentioning this theme is an entry for 18 January 1927:

> Was thinking about imagination and intellect and the unholy muddle I am in about them at present: undigested scraps of anthroposophy and

psychoanalysis jostling with orthodox idealism over a background of good old Kirkian rationalism. Lord, what a mess! And all the time (with me) there is the danger of falling back into most childish superstitions, or of running into dogmatic materialism to escape them.

After quoting these words, Barfield adds: 'Perhaps it is no accident that the previous day reports "A letter from Barfield to say he is at Air Hill and will come over—always good news".'

Shortly after this entry, Lewis records (25/26 January) that Barfield came for a couple of days. 'It was delightful to see him,' he writes. 'After a confused chat of philosophy and jokes, we settled down to read Aeschylus' *Prometheus* together, as we had promised to do.' They commented approvingly on each other's latest literary creations, and, after a refreshing night's sleep, they 'talked about night fears and whether the death of a person one really cared for would abolish the horror of the supernatural or increase it. He [Barfield] also spoke of the reaction that comes after an evening of laughter among your best friends, when the sort of mental security which you had among them goes out of you, and you realize that no one but yourself can give you that security . . . I was sorry to see him go—these meetings are always beyond expectation.'

And yet the latter part of the above was written on the same day—and probably at the same sitting—as the following passage, which describes what had meanwhile been going on at Mrs Moore's current residence of Hillsboro:[121]

Mrs. B[arfield] has apparently been having a heart-to-heart with D. She 'hates, hates, hates' Barfield's Anthroposophy, and says he ought to have told her before they were married: which sounds ominous. She once burnt a 'blasphemous' anthroposophical pamphlet of his, which seems to me an unpardonable thing to do. But I think that they really get on very well, better than the majority of married people. Mrs. Barfield is always glad when Barfield comes to see me because I have 'none of those views'.

In what follows, an attempt will be made to trace the unfolding of this relationship—living as it did between loving friendship on the one hand and outright hostility on the other—from the standpoint of Barfield's own experience. (Lewis's experience of the relationship has been characterized on more than one occasion both by Lewis himself and by his biographer and editor, Walter Hooper; and several of Lewis's letters to Barfield—though not Barfield's to Lewis—have been published.[122]) The method of presentation—as with the Saul Bellow correspondence that introduces the latter period of Barfield's life—will be largely chronological. In this respect, three distinct phases may be distinguished: the first lasting for approximately a decade after 1919 and more or less coinciding with the period before Lewis's conversion to Christianity (dominated by the 'Great War'); the second continuing until Lewis's death; and the third comprising several essays, lectures or interviews touching upon the relationship of the two men given by Barfield since 1963, many of which have been gathered together under Professor G.B. Tennyson's editorship in *Owen Barfield on C.S. Lewis* (1989).

There are no written records—so far as I am aware—of any correspondence between the two friends before January 1926, when Lewis wrote most appreciatively to Barfield to acknowledge receipt of his newly published book *History in English Words*. Until Barfield took his BA degree in 1921 they were of course in close physical proximity to one another (Lewis remained in or near Oxford until 1955); and neither his move to Bee Cottage in nearby Beckley (where he read for his B.Litt thesis) nor, after his marriage in April 1923, his withdrawal to Long Crendon (which remained his home until fully moving to London in 1929) would have seriously hindered personal encounters. The latter part of the 1920s saw a spate of intense written exchanges named by Lewis the 'Great War'. This correspondence arose not so much out of a need to bridge spatial distances but rather from Lewis's endeavour to convince Barfield of the folly of pursuing his interest in anthroposophy. He had been vehemently opposed to any trace of Steiner's influence on his friends (i.e. in particular Barfield and Harwood) from the time of their first encounter with his ideas in the summer of 1923. On 7 July 1923 he had recorded his thoughts on the matter in his diary:

> Harwood told me of his new philosopher, Rudolf Steiner... [He] seems to be a sort of panpsychist, with a vein of posing superstition, and I was very much disappointed to hear that both Harwood and Barfield were impressed by him. The comfort they got from him (apart from the sugar plum of promised immortality, which is really the bait with which he has caught Harwood) seemed something I could get much better without him.

Exactly when the 'Great War' began in earnest is difficult to say, but there is no compelling reason to think that any of the extant documents that are reckoned to belong to it date from before 1927.[123] On the other hand, by no means all the letters—and this applies particularly to the earlier ones—have been preserved. What would appear to have goaded Lewis into launching his initial assault (the military metaphor is by no means inappropriate) was that by 1925 Barfield had completed the initial draft of his B.Litt. thesis, which was in a slightly amended and expanded form published as *Poetic Diction* in 1928. Although Lewis welcomed much of what Barfield had to say in so far as it related to poetry as such, and in particular to understanding the reason for the beguiling spell that good poetry casts on the reader, he felt obliged to—in Lionel Adey's words—record 'his disagreement with Barfield's contention that poetry initially conveyed knowledge and that therefore imagination disseminated truth'. He sensed, quite rightly, that lurking behind Barfield's conclusions from his research there lay that same philosophical (and ultimately religious) standpoint from which he had so strongly recoiled in his brief, indirect encounters with anthroposophy.

Barfield is generally considered to have had the better of Lewis in the 'Great War'. This was certainly Lionel Adey's view, as he sought to make an objective appraisal as an impartial scholar.[124] Barfield's mind, he says, was 'less organized than Lewis's but more attuned to reality. To speak frankly, he often seems more grown-up. Though unable to match his opponent's dialectical figure-skating, rhythmic phrasing and gift for analogy, he shrewdly exposes contradictions in terms and misuse of language, and eventually feels his way toward undiscovered country.'[125] And at the end of his study he concludes: 'That Barfield's thought is both more original and more profound I have come to believe while studying these controversies ... I have come to think him the more important figure ... Future students of twentieth-century thought may well find Barfield ... among the diagnosticians of a profound change in human consciousness, one comparable to the Reformation or Enlightenment ... [whereas] Lewis's writing, on theology in particular, is an effort not of creative Reason but of Understanding that looks backward over the path traced by earlier scholars.'[126] Even a scholar such as Stephen Thorson, who approaches the 'Great War' exchanges very much from a standpoint of sympathy (religious or metaphysical as opposed to epistemological) to Lewis, can state after he has summarized the opposing arguments of the 'contestants': 'Now, in my opinion, Barfield's argument is sound. It seems to be unanswerable from *within* his and Lewis's system.'[127] However, this is not a study of the 'Great War'.

Nor is it of present concern to consider Lewis's serious misrepresentations of anthroposophy, whether in the 'Great War' documents, in his Diary, *All My Road Before Me*, or elsewhere. It is sufficient at this point to state that his *a priori* rejection of Steiner and his determination to cling on to his own caricature of what anthroposophy was standing for was not only responsible for the quasi-Thomist or crusader-like character of his contributions to the 'Great War' but has made it difficult for Lewis scholars (and Lionel Adey and Stephen Thorson are glowing exceptions in this respect) to appreciate what Barfield was actually saying. There is no doubt that Lewis himself took note of it.

What matters for present purposes is to try to understand the actual issues between the two friends—and they were essentially epistemological rather than metaphysical in origin, although they had strong religious associations—from Barfield's point of view. The main focus will therefore be placed on the few extant contributions by Barfield himself (Lewis very rarely kept incoming letters). Because Lewis hardly ever dated his own letters, it is sometimes impossible to discern their order with any certainty, especially as some of the letters on both sides in the sequence are missing. As for the dating of this 'Great War' correspondence, I would strongly surmise that its focus was the years 1927 to 1929.

The sequence begins (even though it was clearly not the beginning) with a lengthy letter from Lewis which plunges right into the heart of his issue with Barfield:

> Now I take it for granted that truth and falsehood can *not* be asserted of 'imagination' in the common meaning ([Greek] fantasia, the *imaginatio* as a psychologist understands it) . . . From all this I conclude—and here I am v. anxious to know if you agree with me—that, granting the truth of poetical imagination [in the sense put forward by Barfield in *Poetic Diction*], we can never argue from it to the truth of any judgement which springs up in the mind as it returns to normal consciousness.

In other words, a state of poetic imagination cannot be as it were translated into the real world and be used to make an authoritative statement about it. Lewis is already aware from a previous letter of Barfield's what his response is likely to be:

> You seem to suggest that the only alternative to holding that poetry is veridical is to hold that poetry is 'fantasy': by which I think you mean to imply something of falseness or triviality.

Another, much shorter, letter which must—through internal evidence—have preceded the first of Barfield's extant letters consists of a four-point statement headed 'The *real* issue between us':

> 1. *Agreed* (by you and me, also by Kant, Coleridge, Bradley etc.) that the discursive reason always fails to apprehend reality, because it never grasps more than an abstract relational framework. The question then is whether it is possible for us to know that Concrete in which alone the thing we have abstracted was *real*.
>
> 2. *Agreed* (by us both, and many others) that the abstract reason *plus* sense experience *plus* habits etc. gives us, in the phenomenal region, a substitute for knowledge which works tolerably well for *practical* purposes. [Barfield at this point has commented: 'No. True for period Thales—Kant.']
>
> 3. *You* maintain that this reason & experience & habit can and ought to be used to produce a knowledge of the supersensible, as confidently as [they are] used in the sensible.
>
> 4. *I* maintain that the distinction is between the real and the phenomenal, not the sensible and the supersensible . . .

These statements are followed by a series of comic sketches, aimed at poking fun at Barfield or warning him of the dire consequences of persisting in his folly.

Barfield replied in a twelve-page letter dated 28 July 1927:

> Truth to you (correct me if I am wrong) is something you *look at* (mentally of course), while reality is something you *are* but never *see*. And I think I am also right in supposing that you restrict the sphere of 'true-false' to the *phenomenal*, while the *real*, you think, one only 'contacts' via moral (and possibly aesthetic) intuition. You then affirm that you see no reason why these intuitions should have *any connection at all* with judgements, except as possible objects of them . . . What I want to say at the moment is that I do not normally think of truth in that manner at all. To me it is not a sort of accurate copy or reflection of something, but it is reality itself taking the form of human consciousness. At the stage at which truth appears, or true thinking, there is no distinction possible between the thought and the object thought of . . .

This latter point can hardly be overestimated in its importance for characterizing the 'great divide', as he saw it, between himself and Lewis, who was thoroughly Cartesian (or un-Coleridgean, one might say) in his insistence in assuming a separation between 'mental complex' and 'fact or object', between the self and what is other than self.

Barfield goes on to try to clarify what he means by supersensible experience, using a highly descriptive verbal image (accompanied by a pictorial sketch) which Lewis could have made sense of only if he had been prepared to accept that subject and object, I and the world, are, in Adey's words, 'grounded in a primal reality that includes them both'. But he was not. Barfield knew this, and the next section of his letter contains a diatribe against the 'arbitrary torn-out-of-a-mobile-reality nature' of the logical mode of judgement as represented by Lewis:

> . . . in order to make a proposition *mean* anything, the terms have to be artificially taken out of time and deposited on an imaginary shore in the land of Nowhen, while the whole thundering torrent of reality (i.e. the whole river minus two drops) is quietly 'impounded in *ceteris paribus*'. It makes me feel quite uncomfortable and ashamed.

He then once again emphasizes what he sees as the reality of the everyday process of perception:

> The point is that the idea of reality being a temporal continuum which we have to arrest and break up for the purposes of speech and logic is to me not merely an interesting fact which I admit and then take no further note of, like the fact that I cannot jump over the Moon. It is a part of the whole meaning of the words 'logic', 'term', 'judgment' etc. to me, and is present in my consciousness every time I use them or hear them used . . .

Barfield now tackles Lewis's insistence upon ascribing to knowledge only the realm of so-called objective fact, which he refers to as the 'hoti-sphere' ('hoti' [Greek letters] is a Greek particle here meaning 'that') and which in later years he would have termed 'the sphere of literal awareness', of 'idols':[128]

> The question before the House is the relation (if any) between the 'hoti-sphere' and inspiration-imagination consciousness. A subsidiary question is: (i) should words such as *knowledge* and *truth* be applied *only* to consciousness in the 'hoti-sphere', (ii) should they be applied *also* to inspiration-imagination, or (iii) are they applicable *at all* to 'hoti' consciousness? So far as I am aware, at present your position here is (i) Mine is nearer to (iii) . . .

He then proceeds to describe how, in concrete terms, he sees the imagination to be playing a part in the acquiring of knowledge about reality:

> The relation between imagination and 'hoti' is psychological, is determined in time, and is *analogous to the relation of a fruit or pod to its*

> *flower.*[129] You will please note that I am *obliged, ex hypothesi*, to convey my meaning by analogy at this stage. Inspiration (= 'lights out' stage) and imagination are, *in that order*, intermediate stages
>
> I Between reality and the 'term' and (more directly)
>
> II Between reality and the proposition.

Barfield illustrates this by a further analogy.

> Please take the word 'sun' (a) as used by Dante and (b) as used by any modern astronomer (any fixed star). The transition from term (a) to term (b) was initiated by imagination. I at least cannot conceive of its happening in any other way than this: that some individual having in his mind (i) a pictorial image of the Copernican solar system and (ii) a pictorial image of some fixed star with planets, etc., suddenly *fuses the images together* . . . by means of that faculty which Coleridge accordingly dubbed 'esemplastic'.

Building on this analogy, Barfield concludes that 'inspiration-imagination is, for me, the source of *meaning*'. Abstract terms, he points out, 'perpetually tend to lose their meaning and become tautologous', because of the demands of strict logic and the laws of thought. 'Meaning is, however, renewable at the fountain of inspiration, flowing through imagination to analogy, and thence either (a) into metaphor and so poetry or (b) into hypothesis and so science.' Thus 'the poet, *qua* poet, is a maker of terms'. Barfield acknowledges that he may make 'bad terms', because his '*accidental* self' may be interpolated as a screen 'between the observer and the reality observed . . . It is because I am so vividly aware of [the pitfalls in that direction][130] that I believe in training oneself to endure increased self-consciousness which implies self-knowledge—that I believe in solving what I called in my Thesis "the paradox of inspiration" by learning to be in full possession of one's power of discrimination . . .'

Lewis remained unconvinced. In a subsequent letter,[131] he summarizes the state of the argument as follows, so far as he understood it:

> (1.) B[arfield] and L[ewis] *agree* that there is a valuable activity called imagination—which is not the same as *imaginatio*, fantasia [Greek letters], the image making faculty—the exercise of which is necessary for the connaissance of meaning.
>
> (2.) B. and L. *agree* that the exercise of this faculty does not enable us to make true statements of judgments (though of course no statement, even a false one could be made without it, as is shown by (1.)).

(3.) B. *maintains* and L. *questions* a doctrine that this faculty produces Truth, tho' not true statements or judgments; and that this is the only veritable Truth, 'true' judgments not being really true.

(4.) B. *maintains* and L. *denies* a doctrine (advanced, I think, as interpretation of (3.)) that the mind can become aware of its own activity in thinking as something other than the content or object of thought.

L. is at present in doubt as to the exact connection between (3.) and (4.).

In the only other letter from himself to have been preserved (apart from the semi-formal treatises that formed the core of the 'Great War' correspondence), Barfield complains that Lewis is failing—or refusing—to understand his analogies. He was clearly somewhat exasperated with Lewis's rationalist pedantry, and—because he thought his friend ought to know better—he was rather less forgiving of Lewis's tendency in this direction than he would subsequently become of the devotees of 'R.U.P.'[132] He painstakingly explains that his 'pod' analogy 'was meant to emphasize the relation between a "becoming", and thus *mobile* and *alive* state of an entity and its "become", *still, dead* state. When a flower reaches the pod stage, it has completed its cycle of changes, its history, and is at rest in death . . .' He then disagrees when Lewis says (in a letter now lost) 'to know the man is not to know the embryo'.[133] 'To know the whole man,' Barfield insists, 'does mean to know the embryo, and the man is the embryo. Your statements are only true for what I call "static" thinking, which labours under the delusion that it can eliminate time and still know something . . .'

To make his point clearer, he uses another metaphorical image:

> Supposing you are looking through a piece of coloured glass without knowing it. Now suppose someone tells you that this is so, and you set to work to rub off the colouring matter. You will then see more perfectly the reality which you have always been seeing to some extent, i.e. *as coloured*. The glass and its colouring matter being part of reality (though more your private concern than the rest of it), you may say, if you will, that you are now seeing a *different* reality; but since you never really saw the colouring matter, but only *through* it, while now, though you can no longer see through it, you can actually see the powder lying about on the ground, your objection is perhaps on the peevish side. It amounts, in fact, to saying that you cannot both look and not look through coloured glass at the same time.[134]

Barfield then goes on to say that he is all the more distressed by what Lewis writes about metaphor because he had thought that:

> We had a *measure* of agreement on this head, which was the principal subject of my Thesis. If there is none, we are going 'further back' with a vengeance. Whatever your view of knowledge, you surely do not think that it can be *administered*—provided the exact formulae are found—to a purely passive recipient? You would agree, I take it, that the most a conversation can do—and above all a philosophical conversation—is for A, by uttering symbols which are the result of his inner activity, to bring it about that B develop a corresponding activity... What I am asking you to do, and what I am trying to do myself, is to apply the same delicacy of perception and willingness to build for yourself on the basis of what is suggested, as you already do when confronted with anything that is an acknowledged form of 'art' or 'poetry'. But, instead of this, you seize on my metaphor with rough hands and try to fit it into a straight waistcoat. For shame! Suppose you were reading *Prometheus Unbound* aloud to me, and I were to shout out 'Stop! He says his soul is an enchanted boat. Right! Boat moves over water, therefore his soul must move over her singing. But that is absurd!' Would you have enough spirit to kick me downstairs? I believe, at any rate, that you would succeed in 'dissembling your love'. Man alive, you *can't* approach the mysteries of creation *except* by the use of poetic tact... You cannot proceed from the One to the Many, as long as you think in terms of things extended in space...

He concludes this seven-page letter by acknowledging that he has become somewhat heated, and begs Lewis's help in reassuring him that they do at least share some common ground.

It is highly likely that one of Lewis's responses to this plea from Barfield was to write his main 'Great War' treatise, his *Summa Contra Anthroposophos* (to give an abbreviated title), which he dated November 1928. Whether this preceded or followed other letters from him in the sequence is difficult to say. I do not propose to say much about the remaining letters, which would appear to have been conceived not so much as responses to Barfield's second letter (this was, rather, the task of the *Summa*) as attempts to dissuade his friend from pursuing his interest in what he (Lewis) regarded as an irrational set of beliefs. Thus in one of these letters Lewis makes the following admission: 'I am often surprised at the extent to which your views occupy my mind when I am not with you and at the animosity I feel towards them.' In another letter he expresses a grave misunderstanding (this is certainly how Barfield would have regarded it) of the extent to which Barfield was beholden to authority through anthroposophy.

With the *Summa*, and the further treatises in both directions that it generated, we reach the climax of the 'Great War'. Its very title, *Clivi Hamiltonis* [Lewis's pseudonym] *Summae Metaphysices Contra Anthroposophos Libri II* ('Clive Hamilton's Treatise on Metaphysics Against the Anthroposophists in Two Books'), denotes Lewis's intention to elevate his treatise to the level of a medieval disputation, specifically Aquinas' *Summa Contra Gentiles*. It consists of 68 pages of densely written prose, together with 15 pages of subsequent notes to Barfield's *Replicit* ('Note on the Law of Contradiction' and 'Replies to Objections in Detail'), and is divided into two parts: I. 'Being' (largely concerned with questions of epistemology); and II. 'Value' (focused on ethics). Adey[135] describes it as 'the most difficult and curious piece of prose Lewis ever wrote'. Through it, he goes on to say, Lewis 'intended to discredit anthroposophical teaching because of its authoritarian and "bulverist"[136], even paranoic tendencies, because its identification of imagination with truth would for him have destroyed the unique value of myth, legend, epic and lyric poem, and because he distrusted the practice of self-contemplation'. It is impossible to even pretend to do justice here to the *Summa* (and, as already indicated, it would be of no more than marginal relevance to do so), which is indeed a mixed bag of pure positivist reductionism (whether tongue-in-cheek or not is often difficult to tell), an attack on Steiner's (and Barfield's) assertion that it is possible for the human soul to gain knowledge of spiritual truths or, indeed, of other human beings, and some gloriously eloquent passages—highly praised by Barfield—such as the one about imagination (Part II, Section XIII).

Barfield's reply to the *Summa* is in two parts. The first, entitled *Replicit Anthroposophus Barfieldus* ('Barfield the Anthroposophist Replies'), consists of his commentary and critical notes on certain of the 21 sections of its first part and the 25 sections of its second part. However, what is of more interest for present purposes—in that our concern is not so much what Lewis thought about Barfield's ideas but what Barfield himself thought—are his more general reflections, which he presented under the title *Autem* ('However'). There are 19 pages of notes, with *Autem* occupying a further 17.

In the *Autem*, Barfield makes three main general criticisms of the *Summa*. The first is that, in his opinion, too absolute a value is given to the distinctive aspect of the concepts of enjoyment and contemplation. His point is not that he thinks it is wrong to attach importance—even considerable importance—to the distinction between (perceptual) enjoyment of phenomena and (conceptual) contemplation of them, but '*having* seen this, it is of equal importance to realize that they cannot be separated. The sharp distinction between "concept" and "percept" seems to me to be the psychological aspect of the same thing...' It was an integral part of Barfield's monism to unite the duality inherent in Lewis's way of understanding the process of perception.[137]

His second criticism, which is more fundamental, is that 'the very *structure* of thought which is applied is inadequate, and necessarily inadequate, to the subject. This criticism applies more particularly to the first and more metaphysical part, between which and the second (practical and aesthetic) part I find serious discrepancies.' Barfield's problem is that the highly reductionist philosophical framework of the treatise does indeed have a bearing on the mineral world but is not applicable to the vegetable and animal worlds or to the human soul.

This brings Barfield to his third, and main, criticism, which he humorously writes under the name of Aloysius Bulver. For his major objection to the *Summa* is the relative absence of feeling in its scheme of things. Everything is viewed in terms of a duality between thinking and willing, between spirit and soul. Indeed, feeling is classed as egotism. But feeling is very important as being the bridge between the finite soul and the infinite spirit in me. He then goes on to describe the importance of polarity as a means of avoiding the contradictions inherent in an 'either-or' framework and thus of expressing the relation between the *three* basic principles. This would, he adds, enable the warmth implicit in the author's treatment of the virtue of charity to enter into the ideas expressed. Courage (cor-age) is thereby added to the Stoic virtue of fortitude.

> If we omit the element of feeling from our consideration the result is Part I of the *Summa*. We discover that we can only 'contemplate' another thing or being by ceasing to *be* it and conversely that we can never 'contemplate' what in the deepest sense we are (i.e. we can never 'know ourselves'). This sounds unimpeachable. And as *tendency* it is true. In actual fact there is a force which is overcoming this tendency at every moment. All human intercourse depends on the functioning in some slight degree of this force; for without it another soul would either be so detached from me as to be undistinguishable from a lifeless

object, or it would disappear into me altogether. This force is known as Love. Its whole nature is such that it enables me to become another soul *and yet* to remain separate, to go out into another being and yet remain within myself. Its whole function is to mediate between the One and the Many.

Because this force is at the core of all human conscious experience, it is impossible to speak of it. It is only possible to attempt to live it. For directly I speak of it, what I have spoken of is something other than pure love, and I seem to have desecrated the mysteries . . . When this force is so strong that it overcomes the separation-and-unity not only of two souls, but of a soul and other objects or beings, it is called inspiration. Inspiration : Love :: Imagination : Charity. It should be clear from the above that Inspiration is at the same time Love & Self-knowledge.

Setting this theme into the context of history, Barfield continues:

. . . What if Spirit were of such a nature that, as time passed, it became less and less *merely* enjoyed and more and more contemplated in the form of 'objects'?[138] What if it chose the moment in history at which this process had gone furthest, and when the destiny of the world was being tossed to and fro between the blind, undirected private wills of individual souls—if it chose this moment to allow itself to be simply contemplated as *One Man* while still continuing to be diversely enjoyed as many men? We may at least say this: that if such were the case, the One Man would have been 'conscious of being at home' in every environment, so that he would have called the multitude his mother and his brethren. And that his whole life would have been both history and myth, both an event in time and a symbol of the timeless. In an accurate biography of him the truth of fact and the truth of imagination would for once coincide.

The final section in the 'Great War' correspondence to be considered—and it was almost certainly the last to be written, probably in 1930—consists of Lewis's 15-page essay on morality, *De Bono et Malo* ('Good and Evil') and Barfield's reply, *De Toto et Parte* ('Whole and Part'). According to Professor Adey: 'In *De Bono et Malo* Lewis set out to refute Steiner's antinomian postulate of an "inner law-giver" by asserting his own Kantian ethic in which . . . duty took precedence over all other moral imperatives. As a counterblast, Barfield wrote his treatise *De Toto et Parte*, expounding an ethic of self-realization that he expected Lewis to dispute. After penning a rather acerbic page or two under the heading *Commentarium in De Toto et Parte*, Lewis lost interest . . .'

There is certainly something to be said for the idea that *De Bono et Malo*—and the same could in some ways be said of the *Summa*—was conceived as a kind of military onslaught rather than out of a wish to engage in dialogue. It is therefore understandable that, in the first section of his reply, Barfield should gently dismiss much of its content as peripheral to his own ideas and concerns. For that very reason it does not seem relevant for our present purposes to enter any further into what Lewis actually wrote in his essay. But it is important to note some of the points that Barfield made in *De Toto et Parte*, since after distancing himself from much of what Lewis wrote he went on to formulate some very interesting ideas of his own; and of course he was greatly in Lewis's debt for the spur to think out his own thoughts in a form that his friend would regard as logically sound.

Barfield's main problem with *De Bono et Malo* was that, because of Lewis's insistence (evident throughout the 'Great War') on placing an unbridgeable gulf between the human soul (as part) and the Absolute, or divine Spirit (as whole), he could not inwardly understand or acknowledge the system of the relation between part and whole as expounded in this treatise and also the *Summa*. Having stated his difficulty, he now proceeds to offer an alternative way of looking at such a relation, one where the whole is neither the quantitative aggregate of a number of parts (for example, the grains of sand in a heap) nor dependent, in its relation to the part, on factors of time and space. 'Can we,' he writes 'specify this relation more closely? It appears to me that we can. The relation between this kind of whole and its parts is such that *in some way* each part, taken separately, expresses or contains the whole.' Such a relation can be discerned in nature, in human physiology and in works of art. 'In a work of art we know that the whole must be present to, and active in, the artist's imagination at every moment of his work, while he is creating [even] the very smallest part. In so far as we feel this to have been the case, we say that a work of art has "*form*", and that he is a good artist.'

Barfield goes on to clarify the distinctiveness of his own conception of 'form' in this respect:

> The apprehension of form is intuitive. Consequently, if it is further asked, *in what way* in such cases the part contains the whole, little can be said. Negatively, however, it is clear that such a relation between part and whole is not merely *independent* of time and space, but that, just in

> so far as the parts are parts merely in time and space, it cannot exist. Time and space themselves can give no other relation than aggregation or succession. In so far, therefore, as they 'are' merely in time and space, the wholeness of the Ninth Symphony and the Last Supper differs in no respect from that of a heap of sand or so many ticks of a clock. Therefore the setting out in time and space is inessential, or rather opposed, to form. This is what we mean by speaking of the opposition between 'matter' and 'form', for 'matter' is our name for the wholeness given by mere aggregation and succession.[139] Thus progress in the aesthetic faculty consists in coming to see the creations of art less and less as matter and more and more as form.

Moreover, 'self-consciousness or integrity, as I know it (and in what other sense can I speak of it?) depends absolutely on an interplay between this being the Whole on the one hand and, on the other, being a part (together with other parts)'; whereas time and space '. . . are always threatening to disintegrate me, and all my integration consists in devices for escaping from my subjection to them'.

Barfield goes on to ask whether the Cosmos, or such a Whole as he can conceive, is indeed a whole of this nature, i.e. is 'the realization of form'. All that he can be sure about, he says, is 'that there is at least one part of it, of which it may be said that the Whole is the part . . . because I myself am that part'.

There then follow some Definitions and Notes on the Definitions. Twelve of these were outlined in general terms,[140] but Barfield wrote detailed notes on only six of them. The most important of his observations arise out of his definition of will as 'that which sunders part from whole and from other parts'. By the same token, it is also 'that which makes me a part', and is that faculty which is crucially the vehicle, within the whole, of the individual, or personal element. 'I must be a part, *in order to* be the Whole, or: it is my duty to be a part and my privilege to discover that I am the Whole. Ethically, such a discovery, as far as it goes, is *grace*; cognitively it is *revelation*. All genuine art is revelation and all genuine religion the result of it.' Moreover, 'by sundering part from Whole, will makes possible the realization of form.'

To conclude this section on *De Toto et Parte*, and, with it, the 'Great War', I shall quote the concluding portion of Barfield's notes on the definition of Form—'the central point of my system'—which he formulates as 'the whole being a part', that the Whole is each of its parts—a definition which he describes as 'axiomatic'. This conclusion sums up the core of what he is driving at in this essay and makes the metaphysical context out of which he is writing clearly evident:

> Form, which preserves unity, is the opposite of will, which produces multiplicity. Both are indemonstrable. Will constitutes one pole and Form the other of that invisible axis round which the whole cosmos, and in particular the little universe of discourse, revolves.
>
> Ethically and theologically, Form is the everlasting mercy and forgiveness of God. However sundered, however 'party', I become, He still is and I am still in Him. If I ascend into Heaven, He is there, and if I go down to Hell, He is there also. He is with me always, even unto the end of the world.'

* * *

It should not be forgotten that while this intense intellectual and spiritual drama was taking place outward life between the two friends continued much as normal. A typical feature of their friendship was their walking tours, of which Barfield and Cecil Harwood would appear to have been the chief originators. Whenever they saw the possibility, Lewis and Barfield, together with some other regular participants such as Harwood, Leo Baker and Walter Field (Tolkien also sometimes joined the party), would set off for the weekend to some rural part of (usually) southern England to enjoy a good walk and the delights of traditional English hostelries. The essential quality of these occasions seems to have been good humour, as is amply reflected in *A Cretaceous Perambulator.*[141] In this memoir, which is largely composed of the Examination Papers that Lewis was apparently set as a good-humoured joke in 1936 by Barfield and Harwood,[142] there are, for example, references to expeditions in April 1927, April 1928 and April 1930.

According to Barfield[143] between around 1930 and Lewis's death in 1963 they met up with one another at the most around half a dozen times a year, exchanging notes or letters approximately once a month. Some of the meetings would have included the Friday evening gatherings of the Inklings in Oxford, when something of their former intellectual camaderie would have been able to shine forth. A further strand in their on-going relationship arose from the fact that, once he joined his father's firm of solicitors in or around 1930, Barfield became Lewis's solicitor, a task that is reflected with uproarious humour in 'The Things That Are Caesar's', a chapter in Barfield's book *This Ever Diverse Pair* (1950) that deals with the legal affairs of a highly successful, but somewhat unworldly author called Ramsden, who is a fictional portrait of Lewis. A further humorous literary relic of the legal aspect of their relationship is *Mark vs. Tristram,*[144] a correspondence between Lewis and Barfield couched in the guise of an exchange of letters between two legal firms.[145]

A study of Lewis's many letters to Barfield reveals for the most part their good-humoured friendship and his warm responses to Barfield's publications and other writings that he sent for comment. Thus the earliest of Lewis's letters to be preserved is one dated 24 January 1926, when he had just received a copy of *History in English Words*. While expressing disagreement with Barfield's account of Plato and Aristotle, Lewis's main response was wholly positive: 'I found it all interesting and enjoyable. I was nowhere inclined to skip, or anxious to get to the next chapter. In other words it fulfils the first elementary condition of a good book: the basis without which higher merits are of no avail. It is completely and certainly *readable*.' In an undated letter, probably from 1928, he writes that he has just acquired *Poetic Diction*, which of course he had already read in draft form. After describing his amusement at an uncomprehending reviewer's perplexity and his (vain) efforts to persuade a colleague or friend to borrow the book, he states: 'I think in general that I am going to agree with the whole book more than we thought I did.' On 21 October 1929 he writes the second of two approving letters about Barfield's long novel 'English People',[146] shortly followed by another letter giving a much higher opinion about some passages that he had had difficulty with. A letter from 1930 expresses Lewis's delight that Barfield has had something accepted by Eliot's *New Criterion*: 'Thank God you've got your foot into the New Criterion. Let them have five rounds rapid of sense . . .' In another letter probably dating from 1930, he relates that Tolkien, when dining with him, had said that 'your conception of the ancient semantic unity had modified his whole outlook and that he was always just going to say something in a lecture when your conception stopped him in time. "It is one of those things," he said, "that when you've once seen it there are all sorts of things you can never say again." '[147] Equally appreciative is his letter of 28 June 1936, relaying glowing praise of *The Silver Trumpet* (Barfield's children's story first published in 1925) from the Tolkien household:

> I lent the *Silver Trumpet* to Tolkien and hear that it is the greatest success among his children that they have ever known. His own fairy-tales, which are excellent, have now no market; and its first reading—children are so practical!—led to a universal wail 'You're *not* going to give

> it back to Mr. Lewis, are you?' All the things the wiseacres on child psychology in our circle said when you wrote it turn out to be nonsense. 'They liked the sad parts,' said Tolkien, 'because they were sad and the puzzling parts because they were puzzling, as children always do.' The youngest boy liked Gamboy best because 'she was clever and the bad people in books usually aren't'. The tags of the Podger have become so popular a[s] to be almost a nuisance in the house. In fine, you have scored a direct hit.

At the end of his letter of 2 June 1940, where Lewis offers Barfield his condolences for the loss of his mother, he writes: 'Blessings on you for everything in our common life these twenty years'. On his receipt of *Saving the Appearances*, he writes to express his warmest congratulations:

> My dear Owen [he used Barfield's Christian name for the first time in a letter dated All Saints Day 1949],
> The book is a stunner. It swept me out of myself at a time when I needed nothing more & expected nothing less. Like Hardie says it is 'exciting'.

Finally, in a hand that betrayed his growing physical incapacity, he wrote on 29 March 1962 to tell Barfield what he thought about *Worlds Apart*. This was the last letter that he wrote to Barfield.

> My dear Owen,
> I have read *Worlds Apart*. My trouble is that I can't help reading it far too quickly. I must presently tackle it again and less greedily. Your language sometimes disgruntles me. Why must it be *polyvalence* instead of *multivalence*? And why do you use *base* as an intransitive verb—'he bases on' meaning 'he bases his argument on' or 'starts from'? Yes—I wondered whether I were any relation to Hunter.[148] Ranger is an attractive boy.
> Yours, Jack.

I have quoted these remarks at some length to give some context to the legacy of the 'Great War' which *did* spill over into this latter half of Lewis's life. Let us now look at these remnants more or less in chronological order, beginning with testimonies from Lewis.

The first of these is a Sonnet, written from his father's home, Little Lea, Belfast, probably in 1929 (or possibly 1930). It is important to include this for its status as the most intimate and tender record of Lewis's emotional opposition at that time to Barfield's spiritual path, an opposition which he tempered or counterbalanced to some extent in a letter from the mid-1940s which will be quoted from below.

> *Fidelia Vulnera Amantis*
> Two wings upbear the eternal Shadow's flight;
> One whirrs us into sleep, the other wakes,
> One steals with downy theft, one heavily breaks
> Our hearts. And *False Security* the right
> Is called; but the sinister *Gloating Fright*,
> Which evil first for power, then power mistakes
> For greatness, and in shuddering worship slakes
> Masochist thirst at the fat dugs of night.
>
> How often I have been the fool of the first,
> Strutting heroics where the true brave durst
> No battle, you well know. Let it not stand
> For insolence if I too show the curs'd
> Black-vaulted wave behind you, ripe to burst;
> For faithful are the wounds of a friend's hand.[149]

A further reference to the 'Great War' comes in the same letter (28 June 1936) that contains the tidings of the reception of *The Silver Trumpet* by the Tolkien children:

> I wish I could Christianize the *Summa* for you—but I dunno, I dunno! When a truth has ceased to be a mistress for pleasure and become a wife for fruit it is almost unnatural to go back to the dialectic ardours of the wooing. There may come a moment—one of those recoveries of virginity, or to speak more suitably to the subject, one of those N.th deaths, and then I'll try . . .

The next memory of the 'Great War' to echo from Lewis's hand is a somewhat mysterious—mysterious in that there is neither explanation nor apparent antecedent for it in the correspondence—document dating from 1944 or 1945 (or, from internal evidence, possibly from as early as 1940) about anthroposophy or at any rate about those professing themselves students of it. There is no dedication to the letter, which may suggest that it was written for some specific purpose:

> Though I reject (in so far as I understand them) the philosophy and theology of Dr. Rudolf Steiner and the anthroposophical movement, I have been intimately acquainted with some who adhere to it for over seventeen years. One of them [Barfield] is the man of all my

> acquaintance whose character both moral and intellectual I should put highest, or very nearly so. Another [Cecil Harwood] has written a work on education called *The Way of a Child* which seems to me full of good sense. Another (perhaps the most enthusiastic anthroposophist of the three) [Daphne Harwood] has continued throughout the time of our acquaintance to be an excellent mother to five children . . . Believing the doctrines of Dr. Steiner to be erroneous (though not more so than many philosophers who are more widely influential than he in modern England) and being frequently engaged in controversy with my anthroposophical friends on this subject, I believe I should have been very quick to notice any evidence that adherence to the system was producing either intellectual or moral deterioration. Of such evidence I have found not a shred. The friends of whom I speak are all highly educated people and I have not found anything to diminish my respect either for their characters or their capacities. I should perhaps add that the works of Dr. Steiner are extremely difficult reading: unassisted popular opinion of them is likely to be no more reliable than the same opinion on Kant or Whitehead.[150]

Lewis's last written reference to the 'Great War' is contained in a letter dated 23 June 1949 marking Barfield's baptism into the Church of England:

> I am humbled (I think that is the right word) by your news. I wish I could be with you. Welcome and welcome and welcome. No, of course it won't mean the end of the 'Great War' . . .

As none of Barfield's personal records of his relationship to Lewis after the 'Great War' have survived (though there is one exception), we are largely dependent for the insight into how he experienced his friend in his post-conversion years upon one lecture which he gave to the Oxford C.S. Lewis Society on 19 November 1985.[151] In this lecture he not only shared reminiscences about Lewis from one point of view or another but spoke explicitly about how he himself experienced the aftermath of the 'Great War'. First he confirms that, 'after Lewis's conversion, we rarely touched on philosophy or metaphysics in our exchanges and, I think I can say, never did we touch at any length on theology. What we did do was just enjoy ourselves.' But this was not a matter of indifference to him: 'I confess that I felt a certain amount of distress when I perceived that we never could have any sort of philosophic/metaphysical interchange of the old kind, because I felt it might have been fruitful. I had the feeling sometimes, when we were enjoying ourselves, *C'est magnifique mais ce n'est pas la guerre.*' This leads Barfield to speak about one particular incident which he had never shared with anyone before. It happened during a mini walking tour (i.e. the one night or one weekend variety) late in the year, when he and Lewis were alone together. He remembers that they were staying the night at Wallingford.

'It was shortly after his conversion [September 1931]. Just before we went to bed, I tried, you might say, to go on from where we had left off. What I wanted to do was to see what relation there was between his "stance" after his conversion and the kind of opinions he had before it, and also to see how far we were still in accord. As soon as the conversation took that direction, he broke it off sharply. I don't think I ever heard him speak with such emotion. He simply refused to talk at that sort of depth at all. I remember his saying, and again with more emotion than I ever heard him express: "I can't bear it!" And I do remember also feeling deeply distressed—indeed agitated—on that occasion. He went off to bed, and I went out (it was after dark) for a walk, like Prospero "to still my breaking mind". I had the feeling something was broken.'

The only surviving document in Barfield's hand that gives any insight as to his considered opinion about Lewis's refusal to enter into any further discussion about the matters which continued to be so central for Barfield's life, and which, for Lewis, were the occasion for the 'Great War', was originally written in Greek—in conscious imitation of the beginning of St John's Gospel—probably between 1941 and 1946. In August 1969 Barfield added a note to the manuscript: 'I don't think I ever showed it to him, though I felt a strong impulse to do so. If I did, then he paid scant attention to it; if I didn't, it was because I was afraid of his paying scant attention to it.'

C.S.L.

Biographia Theologica[152]

Behold, there was a certain philosopher!
And the philosopher knew himself that he is one.
And the Word, having become in the philosopher, was one God.
And the Word was the light of his philosophy.
And the Light was shining in his philosophy,
And the philosopher knew it not.
The Light was in the philosopher,
And his philosophy came into being through the Light,

And the philosopher knew it not.
The philosopher said that no one
Under any circumstance could ever behold that Light.
And when he had beheld that Light, the philosopher insisted
That its name was LORD.
And his philosophy bore witness about the Light,
That it is the Word and the life of mankind,
And about the philosopher,
That he was not born of the flesh,
Nor of the will of the flesh,
Nor of the will of man,
Nor through a command of the Lord,
But of God.
And the philosopher did not receive the witness.

⋆ ⋆ ⋆

After Lewis's death, Barfield often had occasion to look back upon his relationship with him and especially the difference between his outlook and his own. Quite apart from the more emotional, personal aspect which has been considered in the previous section, there were certain respects in which, as he wrote in his essay 'C.S. Lewis and Historicism' (1975), he still sometimes found himself 'mentally arguing epistemology' with him after his death, a practice which, as already indicated, ceased to feature in their earthly friendship after the end of the 'Great War'. There was also, of course, much that he and Lewis had in common as regards their points of view, and when he was asked in later life to speak about Lewis (as he frequently was) he would always do his best to emphasize the areas where they were in agreement. Nevertheless, he indicated that, for all the positive comments that Lewis made about his books, his friends and also himself, there were certain areas where he simply could not agree with Barfield, notably those of historicism or evolution, in particular where it concerned an evolution of consciousness, the function of imagination as a means of acquiring true insight into the nature of reality, and Christian doctrine. However, the fundamental barrier in the case of all these areas to Lewis's willingness to take seriously what Barfield had to say was that he could not accept the concept of polarity, as defined by Coleridge, as a living reality in his own mind.

This crucial concept, this underlying barrier between not only Lewis but the other so-called Romantic theologians and mythmakers and himself, is the subject of Barfield's 'Either: Or. Coleridge, Lewis and

Romantic Theology'.[153] Barfield begins by quoting Coleridge's definition of imagination and fancy with which the latter concluded the famous Chapter XIII of the *Biographia Literaria*, and then indicates that his intention is not so much to speak about this but about the definition of polarity with which Coleridge began this chapter. In conscious imitation of Descartes' dictum 'Give me matter and motion and I will construct you the universe', Coleridge substitutes 'two contrary forces, the one of which tends to expand infinitely, while the other strives to apprehend or *find* itself in this infinity'. In Barfield's words, 'he adds that the two forces are forces "of one power", that they "counteract" each other, and that they are "both alike infinite and both alike indestructible"'. Barfield emphasizes that unlike Descartes' matter and motion, which 'are phenomena', Coleridge's polar forces, being operative (in Coleridge's words) both 'in the living principle and in the process of our self-consciousness', are 'prephenomenal', that is, they not only 'underlie the phenomenal world and constitute its ultimate being' but 'are also to be found "in the process of our own self-consciousness"'. It will be readily seen that in the concept of polarity as developed by Coleridge there lies the key to overcoming the sense of 'outness' which we so readily feel with regard to the world of phenomena, or in other words, the Cartesian dichotomy between matter and mind, which—as Barfield indicates—'Coleridge expressly repudiated'. Barfield goes on to make the contention 'that the apprehension of polarity is *the* basic act of imagination, that it is the fundament of imaginative thinking, in the same way that the apprehension of identity is the fundament of discursive thought...' He then further clarifies this essential thought: 'In short, where logical contradictories, like solid objects in space, *exclude* one another, polar opposities *contain*, and, in doing so, enhance, one another. Moreover, this mode of duality—concrete in place of abstract—is always at the same time a trinity. A "paradox" is a bare, logical abstraction; but the "tension" between two concrete and energetic opposities is a process and, as such, is itself a third reality. For nature, indeed, it is the paramount reality, because it is this process of energetic interpenetration that underlies the sense world as a whole.' He proceeds to draw out some of the implications that Coleridge discerned in this conception of polarity not only for philosophy but also science, political theory and of course theology. There are also, he adds, some very considerable implications for everyday human experience, for without this 'imagination' of tri-unity it is not really possible to make sense of the dilemma which self-consciousness brings, the experience that I am either separate from everything else (with all that this implies) or else my sense of separateness—and hence my awareness of myself as an individual—is an illusion.

Barfield now goes on to focus on this experience, or dilemma, of self-consciousness. There are, he says, three contexts in which the individual self experiences this sense of separation: with regard to nature; in connection with one's fellow human beings; and in one's relationship to the divine creator or ground of one's being. He regards the Romantic poets such as Coleridge as being primarily concerned with the first of these realms, citing in particular the words from Coleridge's *Ode to Dejection*, where the poet refers to 'joy' as a word expressing a sense of oneness with nature:

> Joy, Lady! is the spirit and the power,
> Which, wedding Nature to us, gives in dower
> A new Earth and new Heaven . . .

Barfield then takes up the connection which Professor John Lawlor made in his essay '"Rasselas", Romanticism and the Nature of Happiness'[154] between this joy celebrated by Coleridge and 'the "joy" that is so essential an ingredient in the Christian philosophy of that little group of English writers who are sometimes referred to as "Romantic Theologians" or the Oxford Inklings, and especially of their best-known representative, C.S. Lewis'.[155] This is of course a reference to that joy which, in *Surprised by Joy* (1932), Lewis describes as, in Barfield's words, a 'longing for a "paradisal" reunion with the Absolute, or with the spirit informing the life of both man and nature'. Barfield now goes on to describe how Lewis, in particular, resolved this dilemma: 'The solution of the irreconcilable antagonism implicit in this longing . . .—or (to put it another way) the right way to "handle" a desire by its nature unattainable—lies (so Lewis gradually discovered for himself) in taking a further step. The further step consists in discovering for oneself that the very presence of the desire is its own fulfilment; that "what we really wanted" all the time was, not any one of the many successive objects to which the desire deludes us by appearing to point, but the desire itself, or an essential *quality* in it . . . It is only when we experience that indefinable quality, as and for itself, that we experience what Lewis called "joy".'

Coming, finally, to unravelling the meaning inherent in his essay's title, Barfield declares that this Romantic theological way of dealing with the 'Romantic' experience of 'irreconcilable opposition between man at one with nature and man cut off from nature' can be seen as an *either:or* counterpart to the approach popularized by T.S. Eliot and formulated in his critical theory of the 'dissociation of sensibility', which 'consists in placing the two opposites side by side, treating them as contradictories, and contemplating the result with ironical detachment'. However, there are, he says, any number of different aspects of *either:orness*, all of which can be traced back to the Cartesian matter:mind dichotomy.

We find them most all-embracingly in the realm of human social relationships, whether it be in the domain of psychiatry, where—in R.D. Laing's words—'there is the antithesis between complete loss of being by absorption into the other person (engulfment) and complete aloneness (isolation)',[156] or the sociology of mass communication, where whole theories are built up on the basis of careful investigation but also on the assumption that the antithesis between 'isolation' and 'engulfment' is irreconcilable. And the greatest tragedy of all is that, unless the Coleridgean concept of polarity has been very clearly grasped, the most insightful and noble of new ideas or impulses will be presented as an alternative (i.e. an *either:or*) to the existing state of affairs and will therefore fail to break the spell of this conundrum. Thus when we encounter a fellow human being, 'we must recognize that he is not merely an object, but also a subject like ourselves. And this we can really only do by repeating the divine act of [what Coleridge calls] "separative projection", which in human beings is imagination. This we can only do by "a repetition in the finite mind of the eternal act of creation". Thus, the further step from primary to secondary imagination is, to say the least of it, not *less* important here in the making of poetry. For it is only so that we can come to acknowledge, not merely another person, but an autonomous independent spirit of equal status and equal value with ourselves. Moral imagination is the dialectic, or the polarity, of love . . .'

If I may seem to be spelling this out somewhat, it is because the point that Barfield was trying to make was so inordinately important for him, and—even though this is of course a much abbreviated summary of what Barfield says—the reader needs to be at least adequately prepared for the way that he brought his train of thought to a conclusion. For this conclusion, to my mind, represents his clearest statement about where he and Lewis ultimately diverged.

Barfield indicates that any thinker whom he will really describe as 'contemporary' must be one 'who has not merely caught up with Coleridge in this matter of the two forces, but gone beyond him . . .

> [He] will be the one who has found that [even the] antithesis [between *either:or* and 'a silent world of "primordial discourse" '] is bridgeable,

that this major pair of irreconcilables is in fact reconcilable if we are prepared to pursue further, with the imagination-based thinking that alone is capable of grasping them, those two prephenomenal forces, and the relation between them, to which Coleridge pointed again and again, and whose productive operations he had at least begun to study in *detail*, alike in his philosophy of nature and in his philosophy of man... What will matter is that he should have a mind capable of familiarizing itself, and of working, with them; and then of communicating the results of his work in intelligible language. It is because I have found that capacity in Rudolf Steiner, and because I have not so far found it elsewhere, that I am bound to regard his as the one fundamentally 'contemporary' mind that the first two-thirds of the twentieth century has produced.

I have sometimes wondered whether it might have been otherwise in England if, for example, the Romantic Theologians, the Inklings, such as C.S. Lewis, or some of them, had chosen to explore the path Coleridge opened up for the English-speaking world; if they had sought a reconciliation between reason and imagination, not only in the religious, or semireligious, experience of 'joy' as 'the dialectic of Desire', but also by penetrating inward to the point at which logic itself becomes 'polar logic' and the two are actually one. I have wondered if Lewis might have been led to mitigate his occasionally Talmudic emphasis on the divine transcendence, and if Charles Williams's brilliantly mystical doctrine of 'co-inherence' might have gained something in depth and his account of the Descent of the Dove have lost something of tautness, something a little strained, if either of them had pondered the mystery of 'separative projection' as it is expounded in the *Theory of Life*, the *Essay on Faith*, and elsewhere sporadically throughout Coleridge's writings.

This essay of Barfield's illuminates and gives credence to all the many statements that he makes in the essays, lectures and interviews assembled in *Owen Barfield on C.S. Lewis* regarding Lewis's opposition to his ideas in the three main areas referred to above (see p. 176). However, it will be as well briefly to consider each of these in turn. Thus in his essay 'C.S. Lewis and Historicism',[157] Barfield states that Lewis 'emphatically denied any recognizable, certainly any *significant*, evolution or development of consciousness in the course of human history'. Moreover, after carefully considering the contrasting statements on this theme in certain of Lewis's writings (specifically in his essay on 'Historicism' and his Preface to D.E.

Harding's book *The Hierarchy of Heaven and Earth: A New Diagram of Man in the Universe*, 1952), he concludes: 'My abiding impression is that the very notion of *development* of any sort was somehow alien to Lewis's mind'. And even though he seemed at times to allow the possibility for some notion of development in the mind of God, he remained adamant in his denial that 'men can discover an inner meaning in their history by the use of their "natural powers" ' or, indeed, gain any real understanding of what former ages of human history were like.

As regards the function of the imagination as a means of gaining knowledge of the nature of reality, Lewis consistently believed that there is a wall separating the world of imagination from that of objective truth. In his lecture 'Lewis, Truth and Imagination',[158] Barfield spoke of the dichotomy between two distinct Lewises (there were also other Lewises, but these by and large could be seen as merging with one of the two dominant ones): a combatively logical, rational Lewis, and a gently imaginative Lewis. Barfield states that Lewis's concept of imagination had no or little relation to his concept of truth; and he also confirms that, after the 'Great War', he 'was disinclined to give any attention' to the question as to whether the imagination can be 'a vehicle of revelation', a means 'through which the world around us may acquire, or recover, its true nature as a theophany', or should merely be regarded as 'among many permissible recreations for creaturely minds'. Barfield put this thought in slightly simpler words when speaking with Clifford Monks: 'That's what the Great War is about, whether imagination is a vehicle for truth or whether it is simply a highly desirable and pleasurable experience of the human soul.' Similarly, in 'Reflections on "The Great Divorce" '.[159] Barfield recalls that 'Lewis had practically no use for theories about myth and very definite ideas about its relations to anything that could be called belief or knowledge. He held, in short, that there was no relation at all, or certainly no discoverable one ... Knowledge, or belief about matters of fact was one thing; myth and all it stands for, another ... However it might be in heaven, for man on earth to search for any link between myth and fact was for him a crucial error.'[160]

In both 'Lewis, Truth and Imagination' and in the 'Conversation between Owen Barfield and Clifford Monks' (1984), Barfield gives a further clue as to what lay behind Lewis's determination to keep imagination separate from daily reality. In the first place, as Barfield told Clifford Monks, Lewis 'accepted the conventionally scientific basis of knowledge and that all real knowledge depended on scientific evidence drawn from sense experience. [He] would not admit that the kind of experience that came through imagination had anything to do with knowledge of reality...' But his wish to deny imagination this role was not because he did not value it. In both the contexts referred to, Barfield indicated that Lewis was in love with the imagination rather as a medieval knight wooed his lady and put it on a pedestal, wishing thereby to protect it from the harsh world of reality, to insulate it from having anything to do with fact. 'He was in love with [the imagination] ... but I wanted to marry it.'[161]

As for the third area of disagreement, that of Christian doctrine, the main point to bear in mind is that Lewis's God was transcendent and not immanent. In this sense, there is something to be said for the idea that, whereas Barfield's God, as God the Son, did indeed come down from heaven and die on the cross, Lewis's God the Father Deity remained firmly in the heavenly worlds. Thus on the one hand, Lewis abhorred what he saw as Barfield's tendency towards a deification of man, and on the other hand Barfield referred to Lewis's Christianity as 'devotional reductionism'. The relationship between man and God was not, for Lewis, an evolving one, i.e. from subjection and obedience to cooperation and freedom (the latter pair of which concepts corresponded to Barfield's view). In this connection, Barfield recalled the sentence that Lewis quoted: 'I was not born to be free; I was born to adore and obey.' By the same token Lewis held that one could have a religious belief but not religious knowledge. It was consistent with his religious views that Lewis welcomed hierarchy in the social sense. Finally—and this links onto the evolution of consciousness theme—Lewis, who always emphasized the chasm between Creator and creature, held that revelation has occurred once and for all in the past and is finished.[162]

* * *

In thus endeavouring to reflect Barfield's considered thoughts about his differences with C.S. Lewis and, indeed, the Inklings as a group (in so far as they are a group), I am very conscious that I am—from one point of view—undermining the main connections that link him to the wider world of academic and, to some extent, popular discourse. After all, the average man in the street—whether in Britain or America—has not heard of Owen Barfield; but if one says that he was a friend of C.S. Lewis and an occasional member of an intellectual circle that included not only Lewis but also Tolkien, one's preoccupation with Barfield is more than likely to meet with a nod of recognition. It is somewhat similar in the academic world. Apart from a few scattered professors and other academics here and there who have an expertise in Barfield studies or have respect for his writings, the only university campus where Barfield can be said to have a home is that of Wheaton College, Illinois, where at the Wade Center manuscripts associated not only with Barfield but also G.K. Chesterton, Lewis, George MacDonald, Dorothy Sayers, Tolkien and Charles Williams are housed and an annual journal, *Seven* (or more usually *VII*), produced to further the study of these seven British authors. To my knowledge there is no Barfield Society anywhere in the world, although there are one or two study groups or training centres within the Anthroposophical Society in America that bear his name (they are not set up necessarily to study or in any way directly further his own work). And yet it is no good trying to hide the fact that Owen Barfield sits uncomfortably within a university campus where the Billy Graham Center has its home and where C.S. Lewis's 'devotional reductionism' appears to meet many people's spiritual needs (it is not without significance that Barfield has the most tenuous connection of all the seven authors referred to with the university bookshop). Nor is it possible to pretend that Barfield has more than a very indirect link with the quarterly journal *Mythlore*, which is probably the main vehicle for furthering the work of Tolkien, Charles Williams and the Lewis of the Narnia stories. For the most part, Barfield retains this tenuous connection with modern Christian mythmakers because of his connections with Lewis and also because he had a certain influence on Tolkien,[163] though the extent of this is open to question. In this respect it is important to note that Barfield, who never found Tolkien to be very approachable as a person, did not like *The Lord of the Rings* (published 1954–5), although he enjoyed and admired *The Hobbit* (written for the most part in the early 1930s and published in 1937) no less than Tolkien appreciated *Poetic Diction*.

So I think it is only fair to my readers, especially those who are reading this book in the way that it was written and in the order that its chapters were intended to be read, to say very clearly at this point that here is the parting of the ways. Those whose interest in Barfield and patience with the present volume have been sustained solely by their enthusiasm for the works of his better-known friends and contemporaries or by a largely academic fascination for his ideas on language are now invited to forsake the well-chartered territory of the Lewis of *Narnia*, the Tolkien of *The Lord of the Rings*, the Charles Williams of *The Descent of the Dove* and so on, in order to make the acquaintance of one for whom crossings of thresholds, journeys into other worlds, encounters with spiritual beings and changing forms of consciousness were not part of the apparatus of an imagined world, in the ordinary sense, but something accessible to serious investigation.[164] For those who wish to follow further this quest to understand the core of Barfield's thought, this is the appropriate point to consider his relationship to Rudolf Steiner, whom he regarded as his mentor and spiritual teacher. It is not really possible to understand Barfield's principal writings of the period under consideration without a genuinely open-minded study of at least the rudiments of Steiner's thought. The chapter that follows will therefore endeavour to serve this aim.

Lest what I wrote at the beginning of this concluding section be misunderstood, I should make it clear that it is my own conviction that a further study of Owen Barfield's work such as is now proposed in the remaining part of this book can illumine and strengthen Barfield's connection with not only the work of those writers with whom he has hitherto been associated but also the wider intellectual and spiritual milieu of his, and our, time.

10. *OWEN BARFIELD AND RUDOLF STEINER*

Barfield has not left us any authoritative written record of the nature and timing of his first encounters with the work of the founder of anthroposophy. However, the general outlines are clear enough from his recollections summarized in the Biographical Sketch (see pp. 11–46), which draws partly on conversations with the author (1994–7) and partly on a section entitled 'Youth' that he contributed to an obituary of Cecil Harwood.[165] Thanks to the detective work of Astrid Diener in the doctorate thesis mentioned in the previous chapter (see Note 126), it is possible to be somewhat clearer—albeit tentatively so—about some of the dates. Thus although Daphne Olivier (Harwood), who joined Barfield and Harwood in touring Cornish towns and villages with an amateur concert party organized by the English Folk Dance Society in both 1922 and 1923, had apparently heard Steiner lecture at Oxford in August 1922,[166] there is no evidence to suggest that Barfield's (or Harwood's) interest in Steiner was kindled before 1923. As Dr Diener records, the first definite date by which Barfield may be said to have made a commitment to anthroposophy is 7 July 1923, when Lewis recorded as much in his Diary (see previous chapter, p. 157). Diener also cites a confirmation by Maria Barguirdjian, Membership Secretary of the Anthroposophical Society in Great Britain, that Owen Barfield joined this society in 1924.[167]

It is also important to bear in mind that this period in the early 1920s was the time when Barfield was developing the ideas—based on his own research into language, inspired in particular by Romantic poetry—which were to find expression in *History in English Words* (1926) and *Poetic Diction* (1928), and that the two processes of his own research and his interest in anthroposophy continued on parallel paths for some while before they ultimately fused. Barfield has described this at some length in his lecture 'Owen Barfield and the Origin of Language' (given at Rudolf Steiner House on 21 June 1977) and more succinctly in his interview with Astrid Diener:

> The essence of Steiner's teachings ... is the evolution of human consciousness ... I, in a way, came to the same conclusion on my own before I heard of Steiner, but in terms of language and of nature. In

effect, you could say that I came to the conclusion that human beings in earlier stages of evolution had what you might call a pictorial consciousness. Steiner, of course, taught that too. He called it sometimes 'atavistic clairvoyance'. It was rather curious that I was taken by his whole metaphysic, but for a long time they were more or less parallel—his thought of 'atavistic clairvoyance' and mine of 'original participation', as I called it later. And I didn't connect them. I remember, quite late, as I'd been reading Steiner off and on for a year or two, suddenly saying to myself, this 'atavistic clairvoyance' he is talking about is what I am talking about. For a long time they went on side by side.[168]

But who was Rudolf Steiner? What was the nature of the ideas with which Barfield came to find so deep a relationship? And in what way did Barfield express his own debt to Steiner?[169]

According to his own testimony in his autobiography,[170] Steiner was born to Austrian parents on 27 February 1861 at Kraljevec, in what was then Hungary and is now in Slovenia. His father worked as a telegraphist on Austria's Southern Railway, and when Steiner was about 18 months old the family moved considerably closer to Vienna. Thereafter Steiner grew up amidst beautiful natural landscapes, linked by the railway beside which the family lived at one time to modern technocratic civilization. This polarity between nature and technology was one from which he derived great stimulus, for although he deeply appreciated the healing qualities of unspoilt nature he also felt the attraction of what the railway represented in its time. Significantly, his family's strong traditional roots were balanced by his father's convictions as a 'free-thinker' with no interest in the church.

These outward polarities were reflected also in Steiner's inner development as a boy and youth. From as long as he could remember he had clairvoyant faculties which left him in no doubt of the existence of a spiritual world 'behind' and 'above' the world of the senses. And yet he was wholly committed to trying to translate this awareness into terms acceptable to the modern analytical mind. To this eight-year-old boy struggling with the dilemma of how to relate his spiritual experiences to the physical world of which he was also so palpably a member, the discovery of a geometry book through the assistant schoolmaster at Neudörfl was like manna to his soul:

> I tackled it with enthusiasm. For weeks my mind was full of congruence, the similarity of triangles, quadrangles, polygons; I racked my brains over the problem of where the parallel lines really meet;

> Pythagoras' theorem fascinated me. To be able to grasp something purely in my mind brought me inner happiness, I know that it was in the study of geometry that I first found happiness . . . As a child I felt, without of course expressing it to myself clearly, that knowledge of the spiritual world is something to be grasped in the mind in the same way as geometrical concepts. For I was as certain of the reality of the spiritual world as of the physical world. But I needed in some way to justify this assumption. I needed to be able to tell myself that experience of the spiritual world is no more an illusion than knowledge of the physical world. I told myself that geometry was something that only the mind by the exercise of its own powers could grasp; this feeling was my justification for speaking of the spiritual world that I experienced in the same way as I did of the physical world. And that was how I spoke of it. These were two concepts which, though vague, had already become an important part of my mental life before I was eight years old. I distinguished things and essences 'that one saw' from those that 'one did not see'.[171]

In the second chapter of his autobiography, Steiner describes how these initial attempts to form a bridge between his inner experiences and the physical world around him were extended to the study of philosophy. When he was 14, he acquired a copy of Kant's *Critique of Pure Reason*, which he read avidly during his history lessons (the history teacher appeared to be lecturing but was actually reading from a book, which Steiner found an insufferable way of being taught anything). Although—because of his father's wish that he become an engineer—he went on to specialize in mathematics and science at the Vienna Polytechnic (Technische Hochschule), he also read widely in the great philosophers of German idealism such as Fichte, Hegel and Schelling (especially the first of these). Referring to this student period of his life, he describes his struggle to make philosophical sense of his own experiences:

> My preoccupation with the concepts of natural science had led me finally to a position in which I saw the activity of the human ego as the only possible point from which to advance towards true knowledge. I put it to myself that when the ego is in action and contemplates its own activity, then a spiritual entity is directly present in the consciousness . . . Before, I had cudgelled my brains in an attempt to find concepts for natural phenomena and on the basis of them to develop a concept for the ego. I now proposed to reverse this procedure and, starting from the ego, to penetrate into the workings of nature. At that time I saw

> spirit and nature as two quite distinct opposites. For me, a world of spiritual entities existed. It was by direct perception that I was aware that the ego, itself spirit, exists in a spiritual world. But there was no place for nature in the spiritual world of my experience.[172]

Steiner's path towards resolving his highly unusual dilemma lay through an invitation that he received when he was 21 to join a group of scholars working on an edition of Goethe's works in the *Deutsche Nationalliteratur*, an authoritative edition of German literature in process of publication at the time. The invitation came as a result of a recommendation by Steiner's German literature teacher at the Vienna Polytechnic, Karl Julius Schröer, who was a leading Goethe scholar. Steiner's task was to edit Goethe's scientific writings. Goethe—whom Steiner described in his introduction as 'the Copernicus and the Kepler of the organic world'—had developed a way of studying nature to which Steiner could relate with complete sympathy, since, in contrast to the generally accepted tenet of scientific 'objectivity', it involved building centrally upon the individual ego's direct *experience* of the natural world as a living reality. This editorial task stretched over several years, its fruits being published between 1884 and 1897. In the meantime, however, Steiner developed Goethe's work in a way that the latter was never able to do; he wrote an introductory book, *Grundlinien einer Erkenntnistheorie der Goetheschen Weltanschauung* (A Theory of Knowledge Implicit in Goethe's World Conception, 1886), and then, prefaced by his doctoral thesis *Wahrheit und Wissenschaft* (Truth and Science,[173] 1891), his own chief philosophical work, *Die Philosophie der Freiheit* (The Philosophy of Freedom, sometimes translated as The Philosophy of Spiritual Activity, 1894).

Before characterizing the essential content of this latter book, which Steiner regarded not only as fundamental to the whole of his subsequent work but also as the book whose influence would outlast all his other books and lectures, it will be helpful to indicate in a few words how Steiner himself understood the relationship of the German philosophical tradition in which he had grown up, and where he found a certain resonance for his own experience of the world, with that of England. This will also make it a little easier to appreciate the difficulties that Barfield, with his recently acquired enthusiasm for Steiner's philosophical ideas, had in building a bridge of common understanding with Lewis, who—as Astrid Diener has clearly demonstrated in her doctoral thesis[174]—reflected faithfully the philosophical views and preconceptions that he (and of course Barfield himself) encountered in the Oxford of his undergraduate years. Thus, to demonstrate the general by one specific example, in his book *The Riddles of Philosophy*, Steiner contrasts the philosophical standpoint of Gottfried Wilhelm von Leibnitz (1646–1716) with that of John Locke (1632–1704), each of whom may be considered as representative of his own respective national philosophical traditions of idealism and empiricism. According to Steiner, whereas Leibnitz's world-picture is 'completely formed out of the "ego" itself . . . out of the inner energy of the self-conscious soul, so the world-picture of his contemporary John Locke rests entirely on the feeling that such a productive construction out of the soul is not admissible. Locke recognizes only those parts of a world conception as justified that can be *observed* (experienced) and what can, on the basis of the observation, *be thought* about the observed objects. The soul for him is not a being that develops real experience out of itself, but an empty slate on which the outer world writes its entries. Thus, for Locke, human self-consciousness is a result of experience; it is not an ego that is the cause of an experience . . .'[175]

Steiner's *Philosophy of Freedom*, while quite explicitly written out of the conviction of the essential reality of inner, soul experience that characterizes German idealism, nevertheless seeks to demonstrate that this inner activity of the soul can also enormously enhance what is generally regarded in the English philosophical tradition as the sphere of empirical investigation (and also moral activity). In this sense, human subjectivity is transformed from something to be excluded in the interests of scientific objectivity into an essential element of man's endeavour to gain knowledge of the world around him. Steiner's underlying aim to build a bridge between the traditions of idealism and empiricism comes to expression in the subtitle to *The Philosophy of Freedom*—'Some results of introspective observation following the methods of natural science'.

The core insight that enabled Steiner not only to overcome his own personal difficulty of relating his innate clear insights into the world of spirit to the sense-perceptible world—and hence assuage his extreme sense of homelessness in this latter world—but also to develop a philosophical foundation for free, moral activity in that world which empiricists regard alone as real is that, through thinking, the individual human ego participates in the evocation of what is apprehended by the mind as the objects of its perception. Steiner sums up the crucial role in the process of perception and cognition that is played by thinking in the chapter 'Thinking in the Service of Knowledge':

> This then is indisputable, that in thinking we have got hold of one corner of the whole world process which requires our presence if anything is to happen. And this is just the point upon which everything turns. The very reason why things confront me in such a puzzling way is that I play no part in their production. They are simply given to me, whereas in the case of thinking I know how it is done. Hence for the study of all that happens in the world there can be no more fundamental starting point than thinking itself.[176]

In other words, by the very virtue of the fact that we think, we are co-creators of the world which we habitually regard as being presented to us as a complete and finished picture by our senses. Steiner devotes a substantial part of the first of the two parts of the book to demonstrating that this is so.[177] The problem is that we do not normally notice that this is happening—we are not usually aware that our mind, far from being a passive receptacle of sense-perceptible phenomena, instantaneously adds a conceptual explanation to the perceptual impressions garnered by our senses: 'The percept [i.e. the object of our observation] is thus not something finished and self-contained, but only one side of the total reality. The other side is the concept [his term for the result of our thinking]. The act of knowing is the synthesis of percept and concept. Only the percept and concept together constitute the whole thing.'[178]

Shortly afterwards in the same chapter, Steiner sums up this train of thought in somewhat different words:

> In contrast to the content of the percept which is given to us from without, the content of thinking appears inwardly. The form in which this first makes its appearance we will call *intuition*. *Intuition* is for thinking what *observation* is for the percept. Intuition and observation are the sources of our knowledge. An observed object of the world remains unintelligible to us until we have within ourselves the corresponding intuition which adds that part of the reality which is lacking in the percept . . .[179]

In the remainder of the book, Steiner draws two very important consequences from the epistemological foundation that he has built up in the first few chapters. One of these has implications for man's cognitive capacity and the other for the actions of his will. Both of these consequences derive from the monistic or 'one-world' nature of his philosophical standpoint, as distinct from a dualistic model. The first implication of this monistic view of reality—as outlined in the above quotations—is that there is not another 'real world' lying mysteriously or invisibly behind what is apprehensible by our senses, there is no 'thing-in-itself' which is inaccessible to our faculties of observation. In Steiner's view, the familiar, or naive, experience of dualism, of living in a world where subject and object are irrevocably divided from one another, is an illusion. The conclusion which may justifiably be drawn from this is that there are no limits to knowledge, and this is the title of the concluding chapter of the first part of the book. The second implication of Steiner's having demonstrated that we live in a unified world and are not separated from what we perceive is that our will-relationship to that world is one of participant and co-creator. Moreover, in contrast to the dualistic model, where the deeds that the individual subject enacts upon an objectively conceived external reality must necessarily be conditioned by authoritative injunctions or rules stemming from this external reality (whether in the form of religious commands or secular laws), in the monistic world-view the individual acts as a free spirit who takes upon himself the full responsibility for his own deeds. Such a free spirit, writes Steiner, 'acts according to his impulses, that is, according to intuitions selected from the totality of his world of ideas by thinking'.[180] In the same chapter, Steiner goes on to define the intuitional process whereby 'man produces concrete mental pictures from the sum of his ideas' as *moral imagination*, which 'is the source of the free spirit's action'.[181] This, together with the *moral technique* of supplementing this moral imagination (as thus defined) with 'the ability to transform the world of percepts without violating the natural laws by which these are connected',[182] forms the basis of the *ethical individualism*, which is Steiner's term for the moral philosophy or attitude to will-activity arising out of the epistemological foundation that he has constructed. In Chapter 9, entitled 'The Idea of Freedom', Steiner defines this latter quality at some length:

> The sum of ideas which are effective in us, the concrete content of our intuitions, constitutes what is individual in each of us, notwithstanding the universality of the world of ideas. In so far as this intuitive content applies to action, it constitutes the moral content of the individual. To let this content express itself in life is both the highest moral driving force and the highest motive a man may have, who sees that in this content all other moral principles are in the end united. We may call this point of view ethical individualism.[183]

Later on in the same chapter he states quite unequivocally: 'Freedom of action is conceivable only from the standpoint of ethical individualism.'[184]

* * *

During his years with the Goethe-Schiller Archive in Weimar (1890–7), Steiner became a popular figure as a lecturer and commentator on current affairs as well as on scientific and philosophical developments. This continued with his move to Berlin in 1897, when he took up editorship of *Das Magazin für Literatur*, a well-known literary periodical (his association was between 1897 and 1900) and became active as a teacher at the Workers' Educational Institute (1899–1904). All in all, his radical philosophical and social views, coupled with his keen interest in educational questions and in his fellow human beings in general, led him to be regarded as a leading member of the avant-garde in Berlin intellectual life at the turn of the twentieth century.

It was therefore something of a surprise, even shock, to his many friends in literary and educational circles that in 1902 Steiner joined the Theosophical Society. In the July of that year he attended the 13th annual convention of the European Section of the Theosophical Society in London, and in October became the Secretary General of its newly founded German Branch. He took this step—which alienated him from many of his former associates—because of the direction that his own research into the world of spirit was leading him, research whose initial fruits were the lectures given in 1901 for the Philosophische Bibliothek on 'Christianity as a Mystical Fact' (a book with the same title was published the following year). Even though in February 1913 he was to assert his independence from the Theosophical Society by establishing his own Anthroposophical Society, the very fact that from the beginning of his forties Steiner started lecturing and writing out of his occult research was enough to make many people forget about the tremendous efforts that he had made during his twenties and thirties to place his clairvoyant faculties upon a scientific foundation. From 1902 until the end of his life in 1925, Steiner focused increasingly upon the task of presenting the fruits of this spiritual-scientific research to those wishing to hear about it (for the most part this came to be members and associates of the Anthroposophical Society), while responding in his later years to requests from people interested in his particular approach for indications regarding practical work in fields such as education, agriculture, medicine, science, the arts, social, political and economic affairs, and pastoral care, including the Christian sacraments.

* * *

Barfield was initially especially struck by Steiner's ideas about the evolution of consciousness, as presented for the first time in books such as *Christianity as Mystical Fact* and *The Riddles of Philosophy* (both dating in their main substance from 1901). This was simply because he found an extraordinary degree of concordance between his own early research on the history of language and the etymology of words on the one hand and, on the other, Steiner's grandiose vistas of the history and evolution of man and the earth (as presented pre-eminently in his book *Geheimwissenschaft im Umriss* (An Outline of Occult Science, 1910)). I shall conclude this chapter with a more extended examination of what the discovery of anthroposophy in his twenties—that is, in the period when his early work on language, culminating in *Poetic Diction*, was coming to fruition—meant to him. However, it will be helpful if at this point some attempt is made to present an impression of the extraordinary temple of knowledge which Steiner constructed between 1902 and 1925 on the epistemological foundation of *The Philosophy of Freedom*. This brief sketch needs to be prefaced by a word of clarification. As is implied in *The Philosophy of Freedom*, with its explicit rejection of any notion of dogma or authority in either the sphere of knowledge or that of moral activity, anthroposophy[185] is not a body of knowledge but 'a path of knowledge, to guide the spiritual in the human being to the spiritual in the universe'.[186] And the reader who remains unconvinced that the large number of insights which arose from Steiner's research—of which a very inadequate indication follows—represent any more than some kind of mystical hocus-pocus is recommended to turn to the selections that Barfield himself made from Steiner's *Von Seelenrätseln* (Riddles of the Soul, 1917) and translated, with an introduction of his own, under the title *The Case for Anthroposophy* (1970); for in the very condensed psychologically based discussions forming the chapters of this little book Steiner focuses on that very frontier where the familiar scientific research based on the bodily senses and the extension of this through the cultivation of faculties of the soul come together. The theme of this latter volume may perhaps be characterized by Steiner's introductory words to the first article in Barfield's sequence, which is entitled 'Anthroposophy and Anthropology':

> The spokesman for Anthroposophy maintains, on the basis of apprehensions that are not merely his private and personal experiences, that the process of human cognition can be further developed after a certain fixed point, a point beyond which scientific research, relying solely on sensory observation and inference therefrom, refuses to go...

> Anthroposophical research, then, reckons to begin from where anthropology [Steiner's term in this context for a methodology of research based on sensory observation] leaves off.

Although Steiner's many further contributions to developing the thoughts implicit in *The Philosophy of Freedom* into a path of knowledge which anyone can follow,[187] and also his systematic extension of the research reflected in *Riddles of the Soul* into a fully fledged psychology, where man is described as a being of body, soul *and spirit* (a fact with tremendous epistemological implications),[188] were of great importance for Barfield, the area of Steiner's spiritual-scientific research which so illumined his own early work on language was the historical and evolutionary studies centering on *Occult Science: An Outline*, which Barfield refers to as 'the principal source-book of anthroposophy'.[189] This book, in addition to containing summaries of the two other elements of anthroposophical research already referred to, has a long chapter entitled 'Evolution of the World and Man' which contains in some one hundred pages the essence of what Steiner developed in many other writings and—especially—lectures on this historical and evolutionary theme.

For those brought up to assume that the Darwinian theory of evolution represents the full and true picture, Steiner's account is just about as stark a contrast as it could possibly be. To begin with, the scale of the whole conception is utterly vast, in that we are presently living in the fourth embodiment of our solar or planetary system, with three more still to come. During the first incarnation of our planetary home, which Steiner called Ancient Saturn, the human physical body was created (albeit not in anything remotely resembling its present materialized form). After a period of pralaya, or rest, Ancient Sun came into being and the human etheric or life body was added to the physical substance of warmth engendered on Ancient Saturn. A further pause followed and Ancient Moon, the next earthly embodiment, now became the stage for the development of man's astral or soul body. Another period of pralaya now heralded the dawning of the present Earth incarnation of our planet, when the human ego or 'I' came into existence for the first time. Meanwhile, all the other bodily sheaths of man's being—the physical, etheric and astral bodies—underwent successive stages of development, so that man's physical body is currently the oldest and most fully perfected aspect of his nature. Steiner goes into considerably more detail about the Earth evolution, which he divides into seven great periods, each of which is subdivided into a further seven lesser ones. The first five greater periods bear the names Polaris, Hyperborea, Lemuria, Atlantis and Post-Atlantis (our present period); while the sub-divisions of the post-Atlantean period, generally referred to by Steiner as cultural epochs, are named the Ancient Indian, Ancient Persian, Egypto-Chaldean, Graeco-Roman and our present fifth post-Atlantean epoch.

In connection with these latter epochs it becomes possible for the first time to speak with a certain degree of precision in terms of dates: each of the lesser periods, or epochs, lasts some 2160 years (the number has an astronomical significance, being related to the moving of the position where the sun rises at the spring equinox with respect to the circle of the zodiac). Steiner dated the fourth (Graeco-Roman) age as running from 747 BC until AD 1413, which brings the beginning of the Egypto-Chaldean age (the great civilizations of Mesopotamia and Egypt) to around 3000 BC, the start of the Persian civilization to roughly 5000 BC and the dawning of Ancient India somewhat prior to 7000 BC. Before then was the Atlantean catastrophe and the inundation of the 'lost' continent, corresponding to the story of the Flood and the great leader of humanity whose Biblical name is Noah (dated around 8000 BC). As we go back to the Lemurian age, which was a recapitulation of the Old Moon period (just as Polaris and Hyperborea were recapitulations, respectively, of the Saturn and Sun embodiments) and witnessed the dramatic event of the Fall (the temptation of Adam and Eve by Lucifer and their expulsion from Paradise), historical dates cease to be of any significance and we enter a purely mythological consciousness of human history. Moreover, it also becomes increasingly problematic to relate Steiner's chronology to geological time (he considered that palaeontologists have tended to fall victim to Lyell's assumption of uniformitarianism (i.e., that change has always been taking place at the same rate as it does now) and grossly exaggerated the age of present fossiliferous remains).

The second point to emphasize about Steiner's vista of evolution is that the moving force behind—or within—everything that happens or has ever happened is the activity of spiritual beings. One has the overwhelming impression of an evolutionary picture which is, however, not static (as a 'creationist' picture would be) but where the Gods have an ongoing involvement in establishing a stage on which man can accomplish a certain task for which purpose the Gods have created him and his earthly environment. Moreover, there is nothing vague about the nature and identity of these spiritual beings. Steiner describes nine celestial hierarchies of heavenly beings who are involved in this immense drama, their names being familiar from early Christian terminology. The First Hierarchy are the Seraphim (Spirits of Love), Cherubim (Spirits of Harmony) and Thrones (Spirits of Will); the Second Hierarchy are the Kyriotetes (Spirits of Wisdom or Dominions), Dynamis (Spirits of Movement or Mights) and Exusiai (Spirits of Form or Powers); and the Third Hierarchy are the Archai (Spirits of Personality or Principalities), Archangels (Spirits of Fire) and Angels (Sons of Life). Man's allotted task over aeons of time is to become a tenth hierarchy whose particular task is to add the quality of freedom, a freedom transmuted by love, to what already lives within the Godhead. Still higher spiritual beings are also intricately involved in this divine-earthly drama, specifically the members of the Holy Trinity, central amongst whom is God the Son, the Christ.[190] It is significant that Rudolf Steiner was first prompted to speak about his spiritual research in 1901 because of the awareness that had only recently dawned within him that the appearance of Jesus Christ on the earth was the central event of the whole of earthly evolution (by which is meant the entire planetary drama that is the subject of *Occult Science*). For although all the heavenly hierarchies have had an essential part to play in the creation and sustaining of man and the world of which he is part (for the details of this drama the reader is referred to *Occult Science* itself or to other detailed descriptions in lectures of certain of its aspects), it was the Christ Being alone who was able to redeem fallen humanity at the point of its greatest separation from the Gods. Steiner devoted a considerable number of lecture-cycles, including at least one on each of the Gospels, to demonstrating how the incarnation of the Christ in the human being Jesus of Nazareth represented the fulfilment and synthesis of all religions and restored meaning to earthly existence. (It is impossible to enter here into further details as to how Steiner explains some of the deepest mysteries of Christian doctrine. Some of these figure in certain of Barfield's books still to be discussed.)

The main aspect of Steiner's conception of evolution that needs to be mentioned here is the effect that the work of all these spiritual beings has had upon the evolution of human consciousness over the ages. For the purposes of making a connection with Barfield's early work on the history of language, it is necessary merely to focus upon the tiny portion of this entire drama that falls within the compass of Steiner's fifth period of Earth evolution, the post-Atlantean age. If one has at the back of one's mind the whole vast story that has been unfolded, it becomes more possible to replace the stereotype of uncouth cave-men, with a similar faculty of perception but different cognitive skills to our own, by an 'imagination' of ancient clairvoyant cultures immersed in a spiritual wisdom which has been gradually lost over the 10,000 years of this time subsequent to the mythical Flood in order that the will of the Gods—that a realm of existence be created with the freedom to ignore their commands and even thwart their designs—might be fulfilled. This has in a quite particular way been the main theme of the successive cultural epochs forming the post-Atlantean age.[191] But running through and connecting these successive phases of cultural development, when a wisdom-consciousness is being gradually clouded by an increasing self-consciousness, there can be discerned a further fundamental mystery of which Steiner came to speak at greater length at the end of his life, that of individual karma and reincarnation. It is appropriate to broach this here in the words of Barfield's 'The Disappearing Trick':

> If self-consciousness can truly be said to have 'evolved', it must have increased gradually. But what does it mean to say that self-consciousness must have 'increased', or must have 'emerged' gradually from another kind of consciousness? If self-consciousness can accurately be said to have 'grown', or 'evolved', from what it was, say, in 10,000 BC to what it is, say in AD 1970, then the same self must be assumed as present in both periods. The same self, though not the same organisms (bodies). What does 'evolving' mean? It makes sense to speak of the species 'horse' evolving through the ages, though individual horses have perished utterly; because there is something that has persisted through all these perishings, namely the species. But if it is individuality itself, selfhood itself, that is to be conceived as 'evolving', what are we to say has persisted? It can only be the individuality. In other words, something called individuality has taken the place of species in the process of evolving. In this case, then, it is not the same species but the same individual that must have persisted through those successive embodiments that reveal its evolution to an observer—becoming, in the process of transformation, gradually more recognizable as what it is today.[192]

Barfield clarified what precisely he meant by the 'self' or the 'individuality' in this passage in a subsequent lecture entitled 'Why Reincarnation?' given in May 1978 to the Cambridge University Anthroposophical Study Group and published in the 1979 *Golden Blade*. Referring to Steiner's way of understanding the concept of reincarnation (which he was seeking to elucidate), he states that 'the entity which he [Steiner] presented as experiencing more than one life on earth, was a transpersonal one. It is not the personality familiar to himself and his friends ... but the core of a man's being, of which he is normally unconscious, that passes from one life to another. Earthly personality is more like a shadow, or mirror-image, of the ultimate Self... Putting it more briefly, it is the spirit and not the soul, that is born again.'[193]

There is a meditation by Rudolf Steiner dating from 1923 which represents a distillation of what Barfield is expressing in these two *Golden Blade* articles regarding the deeper logical implications of the idea of the evolution of consciousness:

> I gaze into the darkness.
> In it there arises Light—
> Living Light.
> Who is this Light in the darkness?
> It is I myself in my reality.
> This reality of the I
> Enters not into my earthly life;
> I am but a picture of it.
> But I shall find it again
> When with good will for the Spirit
> I shall have passed through the Gate of Death.[194]

The most distinctively autobiographical description of what Barfield's initial encounter with anthroposophy meant to him is contained in his 1977 lecture at Rudolf Steiner House, London, 'Owen Barfield and the Origin of Language'. Referring to himself as the subject of his own lecture,[195] Barfield spoke of how he initially *experienced* the picture of evolution of which a very brief overall sketch has just been given:

> It was in 1922 or possibly the end of 1921 that the Subject first heard of Rudolf Steiner, and began to read some of his books and lectures. He approached them with an attitude of caution, even of suspicion; particularly he was put off by a certain residual aroma of the Theosophical Society, which was rather noticeable in those days. He had recently begun working on the thesis afterwards published as *Poetic Diction*, but you would be quite wrong if you imagined him confidently confronting the orthodox picture of an exclusively biological evolution with a totally different picture of his own. The Darwinian theory, the Darwinian fantasy as I am now inclined to call it, was about as firmly rivetted on his imagination as on everyone else's; and of course Rudolf Steiner's picture of evolution is startlingly and, on first acquaintance, disconcertingly different therefrom. So, looking back on that time, he seems to recall that his first really positive, really concrete response to what I would call the 'content' of Anthroposophy was rather strangely

> similar to that older response to poetry, or rather perhaps to language out of which the idea of the book *Poetic Diction* first arose. That had begun ... with the discovery that the forms of language created by poets produced a certain change of consciousness, a change that was both pleasurable, and more than pleasurable—followed by the further discovery that older forms of language [reflecting the mystery-wisdom consciousness out of which they originated] could produce a similar change, as it were of their own accord, without the help of the poet, without the help of art. He now found, simply as a matter of experience, that there was also a third source from which that sort of change of consciousness could originate. The often surprising things that Rudolf Steiner reported with such confidence as the findings of his spiritual research, *acted* on him in the same way as did poetic or figurative language ... It was the same trick, the same sort of change of consciousness as in the other two cases. As in the other two cases, so in this, belief or unbelief were irrelevant. The change *happened*. It was something that was *there*.

Barfield goes on to point out that his agnostic twentieth-century upbringing had given him an inbuilt suspicion of any theory implying that there is a meaning in the world as a whole. He then relates how, nevertheless, his discovery of the central significance allotted by Steiner to the Incarnation of Christ—quite apart from being 'very welcome (and for that very reason how *suspect*)'—fitted in very well with discoveries that he had himself made about the way that certain words have changed their meanings over particular periods of historical time, referring in this context to his lecture 'Philology and the Incarnation'.[196]

It should also be emphasized that, in contrast to the way that his initial acquaintance with anthroposophy has sometimes been described,[197] Barfield did not all of a sudden become a 'follower' of Steiner's, still less slavishly accept everything he said. As he explains, the two processes of studying anthroposophy and developing his own ideas about language 'went on side by side for quite a long time'. And yet after some time he felt able to say to himself:

> This atavistic clairvoyance he [Steiner] speaks of [this refers to the spiritual wisdom possessed by ancient clairvoyant cultures, see p. 196] is none other than that figurative consciousness and awareness of meaning in the environment, of meaning entering *into* man rather than coming *out of* him, that I have been trying all along to point to; the only difference, of course, being that I *end* with it, I have been labouring to

establish from very different grounds that there must have been such a consciousness. Steiner simply starts from it, affirms on the basis of his own direct perception that there in fact was such a kind of consciousness, and then he builds on that as his foundation.

Barfield offers a more generalized picture of his debt to Rudolf Steiner in the introduction to *Romanticism Comes of Age* and also, quite explicitly, in the first of the essays included in that collection, entitled 'From East to West', which contains a useful introduction to Steiner's epistemology. Indeed, most of the essays in this volume contain either references to or interpretations of certain aspects of anthroposophy; and the reader seeking further elucidations by Barfield himself of what has already been said in this chapter concerning, in particular, the philosophical basis of anthroposophy and Steiner's conception of evolution would be advised to read, respectively, 'Rudolf Steiner's Concept of Mind' (1961) and 'The Time-Philosophy of Rudolf Steiner' (1955). But what concerns us in the present chapter is not so much Barfield's interpretative work on anthroposophy—after all, there is a sense in which virtually all the books written by Barfield in his maturity are developments of ideas or insights that he gleaned from Rudolf Steiner, which is why this chapter on Steiner is necessary at this point—but the experiences which caused his determination to study Steiner to take off in his twenties. For this, the Introduction to the volume in question represents the sole additional source.

As in the lecture already quoted at some length ('Owen Barfield and the Origin of Language'), Barfield refers to the acute similarity between studying Steiner's ideas and the delight he experienced in reading lyric poetry. But he also makes other points. Thus 'the second ... thing that struck me most about Anthroposophy ... was that, so far as concerned the particular subject in which I was immersed at the time, that is the histories of verbal meanings, and their bearing on the evolution of human consciousness, Steiner had obviously forgotten volumes more than I had ever dreamed. It is difficult to lay my finger on what convinced me of this. As far as I know there is no special mention of semantics or semasiology among his works. Rather it was a matter of stray remarks and casual allusions which showed that some of my most daring and (as I thought) original conclusions were his premises ...'

After commenting on Steiner's contribution to his own particular subject of linguistics—and referring to his deep resonance with Steiner's teaching in the 'adjoining region' of psychology—Barfield makes his third acknowledgement of his main debt to Steiner at that time: 'The third [thing] was, that Anthroposophy included and transcended not only my own poor stammering theory of poetry as knowledge, but the whole Romantic philosophy. It was nothing less than Romanticism grown up.' Barfield proceeds to expand upon this latter phrase—the keynote of the entire volume and, indeed, of the vision that runs through all his work—by quoting from Coleridge's description of what he and Wordsworth were attempting to do in their *Lyrical Ballads* of 1798, on the one hand, and referring, on the other, to the significance that philosophers such as Coleridge and Schelling—and, in his own particular way, Goethe—attached to the imagination as a faculty that could transcend 'that absolute dichotomy between perceiving subject and perceived object on which our practical everyday experience (Coleridge's "lethargy of custom") is necessarily based'. Barfield then states that, in his view, 'only Steiner, so far as I know, has clearly apprehended this activity as part, and but the first part, of a long, sober process of cognition that may end in a man's actually overcoming this dichotomy—sober, but involving a plus of self-consciousness amounting to a mutation, since it presupposes no less than a crossing of the stark threshold between knowing and being'.[198]

There follows what was quite possibly Barfield's most extended and frank statement about his deep disappointment about the consistent policy in the world of—especially—English letters to ignore Steiner:

> ... I have not merely been disappointed, I have been shocked and puzzled to have it borne in on me over and over again that even those who are prepared to lend a very sympathetic ear indeed to *my own* observations, whether on language and poetry or on the wider issue of the whole evolution of human consciousness, are not in the least interested in the news about Steiner which it has been one of my main objects in life to set before the educated public with all the earnestness and sobriety at my disposal... One is left with the unanswered question: how does it come about that this most responsible of minds so often evokes unwonted irresponsibility in others [Barfield cites C.S. Lewis as a typical example of this 'irresponsibility']?... But I am not thinking so much of positive denigration. I am thinking of that combination of a refusal to investigate with a readiness to dismiss, which can alone account for the absence of at least a *reference* to Steiner from a hundred Indexes where one would expect, simply because of his obvious and extreme relevance, to find it as a matter of course.

However, this eloquent passage concludes—after a diatribe against the extent to which positivism remains concealed in people's thinking even where it has ostensibly been abandoned—with a clear conviction of hope:

> That future historians of Western thought will interpret the appearance of Romantic philosophy towards the close of the eighteenth century as foreshadowing the advent of Rudolf Steiner towards the close of the nineteenth I have no sort of doubt.

This was the conviction which underlay all the writings—both published and unpublished—which it is now our task to consider in the remaining chapters of this book.

11. ENGLISH PEOPLE

Alone of all the writers who were in one way or another associated with the 'Inklings' gatherings around C.S. Lewis in Oxford, initially (1922–45) in Lewis's rooms and latterly (until 1962) in haunts such as the Eagle and Child ('Bird and Baby'), Barfield is not celebrated as a writer of fiction. And yet his most substantial work of any kind is the 550-page novel 'English People', written at the end of the 1920s and completed by October 1929. As already indicated, this work was a kind of test-case for his prospects as a writer of imaginative literature; and its failure even to be published closed that particular door as regards its author's future as a writer and required him to earn his living—somewhat unwillingly—in his father's legal firm.

It is interesting to contrast Barfield's *magnum opus* with another novel written at approximately the same time which was also conceived as a portrait of life in England at the end of the 1920s. J.B. Priestly's[199] *The Good Companions*, which was first published in July 1929 and had by January 1931 gone through 18 new impressions, is a rollicking and gloriously entertaining account of three individuals from different parts of England who, bored by or estranged from their familiar day-to-day lives, abruptly set off on their independent adventures and meet up somewhere in the East Midlands, where they encounter a very depressed group of concert party performers whom they revivify with vigour and inspiration. The entire novel is a tour de force in holiday mood. Everyone has a good time and is carried along (as is the reader) by events, but no one thinks to any appreciable degree or indeed seems to have an inner dimension to his or her life and there is virtually no reference (except in the form of wooden caricatures) to the 'real' world of wider social and political events. It was a brilliant, and highly successful, way of chronicling a country plunging ever deeper into the Great Depression, and celebrated a way of dealing with national crises which has since become the norm: forget about everything, treat yourself to a break!

Barfield's book, by contrast, records the sustained efforts of in particular four individuals to make sense of their day-to-day world and, where appropriate, to restore meaning to it in the widest possible sense. It is, moreover, brimful with thoughts and ideas as experienced or shared in conversation by these leading characters, ideas which extend in a thoroughgoing way to the socio-political context of the time. One could philosophize about the reasons why the one novel was a roaring publishing success and the other a total failure. I would submit that Barfield's book, which, quite apart from its richness of ideas, contains some of the finest passages of poetic writing to be found anywhere in his *oeuvre*, is certainly not inferior in stature or quality to Priestly's. And yet, like much of the rest of Barfield's imaginative writing, it is too autobiographical to quite 'work' as fiction. Even where his chosen genre is ostensibly fiction, Barfield is almost always trying to impart a philosophical or spiritual content to his readers; and 'English People' is to all intents and purposes an imaginative depiction of its author's own soul journey, as expressed through the four principal characters, each of whom represents a certain facet of Barfield himself. Certainly, it would be well-nigh impossible to preface the novel with the conventional statement to the effect that 'none of the characters has an intended resemblance to any person living or deceased'. And it was, apparently, Barfield's refusal to change the name of Brockmann, the Austrian seer whose ideas are inspirational to the book's principal figures, to Steiner which deterred its publication at the Goetheanum, Switzerland, by the Anthroposophical Society. How would it have been if he had allowed this change? But then he would probably have had to change the names of the famous psychologists Lusst and Vogel into their originals of Freud and Jung; and it would also have been intriguing to see how he would have dealt with the highly dramatic, and ultimately sinister, events involving leading figures of the Industrialists' Party, whose resemblance to particular individuals in Ramsay MacDonald's Labour Government (1929–31) is much too close for them to have been figments of Barfield's imagination.

The fact is, of course, that Barfield thoroughly disliked fiction. Not only did he say as much in personal conversations; it is apparent both in his whole approach to imaginative writing and in his overall philosophical attitude to life. And 'English People' is in the final analysis transparently *not* a work of fiction, whatever its formal classification may be. Although the ambiguity in which the author placed himself so that he could have the greatest possible artistic freedom to say what he wanted to say most likely prevented his novel from being published, there is no work of Barfield's which comes close to being a comparable quarry of essential material for a psychography. In this sense, the novel—far from being an interesting sidetrack from Barfield's formally non-fictional published writings of the period of his life under consideration in this part of the book—is fundamental to them all and to much more besides. It is for this reason that a study of the novel—from the psychographical point of view—must needs precede any consideration of the three main areas of his creative activity as a writer, all of which are present to one degree or another in 'English People': as a historian of language and of the evolution of consciousness; as a poet and writer of verse-dramas; and as a social critic and reformer. The ensuing chapters on these three areas will be followed by a final chapter—the essential substance of which is likewise encapsulated in the novel—on more intimate, personal matters.

Before proceeding to a gleaning of the psychographical insights offered by 'English People', it will first be necessary (not least because of the book's inaccessibility to general readership) to give a fairly detailed, albeit very inadequate, synopsis. The endeavour will be to amplify the bare story with at least a taste of the rich autobiographical content present in the book. The novel is written in four parts, with a continuous chapter sequence which will be followed here.

Part One

I. We are introduced to John Trinder, who has just finished his theological training at Welldon Theological College. The scene is a cricket match in July, and John is thinking of his fiancée Margaret. John's older brother Humphrey is mentioned as 'a chap who has all sorts of ideas of his own that he goes running off after'. That same evening, the Warden of the College, Dr Startop, gives his valedictory address to the departing students. Startop's theme is the difficult challenge of being a clergyman in twentieth-century England; and he enlarges very frankly upon the mockery, indifference and sheer spiritual emptiness which they are likely to expect as they seek to respond to their high calling. He also speaks of the privilege, 'the sweetness', of holding office in an organization which is the only direct link for our modern world with the time when Christ himself walked the earth.

II. The scene shifts to Westleigh, ten miles north-west of the City of London, where John and Humphrey Trinder share a home with their elder sister Janet. We learn through Janet's eyes more about their family background, which was strictly agnostic in nature. Their mother had died at John's birth, and their father Erasmus, a devotee of Samuel Butler, had brought them up amidst a dogmatic anti-clericalism, against which John had reacted by deciding after two terms at Oxford to take Holy Orders. John, who has by now arrived home, longs to be able to tell Janet about his experience of Startop's address (by which he was very moved), but finds himself trapped in a smug, moralizing falseness. Humphrey also arrives at this point. He is a former medical student who suffered from shell-shock in the war and is not engaged in anything particular, although he has thoughts about becoming a 'pukkah psychoanalyst', stimulated by his mysterious acquaintance Dawson. The political theme which will play a fairly large part in the novel is referred to in the form of a debate between John and Humphrey, with John sympathizing with striking workers' demands and Humphrey commenting on their poverty of ideas. Both Humphrey and Gerald Marston—the fourth main character in the book, who is mentioned here—have a great enthusiasm for ideas, and although John is their equal in other ways he cannot keep up with Humphrey. The main information imparted about Janet in this chapter is that she suffers acutely from a stammer. A final point worthy of note is that the Trinders (there is a threefoldness implicit in the choice of surname) affectionately refer to one another as Liberty (John), Equality (Janet) and Fraternity (Humphrey).

III. The next two chapters are mainly focused on John, though the third chapter opens with Janet working at her typewriter and Humphrey going to see Dawson for further training in psychoanalysis. John is mentally preparing for his honeymoon in Italy. He delights in travelling through London by bus to his parents-in-law's flat near Hyde Park, where Margaret is waiting for him. Margaret—who is a little older than he—comes from the kind of refined, cultural background that lacks any real depth or integrity, where the beautiful is everywhere apparent but where the true is (by contrast to the Trinder family) virtually absent. Her father, Sir Otto Hudson, has lots of knowledge but little heart enthusiasm. He works in the City on the fringe of the commercial and financial worlds, where—as we learn subsequently—he exerts considerable influence on national economic and political affairs. Margaret's mother died some years previously, and Sir Otto married his present wife Mary, the daughter of a very wealthy, eccentric old gentleman (of whom more anon). At this present encounter, John is aware mainly of his love for Margaret as a beautiful woman, while realizing that there is part of her which will never leave the comfortable, bourgeois space of her room in her parents' flat, amidst the sentient mood of its predominantly Italian and Southern French books and paintings. He feels a sense of security in this environment, allowing himself—in the narrator's eyes—to be beguiled by it; and after dining with the Hudson's he returns home 'on top of a bus, floating up the Edgware Road as though it were the Grand Canal'.

IV. John's thoughts are on his impending ordination and marriage. We learn in this chapter and at the end of Chapter III more about his understanding of Christianity. He realizes somewhat to his surprise that the view of Christianity to which he subscribes has a strong affinity with the despairing voice of Greek paganism, where—in a favourite passage of John's from an old Greek history—Solon puts forward the view that one should 'call no man happy till he is dead'. John is able to live with this problem (in what the author is hinting is a distinctively English or Anglican way) by establishing in his mind a division between his thoughts and his feelings, an attitude which Janet derogatively refers to as 'transparent Jesuit'. We learn that he had long thought that ideas have so little real connection with their presumed sources in reality as to have no objective validity. Therefore, he does not think about doctrinal matters—or study Ecumenical Councils—but simply accepts them. He avoids thoughts and opinions, and is able to be oblivious to the travails of modern theology. Instead, he focuses on liturgy and images and seeks out the most beautiful services.

By contrast with his brother Humphrey, his reading is extremely limited. To Humphrey, John's notions amount to 'giving up thinking altogether'. John's relationship to thinking is of a practical nature, and is of no value for 'fundamental things'. His favourite philosopher (in so far as he has one at all) is Kant. These thought relationships are then further clarified by a consideration of Janet's relationship to Margaret. Janet is taciturn and reserved, while Margaret is effervescent and gets on Janet's nerves. To Janet, Margaret is affected, a snob and a pedant—but she suffers everything in silence. She also gets irritated with Humphrey's psychoanalysis, which she finds even worse than John's God.

V. Humphrey takes John to a group meeting, which is described as taking place in a dingy second-floor room in a house near Tottenham Court Road. (The name of the group is not given, but it would appear to have some affinity to the New Age movement.) His main object is to introduce John to Gerald Marston, whom he expects to be there. This is achieved, and the reader is introduced to this individual whose perception and humour are to be of an inspirational nature for the entire Trinder family. A lecture is being delivered on 'Mind and the New Social Order' which the narrator summarizes for us. Its central idea is the dearth of any genuine wisdom or guidance amongst those ostensibly in authority, and the enormous need to develop a greater understanding to match the advances in scientific investigation. Two leading members of the group,

Humphrey's psychoanalyst teacher Dawson and Rex Rollo, the turbaned, black-coated president, are also introduced. John feels belittled and rebuffed by Dawson.

VI. Humphrey makes a speech at the group meeting, citing a quotation from a leading newspaper which, he claims, exemplifies the death of intellectualism in modern culture; and he reads out a long complicated set of sentences in which there is no discernible thought whatever. This prompts another speech about present social and economic realities, which is important because of its effect upon John. The speaker complains that labour-saving machinery has led not to increased leisure but to unemployment. People are denied the produce of the labour that has been saved. Despite the abundant means of production, there are unemployed workers and destitute consumers. The speaker blames bankers, financiers and economics professors (and of course politicians, the universal butt of the group's ridicule). It is absurd to think abstractly about money, continues the speaker. What matters are things and people. The world was longing to make, buy and sell—and could not: with the result that unemployment, misery and war abound. Rex Rollo then makes a speech where, seeking in his own way to interpret what was said by the first speaker of the evening, he distinguishes between the head's capacity to make judgements and the belly's capacity to give meaning, as a source of inspiration, myth and poetry. He concludes that the fear emanating from the intellect is balanced by will from the loins, emphasizing a phrase whose meaning is thoroughly obscure even to Humphrey and Gerald: 'the Will of the Self that overcomes the Fear of the Other'. (Rollo is in no sense Barfield's mouthpiece but the caricature of a very different spiritual attitude.)

After the meeting, Gerald Marston is invited to Westleigh to meet Janet, and Humphrey expresses to John what he thinks these meetings are all about, namely, 'all that was worth preserving of the present civilization'. John then wonders whether his beloved Margaret is 'worth preserving'. He is plunged into depression by such thoughts.

VII. John goes shopping with Margaret. Then she joins the three Trinders for supper, together with Gerald, who rescues the evening socially. She spends the night in John's room (he joins Humphrey), and feels ill-at-ease amidst all his books. She lights upon that same quotation from Solon—underlined by John—referred to earlier, and asks herself what she is letting herself in for.

VIII. John continues to be filled with an uneasy melancholy after the meeting in Tottenham Court Road. He goes to visit Gerald. They speak of Humphrey, and of his view of the meetings. 'England is absolutely *full* of them' (people preparing to found new civilizations), says Gerald. They dine at a restaurant in Soho. Gerald expresses his reservations about Dawson, whom he regards as rude, and Rollo. In response to John's asking him why he attends these meetings, he explains that these people have something that most otherwise excellent people do not, namely, 'self-knowledge' or, in Humphrey's pet phrase, 'spiritual guts'. John does not really know what he is talking about. Gerald goes on to share one of his problems with parsons (from which he hopes John is free), that they generally cannot disentangle the intellectual from the moral and emotional aspects of a question. He gives the example of love between the sexes. How can one distinguish between devotional sacrifice and egotism? Likewise with religion—is it genuine and free from self-interest? Gerald is amazed to discover that John (and his brother and sister) was brought up on Samuel Butler, whereas he had had a pietistic upbringing. John wanted to join the Church to get away from negativity. Gerald poses some probing questions about John's reasons for joining the Church, and asks him about his earlier mental development. There is something of a recapitulation of what John regards as his 'great discovery', namely, the relativity of the truth of any statement, at any time, by different people. (In this respect, John represents that distinctively English mixture of intellectual empiricism and respect for the other, as epitomized by John Locke.)

Gerald goes on to speak about his appreciation of the metaphorical aspect of art and of his path towards understanding the medieval imagination. His heart is full of the 'Rose' tradition, 'the great warm, mystical Rose, which is both the lady and the lover's own heart, and yet at the same time is Paradise itself—is the beating Heart of the Universe'. John for his part feels a parsonical pity for Gerald as he thinks and speaks of his approaching marriage. Gerald notices this, but after declaring his independent circumstances makes light of it and speaks of how he tries to earn his living by writing reviews and occasional articles (supplemented with an allowance from his family). He complains about 'a certain liberal monthly with a literary section' whose editor would freely alter what he wrote and refuse to admit any new thoughts. Unbeknown to Gerald, John respects this periodical.

John walks home under the stars, thinking of Gerald's favourite medieval poems 'I sing of a maiden', and 'All under the leaves', with its wondrous transition from

I die Mother dear, I die!

to

Oh the rose, the lovely rose
And the fennel that grows so green!...

Meanwhile, Gerald is contemplating his relationship with the offending periodical, into which he has been sucked as a fresh young writer. He realizes that he is forced to go on writing 'in the slick, patronizing manner he had once admired'. He dreams that night of a monster (himself) benevolently watching a pair of lovers, and woke the next morning feeling unusually cheerful.

Chapters IX to XIV are missing. Barfield lent the manuscript to a certain person who lost pages 78–114 (his name is known, but there seems little point in making a permanent record: suffice it to say that this would be this unfortunate individual's only claim to appear by name in the present volume). These chapters must have included a full description of John and Margaret's wedding and of the reception at Klosters, the Hudsons' country home somewhere in the Cotswolds whither we are somewhat abruptly led later on in the book. One should also assume that a certain development in the principal characters of the novel must have taken place in these chapters, although the missing pages do not present any problem regarding comprehension of the remainder.

Part Two

XV. In this chapter we learn about Francis Leslie Dawson in rather more detail, his character and education, his living circumstances with his mother, and his relationship to the Tottenham Court Road circle. At the time of John's visit to this group with Humphrey, Dawson had grown dissatisfied with this circle of people; and a few weeks later he had gone to Italy to join a group, known unofficially as the *Scuola Internazionale*, run by a friend of Rollo's. From the descriptions given here it is clear that this organization has a strong resemblance to the Gurdjieff work.

XVI. Here the focus is on Gerald, and his struggles to make a living as a writer in London. He regards himself as a confirmed bachelor, though has an active interest in members of the opposite sex which he endeavours to direct along creative channels. He had fallen in love three years previously and had been quietly but firmly rejected. Humphrey offers that the two of them share a flat, as he has decided to leave Westleigh. Gerald decides to join him.

XVII. Janet has been visiting the Hudsons' family home of Klosters, presumably for John and Margaret's wedding reception. She has difficulties with Margaret, though latterly she has been growing more and more irritated with John's 'rather aggressive optimism', his superior claims and airs and 'superior ethereality'. She is thoroughly aware of her uncharitable thoughts. On the train journey back to London she dwells on her sense of her life's failure, of letting her father down. Through the narrator's chameleon-like skill of entering sympathetically into the minds and hearts of the novel's principal characters, we learn about her philosophical view of human beings as a duality of body and mind, with mind having evolved from the body and being dependent on it. This theme broadens out into that of the position of women in society, specifically the importance of women for whom the mind is more important than the body (despite men's attentions). As she looks at the somewhat brash pictures of attractive women in a magazine called *The Rout*, which she has picked up at a station bookstall, she has the feeling of living 'on a little parochial patch excluded from this other world's air of ample tolerance'. She is painfully torn between a sense of eternal spinsterhood and a longing for joy. She feels utterly lonely, and longs for love in her own life.

XVIII. Janet, now arrived home, is in a very depressed state and has difficulty in finding a reason for going on living. Nor does she subscribe to the great self-deception that suffering in this world is compensated by happiness in another. Her thoughts of gassing herself are abruptly interrupted by Gerald telephoning. Then Humphrey arrives to ask if he can stay for a couple of nights. In general, her days have become a series of little unsupported acts of will. She therefore slept well, this being her sole relief. The early mornings are her worst times.

John and Margaret return from their honeymoon in Italy to Dale End, which is on the opposite side of London to Westleigh. Janet spreads an atmosphere of gloom, and this infects the returned newly weds.

XIX. John takes up a curacy at Onslow (presumably a London suburb), a parish of some 10,000 souls of whom 500 regularly attend services. His congregation consists mostly of elderly or middle-aged people. His own focus is mainly on the sacrament. One influence of his conversation with Gerald (Chapter 8) is that he has a much greater appreciation of art history and church history in terms of an evolutionary process. He experiences a spiritual bliss in these early times of his curacy after his marriage and ordination, and meditates for two hours daily.

In his first sermon he quotes Thomas Traherne extensively. He takes a genuine interest in his parishioners and has an instinctive desire to be sympathetic. He tries to avoid moralistically limiting people's freedom (for example, by discouraging dancing, forcing people to go to church). He also does his best to avoid promoting an 'ivory tower' mentality in his parishioners, always trying to substitute 'we' for 'they' when they are referring to goings-on in the wider world. He is fully aware of a rottenness in modern civilization, but he does not feel pity or scorn for it: he *is* it and it is he. He longs to escape from the enforced egotism of 'highbrowness' in which he has been brought up—he wants to be in living touch with 'the average Englishman'. He does not wish to be part of an exclusive priestly circle.

Gerald visits John and Margaret for a couple of nights. Margaret tries to get him some better-paid literary work through her father. Gerald has succeeded in awakening John's interest in poetry, especially that of Spenser; and the three of them share an animated conversation about meaning and aesthetics. There is evidence of a certain tension between John and Margaret, arising in this context out of the fact that Gerald shares Margaret's greater artistic sensitivity.

XX. Janet's profound unhappiness is lightened only by sleep, music and poetry. Her sense of solitude is redoubled by her poetic studies. She compares the lyric poets' experience of love (of a particular breathing woman), 'a good pain ... a lovely poetic pain which bestowed wisdom and grace and the piercing power to sing', with her own, which 'was a silly "left out" kind of pain, like a little pauper girl's as she watches the children going in to a Christmas party ...' She feels deprived of this gift because she has not known a lover: 'this fairest of all graces was reserved among their other benefits to the great freemasonry of lovers'; and she has a fear of withering into old-maidness.

She moved into a boarding house about three weeks after John's return from honeymoon. Despite her interest in the other inmates, she relapses into private gloom. Her mind is ceaselessly active, but she can no longer read novels. After a tormenting walk in a park strewn with people, she tries a breathing exercise (her way of determining to have hysterics). With every breath she feels as though she is sinking into a bottomless abyss, and then the teeming waters of life bring her up again into the light on the outward breath. And then Gerald arrives quite out of the blue.

XXI. Gerald has been visiting his father, who is afflicted with cancer in a nearby London nursing home. He offers to help Janet with revising her English translations (she is making a living by translating stories by a French writer). They discuss the merits of living alone (as Gerald prefers) or with others. Janet vehemently defends 'ordinary people'. 'I don't think we ought to run away,' she says. Gerald interprets her thought: 'You mean you can't really love the people you do love till you can love the people you don't love?' 'Yes, exactly,' Janet replies. They go on to discuss niceness in relation to physical attractiveness. Janet: 'What does the body matter? It's the mind inside that makes a person beautiful or ugly!' Gerald, who is not handsome, observes: 'You can't just *dismiss* the body. We have *got* them!'

The narrator now gives us some clearer insights into Gerald's past. He is currently 27, and when he was a boy of 13 he had an experience of being deeply struck by a pretty 22-year-old girl. Ever since he has always had a distant relationship to 'the passing fair' (performing acts of complete self-annihilation in her favour). He was not one to engage in kisses or embraces. Beautiful women filled him with this romantic notion—filled him to his fingertips with a rich philosophy of life, into which the plain woman simply did not fit' (even though she was often 'a great deal nicer'). He still could find no solution to this problem.

He is aware that Janet is quietly making an appeal to him. She quotes part of a famous sentence from one of Keats's letters: 'I am certain of nothing but the holiness of the heart's affections.' Gerald reminds her of what for him is a crucial addition: '. . . and the truth of imagination'. Because of her upbringing, Janet's mind is trapped in materialistic assumptions about mental processes, and Gerald cannot reach her on this level. They find a common bond through his insight and her suffering when they speak about 'sleep as a friend'. She knows this from her direct experience, and he is able to encourage her to give wings to her feeling instead of thinking solely in terms of the nerves recuperating themselves. 'And you mean,' said Janet slowly, 'that we can learn something from the feeling itself, that the feeling is just as real, whatever the explanation of it is? That's very difficult, I've sometimes thought that!' 'I mean,' said Gerald, looking hard at her once more, and speaking the words very slowly and distinctly: 'So much the better for the body!' A bond of understanding has been forged between them.

Gerald informs Janet that he is currently writing an article on Carlyle for a new Encyclopaedia, a task assigned to him through the mediation of Sir Otto Hudson. After he leaves, Janet eagerly reads some passages from Carlyle that he recommends.

XXII. Janet spends several happy weeks after Gerald's visit, nurturing her delight in lyric poetry. She finds a growing warmth of heart for the natural world and, quite especially, for those around her. A further important question living in her mind concerns what she perceives to be the unreasonableness of her assumption that those preceding her in time (e.g. in the nineteenth century) were in some way inferior or unfortunate; and she challenges herself to find a reason for this assumption.

XXIII. We are introduced to Adela Cranage, who is narcissistically composing a sonnet in her flat in Chelsea. It transpires that she and Humphrey have a relationship. Humphrey arrives, and is subjected to a commanding female presence which masks a gnawing loneliness. She wants him to initiate something physically. When he doesn't do so, he gets a slap on the cheek. He leaves her flat.

Humphrey returns home to the flat he shares with Gerald, who reads him a passage about the origin of language (written by the German philosopher Herder). This is background reading for his article on Carlyle. Gerald is 'especially interested in words' and deviates from the subject of Carlyle's sources to that of the origin of words. Humphrey then asks Gerald about Janet. Gerald likes all three Trinders and is getting to know them well. He has learnt to respect Humphrey's judgement and insight more than he had initially thought he would.

XXIV. Humphrey has reached the end of what he can learn from Dawson, who is encouraging him to become a psychoanalyst. He holds back from this, and he is also losing interest in Rex Rollo's 'nameless society'. His current preoccupation is with mental categories such as the Dionysiac and Appolline. He divides everything into such categories, including aspects of his own life. Although Gerald refuses to take the categories seriously, he uses them very creatively, applying—for example—female and male principles 'in every manifestation of Nature, Humanity and Art'. Humphrey prefers speaking thus with Gerald than with Dawson, whom he finds 'greasy'. Gerald has no interest in Humphrey's projection theories; and 'when Humphrey confided in him with an air of some importance that Nietzsche's vast oriental conception of an "eternal recurrence" was probably the imaginative "projection" of the peristaltic motion of his bowels, he leaned back in his chair and shook with laughter till the tears came into his eyes'. Nevertheless, he strongly encouraged Humphrey's interest in 'a more philosophical kind of psychology'.

XXV. Gerald's best qualities are brought out by sorrow and suffering, a feature of his personality that he recognizes. He visits Janet again, taking Humphrey with him. She notices a long feminine hair (Adela's) on his coat.

XXVI. Gerald finishes his article on Carlyle; it had occupied him for the best part of two months. He is greatly struck by Carlyle's insights, and has developed a keen interest in German philosophers and in works such as Goethe's *Faust*. Lord Bilbury, his contact with the Encyclopaedia's editorial board, is impressed. Gerald is invited to visit John and Margaret at Onslow on the outskirts of London for a few days.

John is dissatisfied, and is longing to get in touch with people in general. He longs to escape from 'highbrowness'. He and Margaret don't see this quite the same way, and it is apparent that a tension is growing between them. His poetic sermon about the Christmas Tree is not 'churchy' enough for his vicar. For Margaret—in John's view—Christianity is 'a kind of allegory of the goodness of the heart'; whereas her view of him is that he is indulging in 'highfalutin mysticism' (his own particular aversion). He is hurt by this, and yet he knows there is some truth in this accusation.

XXVII. Janet is longing to hear from Gerald (he has travelled north to see his father). She is in love with him, and there is a beautiful description of her feelings. At their next meeting, she realizes that they cannot be together. This leaves her in a state of great anguish and suffering, and she senses that she is ineligible for marriage. (She is considerably older than Gerald.) And yet they have a close relation of a different kind.

Humphrey offers to Janet that they resume living together, and that Gerald join them. She declines, then regrets this; but she wishes for the present to avoid meeting Gerald again. About a month later she writes a love-letter to Gerald, which she then burns the following morning. She requests work via Sir Otto Hudson.

XXVIII. In this chapter we enter fully into Barfield's thinly disguised version of certain contemporary political dramas.

Richard Metcalfe is an influential civil servant working under Sir Otto Hudson, whom he likes and respects. He has lunch with Sir Otto. Adela Cranage's poetry figures in their conversation—her name is one to be mentioned in such circles. Then Sir Otto brings the conversation round to a topic which is giving him current concern, namely, the 'Consumer Finance' scheme. In the opinion of what in his view are 'these cranks', the survival of poverty is due to a flaw in the economic system—there is not enough money available to consumers to purchase the goods and commodities produced by labour-saving machinery. If this problem could be rectified, poverty could be abolished. To Sir Otto, this was tantamount to proposing wholesale inflation. The main advocate of these plans is one Alfred Streeter, the Shadow Chancellor of the Industrial Party and a potential Prime Minister when Dodge, the Leader of the Opposition and a former Prime Minister, retired. (Metcalfe is currently also Dodge's confidential secretary.) Sir Otto sets his mind to influencing people against the 'Consumer Credit' scheme, on the grounds that 'the City wouldn't like it'.

Sir Otto tries to get Janet appointed as Dodge's secretarial assistant abroad (Dodge is spending a lot of time in Italy). He also institutes a press campaign against the ideas lying behind the 'Consumer Credit' scheme. These ideas are attributed to Hicks and Cameron, whom Killigrew, another prominent member of Hudson's circle, refers to as the 'currency cranks'.

XXIX. Gerald returns to London. He learns that his Carlyle article has been rejected and becomes despondent. He is currently estranged from Humphrey because of the latter's enthusiasm for Brockmann, an Austrian psychologist, philosopher, historian, doctor, astrologer and prophet with a new religion (in Gerald's eyes). Humphrey seems incapable of reading or talking about anything else.

Irritated by Adela Cranage's writing, Gerald goes out for a walk and is cheered up by some porters' antics outside Covent Garden. He decides to go to see *As You Like It.*

XXX. Margaret and John have now been married for 18 months. She has an innate loyalty to him, and is efficient as a hostess and housekeeper. She also has an active loyalty to the Church. John himself is always preoccupied and troubled. In addition to his marital problems, he is having struggles with his role as a clergyman. Despite his inherent geniality, he has difficulty with the fixed opinions of the elderly ladies in his congregation, who tend to regard the next world as an extension of this one. He hates 'improving on them' however.

The day after Gerald attended a performance of *As You Like It*, John had the duty of calling on one of his elderly parishioners, Miss Butler. He had expected a dismal conversation about death but was instead regaled with a somewhat lewd Limerick, and with a shock realized that she desired him physically. He flees home to find Margaret with Humphrey and Gerald. The ensuing conversation has strong sexual connotations, ranging from the behaviour of spiders to that of Rosalind and the 'emptiness' of romance. John says he thinks that Gerald is obsessed, a charge which Gerald regards as an expression of parsonical humbug.

XXXI. Margaret is wanting to tell John that she is pregnant, but cannot find the right moment. She decides to wait until after a ceremony in which his church's new font is being consecrated. John, who is officiating, is completely caught up in the giant swinging rhythm of the service, at the climax of which an enormous candle—representing the fertilizing power of the Holy Spirit—has to be ceremonially plunged into the waters of the font. Margaret is blissfully aware of the relationship between this divine mystery and the human one being enacted at that moment within her own body; whereas John—with his tendency always to find symbolism or meaning in what his senses are beholding—suddenly finds that part of his consciousness is viewing the scene as it were from above, with the result that the candlelit scene appears in his imagination as 'a naked picture, a picture with a meaning, one single definite meaning, and no other. And when that moment had passed and had become a memory—but not till then—this meaning seemed to him to be hideously gross'.

XXXII. Margaret is longing to tell John her secret; but he rebuffs her, on the grounds that after the ceremony he wants time to himself. He is struggling with his experience of the 'hideous grossness' of the immersion ceremony. For a moment he finds comfort in the notion that he as a priest has to have the strength to bear the burden of understanding the meaning of symbols, a knowledge which most of his parishioners are denied; but then he rebels against this notion of division and superiority. He becomes frightened and angry at the omnipresence of desire in his flock, and angry with Margaret. The next day they have a very painful conversation. Margaret accuses John of being only interested in himself, which is his cue to insist that she tells him what she has been wanting to say. On hearing her news, which she imparts almost against her will, he becomes almost all ablaze with tenderness. But it is too late, and he is aware of the shadow of an awful sadness. Margaret—who never really recovers from this experience—subsequently has a nightmare in which John figures as some menacing sea-creature.

Janet calls the following afternoon. She is leaving for Italy with Mr Dodge, as one of his private secretaries. She feels sorry for John and Margaret, who to her are like 'two helpless, pathetic little creatures caught in the toils of an alien, hostile world, like babes in the wood'. Janet and

John go for a walk outside: 'Both were aware of the soft air, the clear spring light, and the pale blue sky over their heads, as well as of the profusion of eager sticky buds on an occasional chestnut tree, which they passed...' John complains about his difficulty at not getting into closer touch with people. Janet's response is that this is 'the only thing that matters'. There is a terrible weight of sadness in her voice. John realizes that she has understood everything. 'It seems to me,' she says to him, 'we are all busy *working p-poisons out of our systems*!' After references to both Humphrey's intellectual adventures and to Gerald, they walk on in silence; and as they arrive back at the house 'it was as if the last deliberate pebble had been flung into that fathomless pool of holily intimate silence, and their two souls were sitting hand in hand, watching the ripples die gently away'.

Part Three

XXXIV. Humphrey psychoanalyses a book by Karl Brockmann (possibly *Occult Science—An Outline*). After being overwhelmed by his sense of the book's extreme egocentricity (and, hence, suitability for being psychoanalysed), he eventually gives up because he finds it so convincing. Gerald, who dislikes the very mention of Brockmann's name, insists that Humphrey should read Kant. Humphrey accordingly, 'not without considerable misgivings', borrows a copy of the *Critique of Pure Reason* from the library.

XXXV. Margaret has a fever. John devotedly looks after her. The chapter ends with the birds having settled (a recurrent dream image of hers) and everything seeming to be going right.

XXXVI. John is inwardly struggling with 'Jesus in Piccadilly' (a series of religious articles appearing in the daily press which Holroyd, his vicar, regards as a sign of a great religious revival in the popular consciousness). In these articles, Jesus is portrayed as an enlightened socialist with some unfortunate apocalyptic ideas. Although John has a strong social conscience, he finds that this kind of Christian socialism gives him nothing but pain. His inner strivings reflect his love for ritual, and his great respect for the likes of Traherne and George MacDonald. He remains concerned about his congregation's lack of understanding. There is a full description of his dilemma of, on the one hand, wishing to do away with a superior cleverness and, on the other, recognizing a need to keep the understanding of certain things away from people. He says to himself that 'Startop is a Catholic by nature, while I am a Protestant'.

XXXVII. John experiences sorrow at his sense of estrangement from the majority of his fellow men. Through newspapers he experiences 'a universally diffused senile decay of the intellect', manifested not least in the fact that 'everything in the paper was incompatible with something else'. He ceases to regard a division between highbrow and lowbrow as of any great significance; and he begins to understand the inspiration that brought the people at what he refers to as Humphrey's meeting together. He particularly recalls the man who had spoken about the 'Conversion Loan'. His thoughts then range to a recent speech by an American dignitary regarding Europe's 'moral' obligation to repay its debts to America, a speech where—for example—that country's capital investments are referred to quite candidly as 'open-hearted generosity'. This '*smearing over* of all meaning made him feel personally unhappy. It oppressed him almost physically.' How, he wonders, can there be any relation between such 'intellectual debauchery' and the Gospels? 'Am I only trying to *make* myself believe that Christ can have any further significance for the civilization?'

He then ponders the extent to which the average Englishman's imagination is increasingly fed not by ideas but by pictures: 'He suddenly perceived in a terribly clear new light the enormous difference between a picture and an idea; for, whereas an idea which is not comprehended is rendered by that very fact to some extent harmless, a picture, of which the *meaning* is not grasped, may still be *received*, and received in such an intimate way as positively to alter character'. From this train of thought his mind comes to focus upon his sense of 'dark, wise secret forces operating in the background—forces which knew all about the dangerous inner meanings of these pictures, which knew all about the senile decay of intellect . . . which not only knew all about these things, but consciously willed them'.

XXXVIII. John is in despair about 'those dark, implacable forces, before which he himself and the whole of civilization must apparently go down without the power to lift a finger', and about the 'continual imperceptible *smearing* of language'. He resolves to give up reading newspapers until after the baby is born and focus on his life with Margaret and as a priest. He has a serene vision of his and his family's future.

Sir Otto and Lady Hudson visit. They insist that Margaret use an anaesthetic for the birth. She refuses. During the visit, John informs the Hudsons that Dodge has settled in a villa near Luci, Southern Italy, together with Janet. Gerald Marston also makes his presence felt indirectly, in that Sir Otto stumbles upon an open book of his poems.

John and Margaret are drawing closer together into a real communion. The visits of the nurse are described, and Margaret's labour begins. Tragically, the baby dies immediately after birth.

XXXIX. Humphrey has by now read Kant's *Critique of Pure Reason*, and concludes: 'If Kant were right, all he [Brockmann] claimed to have arrived at in this way could really only be a phantasmagoria of pale reflections of sense-experience'. He then goes on to read a book by Brockmann (presumably Steiner's *Philosophy of Freedom*) whence he gains the impression that Kant is 'the arch-seducer of Western thought'. Humphrey is now deeply interested in Brockmann (as distinct from Lusst and Vogel), and is especially pleased that he did not require or desire *belief* from his followers. Gerald refuses to listen to anything about Brockmann. Similarly, he has considerable appreciation of Goethe the poet, but not of Goethe the man. In his conversation with Gerald, Humphrey then refers to Carlyle. He is convinced that Gerald needs Brockmann. Gerald is thinking of giving up writing (out of disappointment) and going into commercial affairs. He feels very lost and insecure.

XL. Humphrey gives up all thought of becoming a practising psychologist, and resumes his medical studies. He decides to devote himself to the medical section of Brockmann's movement, while continuing to study Brockmann and attend lectures and so forth. He persuades John to accompany him to a reading of one of Brockmann's lectures on some subject concerning medieval history. John has a negative reaction to the view of Christianity that he encounters and specifically to the somewhat dismissive attitude to the Roman Church that he finds in the circle of listeners. Deeply oppressed as he is at the time by his domestic circumstances, John's negative reaction to the meeting finds expression in the overwhelming sense of respect for the early church fathers—such as Augustine, Cyprian and Tertullian—that wells up in his soul. At any rate, his mind is firmly set against Brockmann. Humphrey is disappointed.

Humphrey then receives a letter from Gerald, who describes his work at Northern Syndicated Periodicals for whom he has to write 'cheap romances'. Gerald writes that he dislikes the *atmosphere* of Goethe's life, his relations with women. He states that his metaphysical position is similar to that of Ivan in *The Brothers Karamazov*, 'I believe in God but don't accept his world', adding that he has been very struck by a newspaper story of a 12-year-old American girl whose throat was cut after she had been kidnapped. He then describes his own 'inward lechery', his inward tendency to 'live nearly all the time—and quite willy-nilly—in a sort of *bath* of sex' and to 'lick up with great relish every piece of pornography I see in the shop windows'. Finally, he tells of his fears: 'Do you know I often lie in bed at night, literally *quaking* with fear—though, God knows what of!'

Gerald himself abruptly arrives at Humphrey's flat for a couple of nights. They go off to one of Rollo's Wednesday night meetings. Humphrey hasn't been for twelve months. Rex Rollo is present with Dawson. A speaker contrasts the 'egopetitive and altripetitive libidos' (the latter equated with Vogel and with 'a society in which each shall indeed live for all, instead of living for himself alone'). Rollo speaks dismissively of what he refers to as 'intellectual megalomania' (e.g. Hegel and transcendental philosophers, of whom Brockmann would undoubtedly be one), which to him is as much of a problem as emotional megalomania. Humphrey retorts (to Rollo and Dawson) that he can see no point in cursing abstractions with more abstractions; and he goes on to refer to Brockmann's work with the whole human organism. He invites Rollo and Dawson back to his flat for coffee.

XLI. Margaret sits alone reflecting. John joins her for supper. Their relations are strained, and she is having bad dreams. He attempts to 'have it out' with her. He feels as though she treats him like a dinner-party or dancing partner. She tries (unsuccessfully) through her silence to stop him making a fool of himself. In his anger he shakes her violently. She makes him aware that he in a sense killed their child: 'You—we both did it—on the night the font was blessed.' This is a reference to his statements implying that all the people present were just savages. She bewails his inability to *feel*, his incessant thinking, thinking. And yet she isn't wanting to blame him. She leaves the room. John is left in utter despair about his intellectual and pastoral ideals, bemoaning his fruitless search for 'some highfalutin *tertium quid*' and seeing the justification of Margaret's 'instinctive horror'. He turns the radio on and hears what is a kind of parody of words that he himself might have uttered in a sermon, and flings the earphones violently against the wall. He takes a fiendish pleasure in 'hurling every kind of insult he could think of at the Church, whose minister he was'. He puts on an ordinary collar and tie and leaves the house, not knowing where he is going.

XLII. John wishes that he was not a clergyman, having to be responsible for other people's morals. He decides to go to see Humphrey, and runs into the evening gathering. Humphrey is in full flow about the 'endless stream' of impressions 'pouring on us' (cinemas, advertisements, papers, slogans, philosophies, religions) and the power of the individual to blot this out by saying: 'Wup! All cars stop here!' He stresses the importance of thinking as an act of *will*: '*Mere* thinking is not much better than scratching.' Dawson observes cynically that moral judgements imply fear (suppressed). John makes a cutting remark to Dawson, who is fundamentally opposed to any notion of associating thinking with moral activity and links such notions merely with overcoming fear, controlling what one fears and hates. Then Rex Rollo joins in. A massive debate ensues, with Dawson and John at the opposite extremes (representing a pre-/anti-Christian and Christian attitude respectively). 'I *must* interest myself in the weaker' (John). '*Why* must I interest myself in the weaker?' (Dawson). Rollo then introduces the figure of his 'Old Man', who in his view understands everything much better than we do. Humphrey critically relates this figure to the constitution of the Jesuits, where it states that 'every Jesuit must be guided by his superior, as if he were a corpse or a staff *in the hand of an old man* to serve him'. Gerald is reminded of Dostoevsky's 'Grand Inquisitor'. For his part, John realizes that he 'was Christian *because he chose to be*'. Gerald then takes up the thread of the polarity between the subtleties of modern self-consciousness and the wish to get back into the darkness of a 'pagan' consciousness (the latter being supported by Rollo and Dawson). 'Consciousness exists,' he concludes.

John leaves in much better spirits. Rollo and Dawson also leave.

XLIII. Rollo and Dawson walk together towards their homes. Rollo has decided to give up his meetings: 'I discovered that I am not a *whole*. That is why we cannot act. Instead, we only go on talking. When you are not a whole yourself, you must find a whole to which you attach yourself. That is a law. That is what we are to do . . . From now I shall begin to seek for my whole, till I have found it . . . In order to know oneself, one must first attach oneself to a whole that knows itself . . .' And he goes in search of such an external whole.

Rollo and Dawson part. Dawson encounters an old man with some obscene postcards who insistently asks for a night's shelter. He knocks him unconscious and goes home (to his mother's house).

XLIV. Humphrey and Gerald converse once their guests have left. They revert to the subject of body and soul (or mind). Humphrey recounts Brockmann's account of the abolition of the spirit of man in the ninth century at the eighth Oecumenical Council. Gerald continues to be suspicious of Brockmann, and of all 'cults of the individual soul', with their 'fundamental egotism', 'all this Rosicrucian stuff about the individual ego, its colossal importance in the scheme of things'. Humphrey longs to win Gerald's enthusiasm for Central European thought. In Humphrey's view, English culture is obsessed with the split between subject and object, mind and body. German culture doesn't need to be but is, because of the spirit of the age, which 'comes from us'. The English people, he says, can't understand the heart (he contrasts Hamlet and Goethe). Gerald protests that all this self-knowledge business is stopping him from writing poetry. He feels afraid, cold, frightened to go to bed alone. Humphrey reads him something by one of Brockmann's pupils (including a meditation). Gerald is moved, and agrees to read Brockmann and Novalis.

XLV. Gerald's father has a terminal illness. Gerald has a sense of his own uselessness—a 'sclerosis' of the heart. He reads a book by Brockmann on acquiring higher knowledge. His father dies. John writes to Gerald, enclosing a lengthy poem ('The New Scapegoat') in the style of Spenser. He is now living (with Margaret) in the North of England as the vicar of a poor working community called Loomfield, where unemployment abounds. It is his choice that they have moved there from the more comfortable South. 'God save us and bless us!' comments Gerald after reading John's poem, 'What on earth is the man up to now?'

XLVI. John is trying to guide religious discussions in Loomfield, where people have no historical sense whatever (apart from the Communists). He wants to describe Christ as 'a decent sort of chap', but finds no way of getting anything across. There is no beauty in his parishioners' lives, no leisure or personal space—and, moreover, no money to buy goods that those in work have made. Margaret does not share his social passion. He wonders whether they should move to a living in the country amidst art and nature, while realizing that he has made his choice.

Janet arrives. (Dodge is campaigning for a local parliamentary seat.) She advises John to enable Margaret to get away for a bit. She suggests that Gerald go with her to a garden party that her mother, Lady Hudson, is organizing at Klosters (John cannot go, nor can Janet).

XLVII. Gerald arrives at John and Margaret's house. He and John have a conversation, initially about John's poem 'The New Scapegoat' but then moving on to romance, a theme which both men find very important in their different ways. John goes on to speak about the ideas of Hicks and Cameron, insisting that poverty in the twentieth century 'is simply an illusion. There's not an *atom* of *need* for it.' He points out that 'over-production has two quite distinct meanings: (i) producing more than is wanted and (ii) producing more than you can sell'. The solution in the latter instance is to 'increase the community purchasing-power by reducing prices' (via funds emanating from central government). John is becoming increasingly aware of the resistance in certain influential circles to these and other creative ideas ('people are being got at by pictures', in advertising for instance). Thus whereas the real problem today is distributing goods, all is focused on the fictitious one of distributing *employment*. Far too much value is attached to salesmanship and competition. Production has reached saturation point—but we don't use our wealth in a social way. The academic world is also oblivious to creative thinking along these lines, and dons are appointed only when they say what is wanted. A fundamental problem is that people are afraid of freedom. Control is omnipresent, secret control via money. John concludes that 'the one thing people cannot bear is that a man's moral nature is *his own affair*. That he is free to determine his own destiny. That he needn't—that he can't—be "good" unless he wants to . . .' Gerald is deeply interested in John's ideas. However, he doesn't think John's poem could be published. John, for his part, encourages Gerald to write something himself, a suggestion which elicits the melancholy Barfieldian retort that 'those that read don't need: those that need don't read!' They conclude with mutual encouragement.

XLVIII. Margaret's experience of John has become more difficult since the painful conversation that they shared. She feels resentment now, even hostility. She feels that her cooperation is fundamentally not wanted. John himself took the decision to go up north. All she could do was to put the occasional spoke in his wheel.

Janet arrives. They discuss French novels. Margaret has plenty of time for reading. She is going to Klosters with Gerald, who now together with John—who tries to avoid Margaret—joins the two women after their conversation. Janet is still in love with Gerald. She feels filled with the spirit of her own youth, and loses her stammer. Gerald is equally aware of her. He then refers to the political ideas that he and John had been discussing. This prompts a strongly felt comment by John: ' "The politicians are under the City"—and he jammed his thumb down on the surface of a little table so hard that the pressure bent it backwards—"like that!" ' Margaret goes out, ostensibly to pack.

The political theme is then taken further, through a reference to Streeter's interest in Consumer Credit (Streeter is the Shadow Chancellor for the Industrialist Party). However, he has been removed from office by

Dodge through orders 'from some big person in the City' (this information originates from Sir Otto Hudson's assistant Richard Metcalfe). At this point Metcalfe himself arrives asking for Janet. His dramatic news is that Streeter is after all seeking election to Parliament for Ferrocester NW, a change which is Metcalfe's doing (influenced, for reasons which are shortly to become apparent, by Janet). Metcalfe leaves for his hotel with Janet.

XLIX. Metcalfe indicates Janet's indirect part in the above events. Then he announces that he wants to marry her. She refuses him. She thinks they would be incompatible, she says, but keenly senses the compliment. Her own longing is for Gerald.

L. Gerald and Margaret set off for Margaret's family home in the Cotswolds. He muses about the drab lives of the factory girls visible from the train window, pondering thoughts which bring him close to John. They arrive amidst warm summer weather, and a romantic idyll opens up for them both.

LI. Gerald and Margaret are very happy together 'on holiday'. They attend a variety concert in the village hall, and the following morning they go for a leisurely country walk to a neighbouring village church with an interesting old carving of St Michael transfixing the dragon with his sword. There are some glorious descriptions of this natural paradise, the sunlight on the limestone of the church, the magic of an old inn-garden. As the day wears on, they come across a fair in readiness for the evening. A mood of summer evening happiness prevails, children's voices breaking a blissful stillness. They ride on the fairground horses, then discover a circus tent. The climax of the circus performance is when a clown strips himself of his outer garments while riding a horse. Gerald wants to kiss Margaret. He feels blissfully happy—and so does she.

John sends news of Streeter's electoral success.

Part Four

LII. Gerald and Margaret are still enjoying their time at Klosters. Gerald feels like Margaret's courtly lover, delighting in being her servant. He also becomes aware of Janet in this connection. Perhaps because of having read Brockmann's book on attaining higher knowledge, he finds that he is able to gain insights into the hearts of his friends.

The garden party itself now takes place. It does not turn out to be such a magnificent affair as Gerald had imagined, being essentially a means whereby Lady Hudson could at one stroke fulfil social obligations to a number of neighbouring families. The local 'Agriculturalist' (Conservative) Member of Parliament is there, together with several of Sir Otto Hudson's friends from London. Gerald is entranced with the country dancing, and especially the Morris dancers from a neighbouring market-town: '. . . after a few country dances had been disposed of, six men in white shirts and trousers came on with their bells and handkerchiefs and began one of the dances in the local tradition. Gerald, who had never seen the Morris before, was immediately spellbound. The plaintive little melody from the fiddle, set against the angular childlike springings and hoppings of the male dancers, seemed to produce such a blend of humour and pathos with a rare elusive kind of spiritual grace, as made him feel that he had peeped for an instant right into the open heart of England.' However, when he goes up to the leader of the team he discovers that the side consists largely of young men from university as opposed to local people. Margaret helps him to appreciate the great importance of the revival movement. Later in the afternoon, Gerald's mind goes back to this 'same inexpressibly touching vision! The stupidity—and the grace! Ariel . . . Bottom . . . Tears rose to the brink of Gerald's eyes, as for a moment he beheld, whole and incarnate in his imagination, that shadowy Figure, which he *knew*, however thickly it might be overlaid with the corpulent philistinism of one generation or the sexual fiddle-faddle of another, to be the core and living spirit of England.'

LIII. That evening there is a conversation at dinner about—among other things—the merits of (Chinese) ancestor-worship. Gerald is sitting opposite Margaret. Two of Sir Otto's guests, Moulton the well-known theatre manager and novelist and Professor Curbiton the physiologist, are discussing this and other themes against the background of ingrained materialistic assumptions. Much of the conversation is flippant and sardonic. Gerald, who takes very little part in the discussion, is intensely aware of his own distinction between 'awake' and 'asleep' human beings; and he looks round the table of guests at a series of 'alternately crepitating and cachinnating masks. He could almost hear—behind them—the snores. And at the same instant he seemed in a flash to comprehend Humphrey as he had never comprehended him before, and after the fashion in which he had recently "re-understood" John and Janet. A certain superfluous fierceness, which he had often detected in Humphrey's attitude towards various current ideas and mannerisms, stood before him for the first time in a perfectly clear light and, as long as it did so, he was not with the people who sat beside him, but with Humphrey himself. It had suddenly become so absolutely obvious to him that the best possible thing, indeed the only thing of any importance at all, was that this ripple should stop! "Wup!" he thought to himself half-wonderingly, "all cars stop here!" and his lips could not forbear curving into a soft and secret smile at the memory of Humphrey's animation that night in front of Dawson and Rollo. "I shall be seeing him tomorrow!" he thought, and at once felt something inspirited against the emptiness he had been fearing.'

That night he cannot sleep, and goes to the library to look for a book about the history of Klosters (a former monastery) recommended by Sir Otto. He finds it. However, his eye is caught by the new Imperial Encyclopaedia; and he looks up the article on Carlyle included in preference to his own. It is disparaging of the influence of German culture and transcendental philosophy on Carlyle, and the adjective 'turgid' is used many times to denote the author's point of view. Gerald just has time to notice the initials A.C. (Adela Cranage) at the end of the article when Sir Otto and an older man (subsequently to be revealed as his father-in-law) enter the library. They are discussing strategies of influencing newspaper headlines and cartoons and how to subtly 'water' the anti-German impulse (while making it appear that a pro-German impulse is being promulgated). Gerald, who is hidden from view by a screen, feels acutely embarrassed that he is involuntarily eavesdropping and abruptly comes out from his place of concealment. The old man seems outwardly unperturbed, although Gerald notices that he has a 'ferocious and questioning intensity'. Once Gerald has left the room after his unconvincing explanation that he had fallen asleep, we learn that the old man is the leader of some kind of occult brotherhood. He and his son-in-law discuss the possible necessity of employing more 'melodramatic methods' and forms of 'semi-initiation' to achieve their goals.

Gerald leaves Klosters the following morning for London by an early train.

LIV. Gerald realizes that he has become rather fond of Margaret. He reflects on the weekend and hopes that something will come of all the impressions that he has gained. This is for him not a matter of having an affair with his friend's wife (even though Margaret is undoubtedly the focus of many of his thoughts) but rather of hungering for a fulfilment of the romantic longings with which he has been—in his eyes—blessed, a deep wish for 'romanticism' to 'come of age'.

He gets a job in London as a salesman, and encounters a world—radically different from the one he has just been in—where 'time is money'. On arriving as prearranged at Humphrey's flat, he encounters Mrs Hannaford, Humphrey's new charwoman whom he has not yet met and who thinks that Gerald is Humphrey. Gerald thinks that a message intended for Humphrey from Margaret is for him, and is about to seek fulfilment of his immediate romantic feelings when Humphrey returns, thereby saving Gerald from embarrassment and curing him of the illegitimate aspect of his longings.

LV. John has managed to get on with some work in Margaret's absence. He continues to be aware of the difficulties between them. On her return, he warmly embraces her, even though the tension remains there in the background. They have a few happy weeks together, keeping the gulf between their attitudes and perceptions at bay.

Janet announces that political support for Streeter has cooled. A press campaign against 'the new financial measures with which Streeter intends to startle us all' is in progress.

LVI. The press campaign against Streeter is well underway, and there is an elaborate description of these machinations. The Industrialists (Labour) have won the election. Dodge pleads for support from his colleagues for Streeter's reforms (although he is too canny to say what they consist of). Both Lombard Street and Fleet Street (banks and press) campaign against Whitehall, specifically the Chancellor of the Exchequer, Streeter and the Minister of Labour together with the Prime Minister. The 'inflationist Chancellor' is remorselessly attacked, and the exchange rate plummets. Dodge is obliged to make a speech about the notorious 'Releasing Loan', speculation about which is causing all these problems; and it transpires that it has something to do with facilitating emigration to the Colonies or transfer to other parts of the country where there is available work. In the meantime, Streeter's ideas are to be studied by a 'committee of experts', who will 'report on their practicability'. As this group of experts is to include Sir Otto Hudson, there is a general sense of relief that the ideas will be well and truly buried. Dodge concludes his speech with a cry of 'forward to prosperity!' and confirms that it is the Government that runs the country and not the press.

Gerald takes very little notice of all this, but out of an obligation to

John writes him a full account of the conversation between Sir Otto Hudson and his father-in-law.

LVII. Margaret is having a nightmare about John, who in her dream was trying to murder her. She is very sensitive to anything that John says about her father, about 'plotting to keep the people down'. When she protests that John should 'have it out with him', her husband dismisses the idea, on the grounds that Sir Otto would simply say—in Grand Inquisitorial fashion—that it was all done for people's good. Besides, he could never betray Gerald's confidence by indicating to Sir Otto that he was aware of the content of his conversation with his father-in-law. Margaret is also opposed to the ideas of Hicks and Cameron. 'Nobody,' she concludes, 'has any idea of all that people like my father are saving them from. His responsibilities must be terrible.'

They decide to live apart. She leaves by train. It is clear that she supports her father before John.

LVII. John discovers that it is even worse to live without Margaret than with her. He then concludes that his whole life has been a kind of mistake—making battles instead of following signposts.

Margaret stays in London with a lady called Susan Holmes. She and Margaret agree on having two weeks apart. John then proposes a holiday together in Italy for a month. She accepts.

LIX. They leave for Lucci, to join Janet who is staying in Dodge's villa.

Humphrey is preparing for his medical examinations. He has found his path. Gerald has definitely not. He recalls his night fears as a child, and is aware of his fondness for giving way to a temptation. He reflects on the decline and decadence of a civilization, and on the tendency to return to the darkness of the womb all that we have won from it. This overwhelming sense of being called back to the ancient matriarchal altar is associated by some with Romance, by others with Sex. Gerald, who is strongly drawn to these mysterious depths of human existence, decides to seek refuge again in that garden of medieval literature which had brought him such delight, in particular the sensuous love-lyrics of the *Pervigilium Veneris* . . . '*Cherchez la femme!* Yes, and it is time for thee, too, Gerald Marston! Thou too shalt rest. But where?'

He then receives a letter from the editor of a new monthly periodical requesting a specimen of dramatic criticism. To him this is 'like a breath of his forgotten youth'. A ticket is enclosed for a play, so Gerald cheerfully goes to see it. However, the house is nearly empty, the play being one of

Arthur Moulton's few complete failures. Gerald finds the play utterly boring, but considers that he must try to see it through. As the curtain rises on the Second Act, however, a paper pellet hits him on the side of his head, followed by another one at the end of the same Act. On unfolding this second piece of paper he finds that it contains a message: 'In box No. 2.' He goes there and meets a young lady, with distinct physical attractions. They both dislike the play, and she invites him home. They have dinner, then she seduces him. He notices the initials A.C. sewn into one of her garments, which he is carefully—even reverently—folding, and at this point he realizes that she is the author whose article on Carlyle has supplanted his. A battle ensues between his desire and his thoughts. Suddenly, the golden cloud around her, the object of his abject adoration, passes over into himself; and she turns from a glorious creature into a silly dressed-up girl, rather as though she were his own daughter making an embarrassing *faux pas*. But he chooses to bury his thoughts and deliberately does all that it had been intended he should do, in the knowledge that he would be haunted for ever by desire for her image if he does not.

LX. Gerald wants Adela to marry him. She agrees to an engagement. He feels jealousy towards her other (former?) lovers. She does not really respond to his feelings. And yet she is, precisely for this reason, an otherness.

John writes to Gerald from Italy. He (Gerald) should look out for himself. 'Some people may think you know too much!' Gerald is aware that there is no relationship between his feelings for Margaret and for Adela, and he also suspects that Adela may be part of a conspiracy. He asks her if she was put up to it, a question which brings a vigorous denial. But he doesn't altogether believe her, and breaks off the engagement.

LXI. Gerald tells Humphrey about breaking the engagement. Humphrey is beginning to come round to John's ideas about 'secret control', so he understands Gerald's reasons for taking John's advice seriously.

John and Margaret are in good spirits in Italy. Margaret is painting, and John is thinking of getting a chaplaincy out there. Shortly after Humphrey has finished reading John's letter to Gerald, a telegram arrives bearing news of a serious accident and requesting Humphrey's immediate presence. On telephoning Klosters, Humphrey learns that Margaret is having a surgical operation. He agrees to travel to Italy by train with Sir Otto Hudson, while Lady Hudson is to fly over with Margaret's beloved cat Merlin.

LXII. Humphrey and Sir Otto leave for Italy by train. Gerald, having seen them off, returns home alone. His night terrors, from which he suffered incessantly as a child, are troubling him again. Moreover, he is worried that he has lost something of enormous value by giving up Adela. It is not so much that he is missing Adela herself, but he is aware that she had given him confidence, courage and 'a kind of light': 'The light was something which irradiated the whole of nature, sparkled out of his eyes, and shone back to him again from everything—even from the most ordinary human beings with whom he had to deal! Did he seek in his memory for its original source, it appeared always to be streaming out from that moment when she had reappeared to him in the doorway of her room. And this mysterious reassuring, joy-creating light was now gradually fading away . . .' As a result, he feels increasingly like a beached vessel, while also aware of a split between the physical greed of the blood and cold reason of which he has always been conscious except when in love. And yet his awareness of the danger of going back to Adela is even greater. He starts reading Novalis' *Hymns to the Night* (in German) and finds deep inspiration, 'allowing, with the intentness of a thirsty man drinking, drinking, drinking, that holy twilight to rise up and embosom his garish disintegration and self-hatred . . . He wondered if the Ugly Duckling had felt at all like this.'

LXIII. Humphrey and Sir Otto travel together, their destination being the vicinity of Naples. On their arrival, Margaret's accident is described: she was knocked down by a lorry, causing concussion and the crushing of the right hand and arm that held her painting. Her arm is amputated, to John's great disappointment (he had somehow thought that Humphrey's medical expertise could suggest an alternative to that proposed by local surgeons). Merlin the cat disappears.

LXIV. Margaret is aware of his absence, and is terrified that he may be subjected to vivisection. On making local enquiries, John learns that a certain *Villa Malfese*, which turns out to be close to their own villa, is notorious for such practices. The search is therefore focused there. Sir Otto discourages visiting this house; but John is adamant. On seeing John's resolution, Sir Otto repeats to Humphrey three Latin words mentioned in strict confidence by his father-in-law. On being admitted to the house at their second visit, they find a large fresco with a severed human head lying face upwards in a dish. Humphrey observes to John that 'it may mean worse things than vivisection'—through Brockmann's research he is aware, as John is not, of the black-magical occult significance of this image of John the Baptist's severed head. Humphrey taps at a heavy door, and responds to a query by uttering the three Latin words. The door opens to a smell of incense. A group of men are gathered in a sort of crescent formation around the table, on which are a charcoal brazier, surgical instruments and a soft, grey object strapped to a board. In the dim light radiated by the brazier, John recognizes the face of Francis Leslie Dawson among the group. (Humphrey does not see him.) Humphrey seizes the board with the object on it and leaves, shaking his fist at the men. They return to Margaret with the cat. Humphrey wants to go to the police, but he is feeling very faint after this experience and returns to the house with John.

LXV. Gerald is feeling refreshed by his reading of Novalis. In his mind Caliban is vanquished and made a servant. His dreams are impregnated with the images of Novalis' poetry—intense longing for the feminine, deep happiness but also fear, and a memory of a picture in a childhood volume of Shakespeare of the ghost of Hamlet's father, which haunts him until he realizes that the terrifying being of this old man with its cruel, vindictive will was there to crush and annihilate 'a certain paltry, tremulous, guilt-laden weakling, whose name was Gerald Marston', until such time as 'he should have become once more what he ought always to have been'. The old man is banished with this thought. Gerald then falls into a dreamless sleep, awakes in the morning and then falls on his knees in prayer—he knows not to whom. He then hastily composes a poetic meditation, stuffs the piece of paper into his desk and hurries off to the Underground. In the evening he reads what he had written, a kind of Hymn to the Night in tribute to his Bride of Sleep.

LXVI. Margaret is delighted to have Merlin back, and she seems to be recovering her spirits. Humphrey is feeling very weak and giddy. He is less confident than John about Margaret's recovery because of the severity of her head injury. Margaret, anxious to impart something to John, quietly utters to him the words 'I understand ... your light'. She is increasingly oppressed by what seems like a great weight upon her head. There follows a description of her death, as experienced by herself: she was being caught up from above and being rushed through space at enormous speed ... All thought was becoming impossible.

LXVIII. Her funeral takes place the following afternoon. The Hudsons return to England. Nothing can be done by the police, and John,

Humphrey and Janet are advised to leave as soon as possible. Janet breaks off her connection with Dodge.

They go via Lausanne, where they meet Metcalfe and his newly wedded wife, Adela Cranage. Metcalfe is working for an International Bank, the intention of which is that it will lead to the abolition of distinctive national currencies. Adela and Janet meet for the first time. Janet realizes that this is the woman with whom Humphrey was having a relationship (see Chapters XXIII–XXV).

LXIX. Gerald and Humphrey reflect on the events at the Villa. Humphrey comments that there are other ways of achieving clairvoyance and related states of being than those recommended by Brockmann.

Humphrey then reports that John was terribly upset about what he thought Margaret's last words to him were, on the grounds that there was something about him that she couldn't stand: 'I can't stand your light' (see Chapter LXVI for her actual words). (The reader might well wonder why the relationship of these two unfortunate beings is turned by the author into such a path of torture. See Chapter 15 of this present book for a suggestion as to why this is so.)

Gerald speaks with Humphrey about his warm memories of his time with Margaret in Klosters. He feels as though she is '*still here* . . . in some way'. Humphrey makes him aware that John's sense of loss is far more absolute than this. He also imparts to him the content of his own conversation with John, when he had felt emboldened to tell John what he had experienced during his fainting fit, or out-of-the-body experience, in the vain hope that this might help him come to terms with his bereavement. Humphrey had perceived that Margaret's accident was karmic, 'that her Angel had killed her'. It was not their destiny to be living happily in Italy—they weren't meant to live such a life. John's reaction to these tidings was to say some 'very unpleasant things'.

Gerald and Humphrey proceed to have a discussion about reincarnation. Gerald has a problem with people's need to *believe* in things, which Humphrey warmly sympathizes with. This attitude of Gerald's encourages Humphrey to tell him about something else that he experienced during his faint, namely, a glimpse of Gerald's previous life as a woman, a courtesan, in the Middle Ages. The two of them had a relationship at the time in this previous life.

Humphrey then resolves to speak with John about Brockmann—'it may even be his only chance'. *Fear* is at the bottom of people's rejection of spiritual science (he says). 'I can see this thing being suppressed more and more vindictively with every device known to human ingenuity—and the devil's.' Gerald speaks of the virtue—seemingly widely evident—of tolerance. Humphrey replies that there is more than one form of persecution, and that tolerance is practised very selectively. He is aware that his group is regarded by many as slightly mad, and that madness is 'a danger to society'. He predicts that things will get *far* worse in terms of compulsion and control. And yet 'all the time you can see a little group of people, steadily growing larger and larger, who will go on talking calmly and confidently—as a matter of course—about the Angels and Archangels and the rest of the Hierarchies and their own dead friends and relations, just as the rest of the world talks about the bus-conductor.'

Gerald dwells affirmatively upon all that Humphrey has said. He reflects on his life and sees a clear pattern and purpose in its events.

LXX. Sir Otto Hudson's father-in-law is seriously ill in the Hudsons' London flat. Janet sees a foreign-looking visitor enter his bedroom and stay for two hours. (Janet and John have come to town to collect Merlin.) The visitor is Rex Rollo. Janet shows him into the room (or at least encounters him). The narrator alone is party to the ensuing conversation. The old man is anxious to impart a last message before he dies. Semi-initiation (arising from the impulse of German philosophy) is to be crushed always, he says. Brockmann remains a grave threat, and the only hope of defeating his movement is to learn from him. Reincarnation is to be utterly shunned, and active intelligence discouraged. For the purposes of the brotherhood, it is better that England and America lose their separate identity, 'for *we* know that the ultimate future lies in any case with a united West'. The Jews are useful, the universities and publishing trade easy to penetrate, Kant, Lusst and Vogel either beneficial or harmless. Above all, he warns Rollo, you must prevent the Three uniting; for any form of true threefoldness (as opposed to duality) would work 'like dynamite!'. They then speak of what was for them the very worrying situation surrounding Streeter and Dodge, in that for a few days they did not know what Dodge was going to do. The International Bank should be very helpful to their cause in future. As he leaves the room, Rollo assures the old man that, even after death, 'you will be acting, Master!'

LXXI. Humphrey takes John to a social gathering where Brockmann's lectures are being discussed. He encounters a rather fanatical lady (Miss Dominick). In a subsequent conversation with Humphrey, when the latter claims that 'the whole of life makes nonsense without reincarnation', John indicates that he refuses to have anything to do with this concept. Humphrey changes the subject.

LXXII. Mrs Marston (Gerald's mother) moves to a small house near London. Humphrey gives notice to leave his Bloomsbury flat (he intends to go abroad to work in a clinic following his successfully concluded examination). He marks the occasion by giving a farewell dinner-party, to which he invites Gerald, Janet and John.

They talk about the failure of the Releasing Loan policy. John realizes he can do nothing about it, and for this reason is losing interest in political matters: 'I'm really much more interested in the human beings I have round me, *as they are* here and now, than I am in possible new civilizations. A new order of civilization may be absolutely necessary; but in the meantime these people are actually here, forming part of the old one. And they will continue to form part of it . . .' He intends to remain in the Church and at Loomfield—even though he has realized his mistake in entering the Church. Janet will move in with him.

Gerald has been reading Novalis, and is full of thoughts about the heart and the importance of feeling. The English, he observes, have a particular difficulty with this: 'They can't see anything else *but* the body!' This would not be so much of a problem, he adds, if it were realized that the earth—far from being something to be ashamed of—is in fact nothing else than visible spirit. Humphrey then helps Gerald to explain that what he has in mind is no mere 'abstract *idea* of a *via media* between body and mind': 'He [Gerald] wants to make it clear that he's not talking about some neat psychological theory of a balance between Thinking, Feeling and Willing. What he is talking about is a definite *Thing*—a sort of *Tertium Quid*—you have either got it or you haven't.' Gerald—who has by now developed a great admiration and gratitude (though not affection) for Goethe—relates this concept of Humphrey's on the one hand to the Eternal Feminine and on the other to 'the necessity of egoism', in the sense that 'Christianity tells you to *sacrifice* your ego, not to pretend you haven't got one'. He then shares his vision of the seeds of a new civilization, based on a counter-picture of Dostoevsky's image (in *The Possessed*) of a network of little groups throughout the country bound together by fear, working towards the total destruction of civilization: 'The idea has come to me at just this moment that exactly the opposite might be true of the building up of a new civilization—a series of groups, forming independently, bound together by love, and then eventually joining up with one another into a larger whole . . .' Humphrey then asks him if he has written anything. He answers affirmatively, and with the Trinders' welcoming permission plunges into his fairy tale or *Märchen*.

LXXIII. *The Rose on the Ash Heap* or *Tertium Quid*

I. Sultan, Lord of all the Asias, has fallen passionately in love with a white-skinned dancer named Lady or Lucy. She flees westwards, returns to the Temple and then leaves for the West again (her destination being the land of Albion). Sultan's one thought is to find her, and yet she proves very elusive. After following for a long time in her tracks, he arrives in Albion.

II. The Lord of Albion has a newly adopted daughter ('the Princess'). He has a great love of horses, and his prime concern is to preserve the quality of the breed. (As in many a traditional folk tale, horses are symbolic of the faculty of thinking.) Abdol, the Lord's adversary, is mentioned in connection with the slave-mills which, outside the confines of the Palace, alone offer a means of finding a livelihood. Sultan arrives, and he and Lady (for it is she) embrace. The Lord of Albion maintains a domain of perfect freedom. His kingdom is threatened by Abdol, a very rich financier and businessman. Albion has become Abdolbion, where the adage 'Work for me and buy what I wish to sell you' represents the law that everyone is expected to abide by. Abdol breeds a different strain of horses, and specializes in the production and distribution of mineral oils, a vast store of which is being accumulated in the country. One night, without any warning other than the soaking of its surroundings in oil, the Palace is burnt down and reduced to ashes. Everyone inside is presumed to have been killed.

III. Sultan takes refuge in a part of the country which is untouched by Abdol. He is advised by his friendly host to seek out the Poet, who turns out to be an elderly and graceful—and most hospitable—man (with a certain affinity to Walter de la Mare) who, after advising Sultan to visit the Philosopher, sends him on his way with the strains of a moving and thoroughly romantic sonnet.

Sultan travels westwards to find the Philosopher, who has a fascination for telescopes. Abdol's realm is all around. The Philosopher lives in the centre of a dirty town. He is eccentric in the opposite direction from the Poet, but deeply moral. Sultan stays many weeks with him, learning the virtue of constancy (which the Poet, who is mourning the loss of the wife whom he himself has abandoned, does not possess) and brazen individualism: 'Man is only truly man when he can stand four-square to the Universe, as I am standing now, and hurl defiance at its icy ruthlessness, even as I am hurling it now!' Sirius, the dog star, seems to wink at Sultan, changing colour from green to orange.

LXXXIV. (*Tertium Quid*, continued)

IV. Sultan continues westwards in solitude and bereft of friendship, though he finds friends in the stars. Abdol's dominion is increasingly apparent everywhere. Sultan finds comfort in his poems, of which this is one:

I have been very lonely all today,
Above the million voices of the crowd
Hearing one voice I might not set at bay
Of lost imagination, crying loud
How wide the world was it must wander through
And for what empty years—till in dismay
I turned mine eyes up to the stars and knew
Only that they were very far away
    Ah, God, to come this evening to some room
    And, dropping soft the latch on stars and men,
    To find my Lady in its firelit gloom
    Filling it with her loveliness, and then
    To take her in my arms and hear her say:
    'I have been very lonely all today!'

He arrives at the Western outpost of the land through which he is travelling, which adjoins the Pacific Ocean, and reaches a supposedly inaccessible peninsula ending in a rock called Cape Limit. There is, however, a hotel on this rock, 'The Saracen's Head', which belongs to Abdol. He is given a room at the top of this hotel and gazes at the stars, giving himself up to them in mystic abandonment. Sirius, the dog star, speaks to him. He sees and hears the singing of the stars, a vision of colour. The constellation of the Virgin seems to caress him. He gains hope through this, and knows what he must do:

Oh, traveller through the Zodiac
Pass further on—by turning back.

V. Sultan is given a key by the manager of the hotel. It is a gift of Mr Abdol, and will open all doors and cupboards. This is his means of earning a living, since most of the inhabitants of Abdol's world have a habit of losing their keys almost as soon as they have been given them. He calls on the Philosopher and the Poet on his journey back to Albion. Eventually, he arrives at Albion, at the city where the terrible disaster took place. A Funfair has replaced the Palace—it is known as 'Abdol's Great Gift to the Nation' and contains numerous outlets for physical sensation and sensual gratification, including 'Abdol's Palace of Dancing' and 'Abdol's Automatic Tarts'. Everything is a display of Abdol's proprietary monopolies, not the least visible of which is a huge illuminated advertisement for Abdol's vinegar comprising a figure hanging on a Cross refusing a proffered sponge, at which point the words 'It's not Abdol's' light up on the hoarding. Abdol has been '*loading* the people with kindness'. The monarchy has been abolished and a republic established; and the State organization is a parody of Hicks and Cameron's ideas.

Sultan discovers the Ash Heap, which is all that remains of the huge conflagration that engulfed the Palace. This has for some reason been left untouched, though it has become a sort of rubbish heap, a dumping-ground for broken bottles, tin cans and dirty pieces of paper, thus creating an atmosphere of desolation and squalor.

VI. Sultan tries to earn a living with his master-key, and discovers that many people have even forgotten what they have put in their locked boxes, the keys to which they have lost. A typical response is : 'If we have anything valuable we take it to the Bank. Abdol keeps everything for us today—and a good job too!' Nevertheless, Sultan's aim is to earn enough money to return to the East, where he intends to retire for ever to the Temple. Meanwhile, although he hates the Amusement Park he is lured by it (despite the Virgin's call): he has memories of the seraglio, and of a pretty little concubine whose attentions he enjoyed there. He then sees a Rose growing on the Ash Heap—it seems to be *glowing*. Mysteriously, he senses a fulfilment of the Virgin's vision in what he beholds. In obedience to the vision's command, he utters what he knows are—for him—lies: 'I have found the Beloved! I desire nothing! I am at peace!' He plucks the red rose in a lustful way, and hears a woman's voice laughing in low, mischievous tones. The rose glows more brightly than ever, and sings to him:

Earth despairs not, though her Spark
Underground is gone—
Roses whisper after dark
Secrets of the Sun.
Blushing through the bridal night
To the stars above:
'Love grew in the dark—Oh Light,
Seek the womb of Love!'

Sultan visits the *further* side of the Ash Heap, and finds a little door which he is able to open with his key. He enters.

VII. He walks a long way along the underground passageway, eventually finding a large Marquee. This is the home of a little-visited circus that, according to the tall, dignified Ringmaster and Proprietor who welcomes Sultan, Abdol—'the old Deceiver'—would love to close but he does not possess the title deeds to the site. The Ringmaster adds that everyone has a key to the door but most people lose theirs. As a result, very few actually visit the circus. Sultan is keen to join, and the Ringmaster describes the initiation rites practised in this subterranean temple, which is on the surface a riding school where new arrivals have to don clown's apparel. They are only allowed to remove this when they have mastered the skill of removing all their many layers of clothing while riding at speed on horseback around the ring. Sultan chooses the fiery Arab steed Abba. The Ringmaster, who is a kind of Guardian of the Threshold figure, warns him of the dangers of his choice but clearly approves. He then goes on to describe to Sultan the missions which the Godivas, the initiated students, undertake to the outside world. He indicates that the electric dragons in the Amusement Park will one day come alive, that 'everything will come alive' and that only through the dedicated training that he cultivates will anyone be saved from destruction. The Philosopher and the Poet also join the training. In the end, Sultan is the last to pass out, to 'slip his Motley'. Thoughts become realities in this post-initiation world. Then Lady miraculously appears, the Holy One, the white-skinned Dancer, the Darling, the Beloved—on Abba. Sultan leaps onto his back to join her. The temple then bursts forth from beneath the surface, and the initiates battle together against the dragons in the outside world. All without horses perish. Then the Moon approaches, to the alternating cries 'Ah woe! . . . Kiss!' The apocalyptic vision culminates in the union of the Moon with the Earth: '[Sultan] turned his eyes to Lady and, as he did so, the ground opened under their feet. Answering flames shot up from beneath them. Lady returned his ardent gaze. They burst together into floods of tears and fell to kissing one another, and, in an instant, erect on Abba's rippling back they had melted into one, their four lower limbs struggling downwards like intertwining roots while their two touching breasts strained together and upward in an endless ecstasy of desire that was at the same time fruition. The hoofs of the horses thundered on the flames. In the centre of the ever-widening arena stood the Ringmaster, grown now to gigantic stature, his arms outstretched above his head and forming a great cup. Suddenly all took fire, melted into one, became a chalice of living flames, the petals of a giant Sun-flower into which the journeying Moon fell with a long sigh of relief.'

LXXV. John kisses Gerald on the forehead, which for him is an act of remarkable courage and sincerity. They encourage him to write, to get it published. Gerald indicates that he owes everything to Brockmann, in the sense that he does not claim originality for any of the images in his story: 'I would like to lay *Tertium Quid* at his feet . . . supposing he would accept it.' He also acknowledges his debt to Adela Cranage. The final picture in the novel is one of Humphrey, who 'sat motionless and upright in his chair, with his eyes fixed before him, and a curiously anxious look on his face, as if he were watching on some distant horizon the smoke of approaching battle'.

The theme of 'English People', as I understand it, is that of the inner soul journey of a small group of English individuals—who are not merely particularly well suited for such a quest but have a strong affinity to certain aspects of Owen Barfield himself—from the conventional ideas and attitudes with which they have grown up to an understanding and an appreciation of the significance for their time and national circumstances of the spiritual impulse personified in the novel by Karl Brockmann, who represents Rudolf Steiner. Although it would be possible to relate the three Trinders to other significant individuals in Barfield's life—Janet to his mother, John to C.S. Lewis, Humphrey to Walter Field, to suggest some likely affinities, there is a deeper relevance for present purposes in associating elements in each of the Trinders with Barfield himself, and then making the very obvious connection with Gerald. One way of making this association is prompted by the Trinders' own nicknames for themselves, Freedom (John), Equality (Janet) and Fraternity (Humphrey), from which follow the relationship of John to the head-oriented thinking aspect of Steiner's threefold view of human psychology and its social manifestations, of Janet to the heart-oriented feeling aspect, and of Humphrey to the future-oriented will. Alternatively, one may discern a relationship in terms of John's bluff good-nature and humanity, Janet's temperamental and habitual traits (including her stutter) and Humphrey's boundless enthusiasm for ideas to, respectively, the physical body, the etheric (or life) body and the astral body (or soul)—a series of relationships that points clearly to Gerald's status as the spirit-bearing ego in this fourfold picture. However one views the matter, there is a profound rightness in the scene at the end of the novel, when Gerald has just finished reading his 'fairy tale' to his deeply appreciative audience. It is as though Barfield is showing us how he, as an aspiring literary artist,[200] came to harness the energies of and transform all that he had in one way or another brought with him into his life; and there could be no clearer exposition of his own personal journey from his antecedents in his own background, which was in many ways very similar to the Trinders, to what he had by the end of the 1920s quite decisively resolved to become. The scene that we are left with is therefore a picture of Barfield himself in all his many aspects. What he did with the fruits of this process will be the subject of the remaining chapters of this book. Nevertheless, for a psychographical study the process itself is of even greater interest than the more widely known fruits to which it led.

Such a wealth of psychographical material as is readily available to anyone who would read 'English People' with a good measure of attentiveness is also a timely reminder of the fact that the subject of the present book is not a relic of history. To read 'English People' today is to find oneself in the invigorating and inspiring company of one whose inner path—whatever its temporally limited outward forms—is of at least as much relevance to a modern questing spirit as it would have been to his contemporaries had they had the opportunity of becoming so intimately acquainted with it.

12. *LANGUAGE AS A KEY TO THE PAST*

It is not now generally realized that, at the time when he was writing 'English People', Barfield towered above his now more celebrated contemporaries—in particular Lewis and Tolkien—both as regards his standing as a man of letters and, even, as a writer of children's stories. The story responsible for this latter circumstance, *The Silver Trumpet* (1925), will feature in the following chapter, the subject of which will be the imaginative literature fashioned by a real-life Gerald Marston, a realm which was of such intimate importance to Barfield. But it was his work on the history of language and the far-reaching conclusions that he drew from it which, in addition to representing his own personal development of the philosophical and religious quest inherent in the numerous intellectual dialogues in 'English People', had already established him as a scholarly writer with a distinct, authoritative voice of his own. The aim of the present chapter is to trace in outline the path of discovery that he pioneered in this respect, both before and after the writing of 'English People'. As this requires an encompassing in a relatively brief span of the majority of Barfield's most well-known published works, it may be worth emphasizing that the present intention is to consider them for the light which they shed on a psychographical study of Barfield himself, on his own inner journey. An analysis or critical appraisal of this strikingly individual linguistic and metaphysical research flowing from the inner experiences so abundantly reflected in the novel would require a volume of an altogether different nature, set in the context not so much of Barfield's life but of the work of those few scholars who have followed a similar or related path.

The first fruits of Barfield's research on the history of language may be found in an article entitled 'Ruin' which appeared in the December 1922 issue of *The London Mercury*. (He included the substance of this article more or less verbatim in Chapter VII of *Poetic Diction*, 'The Making of Meaning, I'.) Barfield himself indicates that his interest in the poetic history of the word—and there is every reason to suppose that this research prompted the further etymological studies underlying the two volumes to be considered next, *History in English Words* (1926) and *Poetic Diction* (1928)—was awakened by a remarkable line from an otherwise not especially significant love sonnet by a contemporary poet, E.L.

Davidson. He quotes two passages from this poet's work, the first merely to show Davidson's sensitivity to the beauty of the word in its commonly understood meaning:

> . . . the climbing tentacles
> Of some sleep-swimming octopus
> Disturb a ruined temple's bells
> And set the deep sea clamorous.

But then, like a shaft of light illumining at one stroke the mystery of the recorded semantic history of this little word, comes this startling line from the sonnet:

> I stood before thee, calling twice or thrice
> The ruin of thy soft, bewildering name.

Stimulated by this unusual, though haunting, use of the word in question, Barfield proceeded in his research to trace its etymological history back to its origins in the Greek verb 'to flow', and the Latin *ruo*, 'to rush' or 'to fall', meanings which emphasize the word's original association with movement, the *process* of rushing, roaring, collapsing as opposed to the petrified state conjured up by the mossy relics beloved by eighteenth-century wordsmiths. In his article, Barfield recounts this word's etymological history by means of a number of examples from the poetry of such as Chaucer, Spenser, Shakespeare, Milton, Dryden, Young, Gray, Wordsworth and Tennyson. Finally, he concludes with a passage of sheer poetry, betokening the delight which set his whole process of investigation in motion, a delight at the mystery of the evolution of human language as exemplified, in the case in question, in 'four magical black squiggles, wherein the past is bottled, like an Arabian Genie, in the dark':

> The world is not young, and the burden of the coils of memory hangs heavier and heavier on the race. Always the individual spirit increases, according to its knowledge, its dreadful consciousness of solitude. Language has done this; but language, which was born in order to permit social relationships between men, is striving still towards that end and consolation. As it grows subtler and subtler, burying in its vaults more and more mind, it becomes to those same spirits a more and more perfect medium of companionship. 'In the beginning was the Word, and the Word was with God, and the Word was God'.

In the volume which Barfield published in 1926, *History in English Words*, this article—together with its conclusion (not included in *Poetic*

Diction)—is expanded into a full-length book which, as the title indicates, traces the story of the sequence of cultural developments that are enshrined in the English language. The result is a kind of linguistic geology, an investigation of 'the many ways in which words may be made to disgorge the past that is bottled up inside them, as coal and wine, when we kindle or drink them, yield up their bottled sunshine'.[201] And on the following page, Barfield sums up the mystery that his book is unveiling, characterizing it by means of the phrase which has been most fully associated with his own work: 'Language has preserved for us the inner, living history of man's soul. It reveals the evolution of consciousness.'

History in English Words contains the evidential basis for what Barfield was shortly afterwards to develop in *Poetic Diction* (1928) as a theory of the origin of meaning, or—which is the same thing—his understanding of the general principles of poetic creativity. Here the etymological evidence, which in the former book is presented as a record of words as they have been derived from the vast cultural heritage of the English language, from the spring of Aryan culture several thousand years ago on the banks of the Dniepr to modern times, is systematized around an insight which, while coursing through the whole book, is most explicitly considered in the Preface to the Second Edition written by Barfield in 1951. This insight is that an etymologically based study of language makes it apparent that, far from words having been originally coined by their human creators to refer to external objects and applied metaphorically to certain inner experiences or inwardly perceived realities, these two aspects of experience—the outer and the inner—would seem to have originally been a single, complex whole whence these distinct aspects subsequently diverged. The modern poet, therefore, applies his creative imagination to the task not so much of building metaphorical bridges between the inner and outer worlds where none existed before but of rediscovering those ancient archetypal wholes whence these elements separated out. It is, for example, a historical linguistic fact that the Greek word πνευμα (pneuma) meant (in the New Testament among other places) not merely breath, wind *and* spirit but had a peculiar meaning of its own out of which these three meanings (and maybe also other ones) crystallized; and it is a fallacy to suggest that it originally meant simply breath or wind and was then metaphorically applied to express 'the principle of life within man or animal'.

In his lengthy Preface of 1951, Barfield roundly attacks the philosophical assumptions of Hume and his more recent disciples (such as the Logical Positivists), whose ideas and assumptions are even more completely at variance with the evidence afforded by linguistic history than are those of Locke and Kant; and he sums up his grave concerns on this account as follows:

> Of all devices for dragooning the human spirit, the least clumsy is to procure its abortion in the womb of language; and we should recognize, I think, that those—and their number is increasing—who are driven by an impulse to reduce the specifically human to a mechanical or animal regularity, will continue to be increasingly irritated by the nature of the mother tongue and make it their point of attack. The strategy is well advised. Language is the storehouse of imagination; it cannot continue to be itself without performing its function. But its function is, to mediate transition from the unindividualized, dreaming spirit that carried the infancy of the world to the individualized human spirit, which has the future in its charge. If therefore they succeed in expunging from language all the substance of its past, in which it is naturally so rich, and finally converting it into the species of algebra that is best adapted to the uses of indoctrination and empirical science, a long and important step forward will have been taken in the selfless cause of the liquidation of the human spirit.[202]

For the most part, the argument of *Poetic Diction* is couched in purely linguistic terms, there being little reference to such general philosophical—or other—principles as may be inferred from, or, alternatively, may shed light upon, the reasoned evidence of words themselves. However, both in the original Preface of 1927 and the Appendices, notably II and IV, Barfield makes clear his debt to Rudolf Steiner, not so much because of anything that the latter said about language but more because, on the one hand, of his assistance in demonstrating the extent to which our assumptions about the nature of perception are overshadowed by 'the ghost of Königsberg' (i.e. Kant, and his English counterpart John Locke) and, on the other, because of the capacity of his spiritual-scientific research into the pre-historical consciousness of mankind to enhance such imaginative efforts as one may be able to make to gain some kind of insight into the way that the human inhabitants of these ancient times—including, of course, Adam himself—experienced their world.[203]

Barfield had to delay for some 30 years before publishing the volume where he was to weave his linguistic research and his anthroposophical studies together into a considered and full-fledged treatise of his own on that theme which is essentially a combination of both these areas where, in *Poetic Diction*, he acknowledged Steiner's influence, namely, the evolution of consciousness.

That *Saving the Appearances*, published in 1957 by his usual publishers, Faber and Faber, took so long in the making can on the one hand, of course, be explained in terms of the diversion of intellectual and—even—imaginative energies to the demands of Barfield and Barfield, Solicitors from 1930 onwards. Up to a point, Barfield's agile mind was able to discern an affinity between these two different aspects of his life; and he expressed this in the seminal essay 'Poetic Diction and Legal Fiction'.[204] Nevertheless, the tension between these two worlds remained a very real one; and the anguish of this tension, and also the solution to the problems that it engendered, are lucidly and humorously conveyed in *This Ever Diverse Pair* (1950). In this book, Barfield expresses his frustration that the *alter ego* whom he has created for the purpose, namely Burden, is unable to deal with the humdrum mechanics of a solicitors' office concerned mainly with conveyancing (together with the odd instance of divorce proceedings and so forth) without drawing upon the imaginative faculties which he would much rather keep for his further research on language, poetry and the evolution of consciousness. The solution to this particular problem,[205] which comes to a head when Burden threatens to kill Burgeon (the poetic, literary Barfield) after the latter has gone totally overboard with frustration at some trifling quarrel with a client over a matter concerning litigation, is described—in the chapter entitled 'Astraea Redux'—in terms of a dream recalled by Burgeon, where Burden is duly banished from the office and Burgeon himself is 'punished' by having to take upon his own shoulders the full responsibility for the conduct of the legal practice. In this way it was that Barfield finally reconciled himself to his daily duties. (The figure of Burgeon was to live on as a mouthpiece for Barfield's ideas in his subsequent books *Worlds Apart* and *Unancestral Voice*.)

But the writing of *Saving the Appearances* also required a considerable amount of inner preparation and study. For what he had glimpsed in *Poetic Diction* as a potential task, namely, the writing of a description in his own words of the evolution of human consciousness, necessitated grappling first in his own mind and then amidst the thought-pictures of the leading cultural thinkers of his time with a tension between two intellectual streams which, in the notes that led eventually to the writing of *Saving the Appearances*, he referred to as the 'Nicodemians' and the 'Maccabeans' (the significance of these designations will become clear later on).

His deed of clarifying and resolving this tension in his own mind found expression in his article 'The Psalms of David', originally published in *Anthroposophical Movement* (March–May 1945) and reprinted in *The Mint* (1946) before being republished with slight variations in *The Rediscovery of Meaning*. At the outset of this article, Barfield states his initial aversion to the Old Testament, to the people portrayed in it, their attitude to life and, specifically, their absolute and unquestioning obedience to their stern and vengeful deity, Jehovah. He contrasts this unfavourably with the civilized humanity of the Greeks. But the purpose of his article is firstly to express and then to demonstrate his own later discovery of the immense—and unique—historical importance of the Jews, on the one hand their significance for the time when the Old Testament (and specifically the Book in question) was being written and, on the other, for our own time. For it was the task of the Jewish people to prepare a physical human vessel for the Incarnation of the Son of God, the Divine Ego, the I AM, with all the moral problems entailed by this deed for each individual human soul; and Barfield describes the Psalms of David as the most concentrated and most intimate expression of the yearning and sorrows of the nation entrusted with this task. However, the main significance of this article for present purposes is that henceforth Barfield's thinking becomes inherently Christ-centred in a manner and with an intensity that was not previously possible. This is borne out by several subsequent lectures, one of which, 'The Light of the World' (1953), was given before he wrote *Saving the Appearances*.[206] With this background, it was possible for him to identify and address the aforesaid tension between the intellectual streams that he discerned around him, an endeavour which, as he makes clear in the notes in question, was the springboard for the writing of *Saving the Appearances*.

Barfield begins his enquiry in these notes by suggesting an experiment. He proposes to his would-be reader that he select at random a few contemporary authors who are concerned with the welfare of the human race and its destiny, and himself comes up with H.G. Wells, Middleton Murray, Schweitzer and Toynbee (Oswald Spengler is later mentioned as an alternative to Schweitzer, who—as will become apparent—is a somewhat ambiguous figure in the sense intended). He then requests a repetition of the experiment, but this time limits the choice to writers who could be described as committed Christians. Names mentioned in this category include Kierkegaard, G.K. Chesterton, C.S. Lewis and Charles Williams. While emphasizing that both groups of thinkers affirm similar things, with neither being essentially more intelligent or more wide awake than the other, he discerns between the two groups a fundamental difference in intellectual attitude; and at this point he associates the former group with the name 'Nicodemians' and the latter group with the name 'Maccabeans'. These names, and their definitions, had sufficient importance for him to copy and enlarge a passage from these rough original notes on the theme of 'Time and the Christian Religion' into the front of what was to become the foolscap notebook which contains the notes for the actual chapters of *Saving the Appearances*.[207] The passage in question is worth quoting in full:

> I chose these names for convenience of reference only. There are Nicodemians within the Church, but the main body is outside. For them the essence of reality is the changing soul of Man, its past and future. For the Maccabeans it is God. For the Nicodemians the interesting thing about 'the man of today' is that he is different from the man of yesterday and the day before. For the Maccabeans the interesting thing is that he is very much the same. For the first the significance of history is measured by the change which it is deemed to have wrought in the human soul's relation to God. For the second there is no discernible change. Sometimes men have obeyed Him more than at other times, but mostly they have disobeyed. And history is that same disobedience repeated over and over again.

(It will be clear that I am implying a link—at any rate in Barfield's mind—between the 'Maccabeans' and what he says about the Jewish people in 'The Psalms of David', just as the 'Nicodemians' are representative of the humanistic fervour of the Greeks.) This, then, was the line of enquiry which preceded, and effectively made possible, the writing of Barfield's most important contribution to Western intellectual thought, the remarkably slim volume *Saving the Appearances*, a book where the gulf between the 'Nicodemians' and the 'Maccabeans' is bridged to the point where Barfield's publisher felt able to make the following claim: 'In harmony with the Christian revelation and against the background of the history of human consciousness, *Saving the Appearances: A Study in Idolatry* provides a profound interpretation of the meaning of the age of physical science.'[208]

Within the body of Barfield's writings on the history of language and its implications for an understanding of the evolution of human consciousness, *Saving the Appearances* occupies a central, or focal, position. This is where Barfield says what he had to say to the world by way of an exposition of ideas, where he draws the full implications of his discovery of the spiritual origin of language for man's destiny on earth both now and in the future. Briefly expressed, his argument is that, if one considers this research in the context of the analysis presented in the first few chapters of the way in which we perceive the world in our time (and no one to my knowledge has questioned the validity of this very down-to earth analysis), it is simply no longer possible to accept as remotely reasonable the conventional world-picture presented to us by modern science, the whole weight of which is seen to rest not upon solid, objective fact (as is generally thought) but upon an insubstantial chimera of illusion, or—using Barfield's highly appropriate term—idolatry.[209] But having effectively demolished in a series of brief, closely argued but eminently comprehensible chapters his readers' mental furniture and habitual garments of perception, Barfield offers a way out of this dilemma which harmonizes scientific research and philosophical analysis in a radical reappraisal of Christian theology and of the significance of the Incarnation for an understanding of man and the meaning of human existence. For unlike most critics of materialistic reductionism, Barfield reserves his greatest passion in what is throughout a very deeply felt book for his declaration that paganism, which until the very last word in the book he refers to as 'original participation', is dead, that, in other words, all attempts by modern human beings to depend upon the phenomenal world around them for sustenance, support and inspiration are altogether futile and misplaced. Nature now requires something *from* man, something which the deed of Christ's Incarnation can now enable him to begin to implement. If man fails to respond to this challenge of adulthood and instead continues to hark back to his pagan past, he will—claims Barfield—descend increasingly into a state of puerility.[210]

It is now nearly 50 years since *Saving the Appearances* was first published. Its analysis is just as relevant to our own time, and its dual prophetic message of dire warning and visionary hope addresses the twenty-first century even more directly than it spoke to the twentieth century. For those who wish to see it, the idols of which Barfield spoke in *Saving the Appearances* are considerably hollower and more blatantly unreal than they were when the last great upsurge of interest in matters of the spirit in the 1960s (i.e. in the immediate aftermath of the publication of Barfield's treatise[211]) was diverted into earthly irrelevance by their seeming impregnability. In this context, we will now turn to a consideration of the two further books written by Barfield before he ventured to America for the first time in 1964, *Worlds Apart* and *Unancestral Voice*, the former being an enlargement of the diagnosis expressed in *Saving the Appearances* and the latter of the interpretation of Christianity that he saw as a remedy for the dilemmas inherent in the modern condition of humanity.

Worlds Apart (1963) is an imaginary conversation between Barfield's alter ego Burgeon (described as a solicitor with philological interests) and the seven representatives of diverse academic and scientific disciplines whom he has invited for a weekend's retreat, the ostensible theme of which is the breakdown of communications between the various academic specialisms, imprisoned as they are in their watertight compartments. However, Barfield's theme is not the breakdown itself, and his analysis bears hardly any relationship to that expressed in C.P. Snow's famous Rede Lecture of 1959 on 'The Two Cultures'.[212] The actual subject matter of the dialogue is that of *Saving the Appearances*, though here we view it as seen from the varying standpoints of a professor of historical theology and ethics (Hunter), a rocket researcher (Ranger), a professor of physics (Brodie), a biologist (Upwater), a linguistic philosopher (Dunn) and a psychiatrist (Burrows), with Burgeon himself and Sanderson (a retired schoolmaster) representing certain aspects of Barfield's ideas. The first part of the book centres on an animated discussion between Hunter and Upwater, who respectively represent the Maccabeans and the Nicodemians (see above). The second main element consists of Burgeon's attempt to establish the synthesis between these two irreconcilable opposites as expressed in *Saving the Appearances*, this being largely achieved in a pseudo-Socratic dialogue where he painstakingly demonstrates the utter inconsistency between, on the one hand, what is promulgated by the physical sciences in terms of an investigation of man's spatial environment and, on the other, what is proposed by the earth sciences by way of hypothetical reconstructions or predictions of the dimension or time. This amounts to a devastating attack upon those same intellectual idols which are the principal concern of *Saving the Appearances*, those objects of solidity by which we appear to be surrounded (both spatially and temporally) but which—as we know from the physical sciences and, in a different way, also through philosophical scrutiny—turn out to be in part the creations of our own faculties of perception. The third part of the dialogue is largely devoted to the anthroposophist Sanderson's evocation of an alternative mode of gaining knowledge of the world which is consistent with the findings of the physical sciences.[213]

With this the substance of the dialogue is brought more or less in line with the end of Chapter 21 of *Saving the Appearances* (itself called 'Saving the Appearances'). However, there is at the very end of *Worlds Apart* a hint that Barfield was also planning to unpack also the last four chapters of his *magnum opus*. This is contained in Sanderson's remark about Christianity (p. 206) as 'an historical event that took place in Judaea in the reign of Tiberius', an event which 'was an incarnation' and, hence, to be distinguished not merely from positivism but also from religion as revelation. 'What,' he asks, 'has positivism to do with incarnation? But it is too serious a matter. It would have to be the beginning of a new symposium, not the tail-end of an old one . . .' In a somewhat different way Hunter's dream, which concludes the book, provides a further link with the last book to be considered in the present chapter. It is an established fact that C.S. Lewis is, 'to a limited extent, Hunter's prototype'.[214] Elsewhere Barfield describes Hunter as being 'three parts C.S. Lewis'.[215] The opening image of the dream indeed derived from a dream that Lewis had had of 'great heavy doors *shutting* slowly' (letter of 9 April 1971). In the letter of 31 May 1964 Barfield explains how he built upon this foundation (designated source 1), thereby interpreting the three mysterious images of a solitary head radiating light, a head covered with a magnificent lion's mane, and a headless man (this further step constituting source 2): 'The head and head-system are what *divide* us from the universe, giving us knowledge *about* it, but preventing knowledge *per participationem* [through participation]. The way from the first to the second is by getting the heart (or 'heart-forces') up into the head (head becomes lion) & *complete* union would = disappearance of head (= isolating factor). Hunter is assumed to have known all this in his unconscious & to have suppressed it.' Barfield adds a third source for the dream: 'Somebody told me that a headless man is one of the recognized symbols for an initiate. And it seems to follow from 2.' And finally, in a postscript (and labelled source 4): 'I myself have had a good many dreams (some of them most unpleasantly realistic) of being about to be beheaded.' *Worlds Apart* was one of the last things Lewis read before he died in 1963. Was *Unancestral Voice* (1965), which opens up in a quite unprecedented way for Barfield what lies behind the third picture in Hunter's dream, also an exploration of that aspect of his relationship with Lewis to which he had been denied access (by Lewis) during the previous three decades (at least) of his dearest friend's lifetime?

Unancestral Voice is a book which any reader of the present volume needs to read in its entirety. On the one hand, it represents the culmination of the theme which it has been the task of this chapter to consider. On the other hand, it contains several sustained passages where Barfield reveals more of his own soul-searching and inner striving than he did in any of his other published writings; and its ninth chapter is a pinnacle in this respect. For his chosen method of expanding upon the closing chapters of *Saving the*

Appearances is to present his way of understanding the significance of the Incarnation for our time in the form of a dialogue between Burgeon (who represents Barfield himself) and that being of higher wisdom who 'is the voice of each one's mind speaking from the depths within himself'.[216] This is no imaginary dialogue, concocted in the abstractions of mental invention—although of course in another sense the word 'imagination' is entirely appropriate, in that the book is a sustained example of the final participation defined in Chapter 20 of *Saving the Appearances*.

After the initial vignette focused on D.H. Lawrence's novel *Lady Chatterley's Lover*,[217] Barfield introduces the mysterious Meggid who is the unancestral voice of the title. The Meggid then accompanies Burgeon-Barfield through his further deliberations about key social issues of the time (apart from the *Lady Chatterley* theme the main concerns reflected in this part of the book are the directionless state of young adolescents and the question of the appropriateness of the punitive and the 'liberal' responses to crime). Central to the light which the Meggid sheds upon these outward issues are his indications regarding, on the one hand, the archangelic beings whose task it is to guide successive periods of human cultural development (he specifically mentions and then defines the characteristics of Gabriel, who ruled over that period between the scientific revolution and the end of the nineteenth century when spirit was most fully incarnate in matter, and of Michael, whose field is 'the thinking that has been set free from the flesh').[218] And, on the other hand, there are those adversarial beings who seek (on the surface at least) to interfere with this rightful development: Lucifer—the false Preserver who tries to preserve the past from dissolution—and Ahriman, the false Destroyer who would destroy it utterly and substitute his own invention.

There then comes the sea-voyage when Burgeon has an in-depth conversation with a Roman Catholic named Chevalier and a Buddhist, who rejoices in the name of Grimwade. This is where the central theme which Barfield has been unfolding in the books that have been the subject of the present chapter is taken to its point of fullest development. Again, the springboard for the conversation is a contemporary cultural phenomenon, in this case Arnold Toynbee's *Study of History*, which Burgeon has been reading in its abridgment by Somervill. Burgeon, who is challenged by his astute but not especially sympathetically disposed companions to find a way of expressing his thoughts about human and earthly evolution that touches a chord of recognition in their minds, increasingly finds that the Meggid is speaking through him; and during the latter part of the conversation, when he is speaking with Chevalier alone, he boldly launches into a diatribe against not the makers of the scientific revolution but the Catholic Church, whom he—following Steiner—holds responsible for the dualistic thinking which has always hampered the Western philosophical mind and for the abolition of the spiritual aspect of man's threefold nature of body, soul *and spirit.*[219] What movingly arises in this space between Grimwade's inability to comprehend evolution as such and Chevalier's adherence to a model of Christianity which has no place for its central spiritual core and so 'left the West with that forlorn duality of soul and body, of ghost and machine, which has ever since determined the shape of its science, its history and its so-called doctrine of evolution',[220] is an intimate understanding of that 'interior transforming agent' which is Burgeon's name for the Logos, the Word that became flesh. This understanding is what is expounded in Chapter 9 of *Unancestral Voice.*

The Meggid first speaks with Burgeon alone of the individual human spirit as the 'interior transforming agent' in the evolution of humanity. He leaves him in no doubt that, if it is to be an agent of transformation and not mere substitution, this individual human spirit must persist as an individual unit through the sequence of evolutionary development. But it is only possible to conceive of this if the idea of repeated earth-lives, vigorously suppressed by the Western Church, reawakens in a form very different from the oriental doctrine of reincarnation, thus breaking the great tabu which stands in the way of all further evolutionary development of Western thought and life. Once this has been imparted to him, Burgeon now asks the Meggid to speak more explicitly about the 'relation between all that you have told me, both now and previously, and the birth, life and death of the one man, Jesus of Nazareth'.[221] This leads the Meggid to unfold to him certain mysteries about 'the transforming agent of the earth-planet itself with the race of mankind and all else that lives upon it'[222] which, as he says, some would do anything to keep buried in ignorance, even if this should mean that the earth itself is destroyed. These are the mysteries of the two Jesus children associated, respectively, with the Gospels of St Matthew and St Luke, and of their radically different karmic antecedents, the former being a kingly child with many incarnations and the latter a paradisal soul held back in an unfallen state, the bearer of a divine innocence of which mankind is otherwise bereft; and of the descent into the human vessel ultimately furnished by these twin souls of the heavenly Christ Being at the Baptism by John in the River Jordan. On Burgeon's asking what will happen if the thunderous reality of this interpretation of the Incarnation—or, more generally, of the relationship between man's body (and the physical nature of which it is composed) and his indwelling spirit—is not recognized, the Meggid speaks of the dire threat of the rapid advance of technology, which is the fruit of man's mind '"monkeying" from without with the earth-body [which] it should be striving to inform from within', a process which, as Burgeon acknowledges, is 'a kind of cosmic masturbation' (a phrase enlarged upon, and then transcended, in the discussion about modern physics which forms the last part of the book). Finally, in the last chapter, the Meggid explains to Burgeon why the tabu against recognizing that man is a threefold being with a body, soul *and spirit* has persisted for so long, his interpretation being couched in terms of the fear of crossing the threshold into the spiritual world, the fear of the immense destructive energies buried in man's unconscious will-forces—an anguish which is 'the true origin of materialism', for materialism 'is founded in fear'.

There remains only to consider the nature of this mysterious Meggid who is the source of these revelations. What is of relevance here is not so much the actual content of the insights expressed by this being, all of which can be found amongst Rudolf Steiner's spiritual-scientific research and is available for all to read who wish to do so. For the interest from a psychographical point of view lies rather in the nature of the experiences which led Barfield to write in the way that he did about these central questions regarding the mystery of the Incarnation. The view of the present writer is that *Unancestral Voice* is a work of true inspiration, that in other words the unancestral voice who speaks through the Meggid is indeed, as the name implies, not the reflection of any sort of cultural legacy or abstract memory but a burningly living experience for the author. Nor would Barfield have quibbled with backing this judgement up by referring again to Steiner, who in a few scattered instances spoke of that feminine spirit-being Anthroposophia[223] mentioned in the last paragraph, that being who—in succession to the Theosophia of ancient times and the Philosophia of the classical world prior to the Mystery of Golgotha—now seeks to translate existential man's solitary searchings and strivings into an offering of light, radiating no longer from the Gods to the earth but from the depths of the individual self to the divine world that hungers for man's answer:

The Stars spake once to Man.
It is World-destiny
That they are silent now.
To be aware of the silence
Can became pain for earthly Man.

But in the deepening silence
There grows and ripens
What Man speaks to the Stars.
To be aware of the speaking
Can become strength for Spirit-Man.[224]

With *Unancestral Voice*, Barfield had gone as far as he could in presenting a public exposition of his ideas through the medium of the 'mainstream' press (this work, as were all the books forming the subject of this chapter, was published by Faber and Faber). The reviews received by this book, which, with the exception of those appearing in anthroposophical journals were by and large not so much critical as uncomprehending,[225] were less favourable than those of either *Saving the Appearances* or *Worlds Apart*. It comes as no surprise, therefore, that Barfield's next book, *Speaker's Meaning* (1967), far from taking the process of development further, was essentially an attempt to restate, in lecture form, the arguments initially presented in *Poetic Diction* and elsewhere. Nevertheless, some students of Barfield's thought who have come to most fully appreciate him in his own right, have recognized *Unancestral Voice* to be his most profound and original contribution to the intellectual ferment of his age.[226]

13. POETRY, DRAMA AND MAGIC

At no point in his life was Barfield only interested in deriving philosophical conclusions from the study of language. As a constant thread running through the whole of his life as a writer, there can be traced his ceaseless quest towards the creation of literary works of art. Not surprisingly, the diversity of the forms that he used to express his literary creativity was greatest during the 1920s, i.e. before he became a solicitor. But he remained a poet his whole life long. The focus of the present chapter is this essentially artistic aspect of Barfield's mind, that side of his nature which found expression neither in those relatively familiar books on language and the evolution of consciousness that formed the subject of the last chapter nor in his lesser known zeal as a social reformer (this will be the theme of the following chapter).

Even shorn of these latter two aspects, the breadth and variety of what remains by way of an expression of Barfield's personal voice is fairly extensive, both as regards mood and subject-matter and the forms in which he chose to express himself. Broadly speaking, however, these can be broken down into three main categories: poetry, stories and literary/cultural criticism or comment.

The latter element of criticism and comment belongs almost entirely to the Barfield of the 1920s. Especially his Scrapbook, a collection of brief items culled from various literary publications, reveals his far-ranging interests. Apart from his first published poem, 'Air-Castles', which appeared in *Punch* as early as 1917, the majority of Barfield's initial ventures into print appeared from the late summer of 1920 onwards in the form of literary reviews for the *New Statesman*. It should be borne in mind that he was at the time entering upon the second year of his undergraduate studies at Wadham College, Oxford, having experienced a delay in his return from military service abroad until well after the Armistice in November 1918. From the way that his distinctive voice rings forth in the first of the *New Statesman* articles included in the Scrapbook, 'Form in Poetry' (7 August 1920), one has the sense of a career in the making, whether in the English Department of a university or as a literary critic and writer. In this article, Barfield is already emerging as an independent-minded advocate of the quest for meaning in a literary environment dominated by the likes of Walter Pater, for whom the 'matter' of a work of art (the intellectual content of a poem, for example) is of relative insignificance as compared to the form in which it is expressed. In this respect, Barfield manifests his clear opposition towards the belles-lettres approach to the humanities or literary studies, one which would sacrifice truth to a one-sided aspiration for beauty. Indeed, form in poetry can, says Barfield, be defined as the art of breathing meanings into words through the music of the way in which the poet has combined them; and he illustrates this by giving numerous examples—from the work of especially Blake, Milton and Keats—of the effect achieved of an original juxtaposing of epithets with nouns, as in this example from Blake:

> And I made a rural pen
> And I stained the water clear...

In this way, beauty becomes the vehicle for a truth not previously discerned.

This article was followed in September by the slightly mischievous 'The Reader's Eye' (published in the *Cornhill Magazine*), where Barfield confesses his preference for *reading* poetry (i.e. seeing it in print) to listening to someone else reading it or speaking it oneself from memory, especially if spellings have not been modernized or even corrected. Then followed an article in the *New Statesman* on English ballads dated 2 October 1920 (a review of a collection entitled *Old English Ballads, 1553–1625*) and an admiring review for the same journal of a book of poems by Walter de la Mare (6 November), a poet for whom Barfield had the greatest affection.[227] This sequence of review-articles for the *New Statesman* continues with contributions on *Oxford Poetry, 1917–1919* (20 November), 'John Clare' (25 December) and 'Wilfred Owen' (15 January 1921); and there were a further six articles written for the same journal in 1921. Thereafter, the spate of articles slows down considerably, with one in 1922 and at least two in 1923. Barfield was still contributing to the *New Statesman* in 1926, when on 20 March he contributed a piece on 'Metaphor' which has much in common with the *Poetic Diction* theme; and the sequence concludes in October 1928 with a review of *Collected Essays and Papers* by Robert Bridges.

But this essentially literary endeavour represented only a fraction of Barfield's activities as a commentator on cultural affairs in the 1920s. One of his *New Statesman* articles from 1921 ('Some Elements of Decadence', 24 December), where he attributes the decadence in modern life to an inability to digest experiences and knowledge,[228] may be regarded as his earliest piece of general cultural criticism. But his most significant body of cultural criticism was published in a journalistic magazine rejoicing in the name of *Truth*, which—as Barfield reports in the Biographical Sketch[229]—tried unsuccessfully to enlist him as a permanent member of its staff. It must have appreciated—and doubtless encouraged—the somewhat scurrilous humour manifested in these articles from 1923 and 1924. The majority of these are powerful attacks on prevailing government policy on immunization and foot-and-mouth disease which could almost have been written today (official policy on both issues having remained remorselessly constant, despite strong evidence of its absurdity and ineffectiveness). Other themes in these *Truth* articles range from further more general criticisms of government propaganda to amusing discussions of a (fictitious) 'Domestic Service Inquiry' and of a leader in *The Times* about the agonies of returning to work after the summer holidays. But this humorous vein is quarried to even more elaborate effect in the 'Secrets of Hindu Hair-Killing' and an analysis of the dilemma of 'To Shave or Not to Shave'.

Barfield indicates that he had to sever his connection with *Truth* if he wanted to avoid being turned into a full-time journalistic hack, a separation which presumably took effect from towards the end of 1924. By this time he was already contributing to *The New Age*, a journal which strongly championed Major C.H. Douglas's ideas on Social Credit but which was also happy to publish Barfield's perceptive thoughts on 'The Spiritual Basis of Fascism' and his supportive ideas about the League of Nations, while also allowing him to publish (20 March 1924) a letter correcting certain misapprehensions about Rudolf Steiner's relationship to the Theosophical Society previously expressed in a letter to the same journal. The last contribution to *The New Age* included in the Scrap Book dates from 4 August 1927 and is called 'Suggestions for a Film Scenario to be entitled Romance or "The Professor's Love-Story"'. This was conceived as a wordless film, with numerous musical episodes.

The final repository for Barfield's youthful critical fervour represented in the Scrap Book was *G.K.'s Weekly*, which was more conventional in its sympathies than Orage's *New Age*. Items culled from issues dating from 1925 and 1926 include a spirited defence by Barfield—which clearly went against the grain as regards editorial stance—of Douglas's ideas on Social Credit, and an affirmation by him of the significance of the Celts in early Britain in response to a dismissive, pro-Romanist letter from Hilaire Belloc.

These varied literary outpourings were paralleled throughout from a temporal point of view by a steady flow of short stories and—most notably—fairy tales. The first of these to be written (though never published) was 'The Superman'.[230] This is a thinly veiled autobiographical reflection about the mystery of individual human existence, poised between the melée of everyday human affairs and the starry cosmos. As a piece of writing, it is considerably more interesting—and, indeed, a truer reflection of Barfield's youthful spirit—than the story which he *did* succeed in publishing shortly afterwards, 'Dope', included by T.S. Eliot in the first issue of *The Criterion* (July 1923).[231] Nor did Barfield's deeper interests manifest themselves in the three other short stories published during the 1920s, although a penetrating human perception is evident in all of them. 'The Devastated Area' (*The New Age*, 3 July 1924) was the first of these to appear, followed by 'Queer Story: Postman's Knock' (*Truth*, 3 March 1926) and 'Mrs. Cadogan' (*New Adelphi*, March 1928).[232]

The only piece of imaginative prose from this early period which encompasses the full breadth of Barfield's mind, combining spiritual vision with incisiveness and humour, is his children's story *The Silver Trumpet* (1925). This had been completed by 20 October 1923, since C.S. Lewis had read it in manuscript by then and recorded his reflections in his diary: '. . . I began to read Barfield's faery tale *The Silver Trumpet* in which with prodigality he squirts out the most suggestive ideas, the loveliest pictures, and the raciest new coined words in wonderful succession. Nothing in its kind can be imagined better.'[233]

On one level, *The Silver Trumpet* is a fairy tale in the classic mould about twin princesses—representing, respectively, the intellectual and the feeling elements in the human psyche—who are visited at their christening by a relatively benign witch, whose gift serves to bind the two girls together in an inseparable relationship which subsequent events prove to be mutually intolerable. The drama of the story unfolds with the arrival of a prince from another country, who possesses a silver trumpet with magical powers. Violet, the princess with a loving, feeling nature, is enchanted by the prince and by the sound of his silver trumpet, which has a life-bringing quality, bestowing joy and gladness where discord and sorrow reign. Gamboy, the intellectual princess, becomes intensely jealous of her sister's love and hides the silver trumpet, and the kingdom of King Courtesy and Queen Violet is plunged into suffering and starvation. Gamboy takes over the rulership of the country, and even succeeds in turning the potentially redemptive Prince Peerio—who has fallen in love with a portrait of Violet's daughter Lily—into a toad. Fortunately, however, the silver trumpet is found by a stable boy in the hay-loft where Gamboy had hidden it; and its resurrection forces succeed in engineering an encounter between the aforesaid toad and Miss Thompson, the benign local witch, who tells both the transmogrified Peerio and Lily—by now confined at the top of a tower—what they must do if they want to overcome their predicaments. There ensues a true fairy-tale ending, with even the friendly dwarf, the Little Fat Podger, returning to the land of the living.

For Barfield himself it must have become fairly clear—through having to adopt the kind of jerkily intellectual prose style evidently favoured for publication (as exemplified by 'Dope')—that the only way that he could at the time translate his research on the 'felt change of consciousness'[234] inherent in poetic diction into imaginative literature of his own was through writing a children's story. *The Silver Trumpet* was in this sense no mere whimsical diversion but was utterly central to what he was trying to achieve as a writer and artist in the mid-1920s. And yet its only successors—other than the transformation of this fairy-tale element already encountered in 'English People' and 'Night Operation'—were the far slighter stories such as the delightful 'The Child and the Giant' (written for his Upper School English class at The New School, Streatham in 1930) and 'The Lake of Nix' (was this rather brutal undated fairy story written to encourage his children to eat their soup?).[235]

With this we come to what was undoubtedly the major element in Barfield's explorations as an imaginative writer (if we exempt, for the reasons given in Chapter 11, 'English People'), his poetry and poetic drama. Barfield wrote poetry for much of his life, some three-quarters of a century, his poetry growing '*in the face* of or even *in despite of* the literary climate rather *than in the midst of it*'.[236] Several of his poems were published in *The London Mercury* (see especially his 'Nine Sonnets', March 1922[237]). Both these sonnets and most—if not all—of the other fine examples of this form published or republished in the *Sampler* had a biographical source, as will be explored to some extent in Chapter 15. Readers wishing to acquaint themselves with these and other brief poetic reflections on his life are recommended to peruse the *Sampler*, where many of the best of the over two hundred poems that have been preserved can be found. Here is one of the finest examples, a poem which somehow in a few words transmutes obscurity into a mystery that is both translucent and redemptive:

Risen

Dread not my face. Draw near: Let fan me
Thy fluttering, fond, unanswered breath!

Life of life, receive the Spirit
So—from my mouth,
The Word inwith.

Lean near my breast: be all my solitude
Soon in the flame it feeds forgot.
Be not afraid of the peace I give—nay,
Not as the world gave:
Touch me not!

Seek no caress of my compassion:
I, who created Behemoth,
Became the phantom of thy beloved
Charged with ecstasy:
Touch me not![238]

It is clearly apparent that, when engaged in writing poetry, Barfield was not thinking primarily of publication. Similarly, the longer poetic works to be considered in what follows were almost certainly written out of a kind of inner conviction on the part of the author, although he did attempt to get them published. (His prose works were, by contrast, aimed more directly at publication.)

The first of these longer poetic works under consideration here[239] to be written was *Orpheus*. This play, which was referred to in the context of Barfield's correspondence with Thomas Kranidas[240] was written in 1937, received its only production (by Maud Barfield and Arnold Freeman) at the Little Theatre, Sheffield in September 1948 and was published in 1983. For present purposes, the most illuminating aspect of the 1983 publication is Barfield's own Foreword, where he offers some indications about the play's origin: 'I had casually mentioned to my friend C.S. Lewis that I seemed to be feeling an impulse to write a play in verse and was wondering about a subject, and at the same time that I wanted to keep clear of the sort of ulterior motives I have just referred to.[241] I recall the occasion very clearly and, though I am not reproducing his exact words, he said in effect: "Why not take one of the myths and simply do your best with it—Orpheus for instance?" To which my mental reaction was, after some reflection: Well, why not?'

The spirit of *Orpheus* does indeed live in the magic of its poetry rather than in some sort of veiled philosophical statement. Moreover, its distinctive beauty is most fully apparent when it is treated as a play to be acted rather than as substance for the study, as the present writer discovered when participating in an abbreviated rendering at Wheaton College in the summer of 1998. In so far as there is a message over and above the death and resurrection theme of the story itself, the author reflecting upon his play 45 years after he had written it sought to emphasize its focus upon the nature of love, upon the polarities between flesh and spirit, and between egotism and altruism; and he concludes:

> . . . I am inclined to see *Orpheus* asking a question. And the question is: can the radiant warmth of erotic affection be expanded or metamorphosed into what the Germans call *allgemeine Menschenliebe*? Can Eros *become* Agape? . . . I wonder whether the play, taken as a whole, may not be hinting at a transition from, or rather through, Eros to Agape, neither as a Platonic transfer of attention from carnal copy to ghostly original, nor simply of darkness giving way to light, but rather as moonlight brightening imperceptibly into sunshine.[242]

The second of the poetic dramas to be considered in this chapter is 'Angels at Bay', written probably in the early 1940s.[243] It was never published, although a typed version was drawn up at some point between 1955 and 1970, when the Barfields were living at Westfield, Hartley, near Dartford. In this trilogy of short plays, 'The Wall', 'The Human Dynamo' and 'The Paranoia Wing', the passionate concerns about the threshold between the living and the dead which are subtly veiled in *Orpheus* come explicitly to the fore.

The first of the two scenes comprising the first play, 'The Wall', depicts the sense of anguish and hopelessness in the home of Henry Mayne, who is dying from some undisclosed illness. The doctor imparts this terminal news to Mayne's grown-up children, Marjorie and Peter, while insisting that the patient himself should under no circumstances be told the truth of his condition. Death is portrayed as a subject regarding which the only decent thing to do is to keep silence.[244] The second scene, which is set some three months later, takes place in a super-earthly realm. Henry Mayne has just died, and his guardian angel, Kaüret, is conversing with the angels of the other members of his family together with Remiel, an archangel, and his captains Raquel and Shezef. This conversation is characterized by a mood of profound concern and anguish, prompted on the one hand by the strongly earthbound thoughts of those who have recently died and, on the other, by the incapacity of those still living to form any connection with their loved ones beyond the threshold of death. Thus the thoughts of, in particular, Mayne's widow are 'hurled back by a huge Wall' and 'wander about the past', a theme taken up by Shezef:

I know, I know—
He liked this; he used that; would have wished (if he were here today).
I know well the dreams, memories, fears, photograph near the bed—
And oh, never a thought, never a stray fancy for what he likes
Or wants now, what he feels now, what he now wishes for, and hopes or needs! . . .
If they spared only one corner of the love-weighted thoughts they weave
For us—us and their own dead—we could win worlds—you know we could.
I ask pardon! I came near despairing.

The play ends in a concerted effort by these angelic beings to enlist the help of still higher beings in this struggle that they face.

The second play, 'The Human Dynamo', has a similar form, with the first scene being set in the earthly realm and the second—which this time elapses more or less simultaneously with the first—in the angelic spheres. The 'human dynamo' of the title is a newspaper proprietor called Sir Charles Ritson, who exerts sovereign authority over the editorial offices of 'The Sunday Universe'. Ritson is a caricature of the ruthless magnate, his dominant aim being to sell as many copies of his newspaper as possible. In the course of the conversation, it becomes apparent that some 15,000 coniferous trees have to be felled for every bulky issue of this trivial newspaper. After issuing a wealth of instructions to his subordinates, Sir Charles leaves the office building and walks right into the path of an on-coming car, which is prevented from running him over by a bus skidding out in front of it.

The scene now shifts to the mist-enveloped plateau which represents the angelic sphere. The angels are deeply concerned about the increasing meaninglessness of the activities of the human beings in their charge, and Serakel, who is one of the angels of the coniferous trees, laments about the destructiveness that they have wrought. All await guidance from Armaros, who is Sir Charles Ritson's angel. Armaros finally asks leave to recall his soul, although he is aware that Semjaya's hosts (Semjaya represents the dark powers of opposition) will do their best to thwart this aim. What Armaros predicts does indeed happen (as detailed physically in Scene I), and all the angels can do at the end is to offer up their homage to Mansoul and the higher deities.

The third play, 'The Paranoia Wing', is the most far-reaching of the three. Unlike the other two plays, which are set in the present (i.e. the mid-twentieth century), 'The Paranoia Wing' belongs to the early twenty-first century. The scene on stage represents a meeting of a brotherhood of individuals dedicated to combating what they regard as a growing sickness of anti-materialism (the proponents of which they call 'the Immaterialists'). Amongst their number are a doctor of science, a doctor of medicine, an American citizen, an industrialist and a press and television tycoon (belonging to the Ritson Press), with a civil servant and a trade union leader as somewhat ambivalent observers. At the focus of their deliberations is the sole female character, Joan Holdsworth (described as a welfare worker), who is a patient in the Paranoia Wing of Dr Hugh Sedlescombe's hospital. The reason for Joan's presence in this part of the hospital is that she claims to have experiences of being inspired from the spiritual world and, quite specifically, of being able to communicate with the dead. On being questioned, Joan states that nearly all the patients in the Wing have been, or are, engaged in the pursuit of spiritual science. However, the main substance of what she imparts to her interrogators reveals an intimate connection with 'The Wall', while the presence of Maxim Streeter, the tycoon who represents the Ritson Press, links this third play with 'The Human Dynamo'. It turns out that Joan is the daughter of Marjorie Mayne, the death of whose father Henry is the subject of the first play. Marjorie Mayne had been in contact with her father after his death, in the sense of being convinced of his survival; while Joan herself has asserted that her mother has been communicating with her since her death three years previously. This is of sufficient concern to the members of the brotherhood to incarcerate her in the Paranoia Wing, the regime of which is strongly reminiscent of mental hospitals in Soviet Russia. Joan firmly stands her ground during the interrogation. Just before she is led out, she points out that if she and those who think like her are killed, whether accidentally or by design, they will become all the more able to help those who remain.

After Joan leaves the room to return to the Paranoia Wing, there ensues a lengthy discussion about using a new drug ('palinkenophrenomide'), which has the power both to obliterate all the experiences lying at the foundation of a belief in reincarnation and to accelerate a person's mental processes and, hence, to destroy 'the epidemic bug of philosophical Immaterialism'. The scientists' plan is to diffuse this drug via drinking water, a decision which elicits the resignation of the American citizen, Homer Nasmith. However, shortly after Nasmith's departure from the meeting, the telephone rings. Dr Sedlescombe learns to his horror that a huge crane being used for constructing an extension to the Paranoia Wing has collapsed on the old building, killing all the patients (including of course Joan Holdsworth). The members of the brotherhood recall Joan's parting words with deep foreboding.

The scene now shifts to the angelic sphere. Remiel, the archangel, is flanked on either side by Shezef and Raquel. He recalls Shezef's prophetic words (quoted earlier) from 'The Wall', together with his own reassuring thoughts that followed:

Shezef, the hour you prophesied—the hour
You pointed to, exhorting us—is here.
Momently, in this region, the tall Wall
Crumbles, between the living and the dead.
Across our threshold passings to and fro
Grow common . . .

The play concludes with a ceremonial offering up by these three angelic beings to the highest Divinity:

Winged with the will of God,
I will carry His making Word
To Man building a body
For my Lover and Lord.
Quoniam apud Te est fons vitae.
Et in lumine Tuo videbunt lucem!

'Angels at Bay', which oscillates stylistically between the prose of the human drama and the blank verse of the scenes in the heavenly regions, was Barfield's attempt at a modern mystery play. While he was clearly inspired by Steiner's four mystery plays (written and performed between 1910 and 1913), Barfield was as usual very far from merely imitating and was quietly working out of his own experience of the wall between the living and the dead.

What was his hope when writing these three little plays? Did he ever arrange a performance? There is no outward record of any performance and certainly none of publication; nor have I found any indication that they are known in any form beyond the confines of their refuge in the Wade Center, Wheaton College. However, they reveal a considerable amount about their author's inner questings and strivings at around the mid-point of his life.

The last of the three more substantial poetic dramas to be considered here is 'Riders on Pegasus' (originally entitled 'The Mother of Pegasus'). According to Barfield himself,[245] this was written around 1950, that is, contemporaneously with the Preface intended to accompany it.[246] Outwardly, 'Riders on Pegasus' is a fusion of two Greek myths surrounding the figures of Perseus, Andromeda, Bellerophon and the winged horse Pegasus, with Medusa, the Gorgon, and Pallas Athene, the goddess of wisdom, ever-present in the background. But Barfield's purpose is not so much to tell a tale as express something of his own through the vehicle of the story. Indeed, the poem is difficult to follow without a knowledge of Greek mythology, to say nothing of its other literary allusions. The main point for present purposes is to establish what he was seeking to express through the medium of the poem or, in other words, why he wrote it.

Barfield gives us a clue in his introduction to a collection of papers on Lewis edited by Jocelyn Gibb, *Light on C.S. Lewis* (1965).[247] He described a change that he observed taking place in his intimate friend around 1934, since which time he was aware that Lewis was no longer fully present in whatever he said, that in a certain sense his brilliant conversation was of the nature of a hollow pastiche. This impression was reinforced by poems that Lewis would send him for comment, which gave him the feeling 'not of an "I say this", but of a "This is the sort of thing a man might say"'. In the essay referred to, Barfield characterizes this image that he was forming of Lewis as the principal reason for writing 'Riders on Pegasus':

> From about 1935 onward . . . , I had the impression of living with, not one, but two Lewises; and this was so as well when I was enjoying his company as when I was absent from him . . . This experience gradually became something like an obsession with me, and it must have been somewhere about 1950 . . . that I made it part of the emotional base for a long narrative poem. There were other things I felt the need of unloading as well, and I ended by meditating at some length, and ultimately writing, a sort of extension and combination of two well-known Greek myths in such a way that the characters and events should symbolize, at different levels, a good many matters which I liked to think were still at a 'pre-logical' stage in my mind[,] . . . questions to which I did not yet know the answers and knew that, for the purposes of the poem, it was better that I should not know them.
>
> Among the various themes, or experiences, which underlay this effusion or were woven together in it, the thread that ran most clearly through it all, which I rarely lost sight of altogether in the writing, and which most effectively determined the structure of the whole *oeuvre*,

> was the fact that two of the characters loosely and archetypally represented for me 'my' two Lewises. They suffered very different fates. The one (Perseus), after going through a great many difficulties arising out of a preference he had developed for dealing with the reflections of things rather than with the things themselves (the objective correlative here was an excessive use, for administrative purposes, of the mirror which had once enabled him to slay the Gorgon), made peace with what Professor Wilson Knight or Sir Herbert Read would probably call his 'creative eros' (Andromeda) and was ultimately constellated, along with Andromeda and Pegasus, in the heavens. The other (Bellerophon), after slaying the monster Chimera, declined an invitation to ascend to heaven on the back of Pegasus, who had been his mount in the fateful contest, on the ground of impiety. He was thrown by Pegasus and ended his days in increasing obscurity as a kind of aging, grumbling, earthbound, guilt-oppressed *laudator temporis acti.*[248]

Even this does not render the poem readily accessible to comprehension. One might well ask what other themes was Barfield trying subtly to unload. It has already been noted in connection with the writing of *This Ever Diverse Pair* (1950) that he was experiencing a profound struggle over his relationship to the work of a solicitor's office. We shall also learn that this was a very difficult period in his marriage; and the eros/agape theme is never far away throughout this long poem. For the most part, however, 'Riders on Pegasus' is written both stylistically and semantically in a kind of personal code which could prove fascinating to unravel but places it beyond the scope of the present study. This might seem like the shirking of a challenge, were it not for the fact that Barfield's poetry, in common with the best of his writing in general, is never wantonly obscure, a quality that he explicitly and frequently shunned.

The overall quality of the aspect of Barfield's work which is the subject of the present chapter has been well described in an article entitled 'The Defiant Lyricism of Owen Barfield' by Thomas Kranidas.[249] In this article, Kranidas makes the thoroughly valid observation that Barfield's creative, poetic work was, as it were, forced into a backwater of obscurity because of his refusal to follow the predominant fashion of the time, typified as it was by the intellectual ironicism and detachment of much of Eliot's poetry and drama. As Kranidas rightly points out, this was no mere awkward rebelliousness on Barfield's part but an expression of his passionate advocacy of spiritual values as an integral part of the present and future unfolding of modern culture, a conviction which isolated him not only from the fashionable mainstream but also, to some extent, from more familiar members of the Inklings circle such as Lewis, Williams and Tolkien. Barfield, however, was not content with lyrical outpourings of one kind or another but was—as has already been apparent in the previous chapter on his work on language—actively transforming his 'backwater' into a whole new line of development for cultural and, most especially, social evolution. It will be the task of the next chapter to trace the course of this transformatory work, much of which was inspired by—and has largely been contained within—the wealth of activity flowing from the anthroposophical initiatives of Rudolf Steiner.

14. *VISION FOR A FUTURE SOCIAL AND CULTURAL ORDER*

Amongst the papers that Barfield vouchsafed to the author was a box containing a substantial quantity of notes, mostly dating from the 1920s. Not surprisingly, there is a large body of material relating to his research on poetic diction (an extensive source being I.A. Richards's work on the History of Criticism) and the considerable etymological research lying behind the effortlessly flowing prose of *History in English Words*. But there is also much evidence at this early stage of Barfield's interest in wider philosophical questions (and not only in Steiner), specifically of his reading of the most influential English and German philosophers from the eighteenth century onwards. However, what is most striking about this body of material, which is the nearest we have to a series of notebooks chronicling Barfield's reflections about what he was reading, is the large amount of space devoted to matters such as geography, industrial history and economics. The aim of this chapter is to reflect this other main interest of the philosopher of language, while also taking into account certain of the wider cultural themes touched on in these notes which, arising as they do out of a deeply personal quest, do not readily fall into any other category.

Whether or not the body of notes referred to was preserved by Barfield strictly in chronological order, the strong implication from the way that the focus of the sequence alternates between matters pertaining to language and socio-economic themes is that his interest in social affairs was present from the outset and was not the manifestation of the stricken moral conscience of a somewhat aloof, armchair philosopher. Her failure to recognize this is a major weakness in the otherwise valuable book by Astrid Diener on Barfield's early years.[250] I can find no evidence either in his personal papers or otherwise for the impression that she gives of this interest having been tacked on subsequent to his more well-known preoccupations with language (see the Barfield-Leo Baker correspondence, cited in the following chapter, for substantiation of this view).

What we do have, sandwiched amongst studies of etymology and the history of words, are *detailed* notes on, firstly, geography, with numerous facts gleaned from Chisholm's *Commercial Geography* (1922) and Mackinder's *Britain and the British Seas*. This sequence continues with the theme of industrial history, based on a study of Cheyney's *Industrial and Social History of England* and Ashley's *Economic Organization of England*. This is followed by some notes on J.M. Keynes's *The End of Laissez-Faire*, which Barfield studied with evident approval, quoting sentences such as the following: 'To suggest social action for the public good to the City is like discussing *The Origin of Species* with a bishop 60 years ago. The first reaction is not intellectual, but moral.'

A substantial section on economics as such now follows as a logical consequence, beginning with the observation that the London School of Economics was founded in 1895 and that 'in the '90s one Professor was supposed to be able to deal with the whole of Economics'. The ensuing notes on economics are derived from a book by Cannan on *Wealth*, with ample attention devoted to Adam Smith's *The Wealth of Nations* and to basic concepts such as demand and cost, there being some fairly detailed notes on these fundamental elements taken from Cannan's book, from Henderson's *Supply and Demand*, from Robertson's *Control of Industry* and from a book by Taussig.

Interspersed with the studious notes are several comments by Barfield himself, which indicate that he was entering into this process with his critical faculties thoroughly awake. Thus after a passage on the 'laws' of supply and demand we have the following humorous observation: 'And so everything is for the best, Henry! . . . except that *maximum total utility* (secured as above) still does not = *maximum real utility*, owing to *mal-distibution*.' And: '[The] last 100 years have seen unprecedented increase in machines + unprecedented improvement (*sic*) in standard of living, therefore this will go on for the next 100 years! Machine-breaking is misguided, inter alia, because of competition of non-machine-breaking countries.' Finally, a point which Barfield marked as being of particular importance to him: 'Cannan thinks nurses' and surgeons' services to a sick man are less "satisfaction" to him than a champagne dinner to a eupeptic undergraduate. But surely not less of an *economic* satisfaction! On p. 216 he says that x who saves against a rainy day when he will be sick gets more "satisfaction" out of his income than y who imprudently spends while he is well. So also Taussig, Vol. I, p. 131 refers to a distinction between "plain economy" and "pleasure economy" etc. This attempt to correlate economic "satisfaction" with human "enjoyment" or "pleasure" is BAD.'

Further sub-sections on the theme of economics now follow, with a focus respectively on land, on finance and the control of industry and on money, the latter section being guided by Cassel's *The World's Monetary Problems* and *Virtues and Foibles of Current Economic Writers*.

Considerably later in the sequence of notes and dating from 1929 or shortly afterwards is a section entitled 'Notes for Econ. Book'—a scheme which never seems to have materialized along the lines conceived of at the time, although some of the ideas briefly jotted down were amplified in essays which Barfield published in the later 1930s. At the heart of Barfield's concerns regarding economics lay the simplest of thoughts, one which he expressed in note-form as follows:

> Object of life to acquire the best kind of consciousness. Actions etc. only valuable as the expression of good consciousness (or as mediating it in others), from which is deduced [that]
>
> (a) industriousness ... caused by love of gain [and] economic compulsion is no virtue [and]
>
> (b) history of civil institutions views them as expressions [and] servants of the stage of c[onsciousness]. They crack up when c[onsciousness] changes and they do not.

There then follows on the same page of notes a schematic diagram, the meaning of which is not wholly clear but which would appear to be centred on the difference between Steiner's concept—in his basic economics course of 1922—of the crucial importance of arriving associatively at a true price for the fruits of the production process, on the one hand, and, on the other, a relationship between producer and consumer that is governed solely by the profit motive and lacks the influence of a conscious thought process. Barfield himself comments:

> This is quite different from a Student-Christian call to a 'change of heart'. St[einer] carries Christ right into the technique of economic life. It is also different from the insidious 'honesty is the best policy' cry. Christianity *works*—i.e. brings in profit to *me* (Nonconformist—Liberal—Victorian). For it takes attention off profit. C[hristianity] 'works' means it can produce a society in which all can live a human life.

Especially this last sentence represents the essence of Barfield's ideas on economics, and it is amplified in the two other pages constituting these notes for his 'economics book'. Thus from a book by Walter Rathenau he records the following thought about ' "solidarity" as an opposite force to "mechanization" ', with solidarity being defined as meaning 'that within a community the individual becomes aware of the fact that one necessarily stands for all and all for one'. And from a lecture by Steiner of 20 April 1923: '... Wenn man ausgeht nicht von der blinden Produktion, die nur auf das Reichwerden abzielt, sondern von den Bedürfnissen, von der

Konsumption,'[251] followed by Barfield's comment: 'Surplus values only available to a few, because the above not attended to. One must thus ask *why* capital labour-goals are so badly arranged from the point of view of workers' leading a life worthy of human beings. And so we come to a *Geistesfrage* ... An unhealthy spiritual life has produced unhealthy fruits.'

In the meantime, Barfield was actively campaigning for his socio-economic ideals in the public domain. As already mentioned in the previous chapter, he was engaged with the Douglas Social Credit movement in the 1920s as well as with Steiner's ideas on the social order, and his published writings from this decade stem more from the former connection than the latter, the situation being reversed in the 1930s. The watershed between these two stages of Barfield's development in this respect is marked more or less by the writing of 'English People'.

Probably in 1923 (Astrid Diener suggests 1925, though internal evidence would favour the earlier date),[252] Barfield published a pamphlet called *Danger, Ugliness and Waste*. This begins in apocalyptic mood:

> At a time when this country, if not all Europe, if not all civilization itself, needs more urgently than ever before the assistance of the clearest brains it possesses, I do not apologize for trespassing on your time. Nor will I waste it by quoting opinions in support of the foregoing assertion. There is no need to. The last twelve months have heard a quick crescendo of warning, and it is no longer only the politicians or writers, such as the author of 'The Four Horsemen of the Apocalypse', from whom the omens are forthcoming; financiers, economists, scientists, philosophers, artists—almost every day some fresh mind speaks out, corroborating the panic without apparently shifting the load of hopeless apathy beneath which it is suppressed. Professor Graham Wallas has drawn a close comparison between the years 1923 and 423 A.D., and there is scarcely a general conversation among ordinary people which does not end on the note of precariousness and insecurity. When Cassandra is silent, it *is* generally because she is afraid of being dull.

What prompts this tone is Barfield's perception of the grinding miseries of the post-war European scene, with a picture of considerable unemployment and poverty—even starvation—on the one hand and, on the other, the evident underused capacity of factories and distribution facilities. Increased production based on an opening up of overseas markets is seen by many as the only solution. And yet the British taxpayer, complains Barfield, needs these goods himself! Is it really necessary, in such a situation, to go blindly forward, oscillating between periods of boom and slump? And why has the immense increase in the productive capacity of modern industry not led to a corresponding improvement in human well-being? His diagnosis of present social problems is, fundamentally, that 'we lack one thing—a means of transferring the goods from the producer to the consumer. While our *real* credit [nature's bounties enhanced by machines and technology] is colossal, our *financial* credit is so reduced that the whole mechanism of production and exchange is clogged . . .'

Barfield now turns in the second section of his pamphlet to the remedy (as proposed by the Social Credit movement), which is essentially that 'in future financial credit should be based on real credit, or in other words, that the amount of purchasing power issued, instead of being controlled, as at present, by private individuals on an unscientific system, should be regulated automatically by the relation of our national production to our national consumption. That is, that the number of tickets issued should be determined by the seating capacity of the train. At present, since it is not so controlled, there is actually *never* enough purchasing power circulating in the community to buy all, or even nearly all, the goods which the community can produce. The result is that either manufacturers dare not produce because, although there is a dreadful demand for their goods, there is no money to *express* that demand ("tickets"), and therefore "no market" ("passengers") . . .' And he goes on to outline in practical terms how the Social Credit theorists would recommend this to be achieved, criticizing as he does so the limited horizons of otherwise progressive thinkers like 'certain Fabian intellectuals'. Moreover, he sees no reason why such a system of issuing treasury-notes should be thought of as any less unrealistic than the already existing capacity of banks to 'manufacture credit' or 'manufacture money'.

Barfield concludes his essay by emphasizing to his fellow intellectuals and men of letters the moral impossibility of ignoring the socio-economic questions, which he has been addressing, whatever may be one's view as to their resolution:

> [W]e may talk of education and of university extension, and we may be rightly proud of these things; but we know all the time in our hearts that without a general spread of means and leisure the world of culture must remain for ever the bitter farce it sometimes seems—an everlasting Decameron set in an everlasting plague. This social conscience of ours may be a comparatively recent addition to our hearts, but it is a

> permanent one, and now that it has evolved in us, there is no greatness without it. Until its pangs are allayed, the sincerest works of art will also be the most tortured and preoccupied, sacrificing spirit to idea and life to propaganda . . . For a long, long time after Golgotha fancy could still play upon reality without being sickened by the stink of the human manure from which it drew its fragrance. It is no longer so; and I believe that for the future we have to face either a world without these things or a world in which the leisure and refinement which alone make them possible are not drawn in dividends from half-educated millions to whom all chance of knowing them, or even the value of them, is for ever denied. One of two things is true. Civilization is either a ghastly accident, or it is a means to the end of freeing the human spirit in this world. If the former—so; but if the latter, there can be nothing more than a fluttering of wings, until humanity has established its place in the sun.[253]

At the time of the writing of 'English People' in the later 1920s, Barfield was continuing to expand on the theme of financing consumption. Thus he published three articles in *The Nineteenth Century* on this subject in 1929, 'The Lesson of South Wales' (February), 'The Problem of Financing Consumption' (June) and 'Financial Inquiry' (December). Broadly speaking, these articles bring out aspects of Douglas's ideas regarding 'cultural heritage', by which he meant a recognition—in affinity with the socialists—of the common ownership of natural resources and of the means of exploiting them that have accumulated over the centuries. This common ownership also applied, in Douglas's view, to the facilities of industry itself: 'the industrial machine is a common heritage, the result of the labours of untold generations of people whose names are for the most part forgotten . . . therefore . . . society as a whole . . . has a right to the product'.[254] The corollary of this is that financial credit, normally of course regarded as the exclusive right of individuals, should also be thought of as a communal possession. According to Diener's concluding remarks on the subject, 'Douglas wanted . . . society to be in control of economics through its control of financial power'.[255] These same ideas of Douglas's were what largely underlay the economic and political ferment in Barfield's novel 'English People', which was written at about this time. However, the political scenario portrayed in the novel of a Chancellor of the Exchequer, Streeter, espousing the ideas of Hicks and Cameron (basically those of Douglas) was wholly fictional in that the main thrust of a solution to the problems of unemployment and poverty in 1929 (the year when Ramsay MacDonald's Labour Government came to power) was the Liberal impulse of David Lloyd George and John Maynard Keynes to expand production rather than attend to the question of distribution. As Barfield stated in 'The Problem of Financing Consumption' with reference to Lloyd George's election schemes, he detected 'a fundamental dishonesty behind a policy which keeps people's attention fixed on the problem of distributing employment, when the real problem is that of distributing goods—and leisure!' Ultimately it was Keynes's ideas that prevailed,[256] and that window of opportunity which in the late 1920s Barfield had identified as a potential point of breakthrough for Douglas's Social Credit ideas was closed, at any rate in British political circles.[257] Probably partly in recognition of this, Barfield published—and as far as I know, wrote—nothing further under the auspices of the Social Credit movement.[258]

The next, and final, phase in his socio-economic thinking was heralded in 1932 by the publication of his article on 'Equity'.[259] This essay, which is solidly based on a careful study of Steiner's *World Economy* lectures, is in a certain sense the esoteric companion to the more exoteric thrust of a second essay, entitled *Law, Association and the Trade Union Movement,* which was published probably in 1937 and is to be considered below.

Barfield introduces his essay on 'Equity' by presenting the economic context for his considerations. Basing his remarks on a lecture in Steiner's *World Economy*, he ascribes many of the gravest problems of modern economic life to the tendency of capital to accumulate in the form of land-values. In addition to the two stages in the economic process which would be recognized outwardly as taking place, namely, the operation of human labour upon land and the working of the creative human spirit upon this labour so as to make it more productive, there is a third stage which, in a healthy social organism, ought to be being enacted but is not. For the capital which builds up as a result of the second stage ought to be placed at the service of the spirit by being allowed indirectly (via distribution on educative and other spiritual activities) to flow back to the land. Instead, the spirit is omitted, and consequently huge masses of capital pile up in mortgages and land-values. At the foundation of this problem is the widespread illusion that capital is 'wealth', an illusion which arises from the undoubted fact that anyone who is in control of capital can readily convert it into personal wealth. But capital is more truly thought of as a 'difference of potential', a state of disequilibrium or unequal pressure which is the prerequisite of all economic activity. Barfield concludes his introductory remarks with a helpful electrical metaphor: 'If the economic process were complete, these pressures, after doing their work, would discharge to earth again, that is to the land. But the conductor is wanting. Instead, therefore, they pile up *above* the earth, *over* it. This creates a static charge of steadily increasing intensity; and a static charge is, for the people living in it, the atmosphere before a thunderstorm.'

Barfield then goes on to explain how, historically, it became possible for capital to be converted into personal wealth and, also, why it has tended to become congested in the form of land-values. These connections are to be attributed to the law of property, to the way that certain rights that people have as against each other have come to be guaranteed, and enforceable, by the law. But the way that our modern property laws work is compounded out of the legal arrangements recognized in English law as surrounding two very different classes of property, namely, real property and personal property. Barfield's aim in this essay is to disentangle these two aspects and, most especially, to consider very carefully the potential inherent in a deeper understanding of the latter kind of property. For the idea of real property, related as it is to land as such, is relatively familiar and easy to understand, although it may come as a surprise to realize the extent to which this essentially feudal notion of property grew out of 'a social organism in which the land is everything and the human being (except possibly for a few exalted nobles) is attached to it almost after the fashion of a vegetable'. At this time there was as yet hardly any notion of personal rights existing independently of land and accruing to all human beings by virtue of their sheer humanity. Moreover, the true mark of the coming into being of these personal rights lies not so much in the recognition that there are certain objects that one can call one's own ('things-in possession') but in one's capacity to bring a legal action against another person in order to recover a disputed object or (most especially) a sum of money ('things-in action'). For this to happen requires the gradual recognition of a personal '*right* to possess' which, in England, 'is closely bound up with the history of Equity'. Again taking his cue from a statement in Steiner's economics course, where the lecturer explicitly associates the deed of lending with the arising of a relation between two persons, Barfield defines the history of Equity (in English jurisprudence) as being 'precisely the history of the recognition of this relation between two persons by the courts. Equity begins as soon as the "relation between two persons" begins to be recognized as a *thing*, as an object no less "real", in fact though not in name, than a piece of land.'

Barfield then traces the historical origins of this 'right of action' back to thirteenth-century England, by which time it had become possible for people with a genuine grievance for which no remedy was available under the existing (land-based) law to turn to the King's highest official, the Chancellor, for redress. This official, who was invariably an ecclesiastic, was known as 'Keeper of the King's Conscience'; and the gradual formalization of the relief from the constrictions of Roman law furnished to suitors by the Chancellor—giving rise to a set of courts parallel to and yet wholly distinct from those of the common law—came to be known as the Courts of Equity or 'courts of conscience'. These courts are the ancestors of the present Chancery Division of the High Court. Barfield emphasizes the extent to which 'courts of conscience' was an appropriate term, in that what distinguished these courts from those dealing with common law grievances (which existed purely to satisfy these grievances) was that it was their essential task to 'clear the conscience of the defendant', to offer him the opportunity to repent from wrongdoing. The common law did not recognize such personal rights and obligations and could deal only with the technical circumstances surrounding a particular case. Thus 'a man might be a notorious rogue, but nevertheless he could succeed in evicting from a piece of land (if he could show that it was technically "his") another man whose *personal* right to the land was universally admitted to be far better than his own. This was where equity stepped in. When such a situation arose, the sufferer could apply to the Chancellor, and, if satisfied of the rights of the case, the Chancellor would say, in effect, to the oppressor: "It is perfectly true that you have this legal right to the land, and if you choose to go to law to enforce it, the common law will assist you. I cannot stop that. But there is something else that I both can and shall do. The moment you begin any such action, in order to prevent you going on with it, I shall imprison your person for contempt of *my* court".'

Moreover, a person applying for relief via a court of equity had to be able to show that his own conscience was clear: 'He who seeks equity must do equity.' Not only that; the touchstone for bringing such an action was a state of 'knowing with' the other person, in other words, a recognition of his existence as an individual being separate from, and of equal significance to, oneself.[260] On this basis only was it possible for the work of a court of equity to proceed; for whereas the substance of a common law or criminal court has to do with offences against the *group* of which the criminal is a member, the infringement of an equitable right is 'the wronging of *another individual human being*. It depends on a relation between two persons.'

Drawing upon Coleridge (specifically his *Essay on Faith*), Barfield goes on to indicate the extent to which such a capacity of one being to recognize the *equality* of another is the basis of self-consciousness. And it is here that the profoundly Christian aspect of what is under discussion here becomes apparent. For whereas the ancient wisdom embodied in the great religions of the world has revolved around the central discovery that 'I am divine', the crucial contribution of Christianity—and where it uniquely takes a step beyond all other religions—is to bring about the awareness that 'thou art divine', in that 'Christ can only make his home in a "relation between two persons".' It then becomes dimly apparent that this 'roguish thing' of equity which 'springs rather suddenly into prominence in England at the dawn of the fifth post-Atlantean age[261] . . . has a certain breath of fragrance about it and that that fragrance is the fragrance of Christianity itself'.

Barfield now extends his analysis beyond that realm of the legal-political structure of the state where, according to Steiner's view of the social organism,[262] the ideal of equality belongs. For the phenomenon of equity has, by way of changing conceptions of property, become embedded also in economic life. He furnishes an imaginary instance of how an individual's *personal right* to enjoy a piece of land (a right arising from his right of equity) could itself become a saleable proposition, thus enabling the ancient feudal attachments binding individuals to their land to be broken and fade into the background. A new system of ownership therefore arose, 'in which the theory was that, not the land itself was owned, but the personal *right* to enjoy it', which then became as concrete as the land itself and could be bought, sold or left in a will. This made property much easier to transfer from one person to another, and in this same sense 'the equitable doctrines of ownership underlay the whole phenomenon of the growth of commerce and the rise of the free cities. In commerce, the relations of human beings to one another are based not on the land but on cash.'

Again proceeding from an indication by Steiner in *World Economy*, Barfield now points out that, in its original form, a *loan* was not a contract to repay an exact amount (with or without interest) but a tacit understanding that the borrower would also, in his turn, be willing to become a lender should this be necessary. Once more the emphasis is on the relation between one person and another, as words such as 'trust' and 'credit' suggest. 'Trust is the soul of equity', in that equity 'imputes to a man the intention to fulfil his obligations'. The influence which such a conception has had on the development of *money* (in all its various modern forms) can hardly be overestimated. Problems arise, however, when this influence is lost sight of, when people forget that behind every monetary exchange there lies a personal relationship based on trust and mutual confidence. For once this happens, money becomes a mere physical object, and the rights (personal relationships) that it represents get lost in the blind unconsciousness of the economic process: 'When rights begin to be bought and sold and used for the payment of debts, we see them trying to turn into physical things. They become abstracted from the personal relation which is their essence, and the result is confusion.'

We have now reached the crux of what Barfield is trying to impart in this essay. For what do we see when we emerge from a historical survey of the arising of a modern monetary economy from a feudal past? At the time when Barfield was writing, the monetary world was in the midst of a transition from a system based on cash to one based on credit (a transition which in our time has continued to develop further and intensify). There is, he says, nothing wrong with this, any more than there was anything wrong with a system of cash-exchange arising out of one based on the land and the family. But whereas in the latter process there continued to be an awareness of the personal element which underlies equity, on the one hand, and the physical reality of the land, on the other, in modern credit-finance—where to a far greater extent than in Barfield's time vast quantities of credit, of sums that are owed to nobody and represent the world's debt to itself, flow aimlessly all over the world—the personal relations whence this whole process has developed have become a total abstraction, with the result that the only solid element of security is considered to be the land.[263] The remedy, claims Barfield, is that people come to realize 'that confidence is an immaterial substance, not a material one'. His essay concludes with a grim picture of actual realities as he saw them at the time, and his vision of their counterpart:

> The picture is indeed nearly as dark as it could be. Pestilence and famine have come upon men before, but they have come as the result of the natural forces of the earth. Or—over smaller areas—they have been brought about by certain easily identifiable personal crimes. Never before have they been caused, as they are being caused today, by something between the two, by the natural or at any rate impersonal, forces of a sort of second earth, an earth which is not the physical earth at all, but is compacted of the personal relations of men with one another and of the uneasy ghosts and decaying relics of such relations.
>
> Perhaps it is for this reason that more and more people seem to be drawn to the study of money-problems. In the last decade it has been by no means uncommon for souls impelled rather by a vague spiritual

> unrest than by any instinctive interest in economics to apply themselves to the study of such things as credit and currency. Is this because behind the thick darkness in which money, the 'root of all evil'[264], is shrouded, a darkness which has now extended itself from the moral over the intellectual sphere, they divine the mysterious presence of the root of all good? Really to understand money involves understanding that above the decaying, increasingly mechanized physical body of the earth, whose future even science predicts to be increasing cold and darkness, there is coming into being another earth, an earth which is literally composed of the relations of human beings with one another, an earth whose destiny it is to become increasingly one of light.
>
> This at any rate was the teaching of Rudolf Steiner, and it is this picture of the two earths, the 'real' and the personal, of which the old-fashioned 'trust' of settled land appears to me to be a sort of clumsy but honest caricature. Or rather it is more than this. For what is contained in this most characteristic of all the creations of the old courts of equity? Apart from all other considerations, there is contained in it a certain striking and impressive *form of thought*; and anyone who has ever attempted to inculcate an idea with even modest pretensions to being *new*, will understand what an important part of the task is this establishment of a suitable form of thought.

As one considers Barfield's insights in this essay of 1932 from the perspective of a generation beyond its republication in 1961, they appear as an even more incisive comment on present realities than they were in the 1960s. If one seeks to apply his perceptions to the contemporary scene, it becomes clear that the globalizing thrust of the present world economic order is driven not even remotely by an endeavour to meet the physical needs of all the human beings on our planet out of a spirit of brotherhood (the ideal which Steiner associated with the economic sphere of the social organism) but by a fear and a lack of trust which represent the direct opposite of what originally pertained in an equitable relation between one human being and another. Instead of economic processes being governed by a conscious perception of human need (which would be the appropriate extension into the economic sphere of the recognition of individual human rights which was the basis of the courts of equity), economic activity is driven unintelligently and slavishly by blind market forces which are themselves the outward manifestation of the assumption that only rampant egotism—a *prior* stage of consciousness to that which gave birth to equity relations in thirteenth-century England—can be a spur to focused and responsible human work. And the modern state, faced with the dilemma of controlling this egotistic monster of unbridled unconscious will-forces, has—largely thanks to computer technology—become an all-seeing and all-knowing machine for implementing abstractly and mechanically (and therefore in an anti-Christian way) that quintessentially Christian recognition that God is to be sought in the ego of *another* human being. And yet it is also transparently clear that the people with whom one lives and works have moved on well beyond all this, that there is everywhere a readiness and willingness to implement an entirely different socio-economic order founded on the trust between one person and another which was the foundation of the equity courts. Moreover, not a day goes past when one can read articles or books making a plea that we need firmly to resist the notion that, with the collapse of communism and the apparent sovereignty of the *laissez faire* assumptions underlying Anglo-American global capitalism, humanity has reached some kind of 'end of history', that the model of egocentric (and environmentally destructive) consumerism—with its associated web of political control—represents an ideal for human existence on the earth.[265] As Barfield indicates in 'Equity', what is lacking is not the will to make it happen but the 'suitable form of thought' to furnish a model and guide for such an endeavour. And yet, as he was at pains to point out, such a model and guide already exists among us if we could but recognize, acknowledge and make it conscious.

Some five years after publishing 'Equity', Barfield contributed a pamphlet to a series of essays published by The Threefold Commonwealth Research Group, based at Rudolf Steiner House, London. Barfield's pamphlet was entitled *Law, Association and the Trade Union Movement.*[266] These pamphlets were clearly intended to convey a clear, 'exoteric' message to as wide a circle of people as possible; and one may be aware that, in his essay, Barfield was aiming to address the outward socio-economic situation of that particular time (1937 was the most likely date of publication) in the light of, on the one hand, his essay on 'Equity' and, on the other, the recent publication for the first time in English of Steiner's economics course, *World Economy*, co-translated and introduced by himself. In the following summary, the intention will be to consider this pamphlet not so much as a historical document but as a reflection of Barfield's thinking in terms of its continuing relevance today.

Barfield opens his essay in a somewhat similar vein to the way he introduced his other pamphlet, *Danger, Ugliness and Waste*, by indicating to his reader that he is writing within an outward context of potential disaster: 'To me it appears that, if anything can be done *immediately* to arrest the headlong progress of Europe to catastrophe, it will be done by running alongside the demented beast and giving an occasional slight push or tug of the reins in the hope of guiding it along the safer of two parallel but appallingly different paths.' He goes on to state his intention to select from existing social phenomena those elements which seem to him to belong most appropriately to 'the genuine *underlying movement of human consciousness* in this particular age'.

Law, Association and the Trade Union Movement was written at a time when, according to the pamphlet's author, traditional liberalism, with its rigorous advocacy of free trade and unrestrained competition, was widely regarded as discredited. There was an intuitive awareness that association is more important than competition, and a deep antipathy to anything savouring of the bourgeois notions of property. The proffered political alternatives to liberalism were Communism on the one hand and Fascism on the other, neither of which, incidentally, aroused the slightest sympathy in Barfield. What particularly distressed him was, at bottom, that same failure to recognize the reality of that domain of human relationships discerned in 'Equity' as the seed of a new earth. However, the essay under consideration here deals not so much with this inner reality as with the outward effect of such a failure, namely, the threat to this same sphere of individual rights from, on the one hand, a right-wing Fascism that would hanker for the old hierarchical group life of feudalism and, on the other, a left-wing Communism that would abolish individual rights altogether in favour of the communal principle. In this connection, the crucial error—one to which the trade unions have tended to succumb—is to view human labour as a commodity, as something that can be bought and sold.

Barfield's principal thrust in this essay is to suggest what kind of an alternative might arise specifically for the trade union movement (which he regards as, potentially, a thoroughly creative and positive element) if the individual rights upheld by equity were to be acknowledged instead of being clouded and confused with the material objects—and in effect this means, for the most part, property—received as a result of the accruing of these rights. In this connection, he traces a strand in the history of the trade union movement[267] which, in contrast to its familiar focus on the betterment of wages and conditions, has been concerned with a quality which he calls 'solidarity', where many combine to achieve a given goal. He adds that 'Rudolf Steiner called it "fraternity", that human impulse which demands expression and finds it naturally in the economic sphere; just as the demand for "equality" in society can only be satisfied in the sphere of equity, and the demand for "liberty" in the life of the spirit.' Out of this contrasting principle which he detects still at work in the trade union movement in 1937 emerges a radically different vision of what has become ever more established as 'a bargaining movement, as the incorporated salesman of a supposed commodity termed labour, [which] . . . gropes naturally towards a more centralized structure, on the lines of a juridical corporation'—a vision which, he strongly contests, is more congenial to the large part of the trade union membership than becoming a political 'popular front'. This vision centres on the potential function of trade unions as economic associations: 'Suppose the Trade Unions were to become fully aware of their existing, and still more their possible function as true economic associations. Suppose they were to make a new and deliberate choice, emphasizing henceforth the associative principle, pursuing less ardently the other political principle of their being. I believe the effect would be an immediate relief of political tension,' an effect which, as he goes on to explain, would arise from a handing over of the movement's present preoccupation with matters pertaining to the rights sphere (conditions of labour and rates of pay) to where it properly belongs, that is, 'to Parliament, trusting not only to the Parliamentary Labour Party, but also to the general awakening of social conscience in these matters to see that equity is done'. Instead, the trade unions would focus on economic questions: 'We (they would have to say) will henceforth aim at becoming purely economic bodies concerned with the production and distribution of commodities. Labour itself, however, is not a commodity. The conditions under which it is proper for a man to work are a question of human rights, not an economic question at all . . . But when it comes to the best method of dealing with the Distressed Areas, the transfer of workers to new districts and of industries to old ones, the distribution of "surplus" milk to those who need it, the problems of overproduction and of home and overseas markets, these we regard as our province. Behold, we do now invite all other economic associations, such as the Co-operative Societies, the Chambers of Commerce, the employers' associations and perhaps the municipal enterprises and public utility bodies, to join us in this task.'

The remainder of the essay consists of a picture of the benefits that would accrue 'not merely to Parliament (which would be relieved of the economic deliberations occupying a large part of its present work) and the social and psychological health of England as a whole but also to the wider world':

> Suppose there arose into being an 'economic England', not any corporate body defined by a frontier, and still less one pursuing any competitive and diplomatic policy, but a collection of associations with which the associations existing within other nations were able to have mutual intercourse; drawing and imparting strength in the process and becoming more and more conscious of themselves as an actual world organization apart from the political states of which their members were citizens. I believe the effect would be incalculable. It would be a step towards genuine internationalism, without being at the same time a challenge to national sovereignty.

And Barfield concludes by pointing to what is at stake in what he admits is the considerable task of changing the direction of the trade union movement:

> It is frequently suggested, and not only over here, that this country and the Empire hold a kind of key position in the present world crisis.[268] It *may* be that the Trade Union Movement holds a similar key position in the social life of this country, that—economically—it is England within England. If there is even a possibility of this being so, it will be agreed that the occasion is not one for sitting down under difficulties. Difficulties enough! But I am entitled to insist that any judgment passed shall be passed while looking steadily at the actual condition of Europe in the year 1937.[269]

Barfield's plea fell on deaf ears, and the explosive political situation in Europe detonated, inflicting a terrible wound on the spiritual vision and intellectual confidence of the entire continent. The immediate legacy of the Second World War was that the aspiration towards association and community and the antipathy towards competitive individualism detected by Barfield both diminished to a considerable degree, a trend which culminated in, first, the Conservative right and, second, the Socialist left embracing the previously spurned egocentric principles of classical liberalism.[270] But although—with enormous post-war backing from the United States—the conscious trends of social evolution have more or less ground to a halt, a state of affairs that is marked by the so-called 'history is over' school currently (2002) represented by, for example, George Walden and Barry Cox, the underlying evolution-of-consciousness process identified by Barfield in his 1937 essay as a gradual shift of focus from the sphere of rights and politics to the economic sphere,[271] or from individualism to associationism (as he expresses it in this context), has been taking place anyway. The effect of this latter process is strikingly apparent at the time of writing in the virtually complete sovereignty of corporate business interests over governments and political elites.[272] Barfield would not have seen anything wrong in this shift of focus to the economic domain. But the tragic problem which he would have discerned in our present situation is that our 'forms of thought' have, as noted above, ground to a halt, with the result that the modern economic climate—ruled as it is by blind, unconscious market forces—is largely uncontrolled by any human agency. With politicians in thrall to (increasingly apathetic) voters and businesses to shareholders, the present writer can see hope for the fulfilment of Barfield's ideas (as expressed in the two essays considered at some length in this chapter) only in the free, conscious intervention of the consumer in what is ostensibly being done both economically and legally on his behalf. The goal is still as he has outlined it for us, the forming of economic associations founded on the principle of equity or the reverence for the individual. The difference between 1937 and the early twenty-first century is merely that the initiative now rests fairly and squarely with the sleeping giant of the consumer, who therefore needs to awaken, consciously directing his actions so that economic brotherhood can gradually spread from individuals working together over the entire earth, albeit from tiny local centres to begin with. In terms of one's attitude to money, this would then mean that, instead of thinking primarily of how to acquire money, one would put one's consciousness as far as possible into the way one spends one's money. This, and only this, can engender the foundation for economic associations in our time.[273]

* * *

It is impossible to appreciate the full weight and intensity of what Barfield was seeking to present in these two essays written in the 1930s without taking up further thought-seeds that are scattered in note form in the box of papers referred to at the beginning of this chapter. The notes in question relate specifically to an exploration of the theme of Hamlet and Faust, not so much as works of art but as figures who represent, respectively, the English and the German folk souls. These brief indications were then expanded upon in what was perhaps the most creatively original and profoundly personal expression of all Barfield's analyses of contemporary culture, his essay on 'The Consciousness Soul',[274] and developed further in 'The Form of Hamlet'.[275]

Although in Barfield's notes there are some interesting connections between the three spheres of the social order (as conceived by Rudolf Steiner) and particular national cultures and, hence, a direct relationship with the socio-economic theme which has hitherto been the main focus of this chapter,[276] the central question of both the notes and the essay on 'The Consciousness Soul' concerns the relationship between the national cultures of England and Germany, a question which had all the greater potency in these years between the two Great Wars. For Barfield's entire impulse was to build a bridge of mutual understanding and interaction between these two cultures, with the object of enabling the spiritual impulse of anthroposophy, as the crowning fulfilment of Central European culture, to inspire and awaken the full potential of the economic activity arising out of the distinctive genius of the Anglo-Saxon race (see Note 276 above). His vision is of a marriage between two equally worthy partners, pictorially described at the end of the second part of the 'Consciousness Soul' essay (entitled 'On the Intellectual Soul') in the form of the following graphic image:

> Let us try to call up two divinely tall spiritual forms, and suppose them meeting each other for a moment in the intricate figure of a dance. And let us suppose that this dance is also a choral hymn, so that these two gracious, serenely moving spirits interchange not merely motions and positions, but words. As they meet, the Spirit of the German Nation calls across to the Spirit of the English: 'Seek life! Know thyself! Go down with Faust to the Mothers, to the Eternal Feminine, go down into the teeming earth and rise again in full certainty, having found both thyself and the world. Take the confidence that is based on this knowledge. Know thyself! Seek life!' And the English Folk Soul calls back: 'Seek death! Yes, *know* thyself and the world! Do not merely *believe* in the old way, substituting one creed for another. Rather live in the very breakdown of all belief. Even encourage thine own opposition, as men do in games. Immerse in the destructive element! And so learn to tear thy true self free from all thought and all feeling in which the senses still echo. Leap, with Hamlet, into the grave, in order to wrestle there. Seek death!'

This passage comes at the culmination of an essay which has sought to interpret the respective gifts to the world of, in particular, these two peoples in terms of the incarnation process of the individual human 'I' as described by Steiner, which in the case of the English has by and large gone a step further towards a state of in-dwelling the physical body than it has with the German folk. The effect of this is that the English tend to experience themselves as—from a psychological point of view—more separate from the world around them, whereas especially the Germans excel in being aware of this process actually taking place (but not having come to a conclusion). In this sense, there is in the former case a pre-occupation with disintegration and death, and in the latter case an unparalleled capacity for probing into the meaning of life; hence the appropriateness of associating the former with Hamlet and the latter with Faust.

However, this gives only a very abstract interpretation of Barfield's picture of the dance between these two spirits. If it is to be possible to shed some real light on what has been going on in a soul-spiritual sense within English culture during the last few centuries and, hence, why the legal and economic developments analysed in the two essays under discussion earlier on in this chapter have taken place precisely and pre-eminently in England, it will be necessary to enter to some extent into Steiner's evolutionary picture and terminology as relayed by Barfield in 'The Consciousness Soul'.

Barfield does not, of course, present more than one specific fragment of Steiner's picture of human evolution, while making a particular point of setting it within the context of an image representing the whole vast dimensions of this process. The aspect on which he focuses is the incarnation process of the individual human ego into the three bodily sheaths of the astral body, the etheric body and the physical body, a process which—as an *incarnating* thrust—is reaching its culmination in our present post-Atlantean age. Employing Steiner's terminology, he describes how the working of the ego in the astral body leads to the development of the sentient soul, how its further extension into the etheric body brings about the development of the intellectual soul, and how, finally, its incarnation into the physical body is responsible for the third of these three aspects of soul development, a stage which Steiner named the consciousness soul or spiritual soul. (The latter term is helpful in that it depicts a direct connection between the ego, as the bearer of the individualized *spirit*, and the physical *body*.) A large section of the first part of Barfield's essay is devoted to a characterization of the consciousness soul and to an examination of Steiner's intuition that the English nation has a special task in the unfolding of this aspect of man's bodily constitution. Regarding the appropriateness of the latter insight, Barfield is unequivocal: 'Few things are more startling than the sheer *effectiveness* of this occult key to the quiddity of the Anglo-Saxon genius'; and he goes on to illustrate what he means by taking several examples from English literature and by viewing in particular the Scientific Revolution in the context of this observation.[277] Barfield then goes on to speak of the English Romantic Movement as an awakening of a feeling of inner conviction arising out of an experience of nothingness, a feeling which, he says, has been tragically overwhelmed by a desire to explain it away through having recourse to psychological introspection of one kind or another.

At this point he opens up his intimate study of English culture to a consideration of the entire context of human evolution as discerned by Steiner, introducing these thoughts by making a specific connection between the Romantic Movement and anthroposophy: 'Now one way of approaching anthroposophy is to see in it the solution, or, since that has a somewhat facile sound, let us say the λυσις of this tragedy of Romance.' It would scarcely be an exaggeration to say that Barfield's entire creative work is concerned with expanding upon and explaining this seminal thought; and in the remainder of the essay under consideration he presents within the compass of a few pages a concentrated exposition of what he means by stating or claiming that Romanticism has—through anthroposophy—come of age.

This is the moment to make a conscious link with the socio-economic theme which has formed the main body of this chapter; for the dilemma which faces humanity at the present time, both culturally and socially, is whether there is any future development possible beyond the consciousness-soul experience of the separate individual self, as manifested socio-economically—in the early twenty-first century no less than in the 1930s—in the universally prevalent assumption that human beings can only ultimately be governed by egocentric motives. In fully acknowledging and offering an interpretation of this condition of separate self existence, Barfield goes on to enquire what Steiner had to say about the further development of the human ego beyond this stage of the consciousness soul; and he then presents, as an alternative to 'ultimate death or nonentity', a picture of an outward expansion into the macrocosm from the minute centre of the individual human ego which is no less vast in scope and potential than what preceded it in human evolution. Far from being at the end of history, we stand at the very beginning of the spiritualization of man and the earth, which has been made possible by the incarnation of Christ in a human body, an event that took place in the epoch of the intellectual soul (approximately 750 BC to AD 1450).[278]

The remainder of the essay, forming the part republished under the title 'Of the Intellectual Soul', is concerned with expanding upon Barfield's statement that 'anthroposophy is, in one sense, the intellectual soul speaking to the consciousness soul'.[279] In outward cultural terms, this means that the German culture of Faust (of which Barfield regarded anthroposophy as the highest expression) is seeking to make the English culture of Hamlet aware of the meaning of its very meaninglessness, of the vast significance of the apparent null-point in human evolution which—in modern cultural and socio-economic terms—it has come to embody so successfully and with such an immense effect on the totality of modern life.

In the 1930s, these two forms—representing the German and English folk-souls—were to be thrust into a second brutal military conflict, for reasons which go much deeper than the need to rid the world of people with extreme political views. Since the Second World War the influence of the United States of America—in the role of an appendage to the Anglo-Saxon West (the term 'appendage' in this context is Rudolf Steiner's)—has largely eclipsed the dance of two forms of comparable weight and stature, with the result that the death-bearing impulse of Hamlet has seemingly grown to immense influence over the remainder of Christian Europe. But with the increasing sense in Europe of resistance to and frustration with the behaviour of America as a sort of puppeteer rather than a dancing companion, Barfield's image could now serve as an inspiration to Europe's quest to rediscover its cultural identity and sense of purpose. And at the core of the challenges now confronting Europe is the urgent need to focus, with the guiding hand of Barfield's essay on 'Equity', on what is actually going on when two people engage—as we constantly, even obsessively, do in our time—in an act of monetary exchange.

15. BONDS OF LOVE AND FRIENDSHIP

On 26 November 1986, Owen Barfield moved to his last home at the Walhatch, Forest Row. Although he was 88 years old, it was clear to the friends with whom he shared the greatest intimacy—Josephine Spence and Laurence Harwood being the prime movers in this respect—that it was impossible for him to continue to reside in effective seclusion at Orchard View, South Darenth (near Dartford). His wife, Maud, had died some six years before the decision to move was taken in February 1986.[280] However, Orchard View[281] had been something of a mess even during Maud's lifetime; and the inherent difficulties in running the house, coupled with its isolation on a hillside overlooking Darenth and its access by a very narrow lane, overwhelmed the inconveniencies and complications to both family and visitors which Barfield's move to The Walhatch necessitated (Jeffrey Barfield, for example, continued to live with Owen at Orchard View after Maud's death).

The Barfields had lived at Orchard View since 1970, having moved there from the nearby village of Hartley, near Dartford. By the end of Maud's life, and especially after her stroke, Barfield cared for her devotedly and kindly, reading to her and dealing with the effects of her incontinence. A studio had been built in the house for her dance teaching—constructed in accordance with the Golden Ratio—which her stroke prevented her from being able to use. Before this debilitating illness, life with Maud was a real 'hurly-burly', somewhat Bohemian (as befitted a dedicated artist); and after a dreary day in the city Barfield would often return to help with the day's washing up and other household chores. Only in his own study did Barfield maintain some kind of sovereignty and order, his presence in the house (which Maud owned) being of the nature of a permanent guest. Significantly, Owen and Maud probably never talked about deeper questions, about matters of life and death. On the other hand, there was a strong bond of affection between the members of the family, and—despite their inability or unwillingness to understand his ideas—both Maud and the children were proud of Owen, especially appreciating his academic acclaim in America.[282]

This somewhat chaotic life-style would appear to have characterized the Barfields' family arrangements since Owen and Maud's marriage on 11 April 1923. It is difficult to chronicle their movements with any precision, although the general outlines are clear enough. Initially they lived in the vicinity of Oxford, in the village of Long Crendon, near Thame, also taking a flat in London in 1925 to facilitate Owen's literary career. This pattern of a family life divided between town and country continued for many years, with several changes of residence in both London and the provinces. Shortly after the Second World War the Barfields moved their country abode from Chalfont St Giles, Buckinghamshire, to Uckfield, East Sussex, thereafter residing south of the capital, the move to the Dartford area more or less coinciding with (or slightly pre-dating) Owen's retirement from legal practice. There were also periods—especially during the war—when the only foothold they had in the capital was Barfield and Barfield's office at Danes Inn House, 265 Strand. Only with C.S. Lewis's death in 1963 did the link with Oxford, and the excursions to Inklings meetings, finally become severed.

There can be no doubt that Owen and Maud had much in common with one another, not least their generosity of heart and their love of music and drama. However, as Barfield has himself intimated in the Biographical Sketch (see pp. 11–46), his marriage to Maud was seriously afflicted—as 'a sword through the marriage knot'—by her extreme aversion to anthroposophy. These difficulties were apparent from the first four or five years, as attested by a letter dated 27 September 1928 that Maud addressed to her husband:

> I am unstrung and overwhelmed again by the loss of my Mother and at the same time supremely conscious that you are going on what is to you a very important spiritual journey in which I cannot share. I had hoped to keep cheerful to your going and I wanted you to have very happy memories of these lovely September days before it. I have been so afraid that I might not be kind and that something would happen on the journeys. But the breakdown has come and you must do what you like about coming back. You wrote to me to Scotland that you felt sometimes that you could not keep it up. By that I suppose you meant living with me. I am very sorry that I cannot control myself better and I cannot promise that these fits of sorrow will not occur sometimes. I turn to books as this (which apparently you feed on as it goes with you on every journey) to see if I can get any more in touch; but it seems pretty hopeless. Instance—page 35, [lines] 2 & 3 of what I find merely nauseating. If it had been put in the form more as 'my notion of the Life after Death is as follows'; but to put it down as conclusive statement as though it was the only possible arrangement is petty and limiting.[283] I

am too unhappy to write any more on this subject. I want you to know that I have appreciated your effort lately to be more companionable in reading to me and I am glad you showed me the poem you wrote at Munich. I live so much outside your experiences that, at first I thought your misery there was caused by my breakdown there; but you explained to me that it was not that. Again, I made the mistake of thinking you were happy at Milan chiefly because I was with you until I found it was far more due to some emotional effect of the pictures on you. Everything seems just to point to the fact that you are going through discoveries of soul and spirit and that occasionally I am the peg on which you can hang your feelings. I am still able to be thankful that you are engaged on a spiritual path and know I should be satisfied that it is so; but when two people marry the hope is that their journeying may not be entirely separated. From the first you seemed to be satisfied to start off alone without any desire to find out what my mind was like or on what high quest I was travelling. There is not the slightest tribute anywhere in your writings to any blessing you may have received from living with me or my Mother, who surrounded you with their prayers, who never knelt at the highest place of all without stretching out over the void towards you. Once, I wrote of a beautiful thing, a beam of light while I prayed and you never made any reply. You were very good to me when Mother went away; but I think you thought her personality has ceased. I felt your sympathy then very much all the same.

Can you not see how awful it is to me to come up against your superiority. You hold the position that you and your School of Spiritual Science alone have the solution for the age. I am perfectly willing to admit that it is the solution for some people; but I and countless others are not bound in this way. It is no doubt very fine to write verses in answer to a piece of merriment (written to save a situation from becoming more tragic. I am very sorry if it offended you. I think it saved my balance.[284]) in which you link yourself to a glorious company of Fools. It was carrying it a little far to drag in such an allusion to Jesus Christ.—M.C.B.[285]

Although it would be rash to make any assumptions, it would seem unlikely that Barfield ever read these words or that he was intended to do so. It is difficult otherwise to explain why Maud made a copy of her 'letter' 13 years after it had been composed and why Josephine Spence, who found that this notebook had survived the conflagrations intended to engulf all Maud's confidential correspondence after her death at Orchard View, did not pass it on to Owen. My understanding, for what it is worth, is that this was a private outpouring of grief and anger and was never intended to be shared with the person who was the object of these forceful statements. Regarding the difference of opinion over spiritual paths as characterized in the letter, there is little to be added to what has already been said in previous chapters of the present book (in particular those on Lewis and Steiner)—except to emphasize that this gulf between husband and wife persisted throughout their married lives. But the sword through the marriage knot also extended to other aspects of the relationship. Was the Barfields' lack of progeny related to the difficulties expressed in the letter? What was the motive behind their (or was it mainly Maud's?) adoption of Alexander in 1929, then of Lucy in 1935 and the fostering of Jeffrey in 1945? These are not questions that either can or need have answers. But a whole aspect of Barfield's life-relationships would be lacking in this picture of his soul-journey if one were to omit briefly characterizing the other female friendships which sustained and fulfilled this supremely romantic of natures.

By the early 1950s, the tensions in Barfield's personal life (no less than the professional dichotomy between Burgeon and Burden as depicted in *This Ever Diverse Pair*) had developed to breaking point; and it was in 1951 that he met a young woman, Josephine Grant-Watson, at a lecture on Egyptology in Bedford Square, London. The year before, this young woman's father, E.L. (Peter) Grant Watson, had given her a copy of *Romanticism Comes of Age*, a book which he greatly admired, although he had never met its author. This encounter led to a correspondence and then a trip to Spain, unbeknown to Maud, in 1952–3. In 1953 Owen sent Josephine a desperate, pleading letter, in response to which she broke off the relationship, being unable to cope with the stress of the situation, and herself married John Spence on the last day of 1954. (Owen had seriously contemplated splitting up with Maud, a step which he discussed with Alexander.) Shortly after the reluctant break in his relationship with Josephine, Barfield became intimately involved with Marguerite Lundgren, who then (in 1953) married his dear friend Cecil Harwood in Barfield's presence as a witness (Harwood's first wife, Daphne, had died in 1950).

The culmination of this turbulent period in his personal life was a lecture that he gave at Steiner House in 1953 called 'The Light of the World', a theme suggested by Cecil Harwood as a contribution to a series on 'Rudolf Steiner and Christianity'. Running through this lecture, which is a meditation on the mystery of life and death, is the contrast between rejoicing in one's personal light or glory (succumbing to Lucifer's kingdom) and the aspiration towards the light of the Father, which always involves a personal death; and one of the instances from the Gospels upon which Barfield dwells is the story of the woman who has committed adultery. Barfield's analysis of this story is that of a man who has tasted the 'Eros-content of the joy-bringing light', the 'false light of the world', but has quite clearly chosen to remain true to the marriage sacrament as a lifelong commitment of loving sacrifice. The intensity of the relevant passage of this lecture[286] is noticeable enough even without knowing the background to the personal struggle which underlay it.

Barfield maintained close friendships with both Josephine Spence and Marguerite Lundgren (as she was generally known even after her marriage); and after the death of first Harwood in 1975 and then Maud in 1980, these friendships began to coalesce into a more translucent pattern, finally resolving themselves outwardly when Marguerite died in 1983 (1 August).[287] In a letter to Josephine dated 5 February 1981, Barfield opened up his heart as fully and intimately as perhaps he did in any written context:

> So darling—I think I should come straight to the thing that's uppermost in your mind. I didn't mention that I should be spending the week-end at South Harbour [the Harwoods' residence] because at a very early stage you said you didn't want to hear anything about my foregathering with M. I think that's probably a mistake and I am going to say some more about her and myself—not entirely for your 'benefit'. I shall be glad to open up a little and there is no-one else I could open up to on that subject.
>
> You ask why we don't marry. If I find myself asking the same question—as I very occasionally do—or just vaguely contemplating the idea of marriage, I find myself answering that I just can't imagine myself taking on the vast upheaval it would involve, house removal and all that, let alone the responsibility. Not to keep well in mind the possibility, to say the least of it, that I have only a year or two more to live, would at my age be simply ostrichism. Of course there is a possibility of quite a few more years and I dare say that is what, in the secret recesses, I assume. I doubt if anyone, while feeling well and not in obvious imminent danger, really believes he is going to die at all, let alone soon! But it doesn't alter the facts. There would of course be upheavals for her too. I am not all that sure that, apart altogether from the age

business, it would work out absolutely well. Besides loving each other we irritate each other sometimes—quite strikingly.

So there it is, and all I can see ahead is things going on much as they are now. Zwei *Damen* wohnen ach! in meiner Brust—and they are so unlike each other in nearly all respects that they don't seem to interfere with each other's accommodation, or to have anything to do with one another, in that desirable freehold residence, though, as you know, I sometimes have an uneasy feeling that they ought to and that the fact that they don't means I am a bit of a blighter. I sometimes wonder if, and when, you will come to feel the same.

I should perhaps have added that I suspect M. has a certain need of me. Zwei Seelen again—she is strenuous and energetic and determined, but there are times when all that fails her and they are all the more dismaying because there is so much of it, and then she needs to be able to switch from 'coper' to 'leaser' for a bit . . .

No. I was not thinking of myself in the 'end of their tether' bit of the *Light of the World* lecture . . . As to whether I have ever been in that state myself, well yes, I suppose so. Probably the worst time was shortly after marriage—Maud's repugnance to anthroposophy and my dawning conviction to the contrary—a desperate feeling that my ego was being assaulted from right inside itself. As far as I recollect, the nearest I came to 'coping' was by trying to hold on to the 'No longer I live, but Christ liveth in me'. I was helped in this—helped to move a *little* way in the direction of making it an experience and not just an idea—by the fact that soon after coming across anthroposophy, I had for a time meditated rather frequently on the first 14 verses of John 1 and I was helped in *that* by the sort of thing I had tried to express in *Poetic Diction*. I also think it may have been that that enabled me later to arrive at that formulation: Original Participation—Final Participation which seems to have caught on quite surprisingly both inside and outside the A[nthroposophical] S[ociety]. Have you ever tried it? The Greek does help a little. For instance, 'all things were made by Him' should really have been translated 'all things came into being through Him'.

Later, during that experience of bereavement tinged with envy and jealousy,[288] I seem to have fallen back on St Paul again—specially Philippians 1:21.[289] By the way, a curious thing happened at that time. I sat down (or rather started out—I don't start a poem by sitting down in front of a piece of paper) to write a poem giving expression to my woe, and it turned of its own accord into one called 'Prayer for a New

> House', i.e. South Harbour, which Cecil Harwood had just built for the two of them to live in. I engrove it in posh script and sent it to them, and Cecil liked it so much that he framed it and hung it up in his study (now the spare room or lodger's sitting-room according to circumstances), where it hangs to this day![290] It is all very queer. Also it is a long time ago. I believe I have deteriorated since *The Light of the World*, perhaps because during the last 2 decades I have not been continuously unhappy enough to keep me steady. On the contrary, I have had a great deal of happiness, especially in America. Lucy's disaster has been the one big sobering cloud.
>
> I am afraid setting it all down in black and white may have made it sound a good deal grander and more austere than it was . . .

The letter concludes with some responses to Josephine Spence's remarks in her own letter, which contain some points of wider interest:

> By the way, part of the impulse behind *The Light of the World* was a slightly uneasy feeling about [George Adams's] concentration on experiencing the etheric—rather giving the impression that it is a final goal. Not a whisper about the astral. All life, life, life and life as if there were no such thing as death.
>
> I feel just as you do about the applicability of the parable of the talents, suspecting that pretty well everything I have 'achieved' comes from what I brought with me—just resting on my oars instead of *rowing* with them.

In the 14 years following Marguerite Lundgren's death in 1983, Josephine Spence continued to care for Owen, especially after the move from Orchard View in 1986 to Forest Row, where she herself was then living in a little cottage on the fringes of Ashdown Forest, some three-quarters of a mile from the Walhatch. These visits from a beloved friend were what principally sustained Barfield inwardly and emotionally during his final years, and inspired his last piece of sustained creative writing, the novella 'Eager Spring'. Now that Josephine herself has died (on 17 November 2001), she may be recognized as possibly the love of his life. Undoubtedly, she was the subject of some of the sonnets included in the *Barfield Sampler*[291]. This is not to imply that there was any love lacking in his relationships with Maud and also Marguerite. But I would hazard the suggestion—and it can be no more than that—that the bond with Josephine engendered the greatest personal intimacy and warmth.

* * *

In the earlier part of his life no less than after his retirement, Barfield was a man who also cherished and nurtured his friendships with other men. One of these friendships—that with C.S. Lewis—has already been chronicled as an introduction to this part of the book. But there were two other particular friendships with men born in the same year as Barfield which deserve to figure at its conclusion. Before considering these, however, a brief mention should be made of his extensive correspondence with the poet and novelist Walter de la Mare (1873–1956).

To my knowledge, Barfield's letters to de la Mare have not been preserved. At any rate, Barfield did not retain copies of any of them, as tended to be his habit only when he wanted to keep a record of significant thoughts or propositions. What he did retain was a collection of 70 letters from the poet and story-teller, the originals of which he lodged with the Bodleian Library, Oxford, on 16 June 1986. Apart from a brief letter dated 14 January 1926, gratefully acknowledging receipt of a copy of *History in English Words*, the correspondence runs from January 1939 to July 1953. De la Mare opened the correspondence with a request that Barfield allow him to quote two passages from *History in English Words* in a book comprising a collection of poems and passages in prose on dreams, sleep and similar themes, a realm over which he had already cast his distinctive linguistic magic. Barfield's willing agreement led to their first meeting on 2 February 1939, followed on 5 March by an initial meeting also with Maud. For the most part, the letters record the ripening of a literary friendship and reflect the exchange of poems and other writings that took place between the correspondents. The content and quality of de la Mare's letters may be exemplified by the following excerpt from a letter dated 22 March 1948: '"The Unicorn" has trotted in fresh as paint. I have given him a bottle of hay and a bucket of Bucks's best and he seems perfectly contented. I gather that he mustn't stay too long; so if I am too slow in returning him, let me have a p.c. ...' Throughout the correspondence there is not a sour or unappreciative word, all being borne along by the sheer grace of the older man's whimsical love of words and the mysteries they unlock. Without Barfield's contribution, however, there is little that can meaningfully be added in the present psychographical context. Only rarely does the theme of the letters venture into deeper, more intimate waters. Evidently, Barfield himself opened up such avenues, as the following passage from another 1948 letter (19 January) attests:

> There is so much in [your letter], of course, that my tired old brains would find difficult to put into words, though not *so* difficult perhaps as

> to realize precisely what is implied in 'what we experience here as the "subjective" world will be objective and ... vice versa'. It's not too easy, by the way, to distinguish between the subjective and the objective in presence of any earthly scenery; and one feels it is one's own fault to a certain extent that one cannot thus deal with people. Did you yourself originate: 'A "seeing" of the whole of your past life at once—which won't last very long—then, a living-back of your life in about a third of the time it actually took—a sort of repetition awake of the time you passed in sleep'? It is the word 'time' here that rather baffles me. In a sense I can understand the seeing of the whole of one's past life with extreme rapidity, since it would not be slowed up by the sluggish objective. Still, that would involve a good deal of 'time'. On the other hand, I can vaguely see, as it were, the possibility of being conscious of one's whole life in no time at all. It's your phrase, 'about a third of the time', that rather baffles me. It interests me that you should have mentioned *Peacock Pie* in your letter, in this connection, because a large part of the contents of that—the rhymes—were written after midnight, possibly as late as 1 a.m., chiefly as a relief from grinding away reading MSS for Heinemann, as I was at that time ...[292]

In no sense can it be said that Barfield and Walter de la Mare shared a common way of looking at this theme of sleep and night-consciousness which lies at the heart of the latter's work. Very different were Barfield's friendships with Leo Baker (1898–1986) and Cecil Harwood (1898–1975), both of whom were anthroposophists. Leo Baker, who was a fellow student at Wadham College,[293] has the distinction of having introduced Lewis and Barfield to one another and, hence, to have laid the foundations for the Inklings circle. Baker had returned to Wadham in 1919 after military service to read History, and the friendship between the three men was initiated and sustained, at least initially, by a common interest in poetry. Barfield's letters to him, which have been preserved by Baker's daughter (and Barfield's goddaughter) Susan Bealby-Wright, reflect these shared literary interests and altogether shed considerable light on their writer's inner preoccupations. They are therefore worth examining in somewhat greater detail than what we have of the de la Mare correspondence.

The series of 26 letters begins with one addressed from Barfield's family home, Bicknell, Atheneum Road, Whetstone and dated 10 August 1920. Barfield writes of his manifold literary activities undertaken alongside his undergraduate studies (he had reached the end of his first academic year), including a fairly substantial on-going poem in blank verse, a prose article ('of moneymaking interest') and his most recent publications in the *New Statesman* and the *Cornhill* magazine (see Chapter 5). He is nevertheless, he writes, extremely desirous of company and requests that Baker visit him:

> I do hope you will come, as if you don't, I am like to burst. I have been seeing practically no-one, with whom I can talk naturally of the things I want to talk about, and the result is that I am being forced in on myself like an ingrowing toe-nail. It has come to such a pass that I seem to be living in a land of dream. My self is the only thing that exists, and I wear the external world about me like a suit of clothes—my own body included. It—the world—seems to have about as much objective importance as a suit of clothes, and quite often I have a suspicion that I am really naked after all. When I am alone at night, I sometimes feel frightened of the silence ringing in my ears. Something inside me seems to be so intensely and burningly alive, and everything round me so starkly dead, that I am awed by the contrast; though God knows why it should seem awful that there should be a heart beating in me and not in a table or a chest of drawers. I do not think I am going mad!
>
> You see that by coming to see me you will be doing an act of Christian charity.

After some news about Cecil Harwood's and Lewis's current literary endeavours, Barfield concludes with a humorous aside:

> The following is what you must not do (though you may do the first 2, if they do not produce the remainder):
>
> (i) Get your job
> (ii) Get married
> (iii) Settle down to: I Getting up at 7 a.m.
> II Shaving close to 7.30
> III Hiding behind 'The Times' with coffee and bacon
> IV Going to 'the Office'
> .
> .
> .
> V The grand chain (see *Our Mutual Friend*. Podsnappery).

Appended to the letter is a poem, as if to say that there was some part at least of its author which was not to become submerged in 'the grand chain':

Aphrodite
Laughing, like a child at play,
Aphrodite passed this way—
Mapped in yonder dreaming boy
Unknown continents of joy.
Then, when his soul set trembling sail
Drowned it quick with panting gales
In the Ocean whence she came.
And she played another game:
Into London she put hosts
Of chattering, tittering, high-heeled ghosts
With cavernous, sad eyes that say:
'Aphrodite passed this way'.

In the next letter in the series, dated 23 August 1920, Barfield indicates that, while not considering 'Aphrodite' a masterpiece, he agrees with Baker's stated opinion that 'I like it a good deal'. This letter is mainly devoted to comments on a poem that Baker had sent him (called 'Gurydion'), while indicating his progress with his own current magnum opus, 'The Tower'.

The following letter, dated 24 September, opens with a salvo of impatience about Baker's 'protracted silence' and testifies to Barfield's continued flurry of literary activity. In addition, he reports on his first visit to the Cornish folk song and dance scene: 'I have also met in Cornwall some of the most delightful people I ever met in my life—cultured without dilettantism and enthusiastic with[out] gush. I am also feeling very flat, having just come home thence. I have also learned to dance the Pavane, the Galliard, the Canaries, the Giguye, the Minuet and a new (to me) country-dance called Althea which is a thing of pure joy. I am also not engaged. I have also not done any schools work for about a month and am at present too restless to attempt any.'

The sequence continues in the same vigorous, light-hearted but intimate way—mainly sharing literary initiatives or productions, including (25 March 1921) the 'Nine Sonnets'—through the next five letters, the last of which was written in September 1921 from St Anthony in Roseland, Portscatho, Cornwall. There is then a gap of nearly a year (during which he was working on his B.Litt. thesis on 'Poetic Diction'), when he appends to his letter of 1 August 1922 a corrigendum to its first line: 'For "Baker" read "Leo".' Then on 11 September 1922 he reports that he is leaving the following day with Harwood for Devonshire with the Roseland Concert Party. In addition to contemplating publishing a book of poems, he is enjoying himself writing a fairy story. There is also a first mention of the League of National Awakening: 'I am getting very worried by the precarious condition of civilization. All my instincts are at me to leave it alone and get on with the business, but it gets worse and worse—and everything seems to point to Finance as the root of the immediate trouble. Have not joined the League of National Awakening but I confess I am rather hovering.'

The next letter, dated 4 October, is interesting both for Barfield's view about the League and for its reference to Douglas's Social Credit Scheme: '... I am sorry you never heard from the League of National Awakening. I am still interested in it. Your idea of Douglas [Eric Beckett also "identifies himself very completely with Social Credit"[294]] is much more positive than mine, which corresponds more with that of the man who is starting the said League. His platform has the merit of simplicity: (a) War must be averted, otherwise civilization goes phut. (b) the only way of averting war is a reorganization of the Credit System. (c) Douglas's Scheme is the one which seems nearest the right lines. I have thought more of our Spring Offensive at Oxford, but confess that at present it seems to me like a new scheme of diet (a very wise scheme) when what is immediately necessary is an operation for appendicitis. And I feel as though, if the patient isn't operated on quickly, that patient will pass away.' This letter concludes with an announcement that he and Maud are to marry, adding that 'I do not know yet what I am going to do, but in the meantime we are engaged in being happy and practising dances.'

By the time Barfield next wrote on 12 December 1922, he was able to say that there was a promise of a literary career opening up for him in a big way, encouraged especially by the warm reception accorded to his *London Mercury* article on 'Ruin'. He continues to write affectionately of the League of National Awakening, but he was clearly warming to Douglas's ideas: 'I don't mind telling you that Douglas's proposal seems to me now less like a "scheme" than a "discovery" comparable to Newton's discovery of gravitation'. After references to Walter Field and Eric Beckett (who figures briefly on several occasions in these letters), there follows a passage reflecting Barfield's more intimate thoughts at this time: '... I have been thinking a good deal about the hopes & impulses that brought us together at Oxford, and indeed about most things. Looking back, I seem to have been pondering the problem of existence at most hours of the day & some hours of the night for years. I suppose every speculative mind does. It has caused me much acute depression & seems to depend very much on mood, which is itself a depressing thought. I set out to read the Four Gospels through, a chapter or two at a time in bed at night, but found that I dared not be alone with them at that hour. I sent you a piece of blank-verse I wrote. It does not represent my final convictions—I doubt if I shall ever have any. I am amazed at the profundity of Christ's insight into human nature & its needs—& I wish I had been born in Isaac Newton's day. I hate to be divided up into a Chinese puzzle of selves, each one explaining away and mocking, willy nilly, the one it encloses.—Anyway it is one of the very innermost ones that hopes to see you soon, & is glad you are going on at the Old Vic.[295] Maud & I speak of trying to get seats for "The Merry Wives" on Boxing Day. I wonder if it is still possible . . .'

The sequence continues with a letter dated 19 December 1922, which emphasizes the prime importance attached by Barfield already in these early years to economics and practical human concerns: 'Personally I cannot put much heart into any spiritual movement or any modern restatement of the ancient and general truths, till I see some attempt being made to put right this tragic and absurd indigestion in the world's stomach. And to me, the attitude that a change of heart must come first, that we must educate, and that we must talk immaculately to the world now seems perilously akin to the attitude which, not very long ago, was affirming in all sincerity that typhoid and tuberculosis were punishments from God and that it was irreverent to think we could check them with providing the slums with decent W.C.S. . . .'

The intimate friendship pervading these early letters is never regained after Barfield's marriage, nor do the remaining letters give comparable insight into their writer's inner being. Baker's own marriage is noted with jollity in the next letter in the sequence (dated 25 June 1924), and the mood of much of the remaining extant correspondence in the 1920s (a further ten letters) is exemplified by the following announcement in a letter of March 1926 from Air Hill, Long Crendon: 'OYEZ. Whereas it hath been mooted propounded and adumbrated by those twain well-beloved servants of His nobilissimus coney-catching Majesty, King George V—Alfred Cecil Harwood and Arthur Owen B.—that for a number of days to be hereafter determined, about round about and including the Week-end after Easter, there should be a perambulation, or Walk, through the Champain of this our beloved country, to be undertaken and executed by those four ditto-ditto-dittos (or as many of them as shall declare themselves willing, able-bodied, desirous and well-disposed) hereinafter called The Mutts, *videlicet* Alfred Cecil Harwood,

Arthur Owen Barfield, Leo Kingsley Baker, and C . . . S . . . Lewis (née Hamilton). To be situate and encompassed by *either* (i) all that arable and pasturage lying between (approximately) Newbury & Westbury, *or* (ii) His most excellent Majesty's Cotswold Hills. The long and the short of it is, will you come? . . .'

Two further letters, from 9 July 1945 and 21 May 1950, complete the sequence. In the first of these Barfield reports that he has renewed his 'slight acquaintance' with Walter de la Mare and that he has had 'four or five delightful evenings alone with him—just talking'. The second letter acknowledges Baker's warm appreciation of *This Ever Diverse Pair*, while noting his friend's struggle—on his sick bed—with 'The Mother of Pegasus', while repudiating the charge of obscurity:

> Pegasus hi, Pegasus hic,
> 'Twill make you well if you are sick,
> If you are well, 'twill make you sick.
> Pegasus hi, Pegasus hic.

Mention should also be made of a—for the most part—delightfully humorous series of twelve letters to his goddaughter Susan Baker (written between 1942 and 1980), letters which bear out his very evident affection for her. These are in almost every case annual birthday epistles, although one is no mere brief greeting but an entire Masque, in which Susan is portrayed as a kind of divine patroness in a farcical celebration which includes Queen Elizabeth I, William Shakespeare, Samuel Johnson (appearing fleetingly via a trap-door) and assorted Sailors, Clowns, Godfather Neptune, Naiads and Vikings. Entitled 'The Masque of Susan', it was designated for performance by 'the ladies of Dursley on the 22nd day of July in the year One thousand nine hundred and thingummy' (actually 1945), and included songs, dances and a Historical Pageant. Finally, there is a letter dated 21 February 1980 which, for the human touches it contains, may be quoted here in full:

> My dear Susan,
>
> I was so glad to get your letter—and so differently worded from the sympathizers, poor dears, who write 'There is nothing one can say', or words to that effect.
>
> Maud was only in hospital for 4 days and had been hardly conscious for the last 24 hours or so. I do not think she suffered much pain before she died.
>
> Yes. I am tired of course, but have been marvellously supported in all

practical problems both by Jeffrey and by Mrs. Reddick, the woman who has been coming in 2 or 3 times a week. It was not just all the hard work she put in—she thought up sweet little touches, as it had been her own mother.

I am off on a 10 day visit to America on Monday.

A very nice letter from Leo. And we have decided we really are going to meet after I get back. I keep thinking of him and Eileen.

I am sorry William [Susan's husband] has had his bereavement to cope with as well. Please give him my love—after extracting a large share for yourself.

As Ever, Owen

Barfield's friendship with Cecil Harwood, the last to be considered in this concluding chapter on the human bonds that underlay the intellectual and spiritual ferment that was his life's work, was of all his relationships the most long-lasting, constant and—in its own way—unspokenly profound. The essential elements of Harwood's life have already been outlined in the corresponding chapter in the previous part of this book. What remains to be reflected in the present context is something of that intimacy which lives in Barfield's letters to Harwood. So far as I know, all that has been preserved from what must have been a far more extensive, lifelong correspondence is a series of 37 letters from the latter part of Harwood's life (1942–74), in the possession of Harwood's son (and C.S. Lewis's godson) Laurence. There is no evidence that Harwood's letters have been preserved, with the result that Barfield's own letters—such as they are—stand there as markers, charting the depths that lie beneath.

The extent and realm of Barfield's friendship with Harwood are made explicit in a letter dated 20 February 1965 written from Drew University, New Jersey during the first of his many visits to America as a lecturer or Visiting Professor. He was in something of a dilemma, in that he had just received over the telephone an invitation from Brandeis University (near Boston) to spend the following academic year with them as a Visiting Professor. He therefore turned directly to Harwood for advice:

> Of course I have got to make up my own mind, but I would be very glad of your candid opinion, if you feel you can have one, (a) as oldest friend (b) as anthroposophist & (c) as Chairman of the A.S. in G.B. [Anthroposophical Society in Great Britain].

He then goes on to express his own feelings on the matter and weigh up the decision as he writes:

My own feelings are these: My ties to England are so numerous (you & Marguerite, the Society, your present predicament in the Society, Office, Brother and so forth—and even my unsatisfactory children count for something) that I contemplate with something approaching dismay the prospect of another 8 months' absence from England, especially coming so soon after the present one. I was also looking forward to a rest from lectures, or at least from preparing them. (On and off the Campus, I must have given nearly 40 here already.) And it postpones the business of making a book out of them.

For all these reasons, if the offer were withdrawn or a stroke of destiny prevented me from accepting it, the tear of disappointment would be dried by the sigh of relief—and pretty near the source. I don't know that I should even get my nose wet.

On the other hand—actively to *reject it*! I like the work and the *milieu* it invokes and have a sort of blossoming feeling, which is rather curious. The prospect is, I suppose, more exciting and pleasing than it is dismaying. More objectively, why do they *want* me so ruddy badly over here? It looks as if the reputation of my books is not limited to Drew circles, or to theological ones, since Brandeis is not theologically oriented . . .

What seeds may there be in it?—not only for myself, and there won't be much time for *that* lot to germinate anyway. It seems to be simply the case, that I *don't* occupy a key-position in the A.S. in G.B. or in the work of anthroposophy in England, such as would render my renewed absence a real disaster . . .

It seems to me that, unless (& this is where you come in) there is some consideration I have overlooked or underweighted, then, if I do reject it, I may never cease kicking myself spiritually, psychically and financially, for having done so, and the conclusion I have come to, after sleeping on it, is that I should accept. But I will be very glad of a brief line from you, if you can spare the time . . .

There was probably no other person in the world with whom Barfield could have weighed up the pros and cons of this dilemma, no one else who both knew him intimately and who could—by virtue of his position—wholly understand his sense of obligation to the most significant of his concerns, the Anthroposophical Society.[296] Indeed, the whole sequence of letters conveys the spirit of the greeting of the first letter written to Harwood himself (the first is to his wife Daphne), 'My very dear and oldest friend.' In a letter probably from this same year (1950), he writes as follows: 'And then, although we have known each other so long and so well, we are widely different both in temperament and in destiny. By the way, I have more than once felt the wish that we had not *both* become committed anthroposophists. We should in that case have talked much more about serious matters, since reaching maturity.'

The extant correspondence begins with some tender letters written shortly before Daphne Harwood's death from cancer in 1950. By 1954 Barfield is expressing his great admiration for Marguerite, Harwood's second wife, whose stature as an artist was a boundless source of admiration on his part. In 1957, moreover, he was offering some marriage witness's advice about the kind of husbandly treatment he thought she needed, especially in terms of greater peace and quiet and, in particular, protection from certain younger members of the family. After a letter dated 2 May 1959 briefly referring to some esoteric aspects of the Anthroposophical Society, Barfield opens up a theme that is to crop up several times in the course of the correspondence, namely, the 'Museum Street project' and the struggle to cooperate with 'the English Section' of the Anthroposophical Society (a group which did not see eye-to-eye with the predominant group favoured by Barfield and Harwood, the Anthroposophical Society in Great Britain).[297] What is so striking is the way that Barfield's observations never descend into personal animosity of any kind. This is mainly because he consistently saw how essentially trivial all these issues were, a view which he forcefully expressed in a letter dated 21 December 1965:

> . . . It all seems so, *mutatis mutandis*, on the parish magazine level—hopelessly remote from what is actually going on even in the intellectual and cultural sphere, let alone the social and political. And even more remote, I suspect, from anything of significance for the foreseeable future that is going on in the spiritual world. I don't rule out its possible importance for the slowly maturing destinies of the personalities involved, which (with omission of the time, or urgency, factor) may presumably be as significant there as everything else is. But that goes for the parish magazine and its readers, too.

He came closest to expressing his own view of what ought to happen in the Anthroposophical Society in a letter from Clinton, New York, dated 21 January 1968:

> I can't get a mental 'line' on the right way to try and steer the A.S. in G.B. It does seem terribly remote from the rest of the world. One

possibility might be, apart from the Bookshop, to go into Purdah and concentrate on internal group study and group life and the making of a real community, however small, leaving propaganda and dissemination to the members in their own circles and private capacities. The group life would of course include eurythmy, especially perhaps in relation to the festivals—and the more eurythmy the London School of Eurythmy could take out to the public the better. But all this is not a considered suggestion, it is just running off my pen . . .

As with the Leo Baker correspondence, mention is always made of significant publications, albeit in a somewhat dry and disbelieving manner. For example, Barfield writes as follows about what must be a publishing decision regarding *Worlds Apart* (31 July 1962): 'After sitting on my book for three and a half months Fabers have at last made up their minds that they want to publish it.' And after reporting in a letter dated 12 December 1964 that an American reviewer of this same book has referred to him as 'recently deceased', Barfield registers his amazement that his next book has also been accepted by Eliot's old firm[298]: 'I don't know what has happened to Faber & Faber. Some guy has sure taken the lead out of their pants, for they now say that *Unancestral Voice* is to be published late March or early April' (31 January 1965).

A further frequent theme of the letters was initiated by the death on 22 November 1963 of Barfield's friend and erstwhile intellectual sparring partner C.S. Lewis. At the time of Lewis's death, Barfield had full legal responsibility for his affairs; and he would at times share with Harwood his problems and concerns about the administration of Lewis's extremely lucrative Literary Estate, the health and mental well-being of Warnie, Lewis's older brother, and the appointment of additional Trustees. However, these concerns are outweighed in the correspondence by the reports given by Barfield from America of the many lectures that he was asked to give about Lewis in the wake of the latter's death. The main source in this respect is a letter written from Drew University on 27 October 1964. The theme of this, unfortunately incomplete, letter is his long weekend at Wheaton College (near Chicago) and—in American terms—nearby Beloit College, where after referring to his flight over the Great Lakes and 'the reflections, philosophic and moral, which amazed my mind in transition', he reports of 'how I spoke of Jack for an hour to an audience variously estimated at 800 and 1000 and of their really wonderful attentiveness, warmth and response' and 'how one man flew from Los Angeles to hear the lecture, returning the following day'.[299] He goes on to relate that he was 'put in charge of a smashing blonde (student) with instructions to escort me to Chicago and show me round' and treated to a visit to the Art Institute and an orchestral concert at the College by the Warsaw Philharmonic Orchestra. Then came the impromptu 'whistle-stop' visit to Beloit College. Despite being assured that he would only be repeating the lecture given at Wheaton, he jocularly describes

> . . . How 20 minutes after arriving at Beloit, I was marched round to the College Chapel, & on the way, was handed a copy of the printed Order of Worship, on which I observed, about half the way down, the item: 'Sermon. C.S. Lewis and the New Eden. Dr. Arthur Owen Barfield'.
>
> How, after 20 minutes in the vestry to cut my lecture from 1 to $\frac{1}{2}$ an hour, a gown was hung on me, & I was shoved in position behind the entering choir.
>
> How I got through it somehow (congregation about 700) and even remembered on one occasion to turn right round in the pulpit and scowl amiably at the choir behind me.
>
> How I gave 5 lectures in 3 days (or if it impresses you more) 9 lectures and 2 sermons in 11 days.
>
> How I sat up into the small hours on both the Saturday and the Sunday night discoursing with members of the respective faculties on Jack, on his books, on primitive languages encountered by missionaries, which appear to have no 'inner' meanings of any sort, on Homer's similes and the light thrown thereon by Bruno Snell's *Discovery of the Mind*, on the relative merits of Homer and Virgil etc. etc. and how at Beloit, about half way through we were joined, I don't quite know how or why, by a roly poly Roman Catholic Priest who had small Latin and less Greek . . .

In contrast to the mass interest in his offerings on Lewis in America, Barfield's seminars on his own work attracted a mere handful of students. However, he gave Harwood full and regular reports on his American journeys, which clearly meant a great deal to him.[300] He was especially grateful for the capacity of particularly Californians at Santa Cruz and Berkeley (1969) to embrace the relationship of his work with that of Rudolf Steiner, commenting (2 March 1969) that 'Berkeley, in particular, is ripe for a visit from Edmunds[301] or some other energetic youngster able to speak a bit of their language as well as his own.' He also appreciated the academic honours conferred on him, as for example by Hamilton College (New York): 'On June 2nd this place is going to confer on me the honorary degree of "Doctor of Humane Letters"! The fact that Hamilton

College was originally founded with the object of converting Red Indians into Christian gentlemen and has a student body of 800 undergraduates (no graduates) seems to impart a certain not unpleasingly Gilbert & Sullivan touch to the whole proceeding, but that doesn't prevent it from tickling my vanity' (31 March 1968).

Every now and then a dialectical element ventures into the correspondence, as when the question arises as to the 'content' of evangelical movements: 'Apart from good works, what does the perfectly christened Christian *do* except preaching and psalm-singing? What does he spend his time thinking about? But it seems premature to raise it in this "Teenage Challenge" venture. You have got an apparently impenetrable dehumanized crust which cuts the human spirit off from all communication with men or nature or books and, until that is broken through, the question of content cannot even arise, much less be solved. The cry is "Man overboard" and he has got to be hauled back on board somehow before you start worrying how he is to make the most of his time on the voyage.' These lucubrations are prompted by a portion in Harwood's previous letter about the evangelical-Christian analysis of New Testament historicism, *The Cross and the Switchblade*. Characteristically, however, Barfield ends his letter by postulating that the expected coming of the Etheric Christ[302] might take place where it might from a certain point of view least be anticipated: 'Has He found that, in the middle of the 20th century, the best way of "coming" like a Thief in the Night is to appear (of all places!) in the Church?'

There are frequent brief references in the letters to Maud Barfield, who sometimes accompanied Barfield on his American journeys and became involved in local women's groups and other activities. Barfield also reports that Lucy accompanied him to Brandeis University (1965–6), building up as many as twelve piano pupils at the local music school in Cambridge, Massachusetts. Her debilitating illness of multiple sclerosis (she was hospitalized in 1968) was clearly a source of much sorrow to Barfield. In his letter from Orchard View dated 19 April 1974, Barfield presents to Harwood a vignette of these two members of his family: 'There is not a great deal of news. Lucy much the same, mentally as conscious as ever, or more so, but it is terrible to see her unable, even with a stick, to walk more than a step or two without someone to support her. We are exploring the possibility of a small car or powered vehicle of some sort to enable her to get about a bit. Maud is pretty well, the operated eye gradually overtaking the other and expected soon to surpass it substantially in visual efficiency. She is doing quite a bit of gardening, kneels on the ground for it and helps herself up again with a walking frame. I have also been doing quite a bit myself, chiefly weeding, which is not beyond my skill.'

This same long letter, the last but one in the sequence (and the letter of 8 August is a very brief note adding nothing of any substance) gathers up many threads in this friendship of some 65 years. There is much, naturally enough, on the theme of 'brother ass's prognosis' (Harwood was in the Klinik at Arlesheim, Switzerland) and condolences about his missed holiday in Turkey. He then reports on his interviews in April with Shirley Sugerman (for the introductory chapter to the Festschrift *Evolution of Consciousness*), observing laconically that 'the occasional playbacks we had for checking seemed to consist to a large extent of *her* talking and my saying "yes ... yes ... yes" in sepulchral and inaudible tones...' After referring briefly to an article that he had written for a '3fold book' and dispatched to Charles Davy, Barfield goes on to write about his struggles with his Memorandum for the Executive Committee of the Society for the Protection of Unborn Children, on the grounds that a Royal Commission had 'raised in all seriousness, under the heading of "Ante-natal Injuries", the question whether a child born seriously defective should have a right of action against its parents and/or any doctors involved for damages for not having been aborted, that is, for having been born at all! What a good thing W.S. Gilbert was not born in this age, when there is rapidly ceasing to be any such thing as absurdity!'

The letter ends with a reminiscence which at once takes us back to the scene of Barfield's last marital home as depicted at the beginning of this chapter and prepares us for his own psychographical reflections on his childhood and adolescence:

> Our railway station has a very long platform. Waiting for a train yesterday I decided I had just time to get some excercise walking the whole length and back, and while doing it I suddenly remembered a period at school, during which your brother Eric and Bush used to stride to and fro across the playground arm in arm at about 6 miles per hour throughout the whole of the 5 minute morning break. I wonder if you remember.
>
> But enough—and more than enough. I am wondering how long you will be in Arlesheim and whether you will come straight home or get a change somewhere for a bit in Iran or Turkey.
>
> With love from Maud and myself,
>
> as ever,
>
> Owen.

CONCLUSION

In his Afterword to Astrid Diener's monograph, *The Role of Imagination in Culture and Society: Owen Barfield's Early Work*, Elmar Schenkel offers a penetrating analysis of the staggering apathy with which Owen Barfield's death in 1997 was marked by the intellectual community as a whole. Of those few scholars who remembered his early writings on the history of language, the majority presumed that he had died long before. Professor Schenkel then goes on to present his own view of the relevance of Barfield's thought in an age now seemingly dominated by the Internet and by the Human Genome Project (and—one might add—market-driven globalization), and concludes that the distinction made by the author of 'The Harp and the Camera'[303] between inner (spiritual) inspiration and outward (scientific) exploration is not merely as valid as it was during Barfield's lifetime but considerably more so. At the end of a passage where he examines the claims of software, networks of one kind or another and cyberspace to be regarded as representing a new ascendency of the immaterial over the material, Schenkel concludes that, on the contrary, 'Barfield . . . is a gateway to new syntheses of which we are in dire need.'

The purpose of these concluding remarks is, however, not so much to restate what should already be apparent from the rest of this book but to remind the reader that, whatever may have happened on 14 December 1997 and thereafter to the physical body of Arthur Owen Barfield, the subject of this psychography, namely, the soul-spiritual being who bore that name in the earthly life which ended on that day, is still very much (in the wider sense) alive. If the present exercise has had any meaning, it is to have accompanied this soul on its backward journey—as yet still in its comparatively early stages—through the tableau of earthly recollections. As it is in the form of a book intended for other living human beings to read, it has inevitably focused on seeking guidance from this now super-earthly being for what we may now ourselves accomplish; and both the form and content of this study have sought to focus attention on what is of continuing relevance out of that which Owen Barfield has bequeathed to us. But the dialogue has, I hope, not been entirely one-sided, in that every now and then Barfield's thoughts have elicited a response in the form of an indication—at times, frank and inevitably personal—of the circumstances prevailing at the beginning of the twenty-first century.

Finally, there is a sense in which what is here offered is but part of an unfinished project. What is the source towards which this supersensible journey of recollection of some 33 years or so is tending (a journey which, as will have been seen from the last chapter of Part Three, Barfield himself tried so hard—but vainly—to interpret to both Maud and Walter de la Mare)? And who, moreover, shall be its further interpreter? I can claim no immediate answer to either question. One point is, however, transparently clear. I wish to state very firmly that—along with Elmar Schenkel, Stephen Talbott and many other less eloquent admirers—the unfolding journey to which I have referred will remain for me one of abiding interest, not least for the conviction which this indefatigable literary pilgrim has expressed of the non-finality of our present predicament and state of consciousness.

NOTES

1. For a clear exposition of this concept of RUP, see Owen Barfield's 'Conversation with Shirley Sugerman' in the festschrift for his 75th birthday, *The Evolution of Consciousness*, Wesleyan University Press, 1976, pp. 15–17.
2. From C.S. Lewis, *Surprised by Joy*, Geoffrey Bles, 1955, p. 161.
3. This narrative is based on conversations with the author between 1994 and 1997. Unless otherwise indicated, all quotations are taken from the transcripts of the recorded conversations. Inevitably, some of the information supplied by the nonagenarian Barfield does not completely tally factually with other accounts. On the other hand, the paucity of primary documentary evidence pertaining to Barfield's life—at any rate, such has been my experience—is such that it is not always possible to know for certain, for example, when a particular event took place. The tendency here adopted is to err in favour of Barfield's verbally expressed recollections where there are any doubts or discrepancies.
4. Such was the closeness of their friendship that they were sometimes referred to as 'Harfield and Barwood'.
5. An interesting anecdote underlines the consequences flowing from the entirely secular upbringing which Barfield received from his parents. 'When I was much younger we had a new maid, or a temporary one, and she put me to bed and was horrified because I didn't say my prayers. I remember that very well. I was embarrassed by that somehow. Any official religious atmosphere or circle or experience was always embarrassing.'
6. Barfield also mentions Bedford as a place where he stayed during this time, though it is not clear for how long.
7. He had had a poem of his, 'Air-Castles', written while still at school, published in *Punch* (14 February 1917).
8. Both of these articles were published in 1920.
9. They were published under the title *Nine Poems* in March 1922.
10. This beautiful line does not appear in the *Nine Poems* sequence. I am indebted to an anonymous reader in the United States—whose views I have carefully noted but do not by any means always share—for the information that it forms part of a sequence of 20 poems, which, however, I have not been able to trace in published form.
11. Owen and Maud were married on 11 April 1923 at St Cyprian's Church, Clarence Gate, London.
12. Some experiences already described are repeated here in a somewhat different form.

13. The lectures in question were some of those given by Rudolf Steiner during the First World War.
14. In addition to the main lecture-course, *True and False Paths in Spiritual Investigation* (11–22 August) and lectures given to members of the Anthroposophical Society, Rudolf Steiner gave lectures entitled *The Kingdom of Childhood* to teachers who were shortly afterwards to found Michael Hall (or The New School, as it was then called), the first Rudolf Steiner (or Waldorf) School in Britain.
15. *Owen Barfield and the Origin of Language*, printed in *Towards* (June and December 1978) and published as a booklet by St George Publications, Spring Valley, New York.
16. Although the writing of the thesis was completed by 1927, Barfield did not actually take his degree until later (1934).
17. The book must have been completed by the summer of 1931, as it was described in *Das Goetheanum* in an article also published in *Anthroposophical Movement*, Vol. VIII, No. 17, 16 August 1931.
18. It was published in 1950 by Victor Gollancz.
19. Major C.H. Douglas (1879–1952) was an engineer and economist whose 'Social Credit' scheme enjoyed a considerable measure of support in the inter-war years and after, especially in Canada, Australia and New Zealand. Notable supporters in England included R.H. Tawney, William Temple and Bertrand Russell.
20. This remark refers to a pamphlet which Barfield wrote probably in 1937, *Law Association and the Trade Union Movement*, where he pleads for trade unions to foster economic associations rather than focus on political activity.
21. The connection was actually through Barfield's essay 'Poetic Diction and Legal Fiction'.
22. It was published in *Towards* in 1987.
23. The conversation (on 5 February 1996) then turned to the question of founding a Humanities Section of the School of Spiritual Science.
24. This is convenient shorthand for referring to Rudolf Steiner's ideas about the social organism, which incorporate a threefold principle deriving from his conception of man's being.
25. In this connection, Barfield would frequently ask about the health of the Rudolf Steiner schools in this country, for it was his conviction that the education at these schools is based on the nurturing and encouragement of the new, world-transforming forces that children bring with them from the spiritual world and of which society has so great a need (but which tend to be actively discouraged by most so-called education).
26. A crucial aspect of this 'threefoldness' repeatedly referred to by Barfield is a free and autonomous cultural sphere (alongside the sphere of rights and the economic sphere). This needs to be emphasized in view of the fact that most people nowadays think—at best—in terms of a twofoldness consisting

of the latter two spheres, with the cultural sphere as a kind of appendage wholly at the beck and call of the rights (or political) sphere.

27. Communication of information, which—to a fearsome extent—is indeed possible through these media, is utterly different from communication between human beings.
28. Published in *Essays Presented to Charles Williams.*
29. It is entirely characteristic that in 1998 there were two centenary celebrations in Barfield's honour in America, one on the West Coast and one on the East—but none in his native Britain.
30. Some of this correspondence has already been quoted by Ruth Miller in her book *Saul Bellow: A Biography of the Imagination*. This book is, however, understandably enough, written very much from Bellow's standpoint and presents Barfield, some of whose ideas—notably those on the Jewish people—are misrepresented, rather as Bellow must have imagined him by the end of the correspondence.
31. Published in 1975 by Viking and, in England, by Secker and Warburg.
32. It won the Pulitzer Prize for Fiction in 1976, and in the same year Bellow was awarded the Nobel Prize for Literature.
33. The incorrect page number and slightly inaccurate quotation are as given in the letter.
34. Bellow gave the date as 1877, and forgot to sign the (typed) letter—an indication that he was indeed having a bit of a struggle!
35. In a letter of 14 May 1978 to Professor Thomas Kranidas, Barfield reports of the arrival of a Parker-Knoll armchair, the gift of 'a man in Chicago'.
36. In a letter of 6 December 1992 to Thomas Kranidas, Barfield harks back to this period. Probably prompted by some news in Kranidas's latest letter about Bellow's marital problems, Barfield recalls that Bellow's wife 'thought his [Bellow's] especial respect for me might mean I could help in some way. She was about to visit England and suggested coming to see me, and later did visit me at Orchard View. But by that time Saul and I had lost touch. I wrote to him suggesting a renewal of correspondence, but the letter was unanswered.' Most likely the letter referred to here was that of 13 April 1986, when Barfield was still living at Orchard View. (His move from there to The Walhatch, Forest Row, took place on 26 November of that year.)
37. A phrase taken from the quotation from *The Dean's December* that begins Barfield's review.
38. The first edition of *Romanticism Comes of Age* (1944), for example, contained two essays on Coleridge, 'Coleridge's "I and Thou" (a review of *Coleridge the Philosopher* by J.H. Muirhead, first published in *The Criterion*, 1931) and 'The Philosophy of Samuel Taylor Coleridge', which was given as a lecture at the Goetheanum, Dornach, Switzerland in 1932 on the occasion of the centenary of Goethe's death.

39. Barfield's main academic appointments in America may be listed as follows:
    Visiting Professor (Philosophy and Religion), Drew University, Madison, NJ, 1964/5 and again in 1967 and 1972.
    Visiting Professor (English Literature), Brandeis University, Waltham, MA, 1965/66.
    Visiting Professor (Philosophy), Hamilton College, Clinton, NY, 1968.
    Visiting Professor (English Literature), State University of Missouri, Columbia, MO, 1969.
    Visiting Professor (Program of Religious Studies), State University of New York, Stony Brook, 1974.
    Visiting Professor (Cecil and Ida Green Foundation Lecturer), University of British Columbia, Vancouver, Canada, 1978.
    Visits California State University, Fullerton, 1980.
40. These were subsequently published under the title *Speaker's Meaning* (1967).
41. At the beginning of Chapter XIII of the *Biographia Literaria*, Coleridge presents his alternative to the premise of Cartesian philosophy ('Give me matter and motion and I will construct you the universe') by describing 'two contrary forces, the one of which tends to expand infinitely, while the other strives to apprehend or find itself in this infinity'. These two forces are 'of one power' and 'counteract' each other; they are 'both alike infinite and both alike indestructible'. This notion of the 'two forces of the one power' is the key to understanding 'polarity' as Coleridge conceived it.
42. Literary research was at that time—in contrast to the present—dominated by the search for the apparent sources of creativity in what physically predated it.
43. For Barfield's analysis of this marginal note of Coleridge's in Vol. VIII of Tennemann's *Geschichte der Philosophie*, see *What Coleridge Thought* (paperback edition 1983), pp. 96, 101 and 219.
44. Professor Owen's point was that he thought that Barfield had failed to show whether or not the similar language and vocabulary used by Coleridge to refer to mental and non-mental (i.e. livingly natural) states indicated that for him (Coleridge) there was a real (as opposed to a merely metaphorical) relationship between them.
45. In a letter to Craig Miller of 21 September 1973, Barfield asked with reference to Owen's review: 'Did you see a perfectly *ludicrous* review of *WCT* in *Review of English Studies* (May 1973)?'
46. He expressed this succinctly in his Introduction by quoting from the Introduction to J.A. Appleyard's *Coleridge Philosophy of Literature*: 'What is wanting in the sizeable bibliography of literature on Coleridge is a full-scale study of the development of his philosophy which will consider him on his own terms and not as a representative of something else, whether it be German idealism, English Platonism, pantheistic mysticism, semantic

analysis, or depth psychology. The idea or organizing insight ought to be internal to his thought, so as to see what that thought is and not merely what it is like or unlike.'

47. Reprinted in *Owen Barfield on C.S. Lewis*, ed. G.B. Tennyson, Wesleyan 1989.
48. See Chapter 3.
49. According to Professor Robin Jackson, whose edition of Coleridge's Lectures 1818–1819: on the History of Philosophy appeared as Volume 8 in the Collected Coleridge in 2000, with Barfield's manuscript included as an appendix, Barfield was prompted by Kathleen Coburn's terminal incapacity to hand in his unfinished manuscript, which was, with his consent, deposited in the library at Victoria College, Toronto, so that those who wished could consult it. Although he must by then have come to think that his edition was sufficiently complete for him to be able to relinquish what had become a burdensome task, this was not the view of a reader who appraised it for the Princeton University Press. The Press therefore felt obliged to ask another scholar to complete the edition, while maintaining a correspondence with Barfield over this difficult matter. Professor Jackson, who was allotted the task, also took up full liaison with Barfield, visiting him and exchanging letters. He found it impossible, however, to complete another man's work and decided to start all over again—a decision which, he strongly suggests (in a letter to the author dated 7 July 2003), would not have carried Barfield's conviction of its necessity and was a matter of regret to himself, not least because of the considerable reduplication of work involved. Prof. Jackson's conclusion to the letter referred to offers a clear summary of his position and, indeed, of Barfield's relationship to the entire project: 'According to my recollection, when I visited Barfield shortly after being asked to succeed him in the edition, he explained to me that he had undertaken it only on the understanding that Prof. Coburn would be backing up his work, partly because he was getting on in years, and partly because he was not himself an experienced scholarly editor. Their correspondence up to 1985 and the notes made by him and by her on his MS suggest that kind of give and take. I had of course read his work on Coleridge and on some other topics and I very much enjoyed meeting him; I wished then and wish still that he had had the time and the energy to finish his work for himself...'
50. Barfield ordered a copy of *Early Visions* from the library when it came out, so it is safe to assume that he at least familiarized himself with it.
51. 'The Philosophy of Samuel Taylor Coleridge', in *Romanticism Comes Of Age*.
52. *What Coleridge Thought*, 'Coleridge and the Cosmology of Science'.
53. See her Forward to *Evolution of Consciousness, Studies in Polarity* (1976).
54. This public lecture was given at the Vancouver Institute on Saturday, 14

October 1978, and its companions at the University itself on 12 and 17 October.

55. It is unfortunate, to say the least, that the publishers printed the second part of the title in smaller print than the first, thus giving an altogether misleading impression of what the lecture is about.
56. This epithet is taken from the foreword by the biologist Dr E.J. Steele to *Descent of Spirit*, a collection of Grant Watson's writings (Primavera Press, Sydney 1990).
57. In his biography of Adam Sedgwick, Colin Speakman rounds off his description of the geologist's death by quoting words spoken by Professor Selwyn at a public meeting in Cambridge in 1873 in support of a proposal to name a proposed new Geological Museum the Sedgwick Museum. The words quoted are so apposite that they are reproduced here in full: 'Let me say he was a most *primitive* man—of the solid ancient rock of humanity. He appears like a great boulder-stone of granite, such as he describes, transported from Shap Fell over the hills of Yorkshire, dropped here in our lowland country, and here fixed for life; primitive in his name, Adam; primitive in his nature; in his rugged noble simplicity; a dalesman of the north; primitive in his love of all ancient good things and ways; primitive in his love of nature and of his native rock from which he was hewn; primitive in his loyalty to truth, and hatred of everything that was false and mean; a heart if ever there was one, that "turned upon the poles of truth".'
58. Colin Speakman, *Adam Sedgwick: Geologist and Dalesman*, published jointly by The Broad Oak Press Limited, The Geological Society of London and Trinity College, Cambridge 1982. The words in quotation marks in this passage are taken from M.J.S. Rudwick's article on Sedgwick in the *Dictionary of Scientific Biography*, Vol. 12, 1975.
59. Published under the title *Speaker's Meaning*, Rudolf Steiner Press, London 1967.
60. The definition is in Lyell's own words.
61. This Summer School took place at the Waldorf Institute of Mercy College, Detroit from 17 May until 30 July. Barfield contributed a seminar on 'New Horizons for Consciousness—Towards Imagination and Inspiration in Linguistics and Philosophy' (7–25 June).
62. Barfield reiterated many of the thoughts expressed in this lecture a few days later at Drew University, where on 2 March he spoke on the theme 'Two Kinds of Forgetting'.
63. Barfield had devoted a whole adulatory article for the *Denver Quarterly* on Müller in 1976 (see 'A Giant in Those Days').
64. These are the closing words of his essay on 'The Coming Trauma of Materialism'.
65. Examples which come to mind—most of which were featured by *Towards* magazine in the early 1980s—are W.R. Thompson's critical introduction

to the centenary edition of *The Origin of Species* (Everyman edition), Norman Macbeth's book *Darwin Retried: An Appeal to Reason* (1971) and the successful portrayal in a California courtroom of Darwinism as a dogmatic State religion from which individuals were entitled to be defended (2–6 March 1981).

66. Barfield did, incidentally, write to Prince Charles on 24 September 1986 'with some diffidence' following a speech made by the latter at Harvard which evidently made a deep impression on him. He clearly regarded the Prince of Wales as an ally in his quest to undermine 'the tacit assumptions underpinning current materialism', and he offers him some words of support and sympathy in the light of 'the inevitable hostilities' which the views which he expressed in his speech 'will evoke'. The letter ends, somewhat touchingly: 'May I add: God bless you. With admiration and all due respect . . .' The letter received a speedy, and suitably gracious, response.
67. Barfield anticipated this situation in a lecture entitled 'Language, the Evolution of Consciousness and the Recovery of Human Meaning', given shortly after the Fullerton Conference in Vermont at a symposium sponsored by the Charles F. Kettering Foundation in cooperation with Teachers College, Columbia University, entitled 'Knowledge, Education and Human Values: Toward the Recovery of Wholeness'.
68. It first appeared in two parts in *Towards* in 1983/4 (Vol. II, Nos. 4 and 5), and then in *A Barfield Sampler* (1993).
69. This information is contained in a personal letter of 3 June 1998.
70. His central thesis, that trade unions should have as their central aim that of fostering economic associations (economic brotherhood) rather than allowing themselves to be drawn into the essentially political activity of asserting rights, collective bargaining and so forth, was originally presented in his booklet *Law, Association and the Trade Union Movement* (*c.* 1936/37).
71. In a letter to Thomas Kranidas of 9 January 1989, Barfield states that he wrote this story in 1985.
72. Entitled 'Imagination and Science', this essay appeared in the *Journal of the American Academy of Religion*, Vol. LII, No. 3. The translation of this lecture-cycle, with its foreword by Saul Bellow, had appeared in 1983.
73. *On Hope, Evolution and Change*, Hawthorn Press, Stroud 1985.
74. 'Eager Spring' remains as yet unpublished. It was on the point of being published by the Bookmakers Guild, Lakewood, Colorado in 1989 when this company went out of business.
75. This is a reference to Jean Giono's tale of 'The Man Who Planted Trees', written in 1953 and published in *Vogue* in 1954 and subsequently in a number of other magazines. Not only Barfield but many other readers have felt Elzeard Bouffier to be as real a figure as his creator evidently wanted him to be. Indeed, Giono's purpose in writing it was to make people love the tree or, more precisely, to make them *love planting trees*.

76. The Wealden iron industry flourished between the late fifteenth and the early nineteenth centuries.
77. See page 89.
78. This is the main conclusion of *Poetic Diction* (1928).
79. Barfield is here summarizing the content of *Saving the Appearances* (1957).
80. It was originally published in *Toward a Man-Centered Medical Science*, Futura Publishing Company, Inc., 1976.
81. It was first published in *Interpretation: The Poetry of Meaning*, edited by Stanley Romaine Hopper and David L. Miller, New York 1967, and then included by its author in *The Rediscovery of Meaning* (1977).
82. Central to these reasons is the maxim: *De non apparentibus et non existentibus eadem est ratio* ('the non-phenomenal and the non-existent are in effect the same'). Barfield comments: 'On this view what I have been calling a "threshold" between two dimensions or planes of consciousness is not a threshold at all but a terminus. It is the edge of things. If it can be called a boundary at all, it is the boundary between existence and nothing. This was the response of the whole of natural science down to the end of the 19th century; it is still the working assumption of most sciences and of course of popular scientism. It does not make much difference whether you call it materialism, or positivism, or by some other name. Followed to its logical conclusions, it involves denying the existence of the self also, but it is not often thought through so clearly.' (See further in Chapter 4, 'Positivism and its Residues'.)
83. Some of these have already been mentioned in Chapter 5. Others that deserve particular mention are: his review of Douglas Sloan's book *Insight-Imagination: The Emancipation of Thought and the Modern World*, 1983 (the review appeared in *Towards*, Vol. II, No. 5, Summer-Fall 1984); his article 'Introducing Rudolf Steiner' in *Towards*, Vol. II, No. 4, Fall-Winter 1983, parts of which were used for his review of *The Essential Steiner*, ed. Robert A. McDermott, 1984 (the review was published in *Parabola*, August 1984); and his light-hearted 'Reflections on C.S. Lewis, S.T. Coleridge and R. Steiner', an interview for *Towards*, published in Vol. II, No. 6 (Spring-Summer 1985).
84. So far as I know, this lecture has never appeared in print, although a tape recording was made of what Barfield said. The conference itself was conceived as a forum within which invited participants could share—at a deeper and franker level than normal—their thoughts and feelings about the nature of reality. Quotations are taken from Barfield's handwritten script.
85. Barfield's review of Capra's book *Uncommon Wisdom* (1988) will be considered later in this chapter.
86. From Corbin's book *The Concept of Comparative Philosophy*.
87. A phrase coined by Theodore Roszak, author of *Where the Wasteland Ends*, *The Making of a Counter Culture*, etc., with whom Barfield corresponded in

the mid-1970s. In a letter of 15 April 1974, Barfield informed Roszak of an impression which *Where the Wasteland Ends* had made on him: 'The book as a whole does leave an overwhelming impression of seeing the whole historical descent into "single vision" as an aberration, and a rather stupid one, from the main ("spiralling upwards") course of evolution; a *faux pas* for which the Jews and, following them, Christianity must be held responsible.' This is of considerable interest in view of Barfield's effort in this lecture to distinguish between occultism (spiritual science) and a mysticism that essentially denies the validity of the Judaeo-Christian (Western) path of individual freedom.

88. George Adams (1894–1963)—Adams was his mother's maiden name—was one of the great pioneers of anthroposophy in Britain and was responsible for the on-the-spot translations into English of Steiner's lectures when he lectured in England. In 1977 Barfield wrote a deeply appreciative Foreword to a collection of the writings of this eminent spiritual scientist, who combined the disciplines of chemistry and mathematics (see *George Adams: Interpreter of Rudolf Steiner*, ed. Olive Whicher, 1977).
89. Barfield emphasizes that 'to the like extent' should not be confused with saying 'in the same way'. The characters of the two ages are, as he says, very different.
90. See the Biographical Sketch (especially pp. 41-2) for his thoughts on the subject as he expressed them at the end of his life.
91. See Chapter 5, 'Positivism and its Residues'. In a letter that he wrote on 28 March 1991 to Terence Davies (that is, roughly contemporaneous to his review of Capra's book), Barfield supplied the following insight into the reason for this persistency of a residue of unresolved positivism, of—in Davies's words—'trying to remove the Cartesian dichotomy and keep it at the same time': 'Its *cause* is the fact that, after explicitly rejecting Cartesian dichotomy on logical grounds with his intellect, the sufferer continues to retain it in his imagination, and thus as part of his "reality principle". And this prevents a genuine revision, or extension of scientific methodology. It was not only a new way of thinking that Goethe advocated but also, as the foundation of it, a new way of *perceiving*. And that is what is prevented by the failure of imagination to keep abreast of epistemological theory.'
92. Valedictory greeting from Philip Mairet's letter of 11 February 1973 to Owen Barfield.
93. The others are G.B. Tennyson, Professor of English Literature at UCLA (University of California at Los Angeles) and a contributor to the same volume, Thomas Kranidas (Professor of English at the State University of New York), and the Oxford-based American Walter Hooper, Barfield's colleague as Literary Executor to C.S. Lewis.
94. Most notably the essays by Professor R.J. Reilly ('A Note on Barfield, Romanticism and Time'), Professor R.K. Meiners ('On Modern Poetry,

Poetic Consciousness, and the Madness of Poets') and Professor G.B. Tennyson ('Etymology and Meaning'), and of course Shirley Sugerman's introductory 'Conversation with Owen Barfield' and Cecil Harwood's precious two pages recalling his dear friend.

95. University of Missouri Press, Columbia and London 1994.
96. These conversations were originally published separately in the *Brain/Mind Bulletin* and were reprinted together in *ReVision*, Vol. 5, No. 2 (Fall 1982).
97. 11 November 1982.
98. Paper A, 'Fragmentation and Wholeness', is essentially a distillation of his diagnosis of the problems of modern times as he saw them, and Paper B, 'The Rheomode—An Experiment with Language and Thought,' is his remedy for them. Barfield's comments are, typically, warm and favourable.
99. The only book which Cage had published by 1966 was *Silence* (1961); others followed from 1967, according to *The New Grove*.
100. An English translation was published in 1973 by Anthroposophic Press, New York, with the title *The Riddles of Philosophy*.
101. Barfield had written to Roszak in April 1974 in a somewhat more critical vein than his review article *The Coming Trauma of Materialism* would have implied. See the previous chapter, note 87.
102. *The National Review*, 12 June 1981.
103. This article, 'The Quality of Thinking: Owen Barfield as Literary Man and Anthroposophist', illuminatingly explores Barfield's relationship to Rudolf Steiner, in particular his endeavour to make the ideas and insights of his acknowledged teacher more accessible to the circle of his own readers and listeners. The article bears the additional authority of having been perused and commented upon by Barfield before publication.
104. Barfield destroyed most of Kranidas's letters to him, at their author's request.
105. This is a reference to the domestic arrangements around the seminar that Barfield gave at Stony Brook in the autumn of 1974.
106. At the time Walter Hooper and Shirley Sugerman were clearly established, with Tennyson and Kranidas being proposed in addition to Ulreich.
107. *Orpheus* was published by The Lindisfarne Press in 1983.
108. In the letter of 23 October 1979 he mentions that his wife Maud had produced *Orpheus* in Sheffield in 1949 and speaks of the importance of both music and eurythmy for this play.
109. These are the introductory words to Mairet's illuminating eight-page manuscript, 'Some Notes made after reading Owen Barfield's *Saving the Appearances*'.
110. Also known in English as *The Philosophy of Freedom* (see below).
111. The theme of this lecture had been suggested to him by Cecil Harwood.
112. See the following chapter.
113. In *Owen Barfield: A Waldorf Tribute* (Steiner Schools Fellowship, 1998),

three different dates are associated with Barfield's sole venture into the teaching profession, when he taught English Literature to a small class of 14–15-year-olds at The New School, Streatham. The actual year was probably 1929 or 1930.

114. As a token of his deep affection for his friend, Barfield edited a miscellany of Harwood's writings entitled *The Voice of Cecil Harwood* (Rudolf Steiner Press, 1979).

115. This response of his lives in my memory as one of the most striking elements in our conversations. After all, he might very well have said Harwood, or another of his many anthroposophical friends.

116. See Biographical Sketch, pp. 34-5. See also *The Inklings* by Humphrey Carpenter (1978), *The Magical World of the Inklings* by Gareth Knight (1990) and *Christian Mythmakers* by Rolland Hein (1998).

117. Published by HarperCollins in 1991 under the title *All My Road Before Me: Diary 1922–1927*.

118. Lewis used the Greek letter delta in his diary when referring to his Oxford landlady and close friend Mrs Janie Moore.

119. Leo Baker (1898–1986) was also an undergraduate at Wadham College, Oxford in 1919 and introduced Lewis (whom he had already met in 1917, when he matriculated) to Barfield.

120. Barfield and Harwood were living at the time at Bee Cottage, Beckley (near Oxford).

121. Mrs Moore and her entourage, which included 'Jack' Lewis, only moved into their permanent home of The Kilns, Headington Quarry, in 1930. Barfield and Lewis would have met in Lewis's rooms at Magdalen College, where he had been elected a Fellow in May 1925.

122. *The Letters of C.S. Lewis* were originally published in 1966 under the editorship of his brother Warnie, and a revised edition was published in 1988 edited by Walter Hooper.

123. This material, none of which has been published, is kept at the Marion E. Wade Center, Wheaton College, Illinois, where a major research collection of writings by and about Barfield, G.K. Chesterton, C.S. Lewis, George MacDonald, Dorothy L. Sayers, J.J.R. Tolkien and Charles Williams is housed. An invaluable study of the 'Great War' documents by Professor Lionel Adey, *C.S. Lewis's 'Great War' with Owen Barfield*, was published by the University of Victoria Press (British Columbia, Canada) in 1978. This was the background to my own study of the documents in April 2001, and has been drawn upon (where indicated) in what follows.

124. It should be emphasized that Dr Adey is not primarily a Barfield scholar, and he has stated quite explicitly that he is not an anthroposophist—a fact which surprised (and disappointed) Saul Bellow when the two men met at the University of Victoria in the early part of 1982.

125. Op. cit., p. 56.
126. Op. cit., pp. 122–3. This judgement by Professor Adey is paralleled by that of Astrid Diener in her unpublished doctoral thesis, 'The Role of Imagination in Culture and Society: Owen Barfield's Early Work' (Exeter College, Oxford 1998), where she indicates the extent to which Lewis's philosophical views—in contrast to those of Barfield—were a reflection of the dualism (whether materialistic or idealistic) that was so central a feature of the mental furniture of Oxford in the 1920s.
127. 'Knowing and Being in C.S. Lewis's "Great War" with Owen Barfield', *The Bulletin of the New York C.S. Lewis Society*, Vol. 15, No. 1, November 1983. See also by the same author: 'Lewis and Barfield on Imagination', *Mythlore*, issues 64 and 65, Winter 1990 and Spring 1991.
128. Barfield adds humorously that he has invented this Greek term 'because it makes me feel grand, living as I do in Golders Green and not in Oxford'. (At this time he was spending part of his working week in London.) See *Saving the Appearances* for the background to this quasi-Baconian use of the word 'idols'.
129. In this image, the seed-pod is the end-result, the 'that-ness', arising out of the living (i.e. 'imaginative') process represented by the flower.
130. Lewis had indicated that he thought he was not. Barfield regarded this assumption to be altogether unwarranted.
131. It is very difficult to tell whether this letter came before or after Barfield's next letter. However, it is apparent that an intervening letter from Lewis must have been lost.
132. See Chapter 5, 'Positivism and its Residues'.
133. What Lewis is basically claiming, in this and other examples, is that only that which appears in the present can be known as 'real'.
134. Lionel Adey draws some interesting—and I think highly relevant—conclusions from this image of the coloured glass. See op. cit., p. 80.
135. Op. cit., pp. 47–55.
136. A Lewis invention, presumably based on Bulwer-Lytton, to denote a tendency to ascribe the inadequate behaviour of human beings to manipulation by adversarial beings or forces.
137. In the penultimate section of the *Autem*, Barfield speaks of how '. . . consciousness arises out of the conjunction of enjoyment and contemplation'.
138. Barfield is describing what he would subsequently—in *Saving the Appearances*—interpret as the transition from original participation to individual self-consciousness.
139. To further clarify what he means, he quotes Schiller: 'Darin also besteht das eigentliche Kunstgeheimnis des Meisters, dass er den Stoff durch die Form vertilgt' (this is the true secret of the master's art—that he annihilates matter through form).

140. The Definitions are of the following terms: Cosmos, Thinking, Feeling, Will, Self-consciousness, Form, Image, Time, Space, Body, Soul and Spirit.
141. This was published in a limited edition by the Oxford University C.S. Lewis Society (under Walter Hooper's editorship) to mark the 20th anniversary of Lewis's death in November 1983.
142. Walter Hooper explains the origin of this mirthful exercise: '. . . Owen Barfield and Cecil Harwood decided to go on a few days walk in April of 1936. Lewis was invited, but for some reason he was unable to go. Barfield and Harwood spent the last night of their walk in The Red Lion Hotel in Basingstoke, Hampshire. And it was there that they decided Lewis needed a little leg-pulling. In order for him to be re-admitted into the "College of Cretaceous Perambulators" [as the walking friends called themselves] he should have to sit for a "Re-examination" based loosely on the School Certificate. Their first draft of the examination, written on a piece of stationery from The Red Lion Hotel and dated April 1936, included the question "Who were: Owen Glendower, Owen Nares, Robert Owen, Owen Barfield, Vale Owen, Owain, Ywain, Rowena, Bowen, Rovin', Sowin', Growin', Knowin' and Gloin?" '
143. See Georg Tennyson's Introduction to *Owen Barfield on C.S. Lewis* for further details of the human background to this period.
144. This was edited by Walter Hooper and published by The Lowell House Printers, Cambridge, Massachusetts in 1967.
145. This correspondence was inspired by a passage in Lewis's essay 'The Morte Darthur', published in the *Times Literary Supplement* dated 7 June 1947. Lewis's general drift in his essay was to try to minimize the actual (as opposed to the alleged) villainy in the eyes of his contemporaries of Sir Thomas Malory, author of this poem on what is generally regarded as a 'noble' theme; and he concluded the essay with the sentence: 'But how different such nobility may be from the virtues of the law-abiding citizen will appear if we imagine the life of Sir Tristram as it would be presented to us by King Mark's solicitors.' It was this sentence that inspired the 'lark' that followed, with Barfield, on the notepaper of his firm, Messrs. Barfield and Barfield, writing on King Mark's behalf in stentorian tones to Messrs. Inkling and Inkling (Lewis), who represented the hapless Tristram. Messrs. Inkling and Inkling, having metamorphosed themselves into Messrs. Blaise and Merlin, managed to winkle their client out of his hole by means of a mixture of magic and Arthurian politics.
146. This dated letter confirms that the novel must have been completed by then, as Lewis is describing events in its final part and the concluding fairy tale.
147. For an interesting exploration of Tolkien's debt to *and* divergence from Barfield's ideas, see Stephen Medcalf's article 'The Language Learned of Elves: Owen Barfield, *The Hobbit* and *The Lord of the Rings*', *VII*, Vol. 16 (1999).

148. In a letter of 8 April 1971 to Philip Mairet, Barfield confirms that 'Hunter is three parts C.S. Lewis', adding that '*Worlds Apart* was one of the last things he [Lewis] read before he died and he evidently very much enjoyed it'.
149. In his unpublished article, 'The Mysteries of Creation: Some Disputations between C.S. Lewis and Owen Barfield', Lionel Adey makes the helpful observation that in this allegorical poem Lewis is contrasting 'Barfield's tendency to paranoic fear with his own to overconfidence'.
150. In his Postscript to Charles Davy's article 'C.S. Lewis: Science-Fiction and Theology' in the 1976 *Golden Blade*, Barfield makes it very clear that Lewis's opposition to anthroposophy remained absolute throughout his life and gives a useful summary of the elements in this opposition. He also confirms that Lewis 'heard a little, and read less, of the wisdom of Rudolf Steiner'.
151. 'Lewis and/or Barfield'.
152. The translation is by Dr Jerry Hawthorne, with corrections by Owen Barfield.
153. Originally published in *Imagination and the Spirit: Essays in Literature and the Christian Faith Presented to Clyde S. Kilby*, ed. Charles A. Huttar (1971) and reprinted in a slightly different form in *Owen Barfield on C.S. Lewis*.
154. Published in *Friendship's Garland: Essays Presented to Mario Praz on his Seventieth Birthday*, ed. Vittorio Gabrieli (1966).
155. In a footnote, Barfield explicitly excludes himself from this group in connection with Lawlor's treatment of their Romantic theology, even though he confirms that it would be appropriate to associate him with them in other ways.
156. Quoted by Barfield from *The Divided Self*, the chapter entitled 'Ontological Insecurity'.
157. Originally published in the *Bulletin of the New York C.S. Lewis Society*, August 1975.
158. Delivered as the Third Annual Marion E. Wade Lecture at Wheaton College, Illinois on 3 November 1977.
159. Originally appeared as an article in *Mythlore*, September 1976. Reprinted, together with the other essays under consideration here, in *Owen Barfield on C.S. Lewis* (1989).
160. Paradoxically, says Barfield, in 'The Great Divorce' Lewis came closest to bringing the two divided elements together, as a *symbol* of imagination's relation to truth.
161. Op. cit. p. 137.
162. When speaking of Lewis's difficulty in accepting any notion of an evolution of man's relation to God, Barfield introduces another strand in Lewis's thinking which implicitly sets their religious debate in the context of the medieval controversy between the Realists and the Nominalists: 'The very use of the word *man* if one speaks of the relation of man

to God, and does so in terms of evolution or its possibility, implies that one conceives of humanity as a whole constituting an entity, a real being. Now whatever *literary* Lewis has said, *theological* Lewis always writes of the individual man, the individual soul. If he used *humanity* at all, I think it is clear that he thought of it simply as a numerical aggregate of individual souls. So that anything in the nature of evolution or progress or improvement can occur only in the life of some one soul between birth and death. There Barfield disagrees with him; he thinks that man, humanity as a whole, is a spiritual reality and, as I said, that it has been evolving and will continue to evolve' (*Owen Barfield on C.S. Lewis*, p. 112).

163. This is, for example, asserted in Rolland Hein's recent book *Christian Mythmakers* (Cornerstone Press, Chicago 1998), which is devoted to the study of John Bunyan, George MacDonald, G.K. Chesterton, Charles Williams, J.J.R. Tolkien, C.S. Lewis and some modern American writers, including Madeleine L'Engle, Walter Wangerin, Robert Siegel and Hannah Hurnard. See also Stephen Medcalf's 1999 article already cited (see Note 147), and Verlyn Flieger's book *Splintered Light: Logos and Language in Tolkien's World* (Eerdmans, Grand Rapids, MI, 1983).
164. The alternative is currently exemplified by the *Harry Potter* publishing phenomenon, which is a tribute to the vastness of the hunger for some kind of otherworldliness in our so-called technological age.
165. 'Alfred Cecil Harwood: 5 January 1898–22 December 1975', Anthroposophical Society in Great Britain, Supplement to Members' *News Sheet*, February 1976.
166. This was at a conference held at Manchester College, Oxford, entitled 'Spiritual Values in Education and Social Life'. The educational lectures were given on 16–19 August and have been published under the title of *The Spiritual Ground of Education*.
167. Steiner founded the Anthroposophical Society on 20 September 1913 in Dornach, Switzerland, and its British counterpart on 2 September 1923.
168. Quoted from Diener's thesis, pp. 220–1. (See Note 126.)
169. A very useful answer to in particular the second of these questions may be found in Astrid Diener's thesis, where she rightly points out that this aspect of Barfield's intellectual and spiritual life has for the most part been sorely neglected by Barfield scholars.
170. *Mein Lebensgang*, published in English under the title *The Course of My Life*. Other biographical studies consulted for this section include *Rudolf Steiner* by Johannes Hemleben (1963, English translation 1975), *Rudolf Steiner, Life, Work, Inner Path and Social Initiatives* by Rudi Lissau (1987), and *Rudolf Steiner, the Man and his Work* by Paul Marshall Allen (n.d.).
171. *The Course of My Life*, Chapter 1. Translation by Leo Twyman.
172. *The Course of My Life*, Chapter 3.

173. This was Barfield's preferred translation. The book is also known in English as *Truth and Knowledge*.
174. Op. cit., Chapter 1, 'The Intellectual Context: Owen Barfield, C.S. Lewis and Contemporary Philosophy'.
175. *Die Rätsel der Philosophie* was published in its present form in 1914, although much of its content is based on another book which appeared in 1901. It was first published in Fritz Koelln's English translation in 1973.
176. *The Philosophy of Freedom* (translated by Michael Wilson, 1964, p. 32).
177. Astrid Diener provides a very useful summary of Steiner's argument on pp. 66–9 of her thesis.
178. *The Philosophy of Freedom*, p. 70, the chapter entitled 'The Act of Knowing'.
179. For those wanting an expansion of these cursory remarks about Steiner's epistemology without necessarily aiming to read *The Philosophy of Freedom*, Barfield himself has given his own brilliantly succinct summary in his essay 'Rudolf Steiner's Concept of Mind'. This was originally written for the centennial volume *The Faithful Thinker*, published by Hodder and Stoughton in 1961 and reprinted in *Romanticism Comes of Age* (second edition, 1966).
180. *The Philosophy of Freedom*, Chapter 12, 'Moral Imagination' (p. 162).
181. Ibid, p. 163.
182. Ibid, p. 164.
183. Ibid, p. 134.
184. Ibid, p. 138.
185. In a lecture given on 13 February 1923 Steiner expressly defines his use of the word anthroposophy as follows: 'The true interpretation of the word *anthroposophy* is not "wisdom about man" but "consciousness of one's human nature [humanity]".'
186. Leading Thought (*Leitsatz*) No. 1 in *Anthroposophical Leading Thoughts* (English translation 1973), 17 February 1924.
187. The key book in this respect is *Wie erlangt man Erkenntnisse der höheren Welten?* (1904–5) (Eng. translation *Knowledge of the Higher Worlds: How is it Achieved?*)
188. See especially his *Theosophie. Einführung in übersinnliche Welterkenntnis und Menschenbestimmung* (Theosophy. An Introduction to the Supersensible Knowledge of the World and the Destination of Man, 1904).
189. From the Introduction to the 1966 edition of *Romanticism Comes of Age*, p. 18.
190. The Holy Spirit is conceived as the chief mediator between God the Son and the nine celestial hierarchies, while the realm of the Father lies beyond the furthest confines of our cosmos.
191. As Steiner—and Barfield—never tired of emphasizing, our time is one where this trend of separation and individualization needs urgently to be

transformed into a path of regaining access to the spiritual world, though without sacrificing the treasure of freedom that has been won.

192. Published in the anthroposophical annual *The Golden Blade* (1970).
193. *The Golden Blade* No. 31 (1979), p. 39.
194. Translated by George and Mary Adams and published in *Verses and Meditations*, Rudolf Steiner Press, 1993 (first edition 1961). This verse was given in London on the evening of 2 September 1923. On the morning of the same day the Anthroposophical Society in Great Britain had been founded in Rudolf Steiner's presence.
195. All the other lectures in this lecture series were about pioneers of anthroposophy in Britain who had crossed the threshold of death, whereas Barfield was still present to tell his own story.
196. Originally published in the *Anthroposophical Quarterly* (1969) and reprinted in *The Rediscovery of Meaning* (1977).
197. An example of such a description is in Walter Hooper's obituary of Barfield in *The Independent*, dated 19 December 1997, where we are informed that 'Barfield heard Steiner lecture in London in 1923 and from that time on was an enthusiastic follower'. Not only is this statement a misrepresentation of the truth but the date is incorrect: the lecture that Barfield attended in London was given on 24 August 1924.
198. Barfield is referring here to the three stages of the path of knowledge as described by Steiner, the picture-consciousness of imagination, the perceptive faculty of inspiration and the visionary power of intuition.
199. John Boynton Priestly (1894–1984). Barfield evidently corresponded with Priestly in the early 1920s and kept two of his letters (dated 1923 and 1925).
200. It is not suggested that Gerald Marston is a personification in the novel of Barfield. The point is that, just as the Trinders represent the recipient bodily sheaths, so does Gerald radiate the ego-qualities possessed by his creator.
201. Op. cit., p. 17.
202. Op. cit., p. 23.
203. See above, Chapter 10, specifically the discussions of Steiner's *The Philosophy of Freedom* and *Occult Science*.
204. This essay, which was—as already mentioned in Part Two of the present book—the original trigger for interest in Barfield's work in the United States, was first published by Oxford University Press in 1947, when it was included in *Essays Presented to Charles Williams* (Williams had died in 1945). However, it had, according to Barfield himself, 'been delivered as a paper something like ten years earlier' (from the Introduction to *The Rediscovery of Meaning*, 1977).
205. A second major problem confronting Barfield at this time that is addressed in *This Ever Diverse Pair*—namely his marriage—will be considered below (see Chapter 7). This problem lies behind the theme of Burgeon's first dream ('Home Guard').

206. Other notable lectures with this strongly Christ-centred theme include 'The Son of God and the Son of Man' (1958), 'Philology and the Incarnation' (1964) and 'Meaning, Revelation and Tradition in Language and Religion' (1981).
207. From the dates occasionally inscribed in this foolscap volume, there is clear evidence that work on *Saving the Appearances* was taking place during 1954 and 1955 (and not before).
208. It should perhaps be emphasized that Faber and Faber would not have felt obliged to introduce an author who was already sufficiently well established as an authority on poetic diction as to be invited to give a radio broadcast on the Third Programme on the theme of 'The Influence of Language on Thought: The Poetic Approach' (10 January 1951).
209. See above in Chapters 4 and 5 (especially that on 'Positivism and its Residues') and below in the consideration of *Worlds Apart*. Essentially, what is presented in this regard in *Saving the Appearances* is a graphic picture of the virtually complete breakdown in our time of the coherence of the academic world, in that what is thought to be eminently reasonable by a philosophical mind is not merely unacknowledged by, but is not even conveyed to, those engaged in certain areas of scientific research. The appearances that constitute our familiar (i.e. the scientific) world-picture *must* be saved, whatever the consequences may be for the coherence of our intellectual world. This extraordinary dichotomy is, of course, only possible because modern science is almost entirely lacking in any true *scientia*, being wholly technological in its outlook. (See *Unancestral Voice*, Part Three.)
210. This very clear distinction between 'original' and 'final' participation encapsulates in a sense the extent to which *Saving the Appearances* was a development and clarification of *Poetic Diction*, where there is no such clear differentiation between these very distinct aspects of poetic creativity.
211. Two other significant books, likewise published by Faber and Faber, may be mentioned alongside Barfield's masterpiece: *Man or Matter* by Ernst Lehrs (1950/1958) and *Towards a Third Culture* by Charles Davy (1961).
212. Sir Charles Snow, whose published lecture and its sequel, 'The Two Cultures—A Second Look' (1963), became vastly more well-known than Barfield's book, basically regarded the solution to the problem of the fissure in British cultural life between the humanities and the sciences as lying in an intensification and extension of the scientific and technological revolution. However, to read Snow's celebrated lectures after Barfield's *World's Apart* is to experience the same mental stupor that Barfield is trying to deliver us from.
213. There are good grounds for suspecting that Sanderson is modelled on Barfield's old friend Cecil Harwood, who would have recently retired from teaching at Michael Hall Rudolf Steiner School.

214. From Barfield's letter to Philip Mairet dated 31 May 1964.
215. From Barfield's letter to Philip Mairet dated 9 April 1971.
216. *Unancestral Voice*, p. 165.
217. The case against publishing this novel in full (Regina v. Penguin Books Limited) was heard—and dismissed—at the Old Bailey between 20 October and 2 November 1960.
218. See p. 44.
219. This is a reference to the Eighth Oecumenical Council of AD 869 in Constantinople, whose enactment enabled the Roman Church gradually to annul any awareness of man's spiritual heritage (see p. 102).
220. See p. 101.
221. See p. 110.
222. See p. 111.
223. For a modern study of Steiner's indications about this being, see Sergei O. Prokofieff's book *The Heavenly Sophia and the Being Anthroposophia* (English translation published by Temple Lodge Publishing, London 1996).
224. A verse given by Steiner on 25 December 1922. English translation from *Verses and Meditations*, Rudolf Steiner Press 1961/1993.
225. Frederick Grubb's review of *Unancestral Voice* published on 23 September 1965 in *The Listener* is an exception to this general rule, being not only sympathetic but penetrating in its understanding.
226. The outstanding example in this respect is Philip Mairet, whose correspondence with Barfield was considered in Chapter 8, entitled 'Sir, I thank God for you'. See especially p. 146.
227. There later ensued an extensive correspondence with de la Mare, which will be touched upon in Chapter 15.
228. He refers especially to the effect of the Great War coming on top of industrialism and the Darwinian Theory: 'The Western world,' he comments, 'is like Pope's *Essay on Man*: it knows much, but it has not felt what it knows.'
229. See p. 25.
230. The manuscript of this story bears the inscription 'Wadham College, Oxford', and probably dates from 1920.
231. Eliot had encouraged Barfield to write further stories in the same vein as 'Dope'. In a letter dated 30 April 1924, Barfield explained to Eliot why he did not wish to do so: '. . . I think that the rhythm which you noticed in "Dope" was really something adapted to that particular sketch. I mean it worked itself out from the subject, and was an expression of the sort of passivity with which undeveloped 20th century minds (as far as I can see) watch a mechanical world clicking past their limited field of vision. To repeat the rhythm, it would be necessary to repeat the subject, and I believe at present that it is [a] waste of energy to record an impression of that sort more than once. I am a little tired of literature which can do nothing but

point out ironically that there is nothing much going on but disintegration and decay . . .', a criticism which could, of course, be applied to Eliot's poetry at the time of *The Waste Land* (1922).

Barfield continued to ply Eliot with stories and poems off and on during the next two decades, but *The Criterion* was not wholly content with any of his fictional offerings. However, Eliot did publish Barfield's essay 'Psychology and Reason' in July 1930, an essay where the author criticizes the—at the time—increasing tendency to explain art, literature, philosophy and so forth in terms of personal psychological drives. Mention should also be made here of a letter dated 25 March 1960 from Eliot which Barfield, in a letter of 23 April 1976 to the poet's widow Valerie, indicated that he valued highly. This celebrates Faber and Faber's publishing in 1957 of Barfield's most important book. Eliot writes: '. . . I must take this opportunity of telling you my very high opinion of your last book that we published, *Saving the Appearances*. It is one of those books which make me proud to be a director of the firm which publishes them. It seemed to me too profound for our feeble generation of critics nowadays . . .'

232. All except 'Queer Story' have been republished in *A Barfield Sampler* (SUNY 1993). The introduction to this volume by its editors, Thomas Kranidas and Jeanne Hunter, is warmly recommended as a source of insight into Barfield's life and work.
233. *All My Road Before Me*, p. 275.
234. *Poetic Diction*, Chapter 2.
235. The former story is currently available in *Owen Barfield—A Waldorf Tribute*, edited by Brien Masters (1998). The latter is unpublished.
236. From the Introduction to *A Barfield Sampler*, p. 11.
237. These sonnets elicited the following gracious letter from the Pelican Press: 'Dear Sir, I want to thank you for your nine sonnets in the Mercury. If my opinion in that barren world of comparisons were worth anything at all, this letter would have started with the assertion that they make the finest contribution to English poetry in many years. As it is I have the right to say simply that they moved me profoundly. Death has lately made me ready for them—but there is life there, my friend, longer than hers and yours and mine multiplied together. Yours very faithfully, Francis Meynell. March 14 1922.'
238. See *A Barfield Sampler*, p. 56.
239. It is impossible to claim any complete overview of these longer poetic or dramatic works, since references have been found to one or two which have hitherto proved inaccessible to the present author, despite searches at the Wade Center and elsewhere. Examples of such titles are 'The Unicorn', mentioned in a letter to Barfield from T.S. Eliot dated 1 June 1948 as having been offered to Faber and Faber for publication (' "The Unicorn" is poetry of a different type from that on which we have made our notoriety

and I think might do as well, or better, under a different imprint'), and 'Medea', which Thomas Kranidas offered to the BBC in 1980 as a radio broadcast (the BBC declined). (The source of this latter piece of information is the Barfield-Kranidas correspondence, deposited at the Wade Center.)

240. See p. 140. Barfield's somewhat melancholic words about the reception of the play in published form may also be found here.
241. He had previously stated his determination to avoid trying to impart a metaphysical or philosophical message of his own in the sole aim of writing a good play, one which would be 'good theatre'.
242. See pp. 8–10 of *Orpheus*, A Poetic Drama by Owen Barfield, edited, with an Afterword by John C. Ulreich, Jr, The Lindisfarne Press, 1983.
243. The reason for being fairly confident about the approximate date of composition is that the original manuscript was drafted at Red Roofs, Chalfont St Giles (Bucks), which was where the Barfields lived at this time.
244. In an essay entitled 'Death' written 1929–30 but never published, Barfield had previously presented his critical view of this 'not to be spoken of in the drawing room' attitude towards death. This essay was, according to what Barfield himself attested in a letter to Eliot dated 28 April 1930, conceived as one of a series of six or seven essays 'of a predominantly ethical character' intended for initial publication in a periodical and thereafter in book form. (The first was the 'Psychology and Reason' essay already referred to, which was intended to 'establish the fact that there is a difference between truth and error . . . that it is worth thinking'.) It is clear from Barfield's letter that he put a lot of effort into the writing of this essay, the meditation upon which found expression in both *Orpheus* and 'Angels at Bay'.
245. See *A Barfield Sampler*, p. 178, where a helpful note gives this information and other clues to this most mysterious of Barfield's writings.
246. The date of 1949 is inscribed on the manuscript copy of this 'Preface to the Mother of Pegasus'. Entitled 'Poetic Licence', it was given separately as a lecture in October 1981 at the State University of New York. Within the context of the long (5000 lines) philosophical poem under consideration, this was intended to justify its somewhat archaic style.
247. Reprinted in *Owen Barfield on C.S. Lewis* (1989).
248. *Owen Barfield on C.S. Lewis*, pp. 22–3.
249. Published in *VII*, Volume 6 (1985).
250. *The Role of Imagination in Culture and Society: Owen Barfield's Early Work*, Galda & Wilch Verlag, 2002. This needs to be pointed out on the grounds that this study is, hitherto, the *only* one to recognize that Barfield made any contribution whatsoever to social, political and economic affairs. Most probably this weakness is to be attributed to Diener's lack of knowledge or appreciation of the second part—the non-epistemological aspect—of Steiner's *Philosophy of Freedom* (see Chapter 10, 'Barfield and Steiner'), with

its thesis of ethical individualism and the spiritualizing of the will. Significantly, Steiner's *Nationalökonomischer Kurs* or 'Economics Course' (translated as *World Economy*), which he gave in 1922 and of which Barfield himself was the co-translator (the English edition appeared 1936/37) is not even mentioned in her book.

251. 'If one proceeds not from blind production which has the aim of making people rich, but from needs, from consumption'.

252. There is even less reason to agree with Georg Tennyson's date of 1929, in his Bibliography of Barfield's works appended to the Festschrift, *Evolution of Consciousness* (1976). In the present author's view, the style of this pamphlet is altogether different from articles definitely assigned to 1929 but markedly similar to what Barfield wrote in the early 1920s.

253. *Danger, Ugliness and Waste* (to all Artists and Men of Letters), pp. 14–15. In 1922, that is, the year before this essay most probably appeared, Barfield published a short story entitled 'Seven Letters' in *The Weekly Westminster Gazette* (4 March 1922), which graphically expresses these same sentiments in the form of a fictional correspondence involving the unemployed former employee of a firm that produces fur gloves who had been made redundant through the brute working of market forces. In the present context, the point of the story is revealed only in the last of the seven letters, where a relatively well-off Oxford student has blithely purchased a pair of the gloves that have been produced at such human cost to the person who made them. (See Astrid Diener's monograph, pp. 155–9.)

254. Quoted by Astrid Diener (p. 169) from John L. Finlay, *Social Credit: The English Origin*, Montreal, London: McGill–Queen's UP, p. 112.

255. Diener, op. cit., p. 170.

256. Keynes's *General Theory of Employment, Interest and Money* was published in 1936.

257. According to Diener (op. cit., p. 170), Douglas's scheme continued to be received more favourably in Canada, Australia and New Zealand. She also specifically mentions three well-known continuing adherents—other than Barfield—in Britain, R.H. Tawney, the economist and social historian, the philosopher Bertrand Russell and William Temple, who was to become Archbishop of Canterbury.

258. He did, however, publish an article in *Anthroposophy* (Vol. 8 No. 3, Michaelmas 1933) on 'The Relation between the Economics of C.H. Douglas and those of Rudolf Steiner', which emphasizes both the merits of Douglas's conception of wages (as compared to the familiar way of regarding labour as a commodity) and its proximity to that of Steiner. Only later, in his 1961 postscript to his essay on 'Equity' (see below), did he express the view that Douglas's scheme had been shown to be powerless to bring about any lasting change in the economic relationships of human beings, on the one hand because the Second World War (and its military-

orientated aftermath) had created a vast sponge for soaking up unemployment and financial destitution and, on the other, because of the growing awareness (by the 1960s) of the limitations of the natural environment's capacity to support the kind of industrial development required for the implementation of Douglas's vision of plenty.

259. This originally appeared in *Anthroposophy*, Vol. 7, No. 2 (1932) and was reprinted, with minor revisions and a postscript, in the *Golden Blade* (1961 edition) under the title 'Equity Between Man and Man'.
260. As Barfield points out, the words 'conscience' and 'consciousness' are variant forms of words bearing this meaning of 'a state of knowledge either shared with, or at any rate considered in relation to, *another* being'.
261. That is to say, in the early fifteenth century.
262. Barfield's reference is to *The Threefold Commonwealth*, the then current translation of *Die Kernpunkte der sozialen Frage* (GA 23), published by Steiner in 1919. The English version now available is entitled *Towards Social Renewal*.
263. As these words summarizing Barfield's argument are being written, property prices are increasing—especially in south-east England—in what is reckoned to be an exponentially rising spiral.
264. I fear this is misleading. The allusion is to a remark by Dr Johnson; but what he actually said was: 'The *love of* money is the root of all evil'.—O.B., 1960.
265. Notable worthy examples of such recent books include *The Great Deception* by Mark Curtis (1998), *Captive State* by George Monbiot (2000), *The Silent Takeover* by Noreena Hertz (2001) and *The World We're In* by Will Hutton (2002). The regular contributions of Monbiot to the *Guardian* and of Nick Cohen to the *Observer* are also prompted by a vehement rejection of such a status quo, and not least by a bitter disappointment at the Blair Labour administration's failure to offer a genuine political alternative to the Thatcherite model.
266. Others in the series, of which this was No. 2, included *Towards a Rational Democracy* (G.L. Rowe), *Christianity and Communism* (Charles Davy) and *New Ways of Thinking About Social Problems* (Gladys Mayer).
267. As evidence of this, he refers explicitly to words from an 'initiation ceremony' of 1834, whereby the Woolcombers admitted new members to the union.
268. As will become somewhat clearer later in this chapter, it would be a mistake to view such a statement as an expression of jingoistic nationalism.
269. The reader has to be conscious that these words were written shortly before the turbulence represented by the twin political excrescences of Hitler and Stalin was to burst out in the Second World War.
270. The reference is, respectively, to Margaret Thatcher's Conservative Government from 1979 and Tony Blair's 'New Labour' Government from 1997. As has been remarked by several commentators, it is impossible to

discern any significant difference of fundamental policy between these two Governments, with their espousal of a quasi-Victorian belief in market forces and free trade.

271. According to Rudolf Steiner, the former sphere was associated in a quite particular way with the fourth post-Atlantean age of Greece and Rome (747 BC–AD 1413), whereas the latter relates especially to our present fifth post-Atlantean epoch (lasting until AD 3573).
272. See the books referred to in Note 265.
273. During the many conversations that I had with Barfield at the end of his life, we would translate these thoughts and intentions into a practical involvement in community supported agriculture schemes. Agriculture—as the basis of earthly reality—is fundamental to the development of economic associations today. (See a short article of mine published shortly before Barfield's death, 'Economic Associations and Britain's Task Today', which appeared in *New Economy*, Journal of Associative Economics, March/April 1997.)
274. This essay was first published in two parts in the quarterly journal *Anthroposophy*, Vol. 3, No. 4 (1928) and Vol. 4, No. 1 (1929). It was then republished as two separate essays in *Romanticism Comes of Age* (1944/1966), with the respective titles of 'Of the Consciousness Soul' and 'Of the Intellectual Soul'.
275. Likewise published in *Anthroposophy*, Vol. 6, No. 3 (1931) and included in *Romanticism Comes of Age*.
276. The most relevant section of the notes suggests the following set of relationships:

    '*France* brings in *Political* Equality but falls to *Nationalism*.
    Germany brings in *Spiritual* Freedom (Goethe, Lessing, etc.) but falls to *Materialism*.
    England brings in *Economic* Brotherhood (Strikes etc.) but falls to *Capitalism*.'
277. A reader who wishes to appreciate at greater depth *why* Barfield came to this conclusion is strongly recommended to study both this essay and the following essay in *Romanticism Comes of Age*, 'The Form of Hamlet'.
278. Barfield includes a table, which takes this development through a further three cultural epochs beyond our present one. We are currently about one third of the way through our present cultural epoch of consciousness soul development, each epoch lasting approximately 2160 years.
279. For those familiar with Steiner's way of referring to the tasks of the cultural epochs, such a statement may seem somewhat puzzling. After all, Steiner associated the development of the intellectual soul with the Graeco-Roman cultural epoch (the one preceding our own), just as the development of the sentient soul was associated by him with the Egypto-Chaldaean epoch (approximately 2900–750 BC). However, Barfield points

out that Steiner also spoke of the principle of on-going recapitulation in every period or aspect of human evolution, and that in the epoch of the consciousness soul the peoples of Southern Europe (especially Italy) bear the impulse of sentient soul development, while continental Europe north of the Alps and west of Russia and the Slavic East is the modern vehicle of intellectual soul development. He also clarifies these associations further in the light of Steiner's designation in one lecture of France as the modern intellectual soul nation *par excellence* and the peoples of Central Europe as the bearers of the ego itself, stating that 'from the present point of view—the resurrection point of view—the relation between intellectual soul and ego is peculiarly close. The mystery of the resurrection *is* the mystery of the ego.'

280. Maud died on 13 February 1980, at the ripe age of 94. According to Barfield, she was born on 3 March 1885.
281. The Barfields' house has since been effectively demolished and replaced by a modern house bearing the same name.
282. Lucy Barfield, who of the three children adopted or fostered by the Barfields seemed most disposed to such excursions of the mind, had contracted multiple sclerosis in her early thirties (around 1966) and had been hospitalized for many years. She died on 3 May 2003 at the Royal Hospital for Neurodisability, London.
283. The book by Steiner that most completely corresponds as regards content and page number to what Maud is referring to is *Anthroposophical Leading Thoughts*, specifically Leading Thoughts 53 to 58. These were, as the name implies, incisive summaries of his spiritual insights given by Steiner to the members of the Anthroposophical Society shortly before his death in 1925.
284. This is likely to be a reference to the piece of doggerel verse mocking Steiner's statements about the two Jesus children (see the Biographical Sketch, p. 27).
285. Taken from a copy of the letter inscribed by Maud herself in a notebook from 1941. This notebook came into the possession of Josephine Spence, who passed it on to the present author shortly before her death in November 2001.
286. Published in *The Golden Blade*, 1989 edition.
287. Marguerite Lundgren, the 'beautiful eurythmist' referred to in a letter to Josephine dated 6 June 1980, was the leader of the London Eurythmy School, a venture which Barfield warmly and actively supported.
288. A reference to the turbulent period in the early 1950s as chronicled above.
289. 'For to me to live is Christ, and to die is gain'.
290. It no longer hangs in South Harbour but resides in Cecil Harwood's son Laurence's gracious and welcoming Grasmere home. The poem runs as follows: 'Peace through this house prevail/Though griefs appal/The world, and wars assail/Its outward wall. Here let heart's rosy red/And blood's

indwell/New castle, and old head,/To make them well. Nor fear, nor pining hope,/No more confound:/Here be the Chalice opened,/Closed the Wound. Archangels, Thrones, this place/Uphold and bless,/Where harbours truth with grace/In quietness.' Written by Owen Barfield for A.C. Harwood for South Harbour, Forest Row, Sussex (date estimated as 1955).

291. Barfield himself confesses as such in a letter of October 1980 to Thomas Kranidas: 'All right, yes it is the same Josephine as in some of the poems you selected.'

292. This letter, with all its evident misunderstandings of what his correspondent was trying to convey, indicates that Barfield was still preoccupied with interpreting those same Leading Thoughts which had so baffled and infuriated Maud.

293. Eric Beckett (1896–1966), who would sometimes join in with the walks undertaken by Lewis, Barfield and Harwood and who was to have a distinguished career as a legal adviser to the Foreign Office, was also at Wadham at this time.

294. As did Walter Field, another mutual friend of notably Barfield and Harwood. See Harwood's article 'W.O. Field', included by Barfield in the miscellany of Harwood's writings, *The Voice of Cecil Harwood* (1979).

295. Leo Baker was by profession and inclination an actor, although his acting career was cut short because of the effects of his war injuries. Thereafter he ran a woolcraft business with his wife Eileen in the Cotswolds for a time, became a priest of the Christian Community and also taught at Wynstones Rudolf Steiner School near Gloucester. In his later years he worked as an educational drama adviser.

296. During his many years on the Council of the Anthroposophical Society in Great Britain, Barfield had carried responsibility for its legal affairs and was the author of its Statutes. There are several instances in the correspondence where he writes in this capacity.

297. A detailed discussion of these matters would be of no relevance here. (Barfield himself has given a general outline in the Biographical Sketch.)

298. T.S. Eliot died on 4 January 1965.

299. The lecture in question (16 October 1964) was published in *Owen Barfield on C.S. Lewis* (1989) under the title 'C.S. Lewis'.

300. Despite his great gratitude for what he received from America, he never lost his sense of perspective as to what it actually meant. Thus while he evidently enjoyed his status—so abjectly denied in his native land—of academic hero, he was thoroughly aware of the limitations and peculiarities of the American psyche. Two comments in the Harwood correspondence will serve to illustrate this. The first is contained in one of the first letters he wrote from Drew University: 'The people here are extraordinarily humble, in fact almost tiresomely so. Whatever you say, they remain privately

convinced that you are looking on with a kind of amused and supercilious tolerance; and, if you really succeed in convincing them that you are not, they seem slightly disappointed!' (12 December 1964). The second betrays his sense of the American tendency to get things somewhat out of proportion, but also stands as a more general comment: 'The Americans are children in many ways' (21 December 1967).

301. L. Francis Edmunds (1902–89) was the founder of Emerson College (1962), the anthroposophically based Adult Education College in Forest Row, Sussex, and a frequent visitor to America, whence he garnered students for his college.

302. Steiner predicted in a number of lectures given in 1910 (in particular) that the Second Coming would be a non-physical event taking place from the 1930s onwards. Barfield declares—with a certain pride—in the letter currently under discussion that he himself was responsible for the title *The True Nature of the Second Coming* given to the English translation of two of these lectures (25 January and 6 March 1910) published in 1961.

303. An address given at Wheaton College on 30 April 1969 and published in *The Rediscovery of Meaning* (1977), where Barfield uses the images of the Aeolian harp and the camera to symbolize, respectively, the capacity of human beings to receive inner inspiration from the spiritual world and the characteristics of modern scientific investigation, which for all its technological marvels, can only see the 'outside' of things.

BIBLIOGRAPHY

Lionel Adey, *C.S. Lewis's 'Great War' with Owen Barfield*, 1978

Paul Marshall Allen, *Rudolf Steiner, The Man and his Work*

J.A. Appleyard, *Coleridge's Philosophy of Literature*

Owen Barfield, 'Air Castles', poem, published in *Punch* 1917

—'The Superman', unpublished short story probably dating from 1920

—'Form in Poetry', *New Statesman*, 7. 8. 20

—'The Reader's Eye', *Cornhill Magazine,* September 1920

—Review of *Old English Ballads, 1553–1625*, *New Statesman*, 2. 10. 20

—Review of poems by Walter de la Mare, *New Statesman*, 6. 11. 20

—Review of *Oxford Poetry, 1917–1919*, *New Statesman*, 20. 11. 20

—'John Clare', *New Statesman*, 25. 12. 20

—'Wilfred Owen', *New Statesman*, 15. 1. 21

—'Some Elements of Decadence', *New Statesman*, 24. 12. 21

—'Nine Sonnets', *The London Mercury*, March 1922

—'Seven Letters', *The Weekly Westminster Gazette*, 4. 3. 22

—'Ruin', *The London Mercury*, December 1922

—*Danger, Ugliness and Waste*, pamphlet published probably 1923

—'Dope', *Criterion*, July 1923

—Articles in *Truth*, 1923–4

—'The Devastated Area', *The New Age*, 3. 7. 24

—*The Silver Trumpet*, 1925

—Articles in *G.K.'s Weekly*, 1925–6

—'Queer Story: Postman's Knock', *Truth*, 3. 3. 26

—'Metaphor', *New Statesman*, 20. 3. 26

—'The Lake of Nix', unpublished fairy story

—Articles in *The New Age*, 1924–7

—*History in English Words*, 1926

—*Poetic Diction*, 1928

—'Mrs. Cadogan', *New Adelphi*, March 1928

—Review of *Collected Essays and Papers* by Robert Bridges, *New Statesman,* October 1928

—'The Consciousness Soul', *Anthroposophy,* Vol. 3, No. 4, 1928, and Vol. 4, No. 1, 1929; reprinted in *Romanticism Comes of Age*

—'The Lesson of South Wales', *The Nineteenth Century*, February 1929

—'The Problem of Financing Consumption', *The Nineteenth Century*, June 1929

—'Financial Inquiry', *The Nineteenth Century,* December 1929

—'English People', unpublished novel, completed 1929

—'Death', unpublished essay, 1929–30
—'Psychology and Reason', *Criterion*, July 1930
—'The Child and the Giant', 1930; reprinted in *Owen Barfield—A Waldorf Tribute*, 1998
—'The Form of Hamlet', *Anthroposophy*, Vol. 6, No. 3, 1931; reprinted in *Romanticism Comes of Age*
—'Equity', *Anthroposophy*, Vol. 7, No. 2, 1932; reprinted under the title of 'Equity between Man and Man', *Golden Blade*, 1961
—'The Relation between the Economics of C.H. Douglas and those of Rudolf Steiner', *Anthroposophy*, Vol. 8, No. 3, Michaelmas 1933
—*Law, Association and the Trade Union Movement*, pamphlet, probably 1937
—*Orpheus*, written 1937, published by Lindisfarne Press 1983
—'Medea', unpublished play
—'Risen', poem included in *A Barfield Sampler*
—'Angels at Bay', unpublished dramatic trilogy, written early 1940s
—'The Unicorn', unpublished poem composed before 1948
—*Romanticism Comes of Age*, 1944
—'Poetic Diction and Legal Fiction', published in *Essays Presented to Charles Williams*, OUP, 1947
—'Psychography', unpublished manuscript, 1948
—*This Ever Diverse Pair*, 1950
—'The Influence of Thought: the Poetic Approach', broadcast on the Third Programme, 10 January 1951
—'Riders on Pegasus', unpublished dramatic poem, written around 1950
—'The Light of the World', lecture given in 1953; published in the *Golden Blade*, 1989
—*Saving the Appearances*, 1957
—'Rudolf Steiner's Concept of Mind', published in *The Faithful Thinker*, Hodder and Stoughton, 1961, and in *Romanticism Comes of Age*, 1966 ed.)
—*Worlds Apart*, 1963
—*Unancestral Voice*, 1965
—*Speaker's Meaning*, 1967
—*A Cretaceous Perambulator*, ed. Walter Hooper, published 1983, but written earlier
—*Mark vs. Tristram*, ed. Walter Hooper, published 1967
—'The Disappearing Trick', *Golden Blade*, 1970
—'Either:Or', *Imagination and the Spirit: Essays in Literature and the Christian Faith Presented to Clyde S. Kilby*, ed. Charles A. Huttar, 1971
—*What Coleridge Thought*, 1971–2
—'The Politics of Abortion', *Denver Quarterly*, Winter 1972
—'Industry and the Law', contribution to a symposium on Rudolf Steiner's Threefold Commonwealth, July 1974
—*Memorandum and Oral Evidence on behalf of the Society for the Protection of Unborn*

Children for the Royal Commission on Civil Liberty and Compensation for Personal Injury, 1974–5
—'Night Operation', *ToWards*, 1983/4, and *A Barfield Sampler*, 1993. Written in 1975.
—'A Giant in Those Days', *Denver Quarterly*, 1976
—Postscript to Charles Davy's article 'C.S. Lewis: Science Fiction and Theology', *Golden Blade*, 1976
—Contribution to an obituary of A.C. Harwood, published by the Anthroposophical Society in Great Britain in *Supplement to Members' News Sheet*, February 1976
—'Owen Barfield and the Origin of Language', lecture given 21. 6. 77
—Foreword to *George Adams: Interpreter of Rudolf Steiner*, ed. Olive Whicher, 1977
—*The Rediscovery of Meaning*, 1977; esp. 'The Coming Trauma of Materialism' (1974), 'The Rediscovery of Meaning' (1961), 'Science and Quality' and 'Imagination and Inspiration' (1966)
—(ed.), *The Voice of Cecil Harwood*, 1979
—'Why Reincarnation?', lecture given May 1978, published in *The Golden Blade*, 1979
—*History, Guilt and Habit*, 1979
—'Evolution', lecture given at the Fullerton Conference, California State University, 26–8 February 1980, published in *ToWards*, Summer 1980
—'Language, the Evolution of Consciousness and the Recovery of Human Meaning', lecture given in Vermont, 1980
—Lecture to the Lindisfarne Association Conference of 1982, unpublished
—Review of *The Dean's December* (Saul Bellow), published in *ToWards*, Spring 1983
—Introduction to Steiner's lecture-cycle *The Origins of Natural Science*, 1984, published 1985
—'Imagination and Science', review essay on Steiner's lecture-cycle *The Boundaries of Natural Science*, published in *Journal of the American Academy of Religion*, Vol. LII, No. 3
—'Introducing Rudolf Steiner', *ToWards*, Vol. II, No. 4, Fall–Winter 1983
—Review of *The Essential Steiner* by Robert McDermott, published in *Parabola*, August 1984
—Review of *Insight—Imagination: The Emancipation of Thought and the Modern World* by Douglas Sloan (1983), published in *ToWards*, Summer–Fall 1984
—'Anthroposophy and the Future', lecture given 3 August 1984, published in *ToWards*, Vol. III, No. 1, Fall 1987
—*Eager Spring*, unpublished novella, 1985
—Introduction to Steiner's lecture-cycle *The Karma of Materialism*, 1985
—Lecture at the Summer Conference of the BDAA, Hawkwood College, Stroud, 5–7 July 1985, unpublished

—'Reflections on C.S. Lewis, S.T. Coleridge and R. Steiner', *ToWards*, Vol. II, No. 6, Spring–Summer 1985
—Introduction to a collection of John Davy's writings, *Hope, Evolution and Change*, Hawthorn Press, Stroud 1985
—Review of *Uncommon Wisdom* by Fritjof Capra (1988), published in *ToWards*, Vol. III, No. 2, Winter 1989
—*Owen Barfield on C.S. Lewis*, ed. G.B. Tennyson, Wesleyan, 1989
Saul Bellow, *Humboldt's Gift*, Viking/Secker and Warburg 1975
Simon Blaxland-de Lange, 'Economic Associations and Britain's Task Today', *New Economy*, March/April 1997
David Bohm, *Quantum Theory*, 1951
—*Causality and Chance in Modern Physics*, 1957
—*An Inquiry into the Function of Language*, based on a colloquy held at the Institute of Contemporary Arts, London, 28 March 1971
—and Rupert Sheldrake, Conversations, reprinted in *ReVision*, Vol. 5, No. 2, Fall 1982
Humphrey Carpenter, *The Inklings*, 1978
Kathleen Coburn, 'Coleridge and Restraint', *University of Toronto Quarterly*, April 1969
Samuel Taylor Coleridge, *Biographia Literaria*, esp. Ch. XIII
—*Lectures on the History of Philosophy*, published as Vol. 8 of *The Collected Coleridge*, ed. Robin Jackson, 2000
Henri Corbin, *The Concept of Comparative Philosophy*
Charles Darwin, *The Origin of Species*, centenary Everyman edition, with introduction by W.R. Thompson, 1959
Charles Davy, *Towards a Third Culture*, 1961
Astrid Diener, *The Role of Imagination in Culture and Society: Owen Barfield's Early Work*, doctoral thesis 1998, published 2002
John L. Finlay, *Social Credit: The English Origin*, Montreal/London
Verlyn Flieger, *Splintered Light: Logos and Language in Tolkien's World*, Eerdmans, Grand Rapids, MI, 1983
Jean Giono, *The Man Who Planted Trees*, published in *Vogue* magazine, 1954
Patrick Grant, *Six Modern Authors and Patterns of Belief*, 1979
—'The Quality of Thinking: Owen Barfield as Literary Man and Anthroposophist', *VII*, Vol. III, 1982
E.L. Grant Watson, *The Mystery of Physical Life*, 1964 and 1992
—*Descent of Spirit*, 1990
Rolland Hein, *Christian Mythmakers*, 1998
Johannes Hemleben, *Rudolf Steiner*, 1963, Eng. tr. 1975
Richard Holmes, *Early Visions*, 1989
—*Darker Reflections*, 1998
Gareth Knight, *The Magical World of the Inklings*, 1990
Thomas Kranidas, 'The Defiant Lyricism of Owen Barfield', *VII*, Vol. 6, 1985

—(ed. and Hunter), *A Barfield Sampler*, SUNY, 1993

R.D. Laing, *The Divided Self*

John Lawlor, '*Rasselas*, Romanticism and the Nature of Happiness', published in *Friendship's Garland: Essays Presented to Mario Praz on his Seventieth Birthday* (ed. Vittorio Gabrieli, 1966)

Ernst Lehrs, *Man or Matter*, 1950/1958

C.S. Lewis, *All My Road Before Me: Diary 1922–1927*, 1991

—'The Morte Darthur', *Times Literary Supplement*, 7 June 1947

—*Surprised by Joy*, Geoffrey Bles, 1955

Rudi Lissau, *Rudolf Steiner, Life, Work, Inner Path and Social Initiatives*, 1987

Norman Macbeth, *Darwin Retried: An Appeal to Reason*, 1971

Brien Masters (ed.), *Owen Barfield: A Waldorf Tribute*, Steiner Schools Fellowship 1998

Stephen Medcalf, 'The Language Learned of Elves: Owen Barfield, *The Hobbit* and *The Lord of the Rings*', *VII*, Vol. 16, 1999

Craig Miller, 'Coleridge's Concept of Nature', *Journal of the History of Ideas*, Spring 1964

—*The Unity of Coleridge's Thought*

Ruth Miller, *Saul Bellow: A Biography of the Imagination*

W.J.B. Owen, review of *What Coleridge Thought*, published in *The Review of English Studies*, Oxford, May 1973

Donna Potts, *Howard Nemerov and Objective Idealism: The Influence of Owen Barfield*, University of Missouri Press, Columbia and London 1994

J.B. Priestly, *The Good Companions*, 1929

Sergei O. Prokofieff, *The Heavenly Sophia and the Being Anthroposophia*, Eng. tr. 1996

Theodore Roszak, *Where the Wasteland Ends*

—*The Making of a Counter Culture*

C.P. Snow, *The Two Cultures*, 1959

—*The Two Cultures: A Second Look*, 1963

Colin Speakman, *Adam Sedgwick: Geologist and Dalesman*, Broad Oak Press Limited, The Geological Society of London/Trinity College, Cambridge 1982

Rudolf Steiner, *Die Philosophie der Freiheit*, 1894, Eng. tr. various

—*Die Rätsel der Philosophie*, 1914, Eng. tr. 1973

—*Die Kernpunkte der sozialen Frage*, 1919, tr. as *Towards Social Renewal*

—*World Economy*, tr. of Economics Course of 1922

—*Mein Lebensgang*, autobiography, 1925, tr. 1951 as *The Course of My Life*

Shirley Sugerman (ed.), *The Evolution of Consciousness*, Wesleyan University Press, 1976

Stephen Thorson, 'Knowing and Being in C.S. Lewis's "Great War" with Owen Barfield', *The Bulletin of the New York C.S. Lewis Society,* Vol. 15, No. 1, November 1983

—'Lewis and Barfield on Imagination', *Mythlore*, Nos. 64 and 65, Winter 1990 and Spring 1991

John Ulreich, review of *What Coleridge Thought*, *Arizona Quarterly*, Summer 1972

INDEX